# Political Extremes

The Western tradition of the constitutional state, with its ancient roots, defines political extremes as the epitome of that which must be absolutely rejected. It highlights tyranny, despotism, despotic rule, non-autonomy, ruthless enforcing of interests as 'extreme', contrasting this with a virtuous mean which guarantees moderation. In this volume, the culmination of twenty years of extensive research, Uwe Backes provides a conceptual history of the notions 'extreme' and 'extremism' from antiquity to the present day.

The terminological history of political extremes has been related for more than two millennia with the term mesotês used in Aristotelian ethics and the theory of mixed constitution. Both doctrines influenced the republicanism of the North Italian city-states and later the United States of America as well as British parliamentarism. The positions of moderation and extremes were not joined until the course of the French Revolution with the distinction of right- and left-wing, and this is how it still exists today in the intellectual–political geography. This unique source-based study reconstructs these developments from ancient times to the present.

Tracing the history of the concept of political extremism from Ancient Greece to the present day, this is an invaluable resource for scholars of democracy, extremism and political sociology.

**Uwe Backes** is Deputy Director of the Hannah Arendt Institute for Research on Totalitarianism and teaches political science at the Technical University of Dresden, Saxony.

## Routledge Studies in Extremism and Democracy

Edited by Roger Eatwell, *University of Bath*
Cas Mudde, *University of Antwerp-UFSIA*

This new series encompasses academic studies within the broad fields of 'extremism' and 'democracy'. These topics have traditionally been considered largely in isolation by academics. A key focus of the series, therefore, is the (inter-) relation between extremism and democracy. Works will seek to answer questions such as to what extent 'extremist' groups pose a major threat to democratic parties, or how democracy can respond to extremism without undermining its own democratic credentials.

The books encompass two strands: Routledge Studies in Extremism and Democracy includes books with an introductory and broad focus, which are aimed at students and teachers. These books will be available in hardback and paperback. Titles include:

**Understanding Terrorism in America**
From the Klan to al Qaeda
*Christopher Hewitt*

**Racist Extremism in Central and Eastern Europe**
*Edited by Cas Mudde*

**Fascism and the Extreme Right**
*Roger Eatwell*

**Political Parties and Terrorist Groups (2nd edition)**
*Leonard Weinberg, Ami Pedahzur and Arie Perliger*

Routledge Research in Extremism and Democracy offers a forum for innovative new research intended for a more specialist readership. These books will be in hardback only. Titles include:

1 **Uncivil Society?**
Contentious politics in post-communist Europe
*Edited by Petr Kopecky and Cas Mudde*

2 **Political Parties and Terrorist Groups**
*Leonard Weinberg and Ami Pedahzur*

3 **Western Democracies and the New Extreme Right Challenge**
*Edited by Roger Eatwell and Cas Mudde*

4 **Confronting Right Wing Extremism and Terrorism in the USA**
*George Michael*

5 **Anti-Political Establishment Parties**
A comparative analysis
*Amir Abedi*

6 **American Extremism**
History, politics and the militia
*D. J. Mulloy*

# Political Extremes

A conceptual history from antiquity
to the present

**Uwe Backes**

Routledge
Taylor & Francis Group

LONDON AND NEW YORK

First published in German in 2006 by Vandenhoeck & Ruprecht
First published in English in 2010 by Routledge
2 Park Square, Milton Park, Abingdon, Oxon OX14 4RN

Simultaneously published in the USA and Canada
by Routledge
270 Madison Avenue, New York, NY 10016

*Routledge is an imprint of the Taylor & Francis Group, an informa business*

© 2010 Uwe Backes

Typeset in Times New Roman by
Taylor & Francis Books
Printed and bound in Great Britain by
CPI Antony Rowe, Chippenham, Wiltshire

*British Library Cataloguing in Publication Data*
A catalogue record for this book is available from the British Library

*Library of Congress Cataloging in Publication Data*
Backes, Uwe, 1960–
    [Politische Extreme. English]
    Political extremes : a conceptual history from antiquity to the present /
Uwe Backes.
      p. cm. – (Routledge studies in extremism and democracy)
    Originally published in German: Göttingen : Vandenhoeck & Ruprecht,
2006.
    1. Right and left (Political science)–History. 2. Human rights–History.
    3. Conservatism–History. 4. Radicalism–History. 5. Democracy–History.
    I. Title.
    JC571.B28 2009
    320.509–dc22                                                          2009017222

ISBN 978-0-415-47352-1 (hbk)
ISBN 978-0-203-86725-9 (ebk)

# Contents

# Illustrations

# Series editors' preface

i

For much of the 'short twentieth century', history was characterized by the clash of great ideologies, internal violence and major wars. Although most catastrophic events took place outside the Western world, Europe and the USA were not immune from the turmoil. Two world wars and a series of lesser conflicts led to countless horrors and losses. Moreover, for long periods, Western democracy – especially in its European form – seemed in danger of eclipse by a series of radical forces, most notably communist and fascist.

Yet, by the turn of the 1990s, liberal democracy appeared destined to become the universal governmental norm. Dictatorial Soviet communism had collapsed, to be replaced in most successor states by multiparty electoral politics. Chinese communism remained autocratic but, in the economic sphere, it was moving rapidly towards greater freedoms and marketization. The main manifestations of fascism had gone down to catastrophic defeat in war. Neofascist parties were damned by omnipresent images of brutality and genocide, and exerted little appeal outside a fringe of ageing nostalgics and alienated youths.

In the Western world, political violence had disappeared, or was of minimal importance in terms of system stability. Where it lingered on as a regularly murderous phenomenon, for instance in Northern Ireland or Spain, it seemed a hangover from the past – a final flicker of the embers of old nationalist passions. It was easy to conclude that such tribal atavism was doomed in an increasingly interconnected 'capitalist' world, characterized by growing forms of multilevel governance that were transcending the antagonism and parochialism of old borders.

However, as we move into the new millennium, there are growing signs that extremism even in the West is far from dead – that we celebrated the universal victory of democracy prematurely. Perhaps the turn of the twenty-first century was an interregnum, rather than a turning point? In Western Europe, there has been the rise of 'extreme right' and 'populist' parties such as Jean-Marie Le Pen's Front National, which pose a radical challenge to existing elites – even to the liberal political system. In the USA, the 1995 Oklahoma mass bombing has not been followed by another major extreme right attack, but there is simmering resentment towards the allegedly overpowerful state among a miscellany of discontents, who appear even more dangerous than the militias that emerged in the 1990s. More generally across the West, new forms of green politics, often linked by a growing hostility to globalization–Americanization, are taking on more violent forms (the issue of animal rights is also growing in importance in this context).

In the former Soviet space, there are clear signs of the revival of 'communist' parties (which often masquerade as 'socialists' or 'social democrats'), whose allegiance to democracy is (in varying degrees) debatable. In Latin America, there remain notable extremist movements on the left, although these tend not to be communist. This trend may well grow in response to both globalization–Americanization and the (partly linked) crises of many of these countries, such as Argentina. This in turn increases the threat to democracy from the extreme right, ranging in form from paramilitary groups to agro-military conspiracies.

The rise of Islamic fundamentalism has been an even more notable feature of recent years. This is not simply a facet of Middle Eastern politics. It has had an impact within some former Soviet republics, where the old nomenklatura have used the Islamic threat to maintain autocratic rule. In countries such as Indonesia and India, Muslims and other ethnic groups have literally cut each other to pieces. More Al-Qaeda bombings of the 2002 Bali type threaten economic ruin to Islamic countries that attract many Western tourists.

It is also important to note that growing Islamic fundamentalism has had an impact within some Western countries. The terrorist attacks on the World Trade Center and elsewhere in the USA on 11 September 2001 are perhaps the most graphic illustration of this impact. But in democracies generally, the rise of religious and other forms of extremism pose vital questions about the limits of freedom, multiculturalism and tolerance. This is especially the case in countries that have experienced notable Islamic immigration and/or face the greatest threat of further terrorist attack.

Democracy may have become a near-universal shibboleth, but its exact connotations are being increasingly challenged and debated. As long as the 'evil empire' of communism existed, Western democracy could in an important sense define itself by the 'Other' – by what it was not. It did not have overt dictatorial rule, censorship, the gulags and so on. But with the collapse of its great external foe, the spotlight has turned inward (although Islam is in some ways replacing communism as the 'Other'). Is (liberal–Western) democracy truly democratic? Can it defend itself against terrorism and new threats without undermining the very nature of democracy?

These general opening comments provide the rationale for the Routledge Series on Extremism and Democracy. In particular, there are three issues that we seek to probe in this series:

- Conceptions of democracy and extremism
- Forms of the new extremism in both the West and the wider world
- How democracies are responding to the new extremism

**ii**

The last few decades have seen a wealth of articles and books on the 'extreme right' and, to a lesser extent, the 'extreme left', and definitions of these (and related) terms abound. Oddly enough, very few scholars have focused on the more generic term '(political) extremism'. A notable exception is the German political scientist Uwe Backes, whose work in the field dates back to his influential 1989 book *Politischer Extremismus in demokratischen Verfassungsstaaten. Elemente einer normativen Rahmentheorie* (Political extremism in democratic constitutional states. Elements of a normative framework).

This volume on 'political extremes' is thus the culmination of twenty years of extensive research, and the result is a true tour de force. Backes provides a conceptual history of the term 'extremism' from antiquity to the present day, using an unprecedented wealth of literature spanning over two millennia and some ten languages. He traces the origins of the term to the Greeks, who used 'extreme' to refer to the two pure forms of politics, anarchy (democracy) and despotism (tyranny), contrasting them with a preferred 'mean', i.e. a mixed constitution. Despite debates and slight amendments, the core of the Aristotelian mesotês doctrine and the mixed constitution theory remained dominant until well into the nineteenth century.

It was only really in the 'age of extremes', i.e. the twentieth century, that the term 'extremism' became widely used in both politics and social science. Extremism has become a Kampfbegriff (battle term), mostly used negatively, although some political actors claimed it as nom de guerre. Not surprisingly, this led to both redefinitions and conceptual confusion; extremism became increasingly conflated with other terms, most notably 'radicalism'. It was particularly in postwar Germany that the term 'extremism' became clearly and strictly defined, by both scientists and the state. In this 'extremism theoretical' tradition, linked to the totalitarianism school of Friedrich and Brzezinski, extremism is linked to both a left and a right, but is also separately defined as the antithesis of (constitutional) democracy.

This study provides a historical analysis of a much understudied concept, which is unparalleled in its scope and depth. It traces the lineage of a highly modern term by going back over two millennia. Overlooking the development of the term 'extremism', there are at least two fundamental changes in the use of the term. First, extremism is defined today as the antithesis of democracy, yet for the Greeks democracy was (one form of) extremism. Second, although the Greeks saw the extremes as the primary types of politics, i.e. reducing the desired 'mean' to a mixed constitution, current usages of extremism see it as secondary, i.e. an extreme form of the mean (the primary). Third, and related to both previous points, for the Greeks, the (bad) extremes were constituent parts of the (good) mean, yet in most contemporary uses (notably the extremism theoretical school), the extremes/extremisms are antithetical and should be excluded from democracy.

# Abbreviations

| | |
|---|---|
| ADB | Allgemeine Deutsche Biographie |
| AöR | Archiv des öffentlichen Rechts |
| APO | Außerparlamentarische Opposition |
| APuZ | Aus Politik und Zeitgeschichte. Beilage zur Wochenzeitung *Das Parlament* |
| ARSP | Archiv für Rechts- und Sozialphilosophie |
| BVerfGE | Entscheidungen des Bundesverfassungsgerichts |
| CGL | Confederazione generale del lavoro |
| CGT | Confédération générale du travail |
| ComIntern | Communist International |
| DKP | Deutsche Kommunistische Partei |
| DNVP | Deutschnationale Volkspartei |
| EN | Aristotle, Nichomachian Ethics |
| FDJ | Freie Deutsche Jugend |
| FRG | Federal Republic of Germany |
| GDR | German Democratic Republic |
| GG | Grundgesetz, German Constitution |
| HZ | Historische Zeitschrift |
| JöR | Jahrbuch des öffentlichen Rechts der Gegenwart |
| KPD | Kommunistische Partei Deutschlands |
| NDB | Neue Deutsche Biographie |
| NPD | Nationaldemokratische Partei Deutschlands |
| NSDAP | Nationalsozialistische Deutsche Arbeiterpartei |
| NZZ | Neue Zürcher Zeitung |
| Pol | Aristotle, Politics |
| PVS | Politische Vierteljahresschrift |
| SED | Sozialistische Einheitspartei Deutschlands |
| SEW | Sozialistische Einheitspartei Westberlins |
| SFIO | Section Française de l'Internationale Ouvrière |
| SPD | Sozialistische Partei Deutschlands |
| SRP | Sozialistische Reichspartei |
| SS | Schutzstaffel |
| VfZ | Vierteljahrshefte für Zeitgeschichte |
| ZfG | Zeitschrift für Geschichtswissenschaft |
| ZfP | Zeitschrift für Politik |

# 1 Introduction

## 1 Significance of the topic

*Age of Extremes*, published for the first time in 1994, was the title of the book in which English social historian Eric Hobsbawm took stock of the 'short twentieth century'.[1] The excesses of inhumanity, the way for which was paved by the outbreak of World War I, appear to be 'extremes'. Whether it had to do with the 'initial catastrophe of the twentieth century' (George F. Kennan) or should rather be called the catalyst reaction to conditioning factors from the nineteenth century remains an open question.[2] In any event, the civil society of warring states in its totality, but particularly the German Reich operating on several fronts, was placed in the service of a collective struggle for life and death for the first time in history. The gigantic material battles of the 'total war', as it was later described by Generalquartiermeister Erich Ludendorff[3] with programmatic intent, carried the European nations to the utmost limits of their material productivity. As a result of the war and its aftermath, the livelihoods of countless people became endangered. Millions of soldiers lost their lives, many returned home mutilated and emotionally broken, unable ever again to integrate themselves into civil society. The institutional structure of the constitutional states with its power controls and guaranteed rights that had formed in the course of centuries began to waver under the onslaught of new kinds of soon-to-be-called 'totalitarian' extreme political movements. With World War I, political 'monsters' such as Hitler, Lenin and Stalin, as Hans-Peter Schwarz portrayed them, came to the fore ready to sacrifice hundreds of thousands, indeed millions, of lives for their hubris-driven political visions.[4] Without World War I, neither the Russian Revolution nor, probably, the Bolshevik coup d'état in October 1917 in St Petersburg would have happened. Under Lenin and Trotsky, the new rulers in the Kremlin began a historically unexampled 'cleansing' of Russian society of all those social 'pests' that were seen as an obstacle to the great goal of the world revolution.[5]

The break with history and the conversion to the new empire of socialism/communism justified a pitiless settling of a score not only with all those who denied themselves to the great project or openly opposed it, but also with the ideologically defined 'objective enemies'[6] who, on the basis of their social roles and functions, were to be exterminated as historically 'antiquated' classes and 'parasitic' groups. This goal was hardly covered up. One of the most revealing texts about Lenin's cleansing ideology ('How is the competition to be organized'), which clearly exemplifies the Bolsheviks' break with the basic moral norms of the Jewish–Christian as well as the humanistic tradition, found admission into the official edition of Lenin's oeuvre. In 'achieving the single common aim', the leader of the revolution demanded his followers

> to clean the land of Russia of all vermin, of fleas – the rogues, of bugs – the rich, and so on and so forth. In one place half a score of rich, a dozen rogues, half a dozen workers who shirk their work (in the manner of rowdies, the manner in which many compositors in Petrograd, particularly in the Party printing-shops, shirk their work) will be put in prison. In another place they will be put to cleaning latrines. In a third place they will be provided with 'yellow tickets' after they have served their time, so that everyone shall keep an eye on them, as harmful persons, until they reform. In a fourth place, one out of every ten idlers will be shot on the spot.[7]

With the formation of the Communist International in Spring 1919, the attempts by the 'Centre of World Revolution' began to subjugate the workers' movements of the European states to directives from Moscow. In countries such as Germany and Italy, the efforts by the Communist International sections to strengthen their influence and to drive forward their revolutionary goals led from numerous violent struggles all the way to attempted revolts.[8] The *fascio di combattimento*, founded in Italy in 1919 by Benito Mussolini, a leading representative of prewar socialism, saw itself foremost as a task force against the dangers of bolshevism.[9] In Germany, too, from the ranks of brutal and disappointed war veterans returning from the front, militant nationalist formations were recruited that were assigned to paramilitary units against the 'red danger', fought bloody battles with left-wing extremist fighting units and appeared in terrorist actions against representatives of the system.[10] They achieved their identity in large part from the defence against the 'red beast',[11] developed new stylistic and propagandistic forms of expression, which created an awareness among their contemporaries with the 'March on Rome'. Fascism and its offshoots in other European countries, in connection with the charismatic leader cult and palingenetic ultra-nationalism,[12] became the incarnation of a new extreme right[13] despite obvious borrowings from socialism and revolutionary syndicalism.

This also drew Adolf Hitler, a recruit from World War I, whose right-wing, extremist, aggressively anti-Semitic movement took power in Germany in 1933, sweeping away the Weimar constitutional system already distorted by authoritarianism and erected a regime which, with its officially binding ideology reminiscent of religion, the absolute design claim of the unified party, the socially mobilizing mass organizations, its communication monopoly, its extensive repression apparatus and the internment camps, showed essential parallels with the Soviet system.[14] In 1939, the two totalitarian states formed an alliance against the Western democracies to mark their respective spheres of influence in Eastern Europe. The short period of collaboration between these ideological antagonists ended with Hitler's attack on the Soviet Union and the beginning of a racially ideological conquest and extermination campaign in the east, which, after the US entered the war, led to the systematic, industrially organized elimination of European Jewry.[15]

Anyone listening carefully to the war speeches by propaganda minister Joseph Goebbels could guess what was meant by the 'final solution to the Jewish question'. In the well-known speech at the Sportpalast on 18 February 1943, in which Goebbels propagated the idea of 'total war' after the demise of the Sixth Army at Stalingrad, 'international Jewry' constituted the 'demon of decline', which carried out its destructive work in the capitalist system of the USA as well as in Bolshevik Russia. In this light, only National Socialism (NS) was able and willing to put the Jewish greed for power in its place to avert the threatened decline of the occident. This called for a bundling of all available energies and a ruthless use of every possible means: 'Today, the most radical is just radical enough and the most total is just total enough to lead to victory! (Hails of bravo, applause)'.[16] The 'most radical' and the 'most total' included genocide, which Reichsführer-SS Heinrich Himmler acknowledged in front of the SS-Gruppenführers as a Herculean task of higher morals. In this select circle, the extreme was openly addressed as the 'extermination of the Jewish people' and, in a complete reversal of basic moral concepts, was raised to the rank of a heroic deed as a 'never to be written glorious chapter of our history'.[17]

The NS regime which, by virtue of its economic, social and foreign policy successes, enjoyed the support of large parts of the populace until into the first phase of the war,[18] not only brought misery and death to the Jews and other peoples but also led to a historically unrivalled act of self-destruction. Beyond the extermination of millions of human lives, the war led to the destruction of German cities and to the expulsion of millions of Germans from their homeland. Within a very short time, the power vacuum that had come about in the east was taken up by the Soviet Union, now allied to the Western forces. It extended its totalitarian rule structure to large parts of Eastern and Central Europe. In the Soviet-occupied part of Germany, the efforts towards a multiparty system that started immediately after the war quickly gave way to a communist dictatorship with a unified party, controlled mass organizations, a binding ideology, a communication monopoly as well as an extensive surveillance and repression system.

The end of the Sozialistische Einheitspartei Deutschlands (SED) regime and the other communist systems in Central and Eastern Europe became possible only with changes in the Soviet Union. The radical change in Poland connected with the name of Solidarność giving the signal and the reforms introduced under the cues of glasnost and perestroika by the new secretary general of the communist party, Mikhail Gorbachev, paved the way for the fall of the Iron Curtain, the system transformation in Eastern Central Europe and, thus, the end of European and German separation. The second millennium break, however, came only in the year 1991, as Hobsbawm rightfully placed it, as a successful military putsch by the army, the KGB and party cadres in Moscow would have reversed some of the things that had been achieved in previous years in the direction of more democracy and legal security within the satellite belt of the Soviet Union. The fall of the USSR can be understood as a historically unrivalled event in as far as never before had a world power fallen at the height of its military power without first having suffered a military defeat.

Whoever speaks of the twentieth century as the age of the extremes, and not only – like Hobsbawm – sets his sights on the excesses of inhumanity but also the isomorphies of certain political ideologies and movements, may give the impression that the extremes had unfolded only at the beginning of World War I and that some last death throes and a final demise were all that was left to be reckoned with in the twenty-first century. However, ideological trends reaching far back to the past had preceded the creation process of the, often called totalitarian, extremist regimes.[19] In the 1840s, an intensive analysis had taken place in Europe due to the new phenomenon of 'communism', which, in theory, could be traced back to the great utopias of a Plato, Morus and Campanella and, in practice, to ascetic, religious communities of late Antiquity that cultivated personal poverty (such as the Essenes at the Dead Sea or the therapists at north Egyptian Lake Mareotis).[20] Essential humanist roots lay in radical enlightening ideas such as those supported by Helvetius, Holbach, Morelly and Mably. Historians of ideas such as Jacob Talmon saw one root of left-wing totalitarianism in Jean-Jacques Rousseau's concept of the 'general will'. In connection with a 'popular sovereignty taken to the extreme',[21] the idea of a rational, predeterminable common good had supposedly favoured political ideas such as the Jacobins had tried to put into practice from time to time during the French Revolution. The development of the French Revolution could be described as a changeable struggle between the more strongly pragmatic supporters of a social power equilibrium and advocates of pure revolutionary ideals as they had found their expression during the 'terreur' and in the ideas of François Noël Babeuf. The Jacobin 'terror of virtue' and Babeuf's agrarian communism were interpreted by Talmon as 'the two earliest versions of modern political Messianism'.[22] When Babeuf's 'conspiracy of equals' was discovered, he and some of his loyal followers had to pay for his plans with their lives. Yet, the fascination with communism did not end there. In 1828, the publication of a book by a collaborator (Philippo Buonarotti), in which the humanity-cheering undertaking was drawn up, ensured new supporters.[23] The same went for Etienne Cabet's model state Ikaria where, according to the plans of the 'dictator' Ikar and thanks to the extensive rational planning by a wise 'committee', the people, relieved of a great deal of suffering, led a carefree life in peace, health and prosperity.[24] Ideas of this sort met with approval from German tradesmen living in Paris and were introduced in Switzerland and to the German-speaking realm among others by Wilhelm Weitling, a journeyman tailor inspired by Christianity.[25] The critical reception of the demanding socialist systems of Saint-Simon, Fourier and Owen reached a first peak in the years before the 1848/1849 Revolution.[26] In the following decades, Karl Marx and Friedrich Engels snubbed this 'utopian socialism'[27] and sought to support communism scientifically, most of all by a history of philosophy based on Hegel's dialectics placed on an economic foundation and at the same time sharply separating the doctrine from anarchism. Thus, these ideological foundations were laid long before communism achieved world status as a result of Lenin's acquisition and the doctrinal design of Marx and Engels' ideas, their canonization after the October Revolution and the Soviet Union's extraordinary development of power.

This applied no less to the new extreme right, which was beginning to unfold in many states of the world according to the pattern of Italian fascism. Karl Popper, in his history of ideas' derivation of totalitarian ideologies, referred to Plato's ideal state, which he interpreted as a programmatic political design. Simultaneously, he emphasized its hierarchic anti-egalitarian and racist tendencies, for the common ownership of women, children and possessions was to have been connected to a caste-like separation of rulers/guards and servants as well as the idea of an aristocratic warring master race led by philosopher kings, which obtained its hereditary substance through eugenic selective breeding, was relieved of having to earn a living and had the sole right to education and carrying weapons.[28] In his historical derivation of ideas, Jacob Talmon started much later. Among others, he interpreted Johann Gottlieb Fichte's *closed trade state* as a model in which nationalist and socialist ideas met in a new kind of synthesis.[29] In her work about *The Origins of Totalitarianism*, Hannah Arendt tried to recapture the humanist roots of anti-Semitism, nationalism and racial imperialism, which reach far back into the nineteenth century.[30]

As the comparison with the programmes of a monarchic absolutist right shows, these ideas broke in some ways with the traditional patterns of the legitimization of autocratic rulership, God's divine providence as well as patriarchal views. New ideological forms had already developed in the last few decades of the nineteenth century, which lent new attractiveness to the extreme right by adapting originally 'left' elements. This already applied to Bonapartism, which, not without success, tried to unite traditional dynastic sources of legitimization with democratic plebiscitary ones.[31] The integral nationalism of Maurice Barrès caused the liberal emancipatory impulses of this ideology to step back behind their authoritarian imperial tendencies.[32] In Germany, biologistic, 'eugenic' and anti-Semitic racial doctrines gained influence from the reception of Darwin's evolutionary theories,[33] which, generally, were foreign to ultra-monarchism and sprang much more from the positivist belief in science popular on the left.[34] The authoritarian nationalist trends took up elements of revolutionary syndicalism especially in France and Italy, thus creating an important prerequisite for the development of fascism.[35]

Therefore, whoever describes the twentieth century as the 'age of extremes' ought not to overlook the roots, which reach far back to the history of ideas and the real. It would be equally inappropriate to connect the end of the bipolar East–West confrontation and the beginning of the twenty-first century with overly strong hopes for the end of the extremes. The attacks of 9/11 have shown the whole world the danger of a 'third totalitarianism', which distinguishes itself from its two secular predecessors in the twentieth century not least by its – seemingly anachronistic – religious fundamentalist orientation.[36] In Iran, the Sudan and Afghanistan, Islamism has (at times) unfolded regime-forming power, and it is highly uncertain whether Gilles Kepel's prophecy of a decline of political Islam will come true.[37] The vitality of fundamentalisms is disclaimed by Francis Fukuyama who, in the face of the epoch-making change of 1989/1990, had proclaimed the 'end of history' in respect to a worldwide irreversible victory of liberal democracy and market economy.[38] Furthermore, it would hardly be appropriate once and for all to pronounce dead the two great totalitarianisms of the twentieth century. So – in leaning towards Marx and Lenin – some efforts towards interpreting the expansion of liberal democracy and market economy as theoretical imperialism are experiencing a certain renaissance in radical globalization-critical milieus.[39] As 'undogmatic' thinking is in fashion there, anarchism is also gaining new attractiveness.[40] Precursors of a so-called new right reveal fascism, communism and liberalism as equally totalitarian.[41] At the same time, autocrats and extremist intellectuals do not tire of pointing to new – dangerous – ways out of an unwell world.

Is it even realistic to start out from the assumption of a possible end to the phenomenon of political extremes? Are not the ways of thinking and behaving related to this structure, which is deeply anchored in man's psychological structure? Cannot the autocratic systems demand older 'rights' for themselves than the constitutional states can? And have constitutional forms not been rather residual entities throughout the centuries?[42] Were not the far and wide dominating autocratic structures able to lean on mentalities and forms of legitimization that had already been typical of the states of the early days of human civilization?

To answer such questions, a history of the terms and concepts of the political extremes is able to contribute. It seems reasonable to suppose that, through linguistic expression, a history of basic reflection is connected to the existential experience of inhumanity, heteronomous influence and repression. If this applies, it might be advantageous to have a closer look at questions such as the following: When did the concept of political extremes develop? Does it primarily record attempts of the democratic age? Or can it be traced back historically even further? Is there – as for many key terms in modern language – an ancient origin? Which imagination- and experience-based world laid its foundation? Can connections be found to the doctrine of tyranny and the constitutional tradition? If so, in which way did the respective thinking and interpretation patterns influence the formation of the modern constitutional state? Did they survive the epoch-making caesura of the democratic revolutions? In which forms did they crystallize? Are the terms used for extremes today the heirs of a far older terminology?

## 2 State of the research

When this author began dealing with political extremism during his doctoral studies more than twenty years ago, there was little known about the history of the terms and concepts of the extremes. In the ample German literature which, with regard to the terrorisms of the Red Army Faction and the lively activities of right- and left-wing extreme organizations, filled the bookshelves in the seventies, there were only a few leads in respect of it. Not a single journal article had been published on the topic. Also, in the Anglo-Saxon and the Francophone countries, there was a lack of respective research material.

Nevertheless, one was able to find important information among the entries in handbooks and encyclopaedias. The large, etymological dictionaries of the English and French languages, the *Oxford English Dictionary* and the *Trésor de la Langue Française*, were the most productive. The *Oxford English Dictionary* identified the nineteenth century as the period in which the term extremism was coined. It was first found in the English daily press. Concerning the German linguistic realm, it was assumed that it hailed back to Friedrich Rohmer's *Doctrine of the Parties* of the year 1844, whereby, however, it did not speak of extremism as such but of the importance of the political extremes 'radicalism' and 'absolutism'.[43] The *Trésor de la Langue Française* dated the earliest usage of the French word 'extrêmisme' to the year 1915, the initial stage of World War I. However, as is generally known, the French differentiation between 'extrême gauche' and 'extrême droite', which was already in use in the nineteenth century, could be traced back to the beginnings of the reorientation of political geography during the course of the French Revolution.

Regarding the other European states, it was also to be assumed that 'extremism' had been derived from the older term 'extreme'. Manfred Funke summarized the state of research at the beginning of the eighties in an entry in the *Handlexikon zur Politikwissenschaft*, published by Wolfgang W. Mickel, and there referred to the Latin terms 'extremus' and 'extremitas', which lend expression to 'that highest marginality that results from its relationship to the measuring or reference point'.[44] He pointed to formulations such as 'extremitas mundi', the end of the world, and respective terms in other languages such as the Italian 'estremo supplicio' (death penalty, in English 'extreme unction') and the French 'Extrême-Orient' (Far East), and assumed that the Greek root 'trema' (opening, path) was found in the Latin adjective 'extremus', so that an 'extreme person' was one 'who leaves the fortification of the polis and, thus, no longer participates in its domestic values'.[45] In Germany, the term 'extreme' did not become established until the eighteenth century.

If anyone attempted to shed further light on the history of concepts in the second half of the eighties, he/she did not find it difficult in view of this rather rudimentary field of knowledge to reach beyond the information found in the respective dictionaries and encyclopaedias. Therefore, in an examination of the first entries in the *Oxford English Dictionary* from the years 1846 and 1850, it was found that they did not deal with articles from the English daily press but with American sources. This clue was then traced to the years before the outbreak of the Civil War and showed that the viewpoints that were the furthest apart concerning the question of slavery were classified as 'extremist'.

At the end of the eighties, this author assumed that the first use of 'extremist' and 'extremism' was to be found in the United States. Ten years later, he learned otherwise when, during a guest semester at the Catholic University of Eichstätt, he found the supplement of a hand dictionary of the philosophical sciences from the year 1838, which came from the supplies of the old theological library and had been used widely in the nineteenth century. Under the term 'extreme', he found the following entry:

> Extremists are called those who do not want to accept a true centre but are pleased with themselves only in the extreme. More usually they are called ultraists.[46]

As the findings proved, the political arguments of the German 'Vormärz' (pre-March, between the revolutions of 1830 and 1848) were important for the history of concepts. The link to the term 'ultraism' made it necessary to shed more light on its history and meaning. As was noted, it did not remain in use for very long. Yet the term 'extremism' also did not gain a foothold in Germany. Rather, it applied to the 'extremes' as the 'furthest' or 'most extreme' right and left, but even more so to the 'radicals' and to 'radicalism'.

Therefore, one had to examine in which relationship the categories of the 'extreme' stood to the 'radical'. The origin of 'radicalism' as a political term seemed to lie in England in the second half of the eighteenth century.[47] The expression *radical reform* had, at the latest, made its rounds and found its entrance into the political language across the Atlantic with John Wilkes, a decided advocate for an 'ultra-radical reform'[48] of the right to vote.[49] In the first few decades of the nineteenth century, the supporters of the democratic philosophy of Jeremy Bentham especially were seen as 'radicals'. In the Romanic countries, the formula was soon adopted by the parties who leaned towards the liberal left and the Republican parties. One is reminded of this still today from the liberal (left) parties carrying the attribute 'radical' in their names. In France, the term 'radical' has been connected to an enlightened Republican programme up to the very present, so that other terms play no role whatsoever. Thus, Gérard Baal, a historian of French radicalism, tersely stated: 'In English as well as in German the term "radical" has kept an extremist connotation, which has become lost in France'.[50] This tradition, but also the Latin roots of the word, explains why anti-democratic and/or anti-constitutional movements had an easier time with calling themselves 'radical' than with the pejoratively loaded term 'extreme' or even 'extremist'. In the English-speaking world, the attribute 'radical' frequently serves as a self-label for movements that follow definite emancipatory goals, wanting to free man from all inherent pressures and longing for a never before available socio-political future that would 'overcome' all previous history.[51] Some like to point out that a political concept that started at the roots of things could not generally be evil. In this respect, the history of concepts of the term 'radicalism' became sidetracked and did not add anything essential to further enlighten the history of terms and concepts of the political extremes.

Another related term proved to be older and more traditional: 'fanaticism'. Its history is not at all lacking in thorough investigation.[52] One entry in the *Universal-Lexicon aller Wissenschaften und Kuenste* from the year 1735 is enlightening. There it says:

> fanatici, from the Latin word fanum, a heathen temple. By this name the heathens themselves first called the priests of Cybele and Bellona, as to most heathens both names designated a god: 'those acted as if they were outside of themselves and full of the spirit of the goddess, which is why they were shaking their heads so that their hair flew about, and then they talked all sorts of things which they wanted to have understood as divine revelations'.[53]

The picture drawn here is historically verified. The Lydian cult around the goddess Kybele was connected with orgiastic rites and celebrations. The goddess with the lion team not only bestowed fertility but also appeared as a demon 'that was able to enter human beings and able to fill them with wild delusions'. In Pessinus, the major location of cultural worship in Asia Minor, the

> divine rage was called forth through the insana aqua of the Gallus river [ ... ] with tympani, cymbali, hand drums and tambourins [ ... ], crotali (rattles), horns and flutes the arousal was goaded [ ... ], then one threw oneself around in a wild dance, howling wildly, shaking one's head and one's long, released hair until one was exhausted [ ... ], flagellating oneself, wounding oneself with sharp knives, often going far away over mountains and valleys [ ... ]; once we also heard of a priest who moved from Pessinus to Sardeis in holy μανία [ ... ]. Men and women [ ... ] lent themselves equally to this ecstacy, the sources often speak expressly of castrated priests.[54]

According to Zedler's *Enzyclopedia*, the 'fanatics' were often called 'eutheos' by the Greeks,

> but after them because also the heathens themselves easily noticed the hereby used fraud, and therefore the fanatici and the bellonarii were

subject to ridicule by everyone. All those who served false gods were called this by the ancient Christians and were therefore assigned to a god, which is why in old chronicles, before his conversion, King Clodonaco is given the name of a fanatici. Later on, one pointed out such persons among the Christians with this word as had boasted of immediate divine revelations and strange sciences thereof, for which reason Ventino Weigelo, the originator of the Rosicrucians, and Jacob Boehme as well as their dependents were given this name. In France, one applied this name to those who, after the revocation of the Edict of Nantes, joined the reformed doctrine there, and especially to those who took up weapons for the defence of their faith in Transylvania or in other areas, since there really were some among them who boasted about such revelations.[55]

Concerning the political extremes, the history of terms and concepts of 'fanaticism' seemed to suggest paying special attention to the religious quarrels in Europe, which in many ways foretold the political conflicts of the parties in the nineteenth and the twentieth century. Indeed, as was to be seen later, the extremism formula had not come into existence in the nineteenth century at all, but had already been used in early seventeenth-century Germany.

Did the origins of the concept therefore stem from the time of the religious civil wars? Or did one have to go even further back in history? In my dissertation in 1987, I still held the opinion that the '"extremism formula" – in contrast to "democracy" and "tyrannis" – did not belong to the concepts that had a long, meaningful tradition'.[56] This conclusion, however, stood in stark relationship to the following remark:

> The topos of the 'midpoint between the extremes', connected to the image of 'moderation' in contrast to the absoluteering of certain ideas rooted in the political thinking of the occident, has entered the ancient doctrine of the 'mixed constitution' but has continued to influence the constitutionalism of modern times and finally found expression in that state form which we nowadays summarize under the typified term 'democratic constitutional state'.[57]

This conclusion seemed suitable and could be reinforced in the course of later research. I became aware of this direction in the eighties due to a hint from my dissertation supervisor Erwin Faul and an essay by the political scientist Martin Gralher from Heidelberg, in which the categories of 'midpoint', 'mixture' and 'moderation' were explored.[58] Therein, the 'extremes' also played a, possibly, marginal role. One direction led to the ethics and the politics of Aristotle, in which the category of the 'extreme' is highly important. These relationships had been sketched out by Gralher but had not been systematically examined. The historian of concepts had to newly research the historical terrain in many areas. For essential insights, I am indebted to a number of investigations concerning the history of the mixed constitution, especially the studies by G.J.D. Aalders, James M. Blythe, Daniel Hoechli, Hans Joachim Kraemer, Wilfried Nippel and Alois Riklin.[59]

## 3 Methodology

Where the historian of concepts is not able to reach back to a treasure of lexical findings, he is not spared detailed detection work. If the entire relevant literature were available in digitized form, it would be easier to recapture the development of the political language. Hereby, we are standing amid a communicative revolution, which may certainly ease the burden of researching the history of concepts in a few decades. A start has already been made with the digitization of the classical works of literature. Nonetheless, vast parts of the books and magazines published since the invention of the art of printing have not even been recorded by titles yet. This, however, applies much more to the German, French, Italian, Spanish and Russian literature than to the English.

Where the historian of concepts is unable to build on extensive previous work, he is forced to systematically rake through political publications. Therefore, those amounts of book and magazine literature, from which the desired findings failed to materialize, are not even mentioned in this volume. During the course of this research, the field of investigation was subject to restriction in as far as it concentrated on the use of the terms 'extreme' and 'extremism', whereas an array of related terms had to be neglected. This can also be justified by the fact that the history of terms and concepts of 'radicalism' and 'fanaticism' has been researched more widely. Still, even if this was not the case, a limit would have had to be drawn for reasons of work economy.

Besides, in the following, the focus will be on *political* extremes. Although their interconnection with intellectual personages from the realm of other topics becomes clear, the development of the history of concepts connected to them (e.g. in the realm of logics, mathematics and physics) has nevertheless been largely omitted. Even though the field of investigation thus lent itself to limitation, it nevertheless kept its breadth in other respects: As – as will be seen later – the history of concepts of the political extremes is inseparably connected from the history of ideas of Old Europe, it was out of the question to limit the research to the *German* political language only. Herein lies an important difference from the monumental, in many ways exemplary, undertaking of the *Basic Historical Concepts* inaugurated by Otto Brunner, Werner Conze and Reinhart Koselleck, which was attempted towards the end of the sixties and was completed in the nineties with the publication of its last volume.

The volumes of the *Basic Historical Concepts* do not comprehend the history of political terms and concepts as a bloodless, linguistic grid slipped over the history of the real, but as a product of the human spirit in the permanent process of change in the social, cultural, economic and political world. The analysis of the political use of the language and the therewith connected contents from different historical epochs is to shed light on the more profound structural changes that German society has had to undergo in the course of the centuries. Thereby, special importance is placed on the relationship between the history of concepts and society. It deals particularly with the question in which specific ways different social groups and levels are aware of and reflect their political surroundings, which descriptive and analytical categories they use in this and how they fill them with content.

In particular, four processes of historic change are paid special attention: first, the *time frame*, meaning in which way the contemporaries classify events into a larger historic context, within which time zones they think, which periodization they undertake, which events they notice as being of utmost importance, whether they devise a teleological picture of history, imagine history as goal oriented or rather think in cycles. The second process consists of *democratization*. This addresses the opening of political discussions to groups and levels of society that had so far been excluded from them. The question of in which way the new communication participants use the linguistic categories of the up to then closed elitist circles is of particular interest. The third process deals with the *ideologizability*, i.e. the enrichment of traditional conceptual categories with extensive interpretations of history, present and future, which meet the demand for orientation in a world that leaves former horizons of meaning, pluralizes itself, becomes socially and intellectually more difficult to comprehend and to a growing extent demands the toleration of ambiguities. Finally, the fourth process is the *politicization*, i.e. the use of facts, arguments and meaningful contents in the political discussion with opponents. Linguistic and analytical categories of the academic language change into fighting terms, are provided with pejorative and positive connotations, take on a euphemistic and dysphemistic slant. All four processes: time frame, democratization, ideologizability and politicization, are often closely connected to, influence and penetrate each other.[60]

This approach, first developed by Reinhart Koselleck, proved important for the work in several respects. Of course, it does not solely have to do with a 'best performance' concerning the history of ideas. Particularly in those parts that deal with the period after the French Revolution, an attempt was made to record a wide range of political publications and to take into consideration the different ideological trends, including rather peripheral ones. Hereby, the intensity of the reception is more important than the scientific and literary value of a publication. In this way, an attempt is made to record the differing perceptions of political historic events in a suitable fashion. Special attention is paid to the specific form of the acquisition of the political term by different political and social powers, be it a (pejorative) external term, be it a (turned into the positive) self-labelling term.

Where the discourses of the history of concepts increased in density, particularly at turning points at which the flow of history accelerates, breaks with tradition occur and novelties unfold, a minute reconstruction of the communication processes was required. At such times, the press was utilized intensively. This applies foremost to the American Civil War, the Russian Revolution and the year of the rise of the fascist movement.

In the multilingual appendix, bearing in mind an interest in conceptualization forms and reciprocal perceptions, the investigation adopts methodological ideas from the English historians of ideas, John Pocock and Quentin Skinner. These authors did not conceive a similarly monumental work such as the *Basic Historical Concepts*, but they have demonstrated their form of the history of terms and concepts in a multitude of insightful studies written by them and their students. The English historians of concepts share a number of characteristics with the Göttingen school; however, they are different from it by placing the emphasis on the relevance of different discourses, i.e. in the ways of thinking, speaking and interpreting, which are not only determined sociologically but express different political views, interests and requirements for exploitation. An important example is the differentiation between a Whig and a Tory version of British history. This is not necessarily determined by the specific levels, but developed first of all due to the contrast between the court and the country party. Through history of the mixed constitution discourses, it can thus be shown how the original Whig concept developed into the official version of the British monarchy.[61]

Even though this approach has left its traces, nevertheless it is a history of terms and concepts puzzle, large parts of which were collected in detailed detection work. Not every find could be suitably placed in the sense of the history of ideas. The historian of concepts 'criminalist' is not always fortunate enough to find a trace that will lead him to other finds. Often, he discovers singular pieces of proof that cannot be fitted into a larger historical context. Some traces end in no-man's-land. Only slowly does a mosaic come together from single finds. Thereby, one always had to resist the temptation of forcing 'uncooperative' building blocks together to construe connotations, where they hardly existed in reality. Let the reader decide if this was successful.

## 4 Structure

The investigation begins with Antiquity (Chapter 2). The category of the extremes is already placed in political contexts in pre-Aristotelian philosophy. Moderation ethics and the art of moderation gained eminent political importance in Plato's late work. The categories of the mesotês doctrine and the mixed constitution systematically unfolded Aristotle's politology. This is presented in detail. The chapter also deals with the reception history of Antiquity and the Middle Ages, particularly extolling the importance of the extremes in the framework of the doctrine of the mixed constitution that is closely tied to Aristotelianism. The Aristotelian teaching tradition based on scholastics transported the conceptual categories and concepts further. Chapter 3 follows this path of tradition from the early humanism of the Upper Italian city-states to the foundation of the United States of America, where John Adams especially kept alive the doctrine of the mixed constitution. As can be shown, the doctrine of the mixed constitution, with the supposition of a natural social divergence of interests based on it, offered favourable prerequisites for the acceptance of the party system that had been banned for centuries.

If Aristotelianism was a dominant trend in the political history of ideas in Europe until the eighteenth century, it can be shown by way of German 'Vormärz' liberalism (Chapter 4) that a break with tradition was definitely out of the question. The category of a 'right centre' between the extremes had become the slogan of the citizen kingdom after the 1830 Revolution in France and had also appealed to England (under different framework conditions). The 'juste milieu' theory built upon the new right–left topography that had expanded across the European continent after the French Revolution. The Aristotelian differentiation of 'moderate' and 'extreme' positions united with the right–left differentiation to a two-dimensional system of coordinates.

One focus of the presentation centres on the 'age of the extremes'. As will be seen, the extremism concept, which was already in use in the USA during the Civil War years, found far-reaching application in World War I as a rather derogative expression for the political project of the Bolsheviks in Russia, which was perceived as a threat to the entire occidental constitutional state tradition. The spreading of the extremism term from 1917 on is reconstructed in an extensive evaluation of the English, French, Italian and German press (Chapter 5). Had it, to begin with, been applied almost entirely to the new extreme left, after the march on Rome, it soon also included the new extreme right, which had formed in Italy and found offshoots and imitators in many other European countries.

'Extremism' established itself – in the broadest sense – as a liberal stigma term for those trends that questioned the 'constitutional' consensus that had increased during the course of the nineteenth century. But in which way did the extreme right and left themselves use this vocabulary applied to them? As is known, the term 'fanaticism' was changed into a positive expression by the National Socialists. 'Fanatical enthusiasm' became the quality trademark of the convinced political fighter. Can this terminological break with the vocabulary of the constitutional state tradition also be proved for the category of the 'extremes'? This question is explored in Chapters 5 and 6. It is also necessary to investigate whether the extreme left dealt with this in a similar way. Did this leave traces in the propaganda of the two dictatorships in Germany? Which terms did the ideocratic regime use for labelling political antagonists? Did the language of the SED regime show any similarities with that of National Socialism? Or were the traditional terms only filled with different contents – in a way this also applied to the pleonastic terms of 'people's democracy' and 'people's republic'?

Concerning the time after 1945, the development of the extremism concept is in the focus of scientific discussion. Originating in the USA, it has spread to the Western European states. In West Germany, it found its way into the terminology of 'militant democracy' and thus took on an official nature (Chapter 7). Nevertheless, some time had to elapse before a uniform terminology developed. By its very nature, the scientific discussion presented in

Chapter 8 remains marked by competing concepts and terminologies. The partially crypto-political nature of the – often highly emotionalized – arguments with those powers regarded as extremist added to this. Chapter 9 summarizes the results of the history of concepts and leads to systematic viewpoints for the conceptualization of the extremism concept. It lacks the thus encircled realm of definitions, develops a typology and closes with an outlook concerning the meaning of the political extremes for the foreseeable future.

# 2 Extremes, mean, moderation and constitutional mixture in Antiquity and the Middle Ages

## 1 Extremes in pre-Aristotelian thought

People have always been attracted, fascinated and horrified by the extremes. To transcend the limits of the trite, the average and the traditional, and to push things to their outermost limit, could, in the last consequence, be seen as the thorn of renewal and progress, but likewise as a danger for the existing, the attained and the tried and true.

The Aristotelian mesotês doctrine became the determining factor for the political tradition and language of occidental constitutionalism. A mean seen as the epitome of virtue constituted the centre of a continuum whose extreme points were equated with extremeness and degeneration. The mesotês doctrine reached back to numerous intellectual traditions already in pre-Socratic time. In the fourth book of the *Politics*, where the preferences of democratic and oligarchic elements of a mixed 'polity' are discussed, Aristotle Phokylides of Milet (approx. 550 BC) states: 'Many things are best for the middling; I would be of the middling sort in the city'.[1]

Whoever goes through the number of literary witnesses from the sixth pre-Christian age on, in which keeping to the right measure and a mean between extreme thought and conduct was recommended as the 'norm for desire and action, for the mastery of the senses and the effects, in short, for all sides of the diversities of human life',[2] comes to the conclusion that, in his doctrine of the mean and the extremes, Aristotle expressed a basic experience of generations of Greek poets and thinkers. Keeping to the right mean in all things of life was seen as the mark of Hellenism; extremeness, for example in the form of cruel revenge, ornate development of splendour, unrestrained orgies, on the other hand, was understood as a characteristic of barbarianism.

The recommendation of keeping to moderation and the right mean between the extremes 'has been a basic element of Greek wisdom since Hesiod. It is voiced by seven wise men (magi) and is hewn in stone at Delphi; the poet of the Boethian farmers' morals preaches it as frequently and as fervently as the aristocratically proud gnomic Theognis and as Pindar, the poet of aristocratic sports. Then, again, it resounds in diverse variations from the tragic stage'.[3]

The idea of moderation runs through the preserved literary fragments of the Athenian legislator Solon (approx. 640–561 BC). Dike (Δίκη), the goddess of truth and law, embodies the principle of good order, the eunomy (εὐνομία) against hybris in the sense of greed, the craving for rulership and recognition. Appropriate action, however, keeps to a mean, a meson (μέσον), between too much and too little.[4] A characteristic place is found in the great state elegy:

> But it is the citizens themselves who
> by their acts of foolishness and subservience to money
> are willing to destroy a great city,
> and the mind of the people's leaders is unjust;
> they are certain to suffer much pain as a result of their great arrogance.
> For they do not know how to restrain excess
> or to conduct in an orderly and peaceful manner the festivities of the banquet.[5]

Thinking about the right measure/moderation and its transgression marks the problem that 'for Solon and his time consciously stood in the center: Gaining a new life norm through the power of insight'.[6]

According to Herodot, the idea of moderation also determines the meeting of Solon with Croesus, who not only thought of himself as the richest and most powerful but at the same time also as the happiest person. The Lydian potentate is lectured by Solon in the following manner after a joint round through the magnificent treasure chambers: 'Many wealthy men are unfortunate, whilst many of only moderate riches are blessed by fortune'.[7]

The political ethical idea of a mean between the extremes, as it has found expression in early poetry and writings of history, might have come into existence by an entangled exchange of thought forms, which led to the exact sciences that had begun to differentiate themselves from the fourth century. The terms 'hyperbole' and 'ellipsis', still used today for certain conic sections directed towards a midpoint, stem from Pythagorean geometry and music theory. The geometric proportion is known from the work of the mathematician Archytas of Tarent (420–350 BC). He speaks of this when geometric surfaces are equal to: $2 : 4 = 4 : 8$.[8] However, this relationship is expressed by a much older term from the Pythagoreans: harmony (ἁρμονία). The Pythagoreans had realized that the lengths of the strings of the musical instruments acted like $1 : 2 : 4$ for the octaves. The discovery of the relationship between the height of a tone and the length of a string led to the development of a mathematical proportion theory, which thus had its origins in the harmony doctrine of music.[9]

It makes sense that similar trains of thought gained importance in art. The method that Polyklet (second half of the fifth century BC) recommended in his *Canon* for the determination of the beautiful consists of finding a 'middle line' (μέσον)[10] and harmonizing the parts of the work of art. Such demands exerted an influence on rhetoric. Isocrates (436–338 BC), who had founded his Athenian school of rhetoric a few years prior to the founding of Plato's academy, recommended to the ruler always to clearly consider his words and actions, never to 'miss his aim', rather finding 'the golden mean [ ... ] in a too little than in a too much'.[11]

The idea of the right mean and the avoidance of the extremes had already entered medicine from natural philosophy in the fifth pre-Christian century.[12] Accordingly, Hippocrates (approx. 460–377 BC) pleaded for observing the right measure/moderation concerning the ingestion of food, discussed the problems of too much humidity or drought, heat and cold. There exists 'the right measure/ moderation for the ingestion of food and the proper amount of physical exercise' for every human constitution. When 'the proper relationship between the ingestion of food and exercise is shifted only one little bit, the body will be overwhelmed by the excess of one of them as time goes by and will fall ill'.[13] Man's natural characteristics and ways of behaviour were to be balanced by new cures.

It is no surprise then that the mesotês idea, which was effective in so many scientific realms, entered Greek literature in multifarious forms. From the wisdom found in the rich treasury of Greek tragedies, let us choose only two especially prominent passages from the works of the important dramatists, Sophocles and Euripides.

In Sophocles' (496–406/405 BC) *Oedipus at Colonos*, the mean and moderation form directional points for a general rule of living one's life. Accordingly, the chorus admonishes:

> Whosoe'er as a boon receiveth
> Life in its uttermost measure of days,
> Him I censure as one who cleaveth
> Froward ever to foolish ways.
> Days that linger are ever heaping
> Loads that are liker to grief and care;
> Lost are the hours Age spends in keeping
> Watch for the place where its pleasures were.
> Soon as the lonely Hades loometh
> Lacking the dance and the choric breath,
> He the Comrade of all men cometh,
> His is the end and his name is Death.[14]

The here expressed ethics of moderation run throughout the dramatic work of Euripides (480–406 BC), the younger poet of tragedies. A typical passage is found in a chorus from the *Antiope Fragment,* where the subject is equanimity in one's love life:

> Happy those who moderately and healthily are blessed with Aphrodite, enjoying to be spared the wild raging of love. For Eros shoots the arrows of love twofold, one for blessed lust, the other for destroying pain, may I drive him out of my room! May love be moderate for me, and sacred the

longing! May I be blessed with Aphrodite but avoid extreme love! Men are of different kind, but always clear is the true good. Chaste education does powerfully contribute to virtue. Shyness is wisdom, it brings the rich payment of clearly understanding what duty means, glorious is this. If the order of something great is living within one's bosom, the public welfare will be increased.[15]

The aidos (αἰδώς), a shyness guided by moral feelings, provides one with the strength to hold fast to moderation and leads to virtue. Morally ideal behaviour consists of finding the proper measure (metriotes – μετριότης, metrion – μέτριον) between too much (hupermetron – ὑπερμέτρον, huperbolê – ὑπερβολή) and too little (elatton – ἔλαττον, endeia – ἔνδεια).

Conspicuous parallels have been found between the logical and the linguistic/stylistic version of this terminology and that of Democrit. This may not be much of a surprise, as the poets of tragedies worked out in literary form the topics discussed by philosophers. The central term of Democrit's (born approx. 460 BC, a student of Leukippos of Milet) ethics is euthymy (εὐθυμία), a pleasant state of mind that is achieved by bringing the body's lust, greed and troubles ('tarachai') to a natural measure/moderation. For, every too much ('huperbolê', 'pleôn') and too little ('elleipsis', 'elatton') would turn into its opposite so that the soul would be shaken up. The 'aidos' would lead him to moderation, letting the soul find a balanced condition.[16] The emphasis on physical lust in the development of pathological conditions shows the influence of medicine on Democrit who held lively discussion with physicians such as Hippocrates. His individualized ethical life doctrine has therefore been called a 'dietetics of the soul'.[17]

Doubtless, Democrit influenced Plato's philosophy (427–347 BC) with his doctrine of the soul and the connection of the natural sciences with ethical reflection.[18] Yet the theoretical constitutional application of the idea of moderation does not go back to Democrit, although it had already been in circulation during his lifetime. An early reference is found in the *Eumenides* by Aeschylos (525–456 BC). Anarchy and despotism embody the political extremes which are to be avoided at all costs:

> Approve thou not a life ungoverned nor one subjected to a tyrant's sway.
> To moderation in every form God giveth the victory,
> but his other dispensations he directeth in varying wise.[19]

Or in another place:

> Neither anarchy nor tyranny –
> this I counsel my burghers to maintain and hold in reverence.[20]

The historian of the Peloponnesian War, Thucydides (ca. 455–397 BC), also knew the mesotês model in its application to the constitutional doctrine. In the eighth book, he praises the Athenians with an expression borrowed from medicine. They had effected a 'μετρία' and 'ξύγκρασις'[21] between the rule of a few and that of many in the summer of 411 after the fall of the oligarchy.

Plato brought together constitutional theory, natural sciences and ethical elements of thought in the dialogues of the *Politeia*. A key place is found in the eighth book of the third major part, where the four main forms of bad constitutions and conditions of the soul and the transformation of democracy into tyranny are spoken of:

> The same ailment which arose in oligarchy, and destroyed that, arises in this regime also – only more widespread and virulent because of the licence it is given. Here it enslaves democracy. Indeed, *excess* [ἄγαν] in one direction generally tends to produce a violent reaction in the opposite direction. This is true of the seasons of the year, of plants and animals, and particularly true of political regimes. [ ... ] since the only likely reaction to *excessive* freedom [ἄγαν ἐλευθερία], whether for an individual or for a city, is excessive slavery [ἄγαν δουλείαν μεταβάλλειν]. [ ... ] the chances are that democracy is the ideal place to find the origin of tyranny – the *harshest* and *most complete* slavery arising, I guess, from the *most extreme* freedom [τῆς ἀκροτάτης ἐλευθερίας δουλεία πλείστη τε καὶ ἀγριωτάτη].[22]

The terms used by Plato: ἄγαν ('very', 'completely', 'too much'), πλεῖστοη ('the highest degree'), ἀγριωτης ('wildness', 'violence') and ἀκροτάτης (from ἄκρον – 'top', 'summit', 'maximal height') in their entity describe a quantitative as well as a qualitative excess. By way of subtle philological investigations, it was proved how the terminology of these considerations correlate with the norm structure of the Platonic doctrine of principles. The hereby used categories of a mean (μέσον) between excess (huperbolê) and deficiency (elleipsis) have a central place in the Platonic doctrine of being.[23] In the *Politeia*, they find their expression particularly by one of the four basic virtues in the state, the mindfulness/sôphrosunê (σωφροσύνη), which is to give direction to private as well as public action, preparing the way for the reasonable and moderate and making the successful coexistence of the individual social levels possible.[24] In this way, the idea of moderation and the mean is connected to the ideal of the reign of philosophy. Extremeness, on the other hand, constitutes the main cause for the degeneration of actual constitutions, timocracy, oligarchy and democracy, yet most of all the most unfair of them all, tyranny.[25] Nevertheless, the idea of a mean between the extremes is connected to the idea of a balancing mixture between opposing constitutional elements only in the later writings.

The descent from the lofty heights of the ideal state to the lowlands of the actual world of the polis is, for the most part, explained by the profound political disappointment that Plato experienced on his three journeys to Syracuse.[26] No doubt, the consideration of second- and third-best political constitutional solutions in his late works, most of all the *Politicos* and the *Nomoi*, gain great importance. Through the introduction of a mixed constitution, the idea of a mean between the extremes moves to the centre of consideration.

The terminology unfolded here is especially well developed in a passage in the *Politicos* where Plato distinguishes between two forms of the art of measuring (μετρητική). The relative form of measuring consists of determining a more or a less, a bigger or a smaller; however, the absolute form defines a too much (πλέον, ὑπερβάλλον) and a too little (ἔλαττον) above a fixed measuring point; thus a third one is situated in the 'middle between two outermost ends' ('τὸ μέσον ἀπῳκίσθη τῶν ἐσχάτων'[27]).

The absolute kind of measuring is expressed by the ranking of political forms, which Plato, in a definite turnabout from the ideal state concept of the *Politeia*, *develops* in the *Politicos*. The only proper ideal constitution marked by the reign of philosophy, which must, however, be set aside from all other state constitutions like a god among men,[28] is here confronted with empirically existing state constitutions.[29] They are divided into two criteria: the number of the ruling and the differentiation into lawful and lawless. Departing from the terminology of the *Politeia*, Plato differentiates between kingship, aristocracy and ordinary democracy as lawful forms and tyrannis, oligarchy and anarchic democracy as lawless ones. In the fifth century, the thus systematically developed scheme of six of the constitutional forms was derived from the older division into three parts (own rulership, multiple rulership and the rulership of many) and had, in an initial attempt, already marked Herodot's constitutional debate.[30] As Plato described in the *Politeia*, the kingdom comes closest to the best state, yet Plato not only passes a mostly negative judgement on the unlawful ones but on the lawful states as well. Their conformity to the law leads to hardening and to the lack of adaptability to changing conditions,[31] and every deviation from once established rules ends in anarchy. Therefore, the true politician is not to shy away from breaking the law, although if he does so without being knowledgeable of the norm realized in the ideal state, the revolution only pulls it even further into the maelstrom of the extremes and into anarchy.

Only in the face of this dilemma does Plato credit legal order with its own value. In the *Nomoi*, the necessity of law is based on the nature of the people living in the present, who lacked understanding and self-discipline and tended towards greed and egotism. In view of the impossibility of erecting the ideal state with the inadequate human beings living on earth, the mixed constitution comes into view as a realistic alternative. In the third book, Plato derives the creation of the mixed constitution from the history of philosophy. From the originally patriarchal rule of the family and the tribe, the aristocracy and the kingdom come into being first of all, later followed by all the other forms. The Doric migration leads to the large Peloponnesian troika empire of Argos, Sparta and Messene, which receives a mixed constitution consisting of a democracy and a monarchy in a contract of rulership between the citizens and the kings, thus constituting a fourth and higher developmental step. Whereas Argos and Messene sink into tyranny as a result of their rulers' weakness of character, Sparta's mixed constitution – inspired by the gods[32] – proves to be durable. Here, the right measure (μέτριον[33]) was chosen for the distribution of power, the influence of the kingdom by the principle of cooperativeness (dual kingdom), the senate in the ephores limited and a system of weights and counterweights established. As the kingdom was of a mixed nature ('σύμμεικτος'), using the necessary ingredients and 'duly moderated',[34] decline into tyranny was avoided. 'The objective law freed of all selfish interests, which has as its aim solely the arete and the eudemia of man, without which all communal existence comes to an end sooner or later, in the balancing connection and mutual control of all partial interests, came into close proximity of reality'.[35]

In the following historical consideration, the term measure (μέτριον) becomes clear. According to Plato, monarchy and democracy are the 'mothers' of all other constitutions. Monarchy is carried to the limit ('ἄκρον') by the Persians, as democracy is by the Athenians.[36] However, if freedom and friendship combined with understanding[37] are to develop, both forms must be connected with each other. In a well mixed state, the values finding their expression by the two constitutions form a synthesis. Every deviation from this synthesis misses the right measure. As soon as one of the elements is 'carried to the extreme' ('ἐπί δέ τὸ ἄκρον'[38]), monarchy sinks into slavery; democracy, however, into anarchy (Figure 2.1).

Plato's explanations are based on a constitution continuum which reaches from tyrannis to oligarchy, kingdom, aristocracy and lawful democracy and, slipping into anarchy, to the lawless rule of the people. Consisting of various elements, the mixed forms are 'not only functionally related to the extremes but come as it were into being through them materially by intensification and dilution'. The optimum lies directly in the mean (μέσον[39]) between the extremes of democracy and monarchy. There, the merits of both sides unite in the form of a synthesis of values, whereby the disadvantages are left behind. In the normative synthesis, not only the boundary forms are present in a certain sense, but also all the in-between forms in as far as they are balanced among themselves.[40]

The better and, at the edges, the worse constitutions are located in the inside of the continuum. The sequence is not determined by the number of rulers but by the intensity of power: 'The concentration and the dispersion of

| Turannis | Oligarchia | Basileia Kingdom | Aristokratia | Dēmokratia Nomos/Law | Dēmokratia Anomia/Lawlessness |
|---|---|---|---|---|---|

*Figure 2.1* Continuum of state constitutions according to Plato
Source: Krämer (1959: 210)

power is the law according to which all conceivable empirical constitutions act toward each other. On both sides of the right mean, in which all of them are more or less positively kept, those mutations which are only problematic in their singularity, are stacked first, then gradually – at a growing distance – also the actual mutations'.[41]

In Plato's mixed constitution, the balance of power and the inner balance are caused by an artful distribution of the competencies to different institutions. With regard to Sparta, Plato mentions the institutions of the dual kingdom, the senate and the ephorate.[42] The mixed constitution of the Nomoi knows the council of the thirty-seven iron guardians[43] and, additionally, a nightly assembly[44] to which, among others, belong the ten eldest iron guardians, the head of the education system (the highest civil servant of the state) and deserving priests, twelve civil servants from the highest state court of justice for the supervision of all the authorities and the system of religious worship as the embodiment of the aristocratic monarchist element,[45] as well as the council (boulê) and the assembly of the people as democratic elements.[46] The integration of the competencies and the different forms of election emphasize the importance of the mixed constitution.

In a letter written at approximately the same time as the *Nomoi*, Plato distinctly mentioned this aspect once more: He points to the Spartan legislator Lykurg who, in the light of the coming into existence of tyranny in Argos and Messene, had pleaded for the control of the kingdom by ephorate and gerusia (council of elders) and advises to transfer any tyranny into a lawful kingdom. For 'dependence and freedom in excess are both very bad, but very good in the right measure'. The avoidance of the extremes and keeping to the right measure brings man into harmony with divine order: 'Moderate is the dependence on God, extreme that on man, but the law to the sensible is God, to the rash it is pleasure'.[47]

Owing to the conditions of earthly existence, a convergence to the principles of the ideal state is made possible by the mixed constitution. It mutually cancels out the negative effects of the extreme constitutional elements and is of a distinct compromise nature.[48] On the one hand, a discord-causing excess of property and goods is to be rejected; on the other hand, poverty as the cause of slavery is to be avoided.[49] On the one hand, people's family ties are to remain intact; on the other hand, the people must be prevented from meeting the common good with disinterest.[50] On the one hand, state bureaucracy controls large areas of life; on the other hand, individual initiative must be given some space. On the one hand, the state is placed on a democratic foundation by the participation of a relatively broad populace; on the other hand, the idea of creating an elite and rewarding exceptional knowledge and performance keep their central status. A cleverly conceived voting system with a vote by ticket and a test of competence guarantees the fairness of a suitable mean between the monarchic and the democratic constitution.[51]

The mixed constitution adapts itself to the value structure of the later mesotês doctrine. Hans Joachim Krämer gave its terminology a two-dimensional expression. The μέσον in the vertical (axiological dimension) embodies the idea of the good (ἀγαθόν) and finds a theoretical constitutional equivalence in the mixed (μεικτή) constitution. It forms the mean of the horizontal (ontological dimension). There, the extreme (ἄκρον) constitutional forms, overshooting the mark beyond (ὑπερβολή) the right measure (καιρός/μέτριον), the slavery (δουλεία) of despotism/tyrannis on the one hand and anarchy (αν-αρχία) of lawless democracy (ανομία δημοκρατία) on the other, embody a condition of moral inferiority (κακόν) (Figure 2.2).

The mixed constitution brings the basic ideas of extreme constitutional elements into balance. Their compromise nature, however, cannot blind us to the fact that the radical traits from the ideal state design of the *Politeia* still persist. The economic foundation of the state with slavery and a prevalently agrarian economic system (the corrupting influence of the commercial port cities is a sore point in Plato) remains intact. The aim of the citizens living a virtuous life in the interest of the greatest possible happiness requires strict education[52] as well as a system of extensive control and interventions that comprises all sectors of life from birth control and 'race selection'[53] to the ingestion of food, the purchasing of goods, travelling, the permission to speak publicly as far as to leisure activities.[54] There is no room for non-conformists. Atheists, for example, are either re-educated or, if this does not succeed, killed.[55]

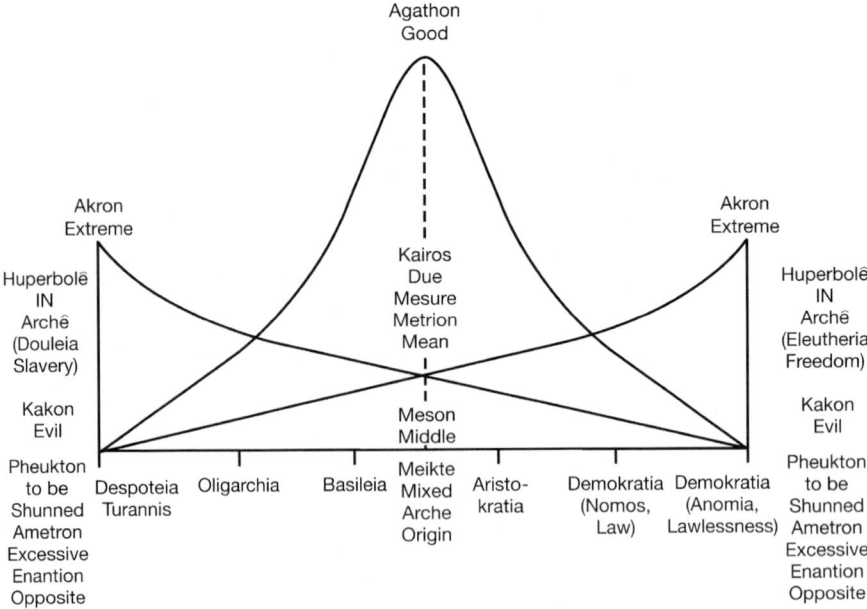

*Figure 2.2* The value structure of the Platonic mixed constitution concept
Source: Krämer (1959: 214)

## 2 Extremes in the mesotês doctrine and Aristotle's theory of the mixed constitution

Plato's student, Aristotle (384–322 BC), critically took up the work of his teacher. In Aristotle's work, there is hardly any analytical or ethical category that was not already to be found in Plato. Still, the student forsakes the dialogue form of explanations, which had led to ambiguities, develops his ideas by strict systems, penetrates nearly all areas of knowledge and organizes them according to disciplines. He departs from the ontologically theological doctrine of ideas, placing his views on a broad empirical basis. Thus, Aristotle can rightfully be called the actual founder of practical philosophy.[56]

The juxtaposition of the mean and the extremes runs through his complete work. In *Metaphysics*, Aristotle develops the terminological logic. The mean and the extremes always refer to each other and form a contrary opposition instead of a contradiction. For 'between the two members of the contradiction', there is 'no mean', whereas 'this is possible with contradictions'.[57] Therefore, the oppositions true/false, to be/not to be, etc., later called contradictory, form no extremes, which is different from the contrary ones such as black/white or good/evil for example. For it is the outermost points of a continuum that are considered extremes. They are formed by those things of a genus that show the 'greatest difference'[58] from each other. Extremes can therefore only be formed by the ingredients of a genus, whereas things, which belong to different genii, are incomparable and 'have no transition into one another'.[59] What is in the middle must thus belong to the same genus as the extremes.[60]

In this implication, the terminological difference is also found in syllogistics. In the *First Analytics*, it says:

> Whenever three terms are so related to one another that the last one is contained in the middle one as in a whole, and the middle one is either contained in or excluded from the first one as in or from a whole, the extremes must be connected by a perfect syllogism. By a middle term I mean one that is itself contained in another and contains another one in itself; this term also becomes middle by position. By extremes I mean both that term which is itself contained in another one and that in which another one is contained.[61]

For 'the last', Aristotle uses the word ἔσχατος, for the position 'outer', he uses ἄκρα (peak, summit). From two premises is derived one concluding sentence, e.g. 'All Greeks are human beings' (premise 1), 'All human beings are mortal' (premise 2); thus it follows: 'All Greeks are mortal' (conclusion). The mean term (later terminus medius) is seen as that predicator that occurs in both premises, and the predicators, which are placed above and below the mean term, respectively, are called 'outer terms' (later termini extremi).

In the *Topics*, Aristotle deals with the position of the mean term between contrary opposites and its relationship to the extremes (ἄκρα). For example, in the fourth book, which deals with the definition of the 'genii of existence' and ' peculiarities', one needs to examine the following:

> If there is an opposite genus as well as an opposite kind of something, and if there is in the definitions something that stands in the middle, yet not so in the others. Namely, if there is something that mediates between the genii, then it exists also in the kinds, and if it exists in the kinds, it also exists in the genii as is the case in 'being good' and 'being evil' (as genii) and 'justice' and 'injustice' (as kinds): in both cases there exists something in the middle.[62]

The mean and the extremes play a central role in the terminological relationship of Aristotle's ethics and politics. In his work, both realms form an inseparable unit. Personal lifestyle and conduct in the polis are the subject of a science focusing on human matters, whereby politics factually complements ethics 'so that our philosophy of humanity might be as complete as possible'.[63] Thus, the ethics, and particularly his mature later work, the *Nichomachean Ethics*, constitute an essential basis for the understanding of the 'Politics'. Ethics and politics represent the two inseparable components of practical philosophy. Their insights are to positively influence human behaviour. Ethics are to create 'good people';[64] Politics shows how a 'good life' can be organized for the citizens.

The close connection of ethics with the writings on methodology and natural sciences is seen where mathematical terms are employed in the realm of ethics. Accordingly, in the *Nichomachean Ethics*, he explains the proportionality of the mean between two equally distanced ends[65] or uses the arithmetic proportion for the definition of fair distribution: When 10 and 2 are assumed as extreme values, the mean is 6. What is located at an equal distance from two ends (ἄκρα, extremes) is called the μέσον (mean).[66] If distributive justice becomes the mean between a wrong from enrichment (person A enriches himself through person B by goods C) and a wrong from theft (person B loses to person A goods C which are his), A–C leads to B+C, thus a re-establishment of a fair condition.[67] If one sees the two unfair conditions A+C and B–C as extremes and assigns to them the arithmetic values 10 and 2, fairness is reached through the arithmetic mean of 6. The mean 6 is at an equal distance, respectively, from the extreme values by the value 4.

However, the use of the arithmetic (and geometric) proportion for the term of justice (dikaiosunê) can somewhat lead one astray. Aristotle himself expressly points out that justice is a form of mean conduct, but 'not in the same way as the other virtues': 'it is concerned with a mean, whereas injustice is concerned with extremes'.[68] For justice does not deal 'with the basic conduct of acting subjects [ ... ] but with what is fair, which is expressed by actions and by thus reached conditions'.[69]

The aim of ethics consists of determining those qualities and virtues (ἀρεταί) a human being can acquire in the polis and thanks to which he can exert influence through his actions. The *Nichomachean Ethics* pay much attention to the discussion of these qualities, devoting themselves in books II–V to the merits of the character called 'ethical virtues' (ἠθικαί ἀρεται), as well as in book VI to the merits of the mind, the 'dianoetical virtues' (διανοητικαι ἀρεται).[70] Hereby, it is shown that virtue in the realm of effects and actions can be determined as a mean between excess and deficiency. Aristotle first verifies this, citing the ingestion of food and doing sports: Whoever eats and drinks too much damages his health as much as whoever eats too little. Whoever does not do any sports is not able to develop his bodily strength; however, whoever overdoes it also weakens his constitution. Here, the influence of the physicians' thinking of moderation becomes visible.[71] Yet, Aristotle also uses this model for character traits such as courage. Here, there is also a too much ('huperbolê') and a too little ('elleipsis'): 'the person who avoids and fears everything, never standing his ground, becomes cowardly, while he who fears nothing but confronts every danger, becomes rash'.[72] This way, a thoughtful and manly individual is destroyed by the too much and the too little, yet spared when he follows the right mean.

Whatever applies to strengths and weaknesses of this sort can be generalized in so far as 'excess and deficiency are characteristics of vice, the mean characteristic of virtue'.[73] When discussing the proper forms of reacting (as in feeling enthusiasm and reluctance, the giving and taking of money, honour and dishonour, feeling anger), Aristotle uses the collective expression 'extremes' (ἄκρα) in the sense of the outermost ends of a continuum instead of the categories 'too much' and 'too little', 'excess' and 'deficiency'. For this, it has to be said that 'in all things the mean is praiseworthy, while the extremes are neither praiseworthy nor correct, but blameworthy'.[74]

The relationship of the mean to the extremes and the extremes to each other is terminologically exactly determined in the *Nichomachean Ethics*. The categories juxtapose each other:

> the extremes are contrary to the mean and to one another, and the mean to the extremes. For as the equal is greater in relation to the less, but less in relation to the greater, so the mean states are excessive in relation to the deficiencies, but deficient in relation to the excesses; this is so both with feelings and actions. For the courageous person seems rash in relation to the coward, and a coward in relation to the rash person.[75]

The interaction and its determination always depends on the situation.

> Since they are set against one another in this way, the greatest opposition is that of the extremes to one another, rather than to the mean. For they are farther from each other than from the mean, as the great is farther from the small and the small farther from the great than either is from the equal. Again, some of the extremes seem rather like the mean, as rashness seems like courage, and wastefulness like generosity. The greatest

dissimilarity is that between extremes; and the things that are farthest from each other are defined as contraries, so that the farther things are apart, the more contrary they will be. In some cases the deficiency is more opposed to the mean than is the excess, in others the excess is more opposed than the deficiency.[76]

The mesotês in Aristotle is not to be understood as a 'middle road',[77] and his ethics is not 'a morality of mediocrity'. For virtue appears as a mean only according to the form of existence, according to its value, however, as a peak: 'Thus, in respect of its essence and the definition of its substance, virtue is a mean, while with regard to what is best and good it is an extreme'.[78] Virtue also shows an ontological and an axiological dimension. Marie Louise von Kahoutek has graphically depicted this two-dimensionality as shown in Figure 2.3.[79]

The influences of people's ethics and medicine on this concept are therefore secondary. In contrast to this, the examination of the terminological categories of Platonic ontology appears more important. However, the Aristotelian phenomenology of the forms of conduct separates the evaluation of reason from Plato's ontological basis. 'Whereas Plato adopts and ontologically proves the traditional evaluation of "justice" as the quintessence of virtues, Aristotle pushes aside this extensive term of justice to turn in depth toward "particular justice", starting from the ambiguity of the term "justice" known from the usage of the language'. Here, he differentiates between a 'distributing' and a 'reconciling' justice (iustitia distributiva, iustitia commutativa). Distributing justice deals with the equal distribution of goods. The unfair thus impairs the sameness.

> Since what is equal is a mean, the just will be some sort of mean. Because equality requires at least two terms, what is just must be a mean, and equal, and relative, namely, just for certain people. And, in so far as it is a mean, it must be between certain extremes (excess and deficiency); in so far as it is equal, it must involve two terms; and in so far as it is just, it must be so for certain people. So what is just requires at least four terms: the persons for whom it is just are two, and the shares in which its justice consists are two. There will be the same level of equality between persons as between shares, because the shares will be in the same ratio to one another as the persons. For if the persons are not equal, they will not receive equal shares; in fact quarrels and complaints arise either when equals receive unequal shares in an allocation, or unequals receive equal shares.[80]

The following analysis of the quantification of justice is oriented to the model of barter trade. Hereby, Aristotle attempts to establish proof that justice as an 'ethical virtue' has a position similar to that of the remaining virtues. Namely, the 'realization of justice' lies in the middle between doing wrong and suffering injustice:

The distinctions we have drawn make it clear that acting justly is a mean between committing injustice and suffering it, since the one is having more than one's share, while the other is having less. Justice is a kind of mean – not in the same way as the other virtues, but because it is concerned with a mean, while injustice is concerned with extremes. And justice is the state in accordance with which the just person is said to be the kind of person who is disposed to do just actions in accordance with rational choice, and to distribute goods – either between himself and another or between two others – so as to assign not more of what is worth choosing to himself and less to his neighbour (and conversely with what is harmful), but what is proportionately equal; and similarly in distributing between two other people. Injustice, on the contrary, is concerned with what is unjust, that is, a disproportionate excess or deficiency of what is beneficial or harmful; thus injustice is an excess and a deficiency, because it is concerned with excess and deficiency. In one's own case, this is an excess of what is unqualifiedly beneficial, and a deficiency of what is harmful; in the case of others, though the general result is the same, the proportion may be violated in either direction. In case of an unjust action, to have too little is to suffer injustice, while to have too much is to commit it.[81]

In both cases, injustice belongs to the realm of the extremes; justice, however, lies in the middle.

In the light of this reason for ethically valuable action, which deviates from the Platonic position, the problem of norms arises. The norm for ethical action is now no longer the eternal and unchangeable but the 'reasonable' as the representative of practical reason and cleverness as well as 'the good one' or rather 'the excellent human being' who, as paradigm, represents the guiding principle and measure for the correctness of ethical action.

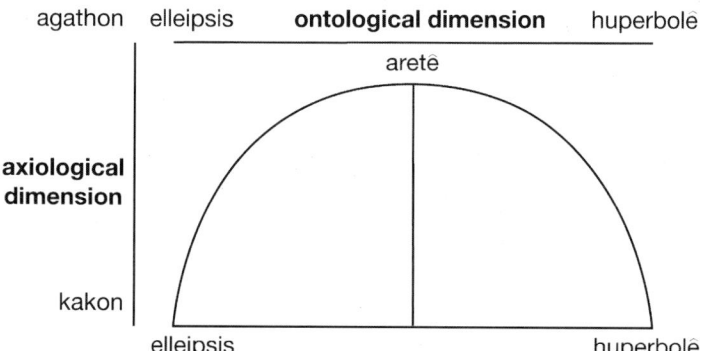

*Figure 2.3* Axiological and ontological dimension of the mesotês doctrine
Source: Kohoutek (1924: 56).

Ethically valuable action refers to practical reason as the guarantor for the choice of the right means but is not bound to the theoretical insight into the structure of being. If formulations such as: the determination of the arête as the mean are carried out as 'the reasonable determine' or 'as proper reason demands' or in general only 'as it need be' sound noticeably vague, it is not norm – subversive sophistic relativism which is contained therein but the attempt to mediatingly join together pre-philosophic life experience and traditions, scientific reason derived from ethnographic and medical thought and elements of Platonic philosophy.[82]

Aristotle's doctrine of virtues is thus located in the middle between a 'relativistic kasuistism and the Platonic direction toward something actually good'.[83]

The *Nichomachean Ethics* closes by pointing out the necessity of examining the political systems to find out which factors 'preserve and destroy cities [ ... ] and what causes some cities to be well run, and others to be badly run'.[84] Although Aristotle developed a typology of the forms of state in the *Ethics* slightly deviating from that of the *Politics*,[85] the relationship to the categories of the mean and the extremes is here not established more closely. In the *Politics*, this then becomes a central topic. In the fourth book, Aristotle particularly emphasizes the connection of the ethical with the politico-institutional level: 'When in the Ethics it was correctly said that a happy life is the one in which the pursuit of virtue is unhindered and that virtue is a mean, so the medium life must be the best, by which is meant reaching the mean that everyone is capable of reaching. And these same rules must also apply to the goodness and the badness of a constitution or state, for the constitution is so to speak the life of the state'.[86]

First, Aristotle strictly distinguishes the state (polis) and its constitution from the household (oikos). Whereas the household, as it were, forms a unit as everyone is subjugated to the head of the household, 'the city is made up not only of a number of human beings but also of human beings differing in kind: a city does not arise from persons who are similar'.[87] Therefore, in the second book, Aristotle criticizes in detail the goods, children and women community which Plato/Socrates recommended in the *Politeia* for furthering state unity.[88]

The state (in the actual sense, therefore as a *political* and not a *despotic* association) thus consists of a multitude of citizens diverging in interests and beliefs who, on the other hand, are defined by their participation in public matters;[89] women, slaves and strangers/metoekes are therefore not part of it. In addition, Aristotle restricts the definition of the citizen in so far as his position can vary greatly in the different state forms. If the citizen is determined by his participation in government, this is, strictly speaking, only possible in a democracy: 'In some [regimes] there is no people, nor is an assembly recognized in law, but [only a consultative meeting of specially] summoned persons, and cases are adjudicated by groups [of officials]'.[90] In practice, the right to being a citizen depends mostly on whether the ancestors possessed this right.

Concerning the typology of the state constitutions, Aristotle leans strongly towards Plato. Regarding their quality, he first subdivides them according to state aim or state ethos. All constitutions that 'look to the common advantage are correct regimes according to what is unqualifiedly just, while those which look only to the advantage of the rulers are errant, and are all deviations from the correct regimes; for they involve mastery, but the city is a partnership of free persons'.[91] Like Plato, he additionally subdivides the state constitutions according to a quantitative criterion, depending on the rule of one, several or many. He distinguishes between the constitutions that are oriented towards common interest, kingship, aristocracy and polity, and those degenerate forms (πάρεκβαςεις), which are solely obliged to the self-interest of rulers: tyranny, oligarchy and democracy.[92] The difference from Plato becomes obvious not only by the different designation for the legal rule of many, 'polity' (a confusing term, as he uses it for the constitution as such), but also by emphasizing that it is still the best – because suitably mixed – constitution most supportive of the citizens' virtue.

The fourth book focuses on this constitution. Here, the terminological system, developed in the *Ethics* in regard to a determination of virtue as the mean between the extremes, primarily finds its application. The polity is introduced as 'a mixture [μίξις] of oligarchy and democracy'.[93] Next, Aristotle differentiates between three principles of combination and mixture.[94] The first consists of connecting oligarchic as well as democratic legal regulations. Aristotle exemplifies this by the dispensation of justice: 'In oligarchies they arrange to fine the well off if they do not take part in adjudicating, and provide no pay for the poor, while in democracies they provide pay for the poor and do not fine the well off. What is common to and a mean between these is to have both [arrangements], and hence this is typical of polity, which is a mixture formed from both'.[95]

The second kind consists of a 'mean' being taken between democratic and oligarchic regulations. One example is the census in the election for the people's assembly, which can be placed at a high (oligarchic solution), low (democratic solution) or middle level (solution of the polity).[96] A third form of this mixture is obtained if combinations of regulations from oligarchic and democratic law are connected: 'I mean, for example, it is held to be democratic for offices to be chosen by lot, oligarchic to have them elected, and democratic not [to do it] on the basis of an assessment, oligarchic [to do it] on the basis of an assessment. It is typical of aristocracy and polity, therefore, to take an element from each – from oligarchy making offices elected, from democracy not [doing it] on the basis of an assessment'.[97] In all three forms, this deals with the distribution of positions and competencies to different powers of state in such a way that it conforms to the spirit and the most striking virtues of both, democracy as well as oligarchy.

A good mixture is recognized in 'that it should be possible for the same polity to be spoken of as either a democracy or an oligarchy, and it is clear that it is because the mixture is a fine one that those who speak of it do so in this way. The mean too is of this sort: each of the extremes is revealed in it'.[98] As an example Aristotle names Sparta's constitution, in which democratic elements such as joint child-rearing, the people's election of the gerontes and participation in the ephorate, and oligarchic ones such as the election of all positions and the highest judicial power lying in the hands of a few are connected.[99]

Nevertheless, the differentiation of these kinds of mixtures should not lead to the assumption that something like a perfect combination is attainable. The question about the best constitution was not to be derived from a virtue, which goes beyond the average measure, or from an education, which requires good natural abilities and fortunate external circumstances, nor from the kind of constitution one might desire, but from the life that the majority are able to live and a constitution that the majority of the states are capable of acquiring.[100] Departing from the basic principle established by ethics, 'that a happy life is one in accordance with virtue and unimpeded, and that virtue is a mean, then the middling sort of life is best – the mean that is capable of being attained by each sort of individual. These same defining principles must also define virtue and vice in the case of a city and a regime; for the regime is the way of life of a city'.[101]

These considerations lead to an examination of the sociological conditions in the states known to Aristotle. He subdivides the citizenry according to the poor, the wealthy and the owners of mean assets (μέσοι). Here, too, those in the middle are given preference over the poor and the wealthy as, under such circumstances,

> it is readiest to obey reason, while for one who is overly handsome, overly strong, overly well born, or overly wealthy – or the reverse of these things, overly indigent, overly weak, or very lacking in honor – it is difficult to follow reason. The former sort tend to become arrogant and base on a grand scale, the latter malicious and base in petty ways; and acts of injustice are committed either through arrogance or through malice. Moreover, these are last inclined either to avoid ruling or to wish to rule, both of which things are injurious to cities.[102]

Hereby, Aristotle goes beyond financial circumstances in his examination and also includes other traits such as outward appearance, bodily strength and origin. Generally speaking: Whoever enjoys an excess of the means of happiness, strength, wealth, followers and the like will develop in such a way that he will

> neither wish to be ruled nor know how to be. This is something that marks them from the time they are children at home, for the effect of living in luxury is that they do not become habituated to being ruled even at school; but those who are excessively needy with respect to these things are too humble. So the ones do not know how to rule but only how to be ruled, and then only in the fashion of rule of a master, and the others do

not know how to be ruled by any sort of rule, but only to rule in the
fashion of a master. What comes into being, then, is a city not of free
persons but of slaves and masters, the ones consumed by envy, the others
by contempt.[103]

Then, the virtue of friendship, so important for the living together of the free,
cannot flourish. As can be seen, Aristotle connects socio-economic and psychological reflections in his reasoning for the advantages of a society founded
on the middling elements.

A state based on a broad middle class is most capable of making liberal
conditions possible. There, the existence of the state is also most secure, as
this kind of citizen does not 'desire the things of others, as the poor do, nor
others their [property], as the poor desire that of the wealthy; and as a result
of not being plotted against or plotting against others they pass their time free
from danger'.[104] In a community essentially founded on the middle class,
there exist the best preconditions for the establishment of a good constitution.
For in such states, where the middle class is strong and superior to the extremes,
or at least to one of the extremes, the middle class is the decisive factor and
prevents exaggeration into the other direction. Where, however, the wealthy or
the poor predominate, 'either [rule of] the people in its extreme form must
come into being, or unmixed oligarchy, or – as a result of both of these
excesses – tyranny [δῆμος ἔσχατος γίγνεται ἢ ὀλιγαρχία ἄκρατος ἢ τυραννὶς].'[105]
The attributes ἔσχατος and ἄκρατος constitute exchangeable terms for glaring
degenerations.

A state based on a broad middle class is spared this: For there are the least
revolutions and factional conflicts among the citizens. For the same reason,
the big states are freer of revolutions, as there the middle class is numerous too.

> In small cities it is easier for all to be separated into two [factions] and
> have no one left in the middle, and nearly everyone is either poor or well
> off. And democracies are more stable than oligarchies and more durable
> on account of those of the middling sort, who are more numerous and
> have a greater share in the prerogatives in democracies than in oligar-
> chies. If the poor predominate numerically in the absence of these, they
> fare badly and are quickly ruined.[106]

As confirmation of this opinion, Aristotle says that the best legislators came
from the bourgeois middle class.[107] He mentions Solon, Lykurg and Charondas,
the legislator of the Cataneans in Sicily. If the middle class is too small, it
follows that either democracies or oligarchies come into existence, as then the
one extreme that has the upper hand, either the propertied classes or the
people,[108] will dominate.

In the twelfth chapter of the fourth book, Aristotle briefly discusses the
general social situations of interests in the *poleis* to, however, return again to
the starting point, the emphasis of the importance of a broad middle class:

Where the multitude of middling persons predominates either over both of the extremities together or over one alone, there a lasting polity is capable of existing. For there is no reason to fear that the wealthy and the poor will come to an agreement against them: neither will want to be the slaves of the other, and if they seek a regime under which they will have more in common, they will find none other than this. [ ... ] The better the mixture of the polity, the more lasting it will be.[109]

In the following chapters, the examination departs from the question of the best state in order to neutrally discuss the different institutional design forms and distribution of competencies with oligarchies and democracies: therefore then, according to Aristotle, the majority of empirically existing states. Hereby, it once more becomes clear according to which viewpoints mixtures of different – extreme – basic forms are possible. Aristotle distinguishes between the deliberative, decision-making and adjudicative powers,[110] and the constitutions can be differentiated according to who possesses these powers and how they are practised. Then the different state authorities are dealt with, whose number, responsibility, length of investment and operational modes vary from constitution to constitution.[111] And, finally, it deals with the court system, where the possibilities of institutional development are likewise discussed in detail.

The fifth book is devoted to the causes of sweeping political changes (μεταβολαί), whereby here, too, the different state forms, preferably aristocracy/oligarchy, democracy and polity, are discussed. Once more, Aristotle emphasizes the importance of the right measure/moderation for institutional and personal development. There is a central cause for the *metabolē*, the constitutional change: neglecting the middling element:

for many of the things that are held to be typical popular overturn democracies, and many of those held to be typical oligarchic overturn oligarchies. Those who suppose this to be the single virtue pull the regime to an extreme, ignorant that just as a nose that deviates form the straightness that is most beautiful toward being hooked or snub can nevertheless still be beautiful and appealing to look at, yet if some [artist] tightens it further in the direction of an extreme, he will in the first place eliminate any moderateness in the part and eventually will got so far as to make it not even appear to be a nose, on account of the preeminence and the deficiency of the opposites.[112]

Here, again, the analogy of the geometric proportion and its application in art is put forward. By the same token, the democracies and the oligarchies can be stable if they do not deviate too strongly from the model of the best constitution. However, if one carries the one or the other to the extreme, one will first worsen the constitution and finally completely destroy it.[113] The legislator must therefore always have in mind the danger of a decline and counteract it with suitable measures.

In the tenth chapter of the fifth book, Aristotle deals with the causes of the fall of kingdom and tyranny. Here, in several places, tyranny and 'extreme democracy' are placed at the same level.[114] The idea will be discussed more closely later on.

> Everything that happens in connection with democracy of the extreme sort is typical of tyranny – dominance of women in the household, so that they may report on their husbands, and laxness toward slaves for the same reason. Slaves and women do not conspire against tyrants, and as they prosper [under such circumstances] they necessarily have a benevolent view both of tyrannies and of democracies (for indeed, the people wish to be a monarch).[115]

In the following book, the sixth book, Aristotle discusses under which preconditions different kinds of democracy and oligarchy can be established successfully. Here, too, he addresses the most extreme form of democracy in which all groups participate[116] and where the right to being a citizen is awarded to as many members of the population as possible. Again, extreme democracy is placed close to tyranny, which would find its expression especially in the uncontrollability of slaves, women and children.[117]

In the seventh book, Aristotle, after the mostly empirical analytical explanations concerning the different forms of constitutions, again returns to the normative question about the best state. Initially, he reveals the hereby to be applied intellectual measures. The best state must make virtuous action possible and thus create the basic conditions for the attainment of a meaningful and fulfilled life.[118] In the considerations as to which norms such a state is to follow, the right balance between a too much and a too little is decisive. Therefore, the state should be neither too small nor too big. The sensible proportion of the citizenry ends where the citizens no longer know each other by their qualities, as then the necessary knowledge for judging fairly and giving the post to the most deserving[119] is missing. Concerning the country's composition/quality, one needs to ascertain that the inhabitants can live generously and in reasonable leisure. Thereby, the 'extremes' of lifestyle, 'penury' as well as 'luxury',[120] are evil.

Concerning the disposition of citizens, the Greek tribes are praised. They not only live in the geographical 'middle'[121] between the cold regions of the European North and the hot ones of the Asiatic South, but also combine their advantages to a fortunate mixture.[122] For the peoples of the North are brave but intellectually and artistically untalented; the peoples of the South, however, are creative but fearful. Only the Greeks are simultaneously brave and intelligent.[123] Also in their temperament do they hold on to a proper mean. Aristotle cites Euripides: 'those who have loved extravagantly will hate extravagantly too'.[124]

What applies to the temperament also applies to urban development: It is recommended to keep to a middle between extreme forms. Accordingly,

Hippodamus of Milet propagates straight lines for houses and streets, yet the older town construction full of nooks and crannies has advantages in war: the attackers get lost in the labyrinth of houses. A combination of both forms of construction is therefore to be recommended.[125]

The art of architecture represents only one minor aspect of discussing the preconditions for the best state. In contrast, education is of central importance, even if it – different from Plato's – does not surpass the institutional dimension. For Aristotle, too, education is the medium for the young to become virtuous, thus being shaped into good citizens. In this connection, the mesotês doctrine is brought up once more at the end of the eighth chapter, where he speaks of the role of music in the classroom. Aristotle distinguishes between three keys in which melodies can be expressed (they were to become the basis of Gregorian chant more than 1,000 years later): 'Mixed Lydian' is rather sad and depressed, 'Phrygian' provokes enthusiasm, and 'Dorian' puts one into a calm, middling condition.[126] Therefore, Aristotle – different from Socrates who, according to the *Politeia*,[127] recommended Phrygian – favoured 'Dorian', as it is the calmest and displays the most manly character. Furthermore, as we praise the mean between the extremes and claim that one ought to seek it, compared with the others, the Dorian harmony shows this feature, and therefore the young people should preferably be taught Dorian songs.[128] But, he then adds, in making this choice one ought not only to take into consideration the 'appropriate' but also the 'possible'. In this way, he comes to a surprising conclusion, once more picking up the idea of the 'mean' at the very end of the eighth book:

> if there is among the harmonies one of a sort that is appropriate to the age of children on account of its capacity to involve simultaneously both order and play, as appears to be the case most particularly with Lydian among the harmonies, it is clear that these three are to be made defining principles for purposes of education – the middle, the possible, and the appropriate.[129]

As can be seen, Aristotle applies the intellectual figure of the mean between the extremes to almost all areas of human life. It runs through his work from metaphysics and analytics to topics and ethics as far as to politics, which again comprises the entity of social relationships and their natural foundations. In ethics, the intellectual figure is assigned an ontological and an axiological dimension: the mean and the extremes cannot only be grasped and measured empirically and analytically in all realms of life, they are also assigned a value dimension. The mean then stands for virtue, the right measure; the extremes are the epitome of all vices, on the other hand.

In politics, the ethical differentiation is placed in the realm of regime forms. The best constitution, polity, realizes a virtuous mean through the mixture of elements, which in their pure, fully distinctive form are evil. This applies to an extreme imbalance of those standing as propertied members of society (predominance of the upper and lower levels) and the resulting political influence as well as to the respective institutional regulations that cause the distribution of powers and the decreeing of positions of the polis to gravitate to the edges instead of moderately balancing them in the interest of the *mesoi*.

At first sight, it is surprising that Aristotle creates a good form out of the mixture of two bad ones. Would it not be more plausible in the framework of Aristotelian argumentation to describe the 'polity' as a mixture of aristocracy and democracy? It has been presumed that in the fourth book Aristotle used the terms 'democracy' and 'oligarchy' in a neutral manner.[130] Another explanation might be that the extremes are evil in themselves, but that a positive outcome will be achieved through moderation and a suitable mixture. For the mean is closer to the extremes than the extremes are to each other, and by causing a balance between the extremes, it causes their basic contents to come into play in tempered form.

If extreme powers are predominant within a constitution, the result is instability. The extremes are the causes for changes in the constitution, the μεταβολε.[131] A stabilization of constitutional conditions requires the balancing of the extremes by mixing social and political institutional elements in a moderate and applicable way. Thus, the contents of the extreme and the mean are changeable in so far as there is a solution according to the idea; yet in reality there is no perfect solution to the problem. On the basis of the given circumstances (to be kept in mind are the differences in the static, climatic, economic, social and cultural framework conditions), the legislator must find a solution to the situation and the matters at hand from the means at his disposal to bring the extremes, which are not equally distinct in all cases, into balance by different arrangements.

The idea of institutional checks and balances is indicated by Aristotle but not systematically developed.[132] He differentiates between three powers but does not develop a programme for the avoidance of power concentration through a division of tasks and mutual control. The argumentation circles around the balance of (extreme) social interests by different modes for the distribution of positions and competencies. In this way, power deconcentration and control are reached factually.

The constitutional forms furthest away from each other are despotic tyranny and democracy ruled by the 'rabble'. On many occasions, Aristotle places both extremes at the same level. If the rulership of the many degenerates to a tyrannical regime by a majority over the minority, a similar climate of fear, distrust, surveillance, flattery, demagogical seduction and incitation of the masses comes about, as it is known from those variants of the rulership of one, which is the furthest removed from the legitimate kingdom.

At this point, the congruence with the constitutional scale as Plato at last developed it in the *Nomoi* becomes obvious again. Aristotle also followed his teacher in respect of terminology. For the history of the terminology of the extremes, the penetration of the Aristotelian doctrines with Plato's terminological categories is of importance in as far as the Platonic and Aristotelian reception strands are often so intertwined that they cannot be disentangled. Beyond that, the influences that did not 'pass through' Plato and Aristotle are to be ascribed especially to Greek folk ethics and medicine.

## 3 The tradition of Plato and Aristotle in Antiquity and the Middle Ages

One can speak about a Platonic–Aristotelian history of reception, the mesotês doctrine and the theory of a mixed constitution in as far as the terminological categories of Aristotle derive, for the most part, from the works of his teacher. The merits of a highly developed system, encyclopedic breadth and empirical foundation explain a certain predominance of the Aristotelian work. However, the doctrine of the mixed constitution did not always 'pass through' Aristotle, e.g. the Greek writer Polybius (c. 200–120 BC), whose importance for the history of ideas can hardly be overestimated, in his Histories, the doctrine of the natural cycle, the Anakuklôsis (ἀνακύκλωσις), connected the six constitutional forms (tyrannis, kingdom, oligarchy, aristocracy, democracy and ochlocracy)[133] most of all to Plato's doctrine of constitutional cycles. Not the least, the new term 'ochlocracy' for the degenerate form of the rulership of many additionally points to other influences, presumably to the peripatetic school. Most likely, Polybius did not know Aristotle's *Politics*. In him, the mesotês idea withdraws behind the new, dogma-historically highly important idea of a balance and a mutual penetration and control (later 'checks and balances') of the constitutional elements.[134] Herein, the image of the mean and the extremes finds no application.[135] Through the idea of the equilibrium, it is explained why mixed constitutions can also undergo a process of degeneration. However, here is possible what in its pure form leads to a transfer to another constitution: the restabilization of the mixed constitution through the establishment of a new equilibrium between the constitutional elements. In contrast to Plato and Aristotle, the basic elements of all three types of constitutions, monarchy, aristocracy and democracy, are brought into balance. The predominance of the people had destroyed the equilibrium in Carthage, whereas in Rome the aristocratic element in the form of the Senate beside the monarchic element of the consuls and the democratic element of the people's tribunals and the people's justice system, whose importance Polybius emphasizes, was strongly expressed,[136] which explained Rome's victory in the power conflict.

Polybius' use of language cannot deceive one into thinking that the formation of the tradition for the history of terms of the *political* extremes based on Aristotle had not been of great importance. Aristotle had departed from the purely normative question concerning the best state, much more so than Plato in his late work, and turned towards the empirical array of forms of the *poleis* in the world he knew. The abundance of sources that was laid out, particularly in the collection of 158 state constitutions (except for the Athenian, they have all disappeared) assimilated by Aristotle, the broad systematic development of the material and its penetration by means of the categories developed in metaphysics, analytics, topics and ethics explain the great importance of the work for posterity.

Nonetheless, the history of reception shows breaks and gaps. The 'esoteric' writings ('pragmatics') written for teaching are all that remain, whereas the 'exoteric' works, already published in Aristotle's lifetime, were lost. Besides, the teaching texts preserved for posterity appear problematic as far as the history of reception is concerned, as they reached a very different editing condition and were put together after the philosopher's death. This also applies to the books of the *Politics*, which are discernibly incomplete (the work ends abruptly) and whose exact order is disputed.

Managing the teaching texts was at first the responsibility of Aristotle's student Theophrastus (c. 372–286 BC), under whose guidance the Peripatos (also called Lyceion), to which around 2,000 students seem to have belonged at times, reached its peak.[137] In the ethical lectures, Theophrastus taught a doctrine of the moral behaviour of man and hereby also adopted the mesotês doctrine. In his best known work, the *Characters*, he outlined in a sometimes amusing form but with a high exactitude of psychological observation forms of human misconduct as Aristotle had juxtaposed them in the *Nichomachean Ethics* as extreme degenerations of a mean seen as virtuous. Individuality, insincerity, flattery, talkativeness, rustic behaviour, vanity, lack of consideration, garrulousness, tendency to gossip, impudence, narrow-mindedness, uncouthness, obtrusiveness, overeagerness, thoughtlessness, smugness, superstition, nagging, suspiciousness, offensive behaviour, tastelessness, small-minded vanity, avarice, bragging, arrogance, cowardice, political arrogance, intellectual philisterdom of the aged, maligning, tendency to seek bad company and greed[138] are dealt with. The character descriptions were used in teaching and may have been devised to serve pedagogical purposes. They later exerted an influence on Seneca and Plutarch.[139] Theophrastus also taught the essential contents of Aristotelian politics with the doctrine of the best constitution as a mix of oligarchy and democracy.[140]

After his death, Neleus, probably the only one of Aristotle's students still alive, inherited the Aristotelian teaching texts. When he was not elected as headmaster of the school, he took them with him to his home town Skepsis and bequeathed them to his descendants. Their interest in the writings was slim; they neglected them so that they were not rediscovered until two centuries later.[141] This is one of the reasons why the teaching texts remained largely unknown until the first pre-Christian century or rather were based on fragments and a few copies as, for example, the Museion of Alexandria had been able to acquire. Even Cicero knew of Aristotle merely through the (today completely lost) published dialogues and the material taught by Theophrastus.[142]

Only at the beginning of the first pre-Christian century did Appelicon of Teos track down the writings in Skepsis and brought them to Athens. When Sulla seized Athens in 86 BC, he is said to have taken the library of the deceased Appelicon to Rome, where he ordered the Greek scholar Tyrannion, who had contact with Cicero, to inspect and sort the manuscripts. In addition, there were also copies of Aristotelian works that Lucullus had brought back to Rome as spoils of war. On the basis of these materials and presumably further available writings, for example from the stores of the Alexandrian Library and the Lykeion in Athens, Andronicus of Rhodes, a student of Tyrannion and presumably of Peripatos, finally produced the complete works of Aristotle in Rome in the years 40–20 BC at the latest, which constitute the basis for the complete tradition of Aristotle. Andronicus complemented the text collection with an extensive work of commentaries, which allowed him to become the 'founder of Aristotle interpretation of Late Antiquity and was essentially instrumental in the displacement and final loss of Aristotle's exoteric writings by the teaching texts'.[143] The work by Andronicus made a first Aristotle renaissance possible in the second half of the first pre-Christian century.[144]

The philosophy of Aristotle and Peripatos, however, found its expression in various ways even before the editorial and commentatorial work of Andronicos in the work of the Roman legislator and scholar Marcus Tullius Cicero (ca. 106–43 BC). Nonetheless, he was more strongly influenced by the doctrine of virtue of the Stoa than by Peripatos.[145] The Stoa draws the mean between goods and misfortunes, so that mean actions are those that are seen as neither virtuous nor depraved.[146] When Cicero warns in the *De officiis* of punishing in anger as one would then miss the mean between too much and too little, he interpreted the mean as mediocrity but not as an incarnation of virtue as the Peripatetics would have rightfully recommended.[147]

In his only fragmentarily preserved text *De re republica*, which was started in the year 55 and published in 51 BC, Cicero conferred the doctrine of the mixed constitution on to the Roman history of the constitution. Doubtless, he was influenced by Polybius who had lived in Rome for many years and knew his *Histories*.[148] However, Cicero's picture, with its sociological and ethical dimension of the mixed constitution, corresponds in various ways more to the circulating versions in Peripatos' work. The establishment of the mixed constitution from elements of the monarchy (regnum), the aristocracy (civitas optimatium) and the democracy (civitas popularis) accordingly took place in several steps: Under King Servius Tullius, the people's assembly was established in the form of the centuriate committees, the republic with the creation of the consulate, and the provocation, the right to a fair trial before a court legitimized by the people, was established, and finally with the creation of the people's tribunal, a complete, mixed constitution was reached.[149] In it, three principles come into play: *caritas*, welfare of the subordinates through the consuls; *consilium*, consultation by the optimates of the Senate; and freedom (*libertas*) were finally guaranteed by the people's tribunal. Connecting the constitutional elements hinders slipping into those excesses that are characteristic of the degeneration of the pure form. Here, Cicero does not speak about the 'extremes' yet about 'every excess' [omnia nimia] when it was too much, be it in the weather, the fields or the bodies, usually turns into its opposite [in contraria fere convertuntur]: 'and especially this occurs in the states, and the all too great freedom [nimiaque illa libertas] turns for people and private persons into great slavery [nimiam servitutem cadit]. Therefore, from this last freedom [hac maxima libertate] comes about the tyrant [tyrannus] and that unfair and hard slavery'.[150] He speaks also of 'faults' and 'vices' ('facile in contraria vitia convertuntur', 'magnis principum vitiis'[151]), which come about from the lack of social integration of the parts of the people. The evenly and moderately mixed constitution of the simple forms ('aequatum et temperatum ex tribus primis rerum publicarum modis'[152]) prevents the 'conversion' ('conversio') from one evil to another.

Cicero also referred to the terminology of the mesotês doctrine in his text about the last aims of human behaviour (*De finibus bonorum et malorum*). Here, in a dialogue from the Athenian Academy of the year 79 BC, he critically discusses the term happiness of the Epicureans and the Stoics and comes to the conclusion that the Peripatetics had found the proper mean for determining human happiness (in reality, this essentially deals with the ethics of Antiochus of Askalon[153]), when they saw it as neither completely independent of outer wealth (Stoics) nor completely dependent on it (Epicureans).

Rather more closely related to Epicurean prudence, *sôphrosunê*, is Horace (ca. 65–68 BC) when he recommends a 'golden mean' in his *Odes*. Here is the most well-known place:

Auream quisquis mediocritatem
diligit, tutus caret obsoleti
sordibus tecti, caret invidenda
sobrius aula.

Everyone who takes the path of the golden mean,
being security-minded, will not let
his house decay due to dirty greed, will not,
prudent as he is, arouse envy in people
with a magnificent building.[154]

The 'Definitions' that Horace gives for the *aequa mens* between the opposite attitudes correspond to the Platonic–Aristotelian differentiation between hyperbole, meson and elleipsis and may be proof of how much these had become general intellectual property. The *Satire* I,2 also shows this. It begins with a number of characters who want to avoid wrong behaviour and instead fall into the opposite extreme: 'If the fool avoids a vice, he finally falls into the opposite [dum vitant stulti vitia, in contraria currunt]'. From this can be gathered: 'measure and mean – are missing [nil medium est]'.[155] In a similar way, the suitable behaviour of a friend is classified between awkwardness and flattery in *Letter* I,18, saying that virtue is the mean between two vices and restrained itself from them: 'virtus est medium vitiorum et utrimque reductum'.[156] Despite this reference, 'it would be wrong to say that Horace swayed between Peripatos and Epicurus. Not he connects the doctrine of the two schools of thought in this point, but they themselves touch each other herein'.[157]

In his *Antiquitates Romanae*, the Greek historian Dionysius of Halikarnassus (ca. the birth of Christ) includes a speech by Brutus after the driving out of the Roman king in which a mixture of monarchy, oligarchy and
democracy is recommended for the avoidance of extreme state conditions
('πολιτείαν ἄκρατον'[158]). Hereby, he might have been influenced by Cicero but
also by Polybius, as his depiction of the constitutional cycle is similar to that
of the Anakyklosis doctrine. Nevertheless, the order of the constitutions is not
as strictly fixed. Democracy as well as aristocracy can degenerate into tyranny, and the rulership of the rabble is not necessarily followed by a decline
into the violent regime of the arch-monarchy.[159]

The further reception of the term of the extremes, in as far as it corresponded to the doctrine of the mixed constitution, left its mark by the development of the constitution of the Roman Empire. It had come into being in
the Greek *poleis* as a solution to the issue of the best constitution. Under the
conditions of the principate, it could – except for the historic and purely theoretical reflection – 'only serve to praise the actually existing constitution as a
mixed one, whereby a rather wilful and violent interpretation'[160] was not to
be avoided.

Echoes are found in the biographical work of Plutarch (ca. AD 45–125)
where the mixed constitution and the term of the extremes sometimes appear
in historic considerations. In the depictions of the arguments with the party
of the aristocratic Athenian politician Cimon, Plutarch characterizes the dis-
empowerment of Areopagus (462/61 BC), which Perikles and Ephialtes joined
in bringing about in favour of the people's assembly and the people's courts,
as a decline into the 'ἄκρατον δημοκρατίαν'.[161] In the panegyric *Vita Lycurgi*,
the term 'mixed' occurs more frequently as 'reasonable' and in contrast to
'extreme'. The durability of Sparta's constitution originates from its mixed
character. One is reminded of the mesotês doctrine when Plutarch places the
establishment of the Gerusia somewhere ('ἐν μέσω'[162]) in between the kings
and the people. Also, when judging ethically on Sparta's mixed constitution,
which served justice, the intellectual heritage of Plato and Aristotle becomes
visible.

With Plutarch, the sources for the term of the *political* extremes dry up for
several centuries. In the course of the lively work of commentators, which
reached a peak in the second post-Christian century, when Alexander of
Aphrodisias held the chair for peripatetic philosophy already founded under
Marcus Aurelius, the numerous usable logical writings (the so-called 'Orga-
non') stood as the focus of attention.[163] Aristotle was foremost seen as a
logician far into the High Middle Ages, and the extremes are met here mainly
as elements of syllogism, which is defined in the *Etymologiae* by Isidore of
Seville (c. AD 560–636) in the following manner: 'The syllogism is thus the
extreme conclusion of the proposition, the assumption and the confirmation,
no matter if under uncertain conditions or confirmed expectations' ['Syllo-
gismus igitur est propositionis et adsumptionis confirmationisque extrema
conclusio aut ex ambigentis incerto, aut ex fiducia conprobantis'].[164]

The Church fathers in the first centuries preferred Plato when they began taking Greek philosophy into service, as they considered his ideas (anchored in a closed divine world system) to be closer to Christianity.[165] Thereby, the interest was concentrated on ethics. The idea of the *mediocritas virtutis* penetrated deeply into Christian ethics, nevertheless mixed with neo-Platonic and stoic elements.[166] Beginning with Hieronymus (ca. AD 342–420), who developed ethics based on the Aristotelian term of virtue in his writings, a long line of Christian theologians can be cited who juxtapose a *temperantia* and a *moderatio* with *vitii* located at the outermost ends. The *extrema*, as Adelard of Bath from the School of Chartres (ca. 1080–1160) called it (during the implanting into the body, the soul had received the task to assure moderation and the mean: 'ut extrema superfluitatis et diminitionis irascens corrigere mediumque tenere cupiditate affectaret'[167]), thus does not always come into play. The ethics of the mean and of moderation marked the *Policraticus* and *Entheticus* by the English humanist and Abelard – scholar John of Salesbury (1115–80). He, too, found the suitable behaviour in the mean between the extremes:

> Temperiem mediae faciunt extrema, iubetque
> Ut medium teneat, qui bonus esse cupit.[168]
> The extremes cause the equilibrium and demand
> him who desires to be good to keep the mean.

The doctrine of virtue was nevertheless frequently not applied to the political realm in the strict sense. This also applied to the Aristotle reception, which was activated in the middle of the seventh century with the Aristotle commentator Stephanus receiving the call to Byzantium/Constantinople. Within the Aristotle reception of the Syrian and Arabian world, the *Politics* did not play a role anyway, regardless of the fact that this strand of the tradition essentially added to the penetration of Aristotelism into the scholarly world in the Europe of the Middle Ages, particularly after many Greek–Arabian scholars had gone to the West – to Sicily, which was occupied by the Arabs in the ninth century, and later to the Califate of Cordoba, where, most of all, Ibn Rushd (Averroës, 1126–98) worked as the most important oriental teacher of Aristotelianism to scholasticism. The Islamic philosophers knew of the existence of an Aristotelian political science; however, they did not know the *Politics* itself.[169]

This does not include the author, who, besides Augustine, probably most influenced early scholasticism. The Aristotle translator and commentator Boethius (ca. 475–525) came from one of the most influential and affluent families in Rome, had obtained an extensive education, possibly having studied in Athens, and possessed excellent knowledge of the Greek language, which was already rare in the Latin West at that time. He had extensive knowledge of the works of Plato and Aristotle. Boethius had intended translating the entire works of both philosophers into Latin and to comment on them. However, for the most part, the plan did not come to fruition – for one, on account of making a career for himself at the court of Theodoric, eventually being promoted to the highest post, that of chancellor; for another, due to falling into disgrace and being executed at the age of 44 for an alleged conspiracy with Byzantium, presumably as the victim of an intrigue. Thus, Boethius was only able to translate and comment on the first logical texts by Aristotle, the writing about the categories and the tract about the sentence. This was essentially the reason why Aristotle's reception in the Middle Ages remained dependent on Arabian sources to such a high degree. What was missing were the Aristotelian real sciences, the doctrine of the soul, biology, physics, poetics, but also metaphysics, ethics and politics. Thus, for six centuries, Aristotle was primarily seen as a logician. As logic was the philosophical discipline that was documented the best, it obtained a paradigmatic function for the thinking of the early Middle Ages. Thinking scientifically means to apply Aristotle's logic to a given field.[170]

Nevertheless, it was known from Boethius and others that there also existed Aristotelian politics. For that matter, Boethius had systematized the sciences, dividing them into 'theoretical ones' and 'practical ones'. To the practical ones belonged the *sciencia politica* such as *philosophia moralis* with the subdisciplines of ethics, economics and politics. Cassiodorus (ca. 490–583), Isidore of Seville, Hugo of St Victor (died 1141 in Paris) and Gundissalinus (attested until 1182, Toledo) were essentially connected with this development.[171] Aristotle's *Politics* themselves were finally translated into Latin in the thirteenth century, and then twice. First, an incomplete version was produced (*translatio imperfecta*), presumably between 1255 and 1261. As also in the case of the second, complete translation (before 1267; *translatio completa*), its translator may have been the Flemish Dominican Willem van Moerbeke (ca. 1215–86) whose authorship of the second translation is undisputed.[172] Soon after, the first commentaries were written. Albert of Cologne (Albertus Magnus, ca. 1193–1280) wrote a commentary in the context of the *studium generale* for the Dominicans of Cologne; his student Thomas Aquinas (1225–74) commented on the *Politics* during a stay at the Dominican monastery of St Jacques in Paris in the years 1269–72.

It was no coincidence that both commentators belonged to the Dominican order. The order, founded in 1216 by the Castilian aristocrat Dominicus, wanted to go through the world preaching, thus turning away from the monastic isolation from the world, and bring the word of God to the people by public lectures and conversations. This required in-depth theological and philosophical studies. Already in 1217, Dominicus had sent seven Dominican brothers to study at the University of Paris. There, and in Bologna, the first universities were established. Among the most pressing intellectual religious issues of the time was the question concerning the reconciliation of the Gospel and Aristotle, faith and knowledge. The early scholastics of the twelfth century had used dialectics as an exegetic method; but through the School of Chartres and the philosophical heresy of Amalric of Bena, the contents of ancient thought had also been offered up for discussion. This was possible because there was no longer only Boethius' translation of Aristotle, his logical and language-logical writings. 'From Sicily and through the translators school of Toledo, but especially through Gerhard of Cremona one obtained the new Aristotle of metaphysics, ethics and the natural sciences since 1150 and found here a genial and closed building of all the sciences, now, however not divided according to the principles of divine creation of the world but according to the subjects of the sensual world and the principles of rational abstraction'.[173] This new Aristotle was, nonetheless, difficult to grasp. The Latin translations were not based on the Greek originals and were full of Arabisms and Hebrewisms. In many places, the commentaries appeared dark and incomprehensible. The best one came from the already mentioned Spanish–Islamic scholar Averroës whose writings were also translated after his death in 1198. Hereby, nonetheless, one had to deal with a faith-endangering heritage as

> the Moslems interpreted Aristotle in the light of Islam and their neo-Platonism; they accentuated sentences such as that the matter of the world had not been created and therefore was eternal, but that the individual human soul was not immortal – some definitely un-Christian doctrines. But what was to become of the university that swore by Aristotle and arduously fought to make room for the freedom to teach just then?[174]

Albert of Cologne realized the excellent intellectual status of the Aristotelian writings, to say the least, when he came across them in the Arabian commentaries. He decided to make the philosophy of Aristotle, whom he saw as a *'princeps peripateticorum'* and *'archidoctor philosophiae'*,[175] available and visible to the scholarly world in a comprehensive way. He wanted to contribute to the objectification of the heatedly discussed theological controversies. He had understood that the Christian faith doctrine and the Church rulership would have to start swaying if the changing society's desire for knowledge was disregarded. Albert – and others – brought about a change after the papal Aristotle bans of 1210 and 1231: Thereby, he already had the greatest difficulty in convincing the brethren of his order that one ought to unprejudicedly examine the writings of the heathens. To have forced back cultural enmity within the religious reform movement of the thirteenth century and to have given a right to the studies of philosophy in theological education is one of Albert's contributions. From then on, the study of philosophy meant mostly the study of Aristotle.[176]

It is disputed whether Albert wrote his commentary about Aristotle's politics earlier than his student Thomas. Undoubtedly, his activities for the reception of Aristotelian politics were groundbreaking. From 1228 on, he worked as a lector in Cologne, then the biggest German city, having returned there after his teaching assignment in Paris during the years 1245–48 to set up the *studium generale* of the Dominicans. From then on, he interrupted his research and teaching work in Cologne only once more in the years 1260–62 when he was Bishop of Regensburg. At this time, there was no university in Germany; for the following 100 years, the intellectual life took place exclusively among the Dominicans, with Cologne as the centre, and in constant exchange with Paris.[177]

From the middle of the century, Albert tried to introduce all of Aristotle's works to the Latin West. He paraphrased the Aristotelian writings, adding excourses at controversial places: 'He explained that in these paraphrases he was not offering up his own theories but those of the Aristotelians. Yet he often enough gave up this reserve to take up the cause of the Peripatetics'.[178] So, Albert explained affirmatively and in detail the mesotês doctrine developed in the *Nichomachean Ethics*. He clearly worked out the dual nature of the extremes: On the one hand, it became manifest by itself at the level of being in the form of depraved counterpoles (excess and deficiency) of a 'mean' type of behaviour seen as ideal ('Virtum autes mediates est duarum mal-itiarum: unius quidem secundum superabuntantiam dictae, alerius autem secundum defectum'[179]); on the other hand, it marked virtue itself at the shall-level ('Virtutem ergo esse in medio, causa est virtutem esse in extremum secundum bonum et optimum'[180]).

However, virtue as an axiological 'extreme' was unimportant for the terminology of the *Politics* as, here, the extremes made their appearance solely as counterpoles, aberrations, exaggerations in reference to a mean expressing moderation – an idea already developed in the fourth book[181] and explained and commented on by Albert: '*mixtures are good* because the extremes are well mixed in the mean' ['*mixtas esse bene*, id est, quia extrema in medio bene mixta sunt'].[182] Albert compared it with the term neuter of the grammaticians and to the balancing effect of several winds in weather occurrences. Afterwards, he explained in detail the combination of oligarchic and democratic elements in Sparta's constitution as it had been described by Aristotle.

In no less detail did he comment on the explanations for the best constitution in which neither wealthy nor poor but many mean existences dominate.[183] Here, the excesses are avoided ('per excessum extremorum'[184]) which, on the one hand, come from the despotic tendencies of a few individuals' greed for power and possessions ('servorum et despotorum civitas: quod est contra rationem civitatis'[185]) and, on the other hand, from the unrestraint of those vegetating in extreme poverty ('in extrema paupertate'[186]). If, however, many owners of mean wealth carry the common system ('civitates [ … ] in quibus multi cives sunt medii inter divites et pauperes'[187]), the dangers of the complete decline into tyranny of the 'extremae politiae'[188] can be avoided. Albert enriched this structure of ideas with biblical wisdom and thus placed it in the service of Christian ethics and world view.

Not only Albert but also his student Thomas Aquinas commented on the Aristotelian writings.[189] At the arts faculty in Paris, there had been violent arguments about Averroism, particularly about the issue of the singularity of the intellect, the negation of free will by reference to the movement of the constellations, the eternity of the world, the denial of the beginning of the world, the impossibility of physical agony in hellfire after death, God's ignorance of the actions of individual human beings, etc. To argue against the theses of the Averroists, Thomas needed detailed knowledge of the Aristotelian writings. Already in Italy, he had been interested in the Aristotle translations by the Dominican Willem van Moerbeke of Brabant. Through his Latin translations, the writings and ancient commentaries became available. In Paris, Thomas commented on almost all the important texts by Aristotle, among them also the *Ethics* and the *Politics*.

As he only dealt with the first three books of the *Politics*, the extremes play no role. However, as expected, they stand in the centre of the commentaries on the *Nichomachean Ethics*. From the numerous respective passages, let there be only those mentioned in which the dual figure of the extremes is explained. Virtue is a mean at the ontological level; however, at the axiological level, it is an utmost.[190]

Yet, the influence of the Aristotelian ethics and politics cannot only be grasped in the commentaries. Already in the *Summa theologiae* still begun in Rome and in the mirror for princes, *De regimine principum*, there are found numerous references to both works. As with Aristotle, it is here too the 'final aim of the society united to live together, to live according to virtue'.[191] But the mean of virtue is reached by the avoidance of an excess of pleasures: 'Sic enim superfluitate vitata facilius ad medium virtutis pervienetur'.[192] These remarks are found towards the end of the tract written for the King of Cyprus, the state of the crusaders. Here, Thomas deals with practical issues, such as which viewpoints the king should keep in mind in his selection of suitable places for erecting cities and fortified places. As 'overly great conveniences of the landscape invite people to excessive pleasures, which, on the other hand, means the greatest damage to the state; it is necessary to enjoy them with moderation'.[193]

The Aristotelian influence is noticeable also in the constitutional doctrine of the Aquinate. Although he pleads for the kingdom, he recommends effectively limiting the competencies of the monarch. Therefore, it suffices in no way to only consider the suitability of the pretender's character. Moreover 'the administration of the kingdom is to be established in such a way that any opportunity of the king to erect a dictatorship is immediately revoked by the constitution. Likewise, his power must also be limited [temperetur potestas] so that he is not even capable to easily turn to tyranny'.[194] The utmost of wilfulness, power and cruelty connected to tyranny is here called 'excessus'.

Much speaks for the idea that Thomas was thinking about the restriction of the kingdom by aristocratic and democratic elements. So it says, after a brief recapitulation about Aristotle's doctrine of state forms, in the 105th examination of the *Summa theologiae*:

> The best order for the princes in a state or in an empire is therefore the one in which one person, who stands ahead of everyone, is placed at the helm according to virtue, and below him stand several who possess leadership according to virtue; and yet such a leadership belongs to everyone: those who can be chosen from among them all and also those who

are chosen from among them all. For the best way to rule a state is that there exists good cooperation in a kingdom when one individual stands at the head, and the best rulership (aristocratia) when many have the leadership according to virtue; and the rulership of the people (democratia) when the princes can be chosen from among the people and the election of the princes belongs to the people.

The importance of this explanation is emphasized by referring to the 'divine law'[195] according to the mixed constitution of the Israelites under Moses and his followers.[196]

Thomas of Aquinas' student Ptolemy of Lucca continued his teacher's fragment.[197] In the thirteenth and fourteenth century, there appeared several texts under the same title (among others, by Aegidius Romanus, Petrus de Alvernia, Engelbert of Admont and Jean Quidort), in which the mixed constitution was dealt with as a realistic design option. The strongest tendency in the direction of an unlimited monarchy is seen in the mirror for princes of 1278 dedicated to Philipp IV ('the Beautiful') of France by the Augustine hermit Aegidius Romanus (also Aegidius Colonna or Giles de Rome; ca. 1243–1316) who had heard Thomas of Aquinas' lectures in Paris and later taught there himself (from 1285 to 1291). The separation of the monarch from positive law does not mean boundlessness.[198] He is bound to natural law, obliged to the common well-being and is subject to the classical responsibilities of virtue, not least of all to moderation ('temperantia'[199]). Aegidius examines the causes and the forms of tyrannis in detail, which, in the Aristotelian tradition, are seen as the worst of all rulership forms. It can come from monarchy, if it follows an 'intentionem perversam', but also from an oligarchy falling into the extreme: 'Tyranny is an oligarchy to the extreme, that is to say: the worst' [Tyrannidem esse oligarchiam extremam idest pessimam].[200]

The connection of the Aristotelian doctrine of the constitution with a discussion of the responsibilities of virtue is also found in Engelbert of Admont's (ca. 1250–1331) *De regimine principum* in the same manner as in the mirrors of princes. In contrast to Aegidius, whose papers he knew,[201] Engelbert however examined the different forms of the mixed constitution systematically and also considered them realistic design forms (aside from the moderate kingdom).[202] Presumably, Engelbert had entered the convent of the Styrian Benedictine monastery as a 17-year-old and had become acquainted with Aristotle's logical and natural-scientific writings during his studies in Prague (1271–74). He expanded this knowledge at the University of Padua, where the laical orientation of the society and the Republican constitution of the commune may have influenced him.[203] After changing to the Dominican university (1281–85), he became familiar with Thomistic theology, still suspected of heresy at that time, which was to shape his world view.[204] The text *De regimine principum*, written after his return from Italy and completed in 1290, impresses in the first two chapters by a systematic discussion of the mathematically possible mixed constitution illustrated with examples from history and the present, whereby he starts with four simple basic forms ('*Olicratia, Democratia, Aristocratia* and *Monarchia* sint *simplices* and quasi *naturales* species regiminis Politici'[205] [the aristocracy distinguishes itself as a virtuous regime from the other forms of the rulership of the minority]) and therefore is acquainted with mixtures of two, three and four elements.[206] The terminology of the mesotês doctrine, for one, appears in the ethical basis, where Engelbert determines the morally correct as a mean between extreme forms of behaviour.[207] For the other, it is a component of the doctrine of virtue broadly developed in the major sections IV–VII for the instruction of the king or prince. So, magnanimity ('magnanimitas') – exemplarily – can be described as a mean between pompousness (pompositas) and narrow-mindedness (pusillanimitas).[208]

At the individual ethical level, Engelbert later broadly developed this topic and thereby fell back on Cicero and Seneca, although foremost on the *Nichomachean Ethics*. In the *Speculum virtutum*, to be dated between 1306 and 1313,[209] he took over the terminology of the mesotês doctrine. Key passages are found in chapters VI and VII of the fourth part, where the mean between the extremes is at first mathematically determined as a centrepoint between the extremes of a distance.[210] Thereafter, Engelbert uses the mathematical figure for the discussion of the virtues, at first for generosity (*liberalitas*) as a mean between prodigality (*prodigalitas*) and avarice (*avaricia*): 'The mean is contrary to the extremes, and the extremes are contrary to the mean, as generosity is contrary to prodigality and avarice and vice versa prodigality and avarice are contrary to generosity'. [Medium autem contrariatur extremis et extrema contrariantur medio, ut liberalitas contraria est prodigalitati et avaricie et econverso prodigalitas et avaricia contrariantur liberalitati].[211] As in Aristotle, all further virtues are afterwards dealt with in this manner and classified terminologically.[212]

For the history of the reception of the political extremes, the translation of the Latin Aristotle into the European national languages was of great importance. A first translation into French came from Pierre de Paris; it was lost.[213] The second translation was carried out by Nicole de Oresme (ca. 1320–82). Oresme was one of the most fascinating thinkers of the fourteenth century.[214] Although he had studied theology in Paris, he became known foremost for his natural-scientific, mathematical and economic studies. He developed a heliocentric theory of the sun system and, along with his teacher Jean Buridan, founded a physics of movement whose sets were finally revised by Newton. He also wrote the first connected analysis about the creation and the characteristics of money.

Oresme translated and commented on important Aristotelian writings from Latin into French on behalf of the French king, Charles V, adding extensive commentaries to the texts.[215] They were to serve the instruction of the monarch and his advisers and help solve practical political issues. In a glossary attached to the *Nichomachean Ethics*, Oresme defined the term *extreme*: 'Extremes or extremities are the outermost ends, the limits of things. But especially in the realm of morality, extremes are the appearances and actions located outside the mean of virtue – in the sense of too much, excess or too little, a lack. This way one says that virtue is located in the mean and the vices in the extremes'.[216] The extremes were described as the outermost deviations from the middle path of virtue: This formula was likewise the quintessence of the second book of the *Nichomachean Ethics*.

In his commentaries on the *Politics*, Oresme connected with the moral philosophical definition of the extremes and transferred the term – as it applied to the concept of the work – to the social and political institutional level.[217] Now, the outermost deviations from the ideal of the well-mixed constitution (such as tyranny and ochlocracy) and the one-sided taking into consideration of the interests of the upper and the lower classes were also seen as 'extremes'. He examined the 'degeneration' ('transgression'[218]) of the three forms in detail, explained the hierarchy of imperfect ('vicieuses') and corrupt ('corrumpues'[219]) regimes, among which democracy represented the lesser evil, because of less abuse of power. In controversial places, he fell back on Albert's commentaries and carefully discussed the pros and cons.

One of these issues concerned the creation of the best constitution out of two degenerations. How is one to imagine that something good could be created from something bad? Oresme used the image of a medicine consisting of too bitter or sweet elements, from whose mixture, however, a healing process would develop. In a similar manner, a good constitution could be composed from contrary elements of constitutional forms which, by themselves, were harmful: 'De.ii. choses nuisibles et contraires est composée une chose moienne, bonne et profitable, si comme l'en fait selon medicine de.ii. choses dont l'une est trop froide et l'autre est trop chaude ou dont l'une est trop amere et l'autre trop douce'.[220] From the balance of the extremes, the 'good' elements contained therein would be developed.

Oresme commented on the socially integrative dimension of the Aristotelian mixed constitution in detail. A good constitution had to be founded on a broad basis of the middle class. Where the extremes of the wealthy and the poor dominated together, or only one of these two groups by itself, there existed unfavourable preconditions for virtuous, stability-guaranteeing conditions.[221] Oresme not only dealt theoretically with the mixed constitution but also illustrated his explanations with examples from the constitutional conditions of his time, e.g. he recommended a limitation of royal power by a representational body called 'parlement',[222] even calling for a mixed constitutional form for the Church as unlimited power in the hands of one individual was a bad thing. Certainly, Oresme was elitist concerning the question of which part of the population was to participate in limiting the power of the monarchy. But in several ways, he went further than other supporters of a mixed constitution of his time. With the idea of a mixed Church regime, he exerted some influence on the conciliary movement (e.g. Jean Gerson and Pierre d'Ailly). His commentaries concerning Aristotle's politics were an 'important milestone between Thomas Aquinas and the conciliar, Florentine, and English theories of limited government and mixed constitution, to be developed in the next several centuries'.[223]

# 3 Extremes and the tradition of the mixed constitution from early humanism to the age of democratic revolutions

## 1 Early humanism

Speaking in humanistic terms, Aristotelism proved to be a powerfully effective trend until well into the eighteenth century.[1] Even though scholastics helped it to blossom, it soon departed from the theological grasp. Also, Averroism had already made its contribution, leading to lively discussions at the arts faculty in Paris, among others.[2] Such tendencies found their continuation in the early Renaissance and in the bourgeois humanism of the northern Italian city-states.[3]

Dante Alighieri (1265–1321) opens the round of the great Florentine state thinkers, yet he holds a special position in as far as he remained connected to the universal monarchy of the Holy Roman Empire, even ascribing it a quasi-sacred function.[4] Nevertheless, he left room in this framework for other design forms and opposed the Church's worldly claim for power in his disputation, *Monarchia*. The works of Aristotle formed the intellectual basis, although Dante broke with it in several ways in his constitutional political programme:[5] He understood the 'human genus' ('genus humanum') as universal and saw its freedom ('libertas') guaranteed only 'under the reign of the monarch': 'Only then, the degenerate state constitutions are shown the right way – meaning democracy, oligarchy and tyranny, which force man into slavery as is clear to everyone who examines all of them – and only then the kings, aristocrats, who are called optimates, as well as those railing for the freedom of the people will reign in an appropriate manner'.[6]

Nevertheless, one encounters the mesotês doctrine everywhere in his work. In the strict order of syllogisms, by which is to be proved that the 'ability to bestow authority upon the empire goes against the nature of the Church', man's position as the mean between the transitory and the intransitory is determined: 'When man thus occupies a certain mean between the transitory and the intransitory and every mean partakes of the nature of the extremes, it is necessary that man possesses both natures'.[7] From this observation, Dante derives two human goals and realms of life, strictly separated from each other: those of earthly life and those of eternal life. Man pursues the goals of earthly life with the help of reason founded on philosophy and that of eternal life through faith aided by the Holy Ghost. Thus, the circle of the authority of the Church is limited and the separation of state and Church justified logically.[8]

As an early representative of Florentine bourgeois humanism[9] after Dante, Leonardo Bruni (1370–1440) must be mentioned, a student of Coluccio Salutati, who was the Chancellor of the Republic of Florence from 1375 to 1406 and whose footsteps he followed in 1410. At this time, the city on the river Arno became the political and cultural centre of Italy, drawing artists and scholars from everywhere. The Tuscan dialect of this city became the national language of Italy and Florence the cradle of the Italian national epic. In Florence, the first modern state system with a differentiated structure of authorities, a cleverly conceived law system, initial forms of the division of powers and a pluralist spectrum of political social powers developed. Culturally, Florence became a world power. A large proportion of the ornate churches, proud government buildings, citizens' palaces and loggias, still admired by tourists today, came into being in the fourteenth and fifteenth centuries. Immeasurable riches were accumulated in the city. The Florentines were able early on to conduct the expanding money market through a banking system of their own. Florentine businessmen and cloth merchants had branches and agencies in the whole world known at the time.

Leonardo Bruni's political thinking was oriented to the ideal of the Greek *poleis*. Florence was to develop into an Athens of the new time. In his *Historia florentini populi*, he interpreted the constitution of the city as a 'regimen mixtum' in the vein of the Aristotelian constitutional tradition. He newly translated the *Nichomachean Ethics* and Aristotle's *Politics* to juxtapose the scholastic texts with a humanist version.[10] Hereby, the mesotês doctrine and the theory of the mixed constitution became the centre once more. In his commentary on the *Politics*, Bruni describes the different possibilities of the mixture of state forms, the thereby existing balance of the extremes, the coming about of tyrannis, among others, 'ex extrema populari licentia'[11] from the extreme generosity of the crowd of the people, the meaning of 'mediocritas' and 'temperantia' and the avoidance of excess (excessus) as well as deficiency (defectus).[12]

With Salutati and Bruni began the long line of Florentine statesmen who made important contributions to the foundation of modern republicanism. The most effective of them was a certain Niccolò Machiavelli (1467–1525), but in his mixed constitutional concept, which was mostly inspired by Polybius, the Aristotelian categories, which he must certainly have known too, did not altogether recur.[13] This was different from one of his younger discussion partners in the Orti Oricellari, Antonio Brucioli (1487–1566). As a young man, Brucioli clung to Republican ideas, participating in the unsuccessful conspiracy against the Medici. He escaped into exile and there wrote, among others, a *Dialogo della Republica*. This he was to publish anew with essential changes in the years 1538–44 during his Venetian exile and troubled by the inquisition, presumably improving his meagre income as an informer for Cosimo I (briefly returning to his native city after the Medici had been driven out in 1527, again being banned as a result of the Bible translator's and commentator's sympathies with German reformer Martin Luther).[14]

Brucioli's dialogue exemplifies how Aristotelian mesotês ethics could also be connected with an unmixed constitutional construction. With Aristotle, the virtue is determined as a medium attitude between depraved extremes ('essa virtù una certa laudibile mediocrità, che i viziosi estremi fugge'[15]). And, just the same, he understands the social forces whose predominance decides the kind of constitution: the wealthy ('ricchi'), the poor ('poveri') and the medium ('mediocri'). The constitutional design, however, does not provide for an institutional balancing of the social forces in the framework of a regimen mixtum, but is founded on a restrictive distribution of bourgeois participation rights: the poor as well as the wealthy are excluded from it.[16] A broad basis of the people is secured through an evened out middle class society in which the *mediocri* carry out a controlled rulership, among others by means of an overlapping rotation of positions and times of service. Despite its realistic intentions, Brucioli's design for a republic cannot hide its idealistic strains against the background of Florentine conditions. This religious humanist was quite obviously not only influenced by Aristotle but also by Thomas More's (1478–1535) *Utopia*.[17]

In comparison, the last important state philosopher of the Republic of Florence, Giannotti (1492–1573), was more strongly oriented to the conditions of real politics. His work, *Della Repubblica fiorentina*, written after its decline in the year 1530 and after the Medici had seized power again, also shows Aristotelian teaching. The Platonic–Aristotelian scheme of six state forms is connected to the Anakyklosis doctrine of Polybius; the necessity for a mixed constitution is explained by the instability of the pure forms oriented along the common welfare. Here, too, the sociological support of the mixed constitution looks very Aristotelian:

> In every city there are citizens of various kinds; everywhere one finds the aristocratic and the wealthy – in other words *grandi* – on the one hand, and the poor and low on the other, as well as the *mediocri* who partake of both extremes. One meets these three groups everywhere, whereby here the one, there the other, is the greater. According to their differences, their leanings are likewise various and different. Since they surpass the others in aristocracy and wealth, the *grandi* want to command, not individually, but altogether. They demand a form of government in which they hold the sole power. Further, there is always one among them striving to reign by himself and wanting sole command. The poor are not interested in reigning, but they fear the arrogance of the *grandi* and therefore only will obey those laws that, without a difference, demand the same from everyone. It is sufficient for them to be free, and whoever obeys the law is free. The *mediocri* have the same tendency as the poor; they likewise strive for freedom. Since fortune is somewhat more even-handed in their case, they demand honour in addition to freedom. We can therefore say that there

are some in every city who only demand freedom (libertà), whereas others additionally demand honour (honore); and yet others strive for greatness (grandezza) either for themselves alone or together with others.[18]

Establishing a stable political order calls for a reasonable representation of the interests of the poor, the wealthy and also of the middle class. This can best be carried out in a 'stato misto' (Table 3.1).

Preferably suited for the establishment of a mixed constitution are those cities in which the *mediocri* predominate. This idea is as aristocratic as the connection to the doctrine of virtue: When the *mediocri* are the majority, neither can the wealthy rise up against the poor nor the poor against the wealthy,

> for in both cases, the rebelling group would have to fear the mediocri. The larger their number, the better the said order can be reestablished in the respective city. According to Aristotle, virtue stems from its position in the mean. From this there follows that the moderate life is perfect and good whereas a life that deviates from this is imperfect and bad. Since the mediocri are neither extremely aristocratic and wealthy nor particularly poor and low, they lead a perfect life.[19]

In contrast, the *grandi* and the *plebei* tend towards the extreme, the former to love of splendour and power and the latter to small-mindedness and slavish attitudes. A mixed constitution not only establishes a balance of interests but also produces those virtues that make a good life possible.

In Giannotti, the interests are divided among the state institutions, which themselves again participate on a different scale in the execution of four state

Table 3.1 Giannotti's mixed constitution

| Social classes | Interests | Institutions | Mixed constitution |
| --- | --- | --- | --- |
| Plebei Popolari Mediocri Grandi | Tranquility | – | – |
| Popolari Mediocri Grandi | Tranquility Freedom | Gran Consiglio | Democratic element |
| Mediocri Grandi | Tranquility Freedom Honour | Senato | Oligarchic element |
| Grandi | Tranquility Freedom Honour Greatness | Collegio Principe | Monocratic element |

Source: Riklin, Donato Giannotti, p. 55.

functions: elections, foreign policy and security policy, legislation and dispensation of justice. Here again, he differentiates between three phases in the decision-making process: consultazione, deliberazione and esecuzione (consultation, deliberation and execution). The 'stato misto' is marked by a complex, power-controlling tangled mass of social interests, state organizations, functions and decision-making phases.[20]

The plans of the Republicans in exile existed only on paper. They were not given any opportunity to put their Republican stabilization programme into action. When Giannotti died in Rome at an advanced age in 1573, the Medici were still in power. His work remained unpublished for nearly two centuries. Finally, in 1721, a first edition was published in Venice.[21] Therefore, Giannotti's cleverly conceived doctrine of the division of power has played no role in the history of ideas.[22] Furthermore, Florence could hardly serve as an example of republican durability. This applied much more to Venice which connected its constitution, which was understood to be republican, with an admirable stability on the inside and an extraordinary development of power on the outside, maintained a hegemonial position in the Mediterranean and became the centre of a worldwide trade empire. Like many Florentine philosophers before him, Giannotti also dedicated a text to the Republic of Venice, which is preserved only fragmentarily and whose explanations concerning the mixed constitution would presumably have been found in its lost part.

The characterization of Venice as a mixed constitution goes back to at least the fifteenth century. Felix Gilbert found the earliest proof in a fragment by Pier Paolo Vergerio, in which he calls Venice an aristocracy, at the same time pointing out the democratic and monarchic elements in its constitution: 'venetorum republica optimatum administratione regitur. Ideoque aristocratiam greco vocabulo licet appelare quae inter regium popularemque principatum media est. Hec vero et tanto est melior quod, quoniam utrique ladabilium extremorum participat, ex omni genere laudabilis recte politice simul commixta est'.[23]

For perceiving Venice as a mixed constitution, the much-read book by the Venetian Gasparo Contarini (1483–1542) was much more important. *De Magistratibus et Republica Venetorum* was presumably written in the years 1523/24 and published for the first time in 1543. According to Leopold von Ranke, Contarini was the famous founder of the doctrine of the mixed constitution of Venice.[24] In his description, the Doge embodies the monarchic principle, and the Major Council the democratic one. Between these two extremes stands the optimatic element as the balancing mean embodied by the Senate, the Council of the Ten and the savii (pre-advisers). Hereby, Contarini does not refer to Aristotle but to Plato's *Timaios*, where God creates water and air as the mean (*meson*) and fire and earth as the connection between the extreme elements (*eschaton*).[25]

Three decades after Contarini's book appeared, Jean Bodin (1529–96) vehemently contradicted the latter's interpretation of Venice as a mixed constitution. It was not compatible with his doctrine of the inseparability of sovereignty. According to him, sovereignty lay with the legislative power, thus with the Major Council. Therefore, Venice had to be seen as a pure aristocracy. In a similar manner, Bodin sought to prove that those regimes that in the past had been called mixed constitutions by Plato, Aristotle, Polybius and other authors (most of all Sparta and Rome) in fact only showed a true sovereignty representative and therefore were to be seen as democratic, aristocratic or monarchic.[26] Aristotle had contradicted himself when he criticized Plato for recommending a mixture of democracy and tyranny, on the one hand, yet himself, on the other hand, had propagated a form mixed of several constitutions: 'En quoy Aristote dispute contre soy-mesme: car si la meslange de deux Republiques est vicieuse, à sçauoir des deux extremités, qui font en toute autre chose le moyen, encores plus vicieuse sera la meslange de trois'.[27] Despite the critique, Bodin used the image of the mean between the extremes in comparing the advantages and disadvantages of different forms of state. The following argument was in favour of an aristocracy: 'Car s'il est ainsi qu'en toutes choses la médiocrité est louable, & qu'il faut fuir les extremités vicieuses, il s'ensuit bien que ces deux extremités vicieuses estans reiectees, il se faudra tenir au moyen, qui est l'Aristocratie'[28] – namely between democracy and monarchy. But after weighing all advantages and disadvantages, the 'monarchie bien ordonnée'[29] received the highest rank, after all. Besides, the extremes turned up again in the discussion of 'harmonious justice'.[30] In this way, Bodin broke with the tradition of the mixed constitution, however, integrating the categories of the mesotês doctrine into his doctrine of sovereignty.

## 2 Constitution of England

Lewes Lewkenor translated Contarini's Venice book into English. The publication contributed to acquaint the educated English public with the aristocratic–republican tradition of the mixed constitution.[31] The work must have impressed so much more as it did not describe an abstract model but the existing constitution of a mighty trading empire of astonishing stability. In addition, England, being at war with Spain and having to make great efforts to 'bring peace' to the rebellious Irish, had to deal with a difficult social and economic crisis in the 1590s. In the light of the unresolved succession issue, the tension at court between rival groups who offered different institutional solutions also intensified. So, Lewkenor may not only have had in mind satisfying the curiosity in foreign countries of the English public. The mixed constitution presented a model opposite to the Elizabethan system with its absolutist tendencies.

With research, the emphasis on the 'Machiavellian moment' and the strengthening of 'civic humanism' during and after the English revolution[32] connected to it led to an underestimation of humanist traditions and the mixed constitution discourse in pre-revolutionary times. But already, court barrister John Fortescue (1394–1476), in his text about *The Difference between Absolute and Limited Monarchy* (ca. 1471), had differentiated in the

Aristotelian–Thomistic tradition between the *dominium regale*, the absolute monarchy, the *dominium politicum*, the republic, and the *dominium politicum et regale*, a mixed form, pleading for the latter.[33] For the following century, the importance of the reception of ancient humanism and the mixed constitution can be proved on a broad foundation of sources.[34] One of many examples: The Bishop of Rochester and Winchester, John Ponet (ca. 1514–56), in his *A Shorte Treatise of politike pouuer* (1556), quoted the mixed constitution: 'wher all together, that is, a king, the nobilitie, and comones, a mixte state: which men by long continuaunce haue indged tu the best sort of all. For wher that mixte state was exerciced, ther did the comon wealthe longest continue'.[35] It seems that Cicero's doctrine of virtue outweighed that of Aristotle in the sixteenth century. Yet the *Politics* was also widely read in the English language early on, whereby the translations and commentaries of the French Renaissance humanist Louis Le Roy served as a model.[36] In the arguments around James I, the mixed constitution belonged to the arsenal of Jacobite argumentations (reference to a 'balanced constitution', which connected the authority of the king and the freedom of the people) and that of the anti-absolutists.[37]

On the eve of the outbreak of the civil war, in his *Answer to the Nineteen Propositions*, Charles I himself took refuge in the idea of a 'mixed government', concerning the interpretation of the kingdom.[38] After the outbreak of the war, the doctrine gained outstanding importance: 'now that the breakdown of the old system had become obvious, the question about who possessed sovereign power could no longer remain open. Now that the entire political system was at disposition, the discussion about the alleged English mixed constitution became a central topic'. It found its closure, for the time being, only after the Glorious Revolution, when the version of the sovereignty of the king-in-parliament asserted itself for all time and the 'belief that England had a mixed constitution'[39] became commonplace.

The Puritan clergyman Philip Hunton (1604–82) made an important theoretical contribution to the English discussion concerning the constitution at the time of the civil war with his *Treatise of Monarchy*, published anonymously in May 1643. In the foreword to the first edition, it says: 'I write not this Discourse to forment or heighten the wofull dissention of the Kingdome, but if possible to cure, or at least to allay it [ … ]. If any condemn me for any thing here, it must be for endeavouring a thanklesse Moderation 'twixt two Extremes'.[40] In his appeal for a 'moderate or limited monarchy', he wanted to mediate between the followers of pure royal sovereignty and undivided parliamentary sovereignty. The solution consisted of ascribing sovereignty to the king-in-parliament, interpreting him, thus, as a part of rulership association consisting of three elements expressed in parliamentarily represented 'estates'. He described a mixed monarchy 'in which three estates are constituted to the end that the power of one should moderate and restrain from excess the power of the other'.[41]

Sir Robert Filmer of Kent, who had been incarcerated by the parliamentary party in the years 1643–45, opposed Hunton in his pamphlet *The*

*Anarchy of a Limited or Mixed Monarchy*,[42] published in 1648, in which he tried to prove the absurdity of the concept of the mixed constitution. In a text published four years later, he also went against the creator of the theory of the mixed constitution. Among others, he rejected Aristotle's interpretation of the polity as 'perfect forme [ … ] made of two imperfect' in a play on words as 'rather a confounding then compounding of government'.[43]

Filmer's positions had, however, been pushed to the edge on account of political developments. John Milton, the main propagandist of the republic proclaimed under Oliver Cromwell, justified the execution of Charles I in his *Eikonoklastes* (1649) by claiming the democratic arch-power of the people and the right to opposition. If the king had reigned well, violent fighting would not have come about: 'For besides that in good Government they [Tumults] happ'n seldomest, and rise not without couse, if they prove extreme, and pernicious, they were never counted so to Monarchy, but to Monarchical Tyranny, and extremes one with another are most Antipathy. If then the King so extremely stood in fear of Tumults, the inference will endanger him to be the other extreme'.[44] The 'errors also of this Government had brought the Kingdom to such extremes'[45] justified the murder of the tyrant in Milton's eyes.

Later, another Republican opposed Filmer's influential attempt to derive the 'natural' and the 'divine' law of the absolute kingdom to the patriarchal arch-power stemming from arch-father Abel. In the meantime, Filmer's major work *Patriarcha* (1680) had been published, 'the flagship of seventeenth century royalism'.[46] In his *Discourses Concerning Government*, Algernon Sidney (1622–83) showed the superiority of the mixed constitution, not least on the basis of Aristotelian ethics and politics, and warned of the dangers of an insufficiently controlled kingdom in the hope 'that the people did not suffer extremities by the vices or infirmities of kings'.[47] After the civil war, Sidney had supported the cause of the exiled Republicans; however, in the meantime, he had moderated his views. Still, he himself did have to suffer 'extremeties' on the part of the monarchy. When he had completed his *Discourses*, he was executed in the same year (1683) for supposedly being involved in the Rye House plot, a Republican revolutionary plan.[48]

The struggle as to how to interpret the mixed constitution soon led to a far-reaching consensus on the constitutional–monarchic basis. The leading doctrine was mirrored in Lord Bolingbroke's (1678–1751) influential *Dissertation upon Parties*, which was published in London in 1739 and in which the freedom-ensuring effect of a special mixture of monarchic, aristocratic and democratic elements was conjured up. In contrast, simple forms of government by necessity led to the abuse of power:

> By simple Forms of Government I mean such as lodge the whole Supreme Power, absolutely and without Controll, either in a single Person, or in the principal Persons of the Community, or in the whole Body of the People. Such Governments of arbitrary Will, and therefore of all imaginable Absurdities the most absurd. [ … ] Absolute Monarchy is Tyranny;

but absolute Democracy is Tyranny and Anarchy both. If Aristocracy be placed between these two Extremes, it is placed on a slippery Ridge, and must fall into one or the other, according to the natural Course of human affairs.[49]

A similar interpretation is found in an essay by the Scottish liberal David Hume (1711–76), which appeared two years later. Hume derived the much praised freedom of the press from 'our mixt form of government, which is neither wholly monarchical, nor wholly republican. It will be found, if I mistake not, a true observation in politics, that the two extremes in government, liberty and slavery, commonly approach nearest to each other; and that, as you depart from the extremes, and mix a little of monarchy with liberty, the government becomes always the more free'. A purely monarchic as well as a purely republican government, as could be found in Holland, tended towards the restriction of individual freedom. Therefore, it seemed 'evident, that the two extremes, of absolute monarchy and of a Republic, approach very near to each other in the most material circumstances'.[50]

## 3 European continent

While the struggle between the king and the parliament in England was decided in favour of a constitutional monarchy, whose interpretation as a mixed constitution had almost become commonplace at the end of the seventeenth century, the concept of the mixed constitution on the European continent, where absolutism was spreading, developed into an interpretative pattern of political dissidence. In Germany, the Calvinist lawyer Johannes Althusius (1557–1638), a professor in Herborn and later at the council syndic in Emden, stood up against Bodin and absolutism, oriented himself at the constitution of the Empire, the cooperative practices of the Swiss city cantons and the republican constitution of the northern Netherlands. Through absolute power, he wrote in his *Politica* published in 1603, 'kingdoms become thieving gangs'.[51] He explicitly referred to Aristotle and Augustine. Althusius still held fast to Bodin's sovereignty dogma, but for him, sovereignty (jus majestatis) was indivisibly connected to the people, from where it could be delegated to different authorities. The administration of the state was carried out by elected representatives of the people, the 'ephores', who represented the rights of the political community towards the person holding the highest power and the Summus Magistratus elected by them. All the members of the community owe respect to God and the laws of the decalogue. In his affirmative depiction of the mixed constitution, Althusius quoted, among others, Aristotle and Gasparo Contarini's description of the Republic of Venice. All there is to it is regulating the power of the state: 'Namely, that power is more secure which sets a limit to the powers, rules over willing subordinates and is explained by laws, so that it does not become arrogant, thus effecting damage on the subordinates and becoming a tyranny'.[52] Althusius held on to the kingdom as the best order,[53] limiting it however by an aristocratic and a democratic element: 'Misformations and degenerate forms which come about from the too much or too little of these three kinds are not to be seen as independent forms but as degenerations and deviations'.[54] The well-mixed constitution is found with an imagined mean between the extremes.

In Germany, absolutism asserted itself in most of the territorial states, which finally established themselves after the end of the Thirty Years' War. In France, on the other hand, the process of the political concentration of power had begun sooner, allowing a new political system to come into existence already under Henry IV (1589/93–1610). The Protestants were interested in a strong central power that protected them and joined the absolutist camp. Only after the abolition of the Edict of Nantes in 1685 did a wave of anti-absolutist critique begin, inspired by the sovereignty of the people thinking of the *monarchomachians*. The *Politique tirée de Propres paroles de l'Ecriture Sainte* by Jacques Benigne Bossuet (1627–1704), the court ideologist of Louis XIV, opposed such tendencies. His student, François Fénelon (1651–1715), took a different path.[55] He defended the rights of the individual against an absolute reign from a Christian standpoint.[56]

The admonishments and advice that Fénelon directed towards the Duke of Burgundy, the presumptive heir to the throne of the ageing Louis XIV, in his *Examen de conscience sur les devoirs de la royauté* (presumably in the years 1709/10), in which he criticized luxury, the prodigal lifestyle, favouritism and the spirit of conquest, read like an indictment against the absolutist regime of the Sun King. In the long list of questions of conscience, which the author asks his reader, the following is also found: 'Do you know [ ... ] wherein anarchy, wherein a despotic rulership and wherein a kingdom regulated by laws, the mean between the extremes, consist of?'[57] Monarchic power should be effectively limited by the Estates-General and an independent justice system. In view of the explosive nature of the explanations concerning monarchic duties, the addressee kept them under strict lock and key until his early death, and the first attempt to publish them in the year 1734 was stopped by the ministry responsible. In 1775, the text was finally published in France with the permission of Louis XVI.[58]

Fénelon never developed his ideas systematically. The educational novel *Les Aventures de Télémaque* (1699), in which a virtuous agrarian utopia serving everyone's welfare is developed in the fantasyland of 'Salente', contains a detailed critique of society but does not construct a subjective, realistic model of state and government. And the plans for a government jointly developed with the Count of Chevreuse at his castle in Chaulnes/Picardy in November 1711 ('plans de gouvernement') for his student, the Duke of Burgundy, who had become the crown prince, only consist of a list of political recommendations.

Scotsman Andrew Michael Ramsay ('Chevalier de Ramsay', 1686–1743), whom Fénelon had led back to the 'right path' of Catholic faith in Cambrai in 1710, making him his protégé, produced an *Essai sur le gouvernement civil* (with numerous changes of title and changed content in the following years), which was published in 1719 'according to the principles' of Fénelon, an interpretation in which the ideas of the master were mixed with those of Ramsay.[59] It contained proposals for how a 'civil government' would be possible and how people would adhere to order without 'feeling like slaves'.[60] There was no perfect state, but one had to always find a balance between those ruling and those being ruled. The uncontrolled striving towards power of the 'sovereigns' would lead to 'despotism', whereas unlimited striving towards freedom of the subordinates would lead to 'anarchy'.[61] This had been the situation in which Rome had found itself at the end of the consulate. The Plebeians feared the tyrannical degeneration of patrician power as much as the Patricians feared the anarchic consequences of the uncontrolled power of the people: 'Between these two extremes a people which was otherwise wise could not find a mean'.[62]

In a well-mixed constitution, the monarchic element would be able to keep the democratic element as well as the aristocratic element within suitable boundaries: 'The kingdom then is like the turning point of a lever that holds the balance between the two extremes by moving closer to the one or the other'.[63] Even though in this way Ramsay expressly accepted the possibility of a stable mixed constitution with a strong monarchic head, he nonetheless endeavoured not to delegitimize French conditions of rule. Therefore, he admitted that a mixed constitution was in no way always better than a true monarchy. In the final part of the essay, he emphasized the necessity of a 'sovereign power immediately derived from God'[64] and distinctly opposed the theory of the 'arch-power of the people'.[65]

## 4 Montesquieu's 'gouvernement modéré'

In 1727, Ramsay read from a new edition of his educational novel *Voyages de Cyros*, which had become a bestseller, at the *Club de L'Entresol*, a discussion circle founded by Abbé Pierre-Joseph Alary in 1720, which did not shy away from dealing with difficult political issues. Among the listeners were Charles-Louis de Secondat, Baron de la Brède et de Montesquieu (1689–1755) who, at this time, had already made a name for himself as the author of the *Lettres Persanes*, a work that held a mirror up to the eyes of the absolutist society of France.[66]

His major work, *De l'esprit des lois*, was to appear in 1748, offering a whole arsenal of ideas and concepts to the 'anti-despotic' and moderately egalitarian trend of the Enlightenment. In the centre, there is the differentiation between moderate and extreme forms of rule. Limiting the antithesis of the extreme was carried out by a closer determination of the principle of 'modération' and its application to the doctrine of the state forms. A preform of this differentiation was already found in the *Persian letters* that anticipated the later systematically developed ideas, often in short prose form, frequently speaking of the 'douceur' (softness) and the 'dureté' (hardness) of legal regulations, institutional precautionary methods and modes of governing.[67] Montesquieu had introduced the term *gouvernement modéré* already in the *Considérations sur les causes de la grandeur des Romains* and the early *Pensées*, a collection of a lifelong syllabus of reading and some immature brain-waving intellectual ideas.[68] However, he did not develop the terms modéré/extrême until the *Esprit des lois.*

Hereby, apparently, the system of categories of the Aristotelian texts played an essential role. How strongly this reading material had been improved in conviction and subjectivity from the descriptive example of the conditions of the English constitution might be difficult to judge. After all, Montesquieu had conceived the sixth chapter of the eleventh book after his return from England, later adding it to the *Esprit des lois*.[69] There, he had acquainted himself with the theory of the constitution. He even knew two advocates of the doctrine of the mixed constitution in person. Lord Bolingbroke had spent six months at his country estate La Brède in 1724, and he carried on a lively correspondence with David Hume. Even more important than the exchange of thought with the two of them might have been the first-hand studies of political life in London. He had contacts with members of the political headquarters, the Whigs and the Tories, and was able to observe the debates of both chambers in parliament on account of good connections; he was also able to convince himself of the great influence of the English press on public opinion.[70] For the theoretical penetration of these kinds of experience, however, the knowledge of the English constitutional discussion does not appear to have been as important as the study of the classics.

In 1734, Montesquieu purchased the two available editions of Aristotle's *Politics*, essentially the French translation by Nicole Oresme and the commented translation by the Hellenist Louis Le Roy, which included the interpretation of the French monarchy in the vein of a mixed constitution by Claude de Seyssel.[71] From these works, he adopted the idea of virtue as a zone in-between extreme basic attitudes and the transmission of this model of politics in the concept of the mixed constitution, which causes moderation through the control of power and the balance of opposing social forces.

As in Aristotle, ethics and politics are also closely linked in Montesquieu. The principle of moderation, which Montesquieu renders the leading idea of his work, applies equally to politics and morals: 'I am saying, and it seems to me as if I had written this work only to prove this: The spirit of moderation must be that of the legislator; and the politically good as well as the morally good is always found in between the two outermost ends'.[72]

The ethical foundation did not hinder Montesquieu any more than it did Aristotle to soberly and differentiatedly discuss the actual variety of constitutions and their manifold spatial, social and cultural conditional factors. Aside from examinations of a natural–scientific kind, ethical reflections appeared again and again. So he connected the doctrine of virtues with the climate theory, as it is found in a similar form in the eighth book of Aristotle's *Politics*. Yet, Aristotle had juxtaposed the moderate, culture-furthering climate of Greece with the unfavourable conditions of hot and cold climates. Montesquieu, on the other hand, praised the favourable results of northern barrenness: The 'Gothic' arch form of the 'moderate state', which he favoured (gouvernement modéré), came from the cold forests of Germania. The 'hot countries' showed an 'extreme' tendency towards craving pleasure,[73] whereas the cold strengthens the circulation, the heart and the brain, seriousness, courageousness, capability and endurance, at the same time dampening emotional excitability. If one considers these natural relationships, one need not be surprised that 'the cowardice of the peoples of the hot climates almost always makes slaves of them, whereas the courage of the peoples of the northern climates was freely maintained'.[74] Montesquieu explains the 'extreme slavery' of Asia,[75] on the one hand, by the fact that there the cold of the 'Tartar' plateaus and the heat of the south collided abruptly, which was why the climate had caused the conquering peoples to immediately be confronted with easily enslaved tribes, which they then made into slaves. In Europe, on the other hand, similarly strong peoples had met up. And in contrast to the 'Tartars', the conquerors from the north, the 'Goths', had founded free state forms everywhere.[76] On the other hand, the expansive organization of Asia had favourably influenced the formation of extensive empires, which could only been ruled by despotism, whereas the more delicate organization of Europe had given rise to political freedom.[77] In a similar way, Montesquieu found connections between soil condition, population density, use of money, religion, customs, mores and the establishment of moderate or extreme rulership conditions.

As tyranny is in Aristotle's work, despotism is the playing field of the extremes in Montesquieu's. In the despotic states, 'extreme obedience'[78] rules, whereby the ruler's will must be carried out unconditionally. At best, religion causes exceptions from this rule: One would even kill one's father if the despot commanded it, but would not drink wine if the religious commandments strictly forbid this. 'Extreme obedience' was the goal of education in despotics; advisement, discussion, objections and doubt concerning the ruler's commands are frowned upon.[79] Owing to 'extreme slavery',[80] tax increases are per definitionem impossible. Women are seen as the property of their masters and are held as slaves in an extreme fashion.[81] In a state in which 'extreme subjugation'[82] is called peace, women must be locked up, as otherwise their intrigues will have a disastrous effect on their husbands. Whereas in moderate monarchies, the representatives of the classes/estates lend firmness to the constitution and discontent among the population only rarely leads to 'excesses', the uprising in despoties, once erupted, always takes on 'extreme'[83] forms.

In the despotic regime, the extremes come to full bloom. Simultaneously, extreme solutions are a danger to all other state forms, especially if the basic principles on which they rest experience great strain. Of (direct) democracy, it is said that its existence would be endangered as soon as a spirit of inequality or a 'spirit of extreme equality'[84] spread. A 'regulated democracy' showed itself in that the citizens and those holding the same office were equal before the law. 'Extreme freedom'[85] and equality of the natural condition was as far removed from freedom compatible with 'virtue' as slavery was. As soon as democracy began to relieve those holding state positions of their functions, it would collapse into 'despotism for all'.[86] If one took 'extreme paths',[87] such as the equal division of real estate property, this would favour corruption. Soon, one would then even buy votes. 'Small tyrants' would establish themselves, from the midst of whom a great tyrant would come forth who would replace democracy that had become decadent with the 'despotism of a single person'.[88]

Owing to titles being hereditary and the spreading of 'extreme corruption' related to this, the aristocracy is ruined. When the high ones no longer keep the laws, a 'despotic state' with 'several despots'[89] comes about. Extreme freedom ruins virtue as much as extreme slavery does. In 'extremely absolute monarchies', the historians divulge the truth, as they are not permitted to tell it. In 'extremely free states', they divulge it because the population falls apart into party affiliations, and everyone becomes a slave to the prejudices of his 'faction'.[90] The freedom of science is thus only assured in a state in which the representation of interests of the social groups is guaranteed and the power is controlled institutionally. Montesquieu's power-balancing mixed constitution, his 'gouvernement modéré', distributes the social forces seen as equal (voting population, aristocracy, king) into a two-chamber parliament, government and courts in such a way that none of these three powers is solely in the hands of a single social force or a single state organization, and every social force participates in each of the three powers.[91]

With Montesquieu's work, the ideas of moderation, mixed constitution and the control of power were updated. The work became very popular. Already two years after its publication, Montesquieu was able to speak of twenty-two editions.[92] In the second half of the eighteenth century, the balance between the extremes was an important topic in Enlightenment circles. In the *Encyclopédie*, Denis Diderot (1713–84) explained in detail the categories of Aristotelian ethics: 'Ce milieu écarte également d'homme de deux points opposés & extrêmes, à l'un desquels il pèche par excès, & à l'autre par défaut'.[93] Voltaire (1694–1778) recommended the examination of the extreme as a method to reach a suitable viewpoint on a controversial matter. If one were to ask oneself if it were useful to encourage the population to popular superstition, one would only recall the worst of the excesses called forth in this way: 'voyez surtout ce qu'il y a de plus extrême dans cette funeste matière, la Saint-Barthélemy, les massacres d'Irlande, les croisades'.[94] This is how the question answers itself.

In Germany, 'extremes' and 'moderation' were also an important topic in the discussion of the Enlightenment, e.g. – to name just one prominent example – the Cameralist Johann Heinrich Gottlob von Justi (1717–71) in his later works occupied himself in detail with the *Esprit des lois*, criticising them individually though adopting essential trains of thought. Justi became acquainted with the book in Vienna, where he had joined the censorship commission against the Jesuit opposition to his authorization.[95] Under Montesquieu's influence, Justi developed from a supporter of the enlightened police state absolutism to a 'consistent supporter of liberalism'.[96] In the *Comparisons of the European with the Asiatic and other supposedly Barbarian Governments* (Vergleichungen der Europäischen mit den Asiatischen und andern vermeintlich Barbarischen Regierungen; 1762), no basic rejection of the unlimited monarchy was to be found. Justi defended the omnipotence of Chinese dynasties against Montesquieu's reproach of despotism, even celebrated the Inca empire for its 'good policies' as ideal order.[97] In contrast, his suspicion against unlimited power in his examinations concerning *Natur und Wesen der Staaten* (1769, second edition 1771) was based on the estimation regarding 'the mixed forms of government' consisting of 'all three simple forms'[98] (according to the manner of England). The principle of moderation was to guide every wise government: 'It shall moderate its power by its own movement assuming that the basic laws of the state are not limited; as all unlimited and immoderate power brings forth effects that are too violent and damaging, which definitely become frightening to people. All violent power burns itself out through its own gravity and through the immoderateness of its effect; alone, a moderate use of the power is lasting, durable and pleasant to God and man'.[99]

## 5 John Adams and the American mixed constitution

With the specific connection of the doctrine of the mixed constitution and the doctrine of the division of power, Montesquieu achieved great influence on the democratic revolutions towards the end of the eighteenth century. According to a quantitative analysis of how often important authors were cited, Montesquieu was the busiest author at the time of the foundation of the USA, and this is true for both federalists and anti-federalists.[100] Although the federalists claimed that they wanted to create an 'unmixed republic' in the vein of a no classes, non-hereditary, non-monarchic system,[101] they still fell back on Montesquieu's ideas in numerous ways.

The doctrine of the mixed constitution was most vehemently represented in the post-revolutionary fights for direction by John Adams (1735–1826) who had represented the state of Massachusetts at the Continental Congress and, together with Benjamin Franklin, Thomas Jefferson, Roger Sherman and Robert Livingstone, had worked out the Declaration of Independence. In 1796, he won the race for the presidency against Thomas Jefferson and governed in Washington until 1801.

Presumably, John Adams was the most educated of the founding fathers. His collected works encompass ten bulky volumes. The core of his state-political convictions was already contained in his early writings, the *Thoughts on Government* (1776). He wrote them down in detail in his three-volume *Defence of the Constitutions of Government of the United States of America* (1787/88), written during his ambassadorship in London, the 'only attempt of a great "Politics" which the American Revolution produced'.[102] Here, he defended the mixed constitution and the two-chamber parliament according to the manner of his home state Massachusetts against opinions as they were presented by Turgot. He saw an unnecessary imitation of the English constitution in the American bicameral division of power and supported the view that a self-governing nation had to assimilate state power into a collective body. In his refutation, Adams summoned all the political experience of the Western freedom tradition from Antiquity to the northern Italian city republics as far as to the constitutions of England, the Netherlands and Switzerland. Thereby, he delved into the history of ideas' variety of sources,[103] Plato, Aristotle, Polybius, Cicero, Machiavelli, Guicciardini, Thomas Smith, John Milton, Harrington, Sidney, Locke, Bolingbroke, Burlamaqui, Montesquieu, Hume, Blackstone, Adam Smith, DeLolme, wrote line after line of quotations, repeated sources according to their content and commented on them to repeat his creed again and again that the simple constitutional forms were always a bad thing and that only a mixed constitution where the power was divided could assure freedom and stability.[104]

In the extensive treasures of the quotations and paraphrased texts concerning the history of the mixed constitution, the extremes recur frequently and always as opposite poles of a moderate constitution guaranteed by a mixture. To give an example: In writing about the dangers a republic such as Florence was exposed to, he falls back on Guicciardini when drawing lessons for the present: 'These things, at all times dangerous in such a government, will be much more so at present, because it is the nature of mankind, when they fly from one extreme in which they have been held by violence, without stopping at the mean, to the other extremity. Thus, he who escapes from a tyranny, if unrestrained, precipitates himself into an unbridled licentiousness, which also may most justly be called a tyranny'.[105]

The danger conjured up here of the transition from one extreme to the other sounded like the ancient doctrine of the constitutional cycle. But the striving characteristic for Adams to draw the constitutional political solutions of the present from the treasure of experience of the Old World was not shared by the founders of American democracy.[106] The fundamental newness of the marriage between democracy and the representative system was emphasized not least by those to whom the traditions of the mesotês doctrine and the mixed constitution concept were not as evident as to John Adams. Some of them suspected Adams of being a monarchist in disguise. Without doubt, his view relativized the constitutional political difference between Great Britain and the USA. The British constitution in his typology of state forms was confirmed as a monarchist republic. This was a pleonasm in the eyes of those who did not think in the categories of the regimen mixtum. However, Adams emphasized the power-balancing mixed constitution of both systems. The system in which the legislative lay in more than one hand was seen as a republic. This was true for both Great Britain and the USA. The participation of the executive authority in the legislative power was, as he corrected himself in a letter to Roger Sherman, in no way an 'extreme not to be imitated by a republic'.[107]

## 6 Extreme social forces

In Europe, the touching of the extremes had been a quotation long before the outbreak of the French Revolution. The much cited chapter heading from Louis Sebastien Mercier's (1740–1814) *Tableau de Paris* (1788) – 'Les extrêmes se touchent' – polemicized against the apparent moral similarity of the socially high positioned as well as the lowly people ('Les grands & la canaille se rapprochent dans leurs moers'[108]), and was deeply rooted in the Aristotelian tradition of ideas, 'the societal political normal philosophy of pre-revolutionary Europe'.[109] The categories of the mesotês ethics – whether they connected to a political institutional arrangement or not – had become facets of general education. Aristotelian as well as Stoic strands of tradition became a part of the 'mirrors for princes' ('Fürstenspiegel'), where keeping to the middle road had become a quotation:

> One used to say
> too much or too little
> is the devil's aim: the middle road
> was the best
> Medio tutissimus ibis.[110]

The Reformation had not caused a break with Aristotelian–Thomistic tradition. Martin Luther (1483–1546) had sharply criticized scholastics, where the 'blind heathen master Aristotle'[111] ruled, who, in his text *De Anima*, had announced the mortality of the soul.[112] At Wittenberg University, the positions of the humanist Aristotelians, who had recently been appointed in 1518, were not filled again when the time came.[113] In the first edition of the *Loci communes* (1521), Philipp Melanchthon (1497–1560) in youthful wantonness judged that Aristotle's doctrine consisted 'generally in a desire to polemicise so that among the writers of moral philosophy he did not even deserve the last place'.[114] But in the course of founding the Reformed university, Luther's student, comrade-in-arms and follower, gifted graecist and ancient philologist seriously concerned himself with the works of the so denounced one. In his ethics commentaries, which came about later, he dealt in detail with the categories of the doctrine of virtues (Mäßigung/Mitte – 'mediocritate', extreme – 'moderatione ab extremis recedens', 'omnes immoderatae actiones in utramque partem nocent naturis'[115]). Through the differentiation of the law and the Gospel, ethics, as that part of the divine laws being devoted to the bourgeois living together was given its own place. Aristotle's moderation and mean thus found – with Luther agreeing – entrance in the Reformed doctrine.[116]

Melanchthon's interest in constitutional political issues was awakened later and never reached the intensity of his philosophical–theological strivings. Yet, one could not escape the topic, already due to the necessity of clearing up the relationship of religion and state. In the *Commentarii in aliquot politicos libros Aristotelis* (1530), he did not pay any attention to the complex explanations regarding the mixed constitution, as he only commented on the first three books.[117] Later, he pleaded for a middle solution for the constitution between monarchy and democracy. The free city of Nuremberg, which did not participate in political power intrigues and owed its rank to the support of science, art and trade, offered the model of a state 'in which many wise and good people compare their plans and rule the state in a common spirit with equal eagerness and faithfulness'.[118] The appreciation of the virtuous middle road, however, did not hinder Melanchthon – as had been recommended by Erasmus – from damning the *via media* between the denominations carried out by some princes of the empire.[119]

The ethical differentiation between 'moderate' and 'extreme' attitudes could easily be used for the characterization of actors' groups. So the mesotês doctrine found its way into the self-finding and boundary-setting process of the denominations, which were each eager to depict their own dogmatics as the salvation-bringing middle road, yet the deviating view of the 'heretic' or 'the anti-Christ' as an extreme aberration leading straight to hell. An early example of the religious personification of the mesotês categories is found in the argumentation of the Bishop of Winchester, Stephen Gardiner (ca. 1483–1555), the leading Church theologian in England, who took a conservative attitude in the religious arguments and definitely distanced himself from the 'new scoole of extremites',[120] the advocates of the reformed viewpoint in the argument concerning the predestination doctrine and the role of personal judgement in the interpretation of the Bible. Such 'extremists' were threatened with being burned at the stake during the reign of the Catholic Tudor queen, Mary I (1553–58).[121]

The feuding camps each claimed keeping to a golden mean for themselves. An anti-reformation argumentation, *de extremis Haereticorum erroribus*, by the Spanish Jesuit F. Joanne Gonzales de Leon from the year 1635/36, represents an impressive testimonial of this kind from the Catholic point of view, in which the 'Veritas Catholicorum circa afficaciam divinae gratiae' between the extreme 'Haereses Pelagianorum' and the 'Haereses Calvinastarum & Lutheranorum',[122] thus the false doctrines of the Palagians, Calvinists and Lutherans, were located. In a similar way, a text, the *sixteene Golden Meanes* of the Anglican Church, which appeared in London towards the end of the Thirty Years' War (1647), sought to set up a boundary against the thirty-one faulty theological teaching opinions of the 'Old Extreme'[123] (of the Papal Church) and the thirty-two no less faulty opinions of the 'New Extreme' (of Puritanism) (Figure 3.1).[124]

The harshness of the religious arguments and the political military organization of the feuding parties in the Thirty Years' War also had an influence on the language, which used the Aristotelian juxtaposition of the virtuous mean and the depraved extremes in order to stigmatize positions that were farthest from one's own standpoint. In such an atmosphere, the derogatory party name of 'extremists' was introduced into German scholarly language of the seventeenth century, which was rich in Latinisms. The word is found (for

*Figure 3.1* Thirty and two Extremes of these times discovered and reduced to sixteene
      Golden Meanes
Source: British Library 669, f 11 et seq. (66), London, 1647.

the first time?[125]) in correspondence by the Calvinist Ludwig Camerarius
(1573–1651), the son of the Nuremberg patrician Joachim Camerarius (1500–
574), a friend of Melanchthon, ancient philologist, theologian and pedagogue,
who had set up the Reformed High School in Nuremberg, reformed the
University of Tübingen and, among others, had become known as the commentator of Aristotle's *Politics* (with a detailed acknowledgement of the
mesotês doctrine).[126] Without doubt, the son obtained part of the father's
extensive humanistic education, aside from taking a different career path, and
developed a Calvinistic argumentative belief that differed from the more
peaceful attitude of the Reformation humanist who was always concerned
with a denominationally balanced attitude.[127] Ludwig Camerarius accompanied the Palatinate 'winter king' to his Bohemian adventure in 1618/19,
worked for years in the diplomatic service of the Kurpfalz and was entrusted
by Swedish King Gustav Adolf with the leadership of his embassy in the
government of the general estates in The Hague in 1626.

   In the letters to his Nuremberg compatriot, Lukas Friedrich Behaim, the
Jesuits, in their irreconcilability and their obstinacy, were affirmed as the
'discipuli of the devil', the evil spirit of the war, and thus the most guilty party
in the devastation of the Empire. The Electoral Palatinate had been unjustly
blamed as having played a decisive role in the unleashing of the war:

> One has blamed the poor Electoral Palatinate and the union as if they
> had wanted to cast a new model to make the Empire into, but they had
> (as I can witness with God and my conscience) no other scopum than
> libertatem religionis, the observance and the execution of the case. Capi-
> tulation and legum fundamentalium, as also on behalf of the letter of the

majesty, so then altogether a neutral iustitiam, which all was thrown over by the deeds of the Jesuits and other extremists.[128]

Camerarius seems to have used the term 'extremists' for the first time in a letter in April 1646, where the hope is expressed that God would not allow that 'the extremists would much longer prevent peace'.[129] Here, too, the spearhead of the Counter-Reformation, the Jesuits, must have been meant.[130]

In the logic of religious civil war, the extreme had to be burned away like an abscess, in order to heal the ill body. There could not be a substantial compromise with evil itself. However, this was not an urgent consequence of the mesotês doctrine. In its sociological application, it could rather support the opinion that a balance between the extreme social groups was to be found. Reminiscences of such an interpretation were found, e.g. in Giannotti's description of the Florentine constitutional conditions, whereby institutional precautionary measures achieved the integration of the extreme groups, the populari and the optimati.

Even before Giannotti, Machiavelli, himself a supporter of a mixed constitution, had made an important differentiation in the *Istorie Fiorentine*. He distinguished between selfish groups on the basis of bribery, patronage and miscarriage of justice, on the one hand, and such as going towards an open, enlivening, power-limiting competition for public office, on the other.[131] In his considerations about Republican Rome, inspired by Polybius, he acknowledged the power conflict between the people and the aristocracy as a reason for Roman freedom, as 'good laws' had come about through 'party arguments that many judged prematurely'.[132] Different from Aristotle, who wanted to strengthen the mean but weaken the extreme social groups, Machiavelli, in his mixed constitution model, supported a balance of the extremes, the grandi and the popolo. The discord between the two social segments had once assured the freedom of Rome: 'e che e' non considerino come e' sono in ogni republica due umori diversi, quello del popolo, e quello de' grandi; e come tutte le leggi che si fanno in favore della libertà, nascano dalla disunione loro, come facilmente si può vedere essere seguito in Roma'.[133] In Machiavelli's mixed constitution, an 'integration figure vested with quasi-monarchic elements'[134] was to bring about the equilibrium of the extreme forces. Also in his *Memorandum about the Reform of the State of Florence*, he observed thus: 'Those constituting a republic must make room for three classes of people that are in all cities, namely the first, the middle and the last [cioe primi, mezzani e ultimi]'.[135]

Montesquieu connected to Machiavelli's understanding of the party when he remarked in his *Considérations sur la grandeur des Romains*: a 'Corps Politique' distinguished itself in comparison to 'Asiatic despotism' in that 'all parties, no matter how opposite they may appear to us, argue about the general welfare of the society as the dissonances in music run together into a complete chord'.[136] This included the representatives of all, in themselves 'extreme', social interests. However, in the famous sixth chapter of the eleventh book of *De l'esprit des lois*, in which he acknowledged the British Isles for its order of divided power as the refuge of political freedom, there was not a word about the role of the parties. Yet, the fight of the parties had been especially fierce during the years of Montesquieu's stay in England (1729–31) and the institutionalization of a parliamentarian opposition directed towards the government and the parliamentary majority had just begun. This might be explained by Montesquieu's being under the influence of the Walpole opponents around Lord Bolingbroke, also when it comes to his perception of parties and opposition.[137] Through their political practice, they were able to measurably contribute to the establishment of the parliamentarian interaction between the opposition party and the government party, but, in their constitutional theory, they fell back to the dualist classes ideas of the Common Law tradition, which could no longer do justice to the developmental position of political systems. Bolingbroke's opposition doctrine in part still breathed the spirit of the resistance law.[138] He saw the predominance of the Walpole government in parliament as estranged from tradition and to be removed anomaly, a 'government by a party' would have to degenerate to a 'government by a faction',[139] thus to a government of selfish interests. A generation later, Edmund Burke entered the scene as the eloquent defender of the party system whose freedom-ensuring effect he emphasized towards the Crown's demands for the government's standing above partiality: 'This objection against party is a party objection'.[140] To him, parties were legitimate organizations of interests for supporting common welfare.

It is certainly no coincidence that advocates of the mixed constitution gradually contributed to a more positive assessment of the party system and the political variety of interests, whereas strict opponents ideologically supported its traditional banning. Jean-Jacques Rousseau (1712–78) is an outstanding example of this, as the rejection of representation, the division of powers and intermediate authorities are closely connected, because they contradict the ideal of an identity of rulers and the ruled.[141] The issue of the political theoretical evaluation of party systems became the more urgent the stronger they made their appearance as important societal forces in the course of the dissolution of the feudal society. This applied not only to the 'moderate', but also to the 'extreme' political powers.

## 7 The French Revolution and the right–left dichotomy

In the eighteenth century, those ideological trends were formed (also as a result of the secularization process connected to the Enlightenment) which were to determine the history of the nineteenth century. Their organizational solidification was furthered by the French Revolution in the context of which also began the language convention of a political taxonomic differentiation into 'rights' and 'lefts'.

The coming about of the differentiation of 'right' and 'left' in the sense of antithetical political terms of direction is usually attributed to the *Assemblée nationale*. Yet the word pair had found its usage already much earlier in the language of the parliamentarian committees: In the French translation of the then much read work about *The Present State of England*, written by Edward Chamberlayne (many editions since 1669), the seating order in the English upper house is described from the perspective of the king residing in the centre and more closely explained which members holding positions and dignitaries take their seat 'A la main gauche' or 'A la main droite'.[142] But this distribution was not connected to an intellectual political geography; typically, the author only applied it solely to the House of Lords consisting of members of the classes and not to the House of Commons with its party oppositions. Therefore, it is correct to trace back the genesis of the right–left differentiation of the political terms of direction to the French National Assembly of 1789. Not even a conscious leaning towards the estates–parliamentarian use of the language of the older classes has so far been proved.[143] In the new era, the seating order no longer remained the mirror image of solid societal hierarchies, but soon expressed the dynamics of the ideological political arguments.

The splitting into two opposing camps of the National Assembly – 'le coté gauche' with a definite push in the revolutionary direction and 'le coté droite' with a more reticent, friendly attitude towards the monarchy – was definitely noticed by political observers in August/September 1789 at the latest, during the discussions concerning human rights and the royal veto.[144] In the parliamentary history published by Philippe Buchez and Pierre Roux-Lavergne in 1834, the meeting of 28 August 1789 is named as the starting date for the left–right grouping of the National Assembly.[145] In this way, the voting behaviour could be determined much more quickly. Other historians name the meeting of 11 September, in which the National Assembly voted with 575 against 325 votes in favour of postponing the king's right to veto.[146] Now, at the latest, the right–left placement had been established. Soon, the spatial adjectives 'right' and 'left' became nouns. One simply spoke of 'la droite' and 'la gauche', and within this camp, one could make out wing groups from 'l'extrémité droite' and 'l'extrémité gauche'.[147] In the *Moniteur*, the official parliamentarian debate periodical, there was also mentioned 'l'extrémité du côté gauche', 'l'extrémité de la partie gauche' and ' l'extrémité de la partie droite'.[148]

The formation of terms came about in the course of the rash revolutionary development, creating unknown contents for which new words had to be found. For the political extremes, there were a number of neologisms. To mark the exaggerations ('exagérés') or the exaltation ('exaltés') of a political position, one placed 'ultra' before a party term. Accordingly, one spoke of 'ultra-royalists', 'ultra-constitutionals', 'ultra-patriots' and 'ultra-revolutionaries'.[149] In a similar way, the old attribute 'fanatical' devoid of its religious content could be used for political trends such as 'fanatico-royalisme'.[150] A destructive, murderous tendency could be marked by the suffix '-icide' borrowed from Latin (e.g. 'liberticide', 'républicide'); a definite opposition could be marked by the prefix 'anti-' ('anti-aristocrat', 'anti-constitutional', 'anti-democratic', 'anti-political', 'anti-revolutionary').[151] Even the very modern-sounding 'alarmism' ('alarmist') was a component of the revolutionary language – for example for the labelling of those Jacobins who constantly called an alarm to create a basis of justification for their bloody trade.[152] However, the 'moderantism' of those who resisted the dirty acts of the 'enraged' did not have a good name with determined Republicans. In the *Republicain* of 28 February 1793, it was said about one of these moderate ones ('modéré') that he seemed to be infected with a damnable freedom-destroying 'moderantism'.[153]

Already on account of the turnaround of the traditional political categories, the new language conventions could not establish themselves firmly in the course of the turbulent development of the revolution. The power takeover of the Jacobins was followed by a rigorous curtailment of the political spectrum seen as legitimate. During Napoleonic rule, the suppression of political pluralism found its continuation only under changed 'prefixes', however in milder forms.

## 8 Extremes as topos of early revolution critique

The right–left differentiation in the French Revolution was connected with the old differentiation of 'moderate' and 'extreme'. In this way, a political–geographic dimension attached itself to the political–ethical one. The Platonic–Aristotelian value terms continued therewith. Speaking about the 'extreme' became a topos of French and non-French revolution critique. Already before the takeover of power by the Jacobins in 1793, observers who were not to be counted among the irreconcilable opponents of the ideals of 'liberté, égalité, fraternité' had expressed their doubts. The English politician Edmund Burke felt himself called to a fundamental critique of events in France due to the plea of a nonconformist cleric, Richard Price, for the right of the people to give themselves a new constitution. In his *Reflections on the Revolution in France* (1790), he emphasized the fact that fundamental forces of the revolution rejected every compromise with pre-revolutionary conditions, wanting to build up the country upon completely new principles. According to Burke's conviction, every solution that had no connection to the tried and true was doomed to fail. He pleaded for 'a mixed and tempered government in either of the extremes'[154] against the republicans in France and cited Aristotle with the observation 'that a democracy has many striking points of resemblance with tyranny'.[155] From this viewpoint, the distance from a pure republic to pure tyranny was not far.

The transfer from one extreme to the other also stood at the centre of the revolution critique of the Prussian liberal, Wilhelm von Humboldt (1776–1835). In his *Ideen über Staatsverfassung* (Ideas about state constitution), published in 1791 after the new French constitution had been adopted, he explained the creation of boundless freedom with the boundlessness of previous 'despotism': 'Mankind had suffered from one kind of extreme, in an extreme it had to seek its salvation'.[156] In a similar manner, Christoph Martin

Wieland (1733–1813), Professor of Philosophy in Erfurt and tutor to the princes in Weimar, in the literary criticism journal *Teutscher Merkur*, used the topos of the transfer of one extreme to another when he warned in 1790 that one would set 'one democratic despotism in the place of the aristocratic and monarchic one'.[157] In September 1792, after the abdication of the king, he examined the foundation of the French Republic and in a historical consideration expressed deep scepticism in view of its chances for stabilization. The history of the Greek *poleis* seemed to prove that a state was never successfully transferred from a monarchy into a 'pure democracy':

> For the so-called *kingdoms of heroic times* such as the one of Argos, Mycaen, Sicyon, Megarae, Athens, Thebes, etc. from which all the small republics of Ancient Greece formed themselves by and by, none here will want to bring up against me [due to their small size, U.B.]. And even those did not go from one extreme to the other. They were small embryos of as yet undeveloped bourgeois societies, mixtures of democracy, aristocracy and monarchy, where the nobility and the people got rid of the King, and the common system sauntered between aristocracy and democracy until the latter finally became predominant and thus accelerated the loss of freedom from within and of independence from the outside.[158]

In addition, a democracy was unthinkable 'without virtue, without moderation, without the purity of the mores (s. o.)'.[159] And just these prerequisites were entirely missing in a country that indulged in luxury such as France. What 'an immense leap' a people such as the French would have to make 'to suddenly change from its former habits to another extreme, that of democratic virtue'.[160]

More optimistic than Wieland, the chamber councillor and writer Gerhard Anton von Halem, who had travelled from absolutistically governed Oldenburg to revolutionary Paris in 1790, judged the course of the revolution: 'some extremes would have been avoided, less passion would have come into play, and the King would not at the same time have remained isolated in the midst of his nation if the representatives of the nation had not been disrupted by the court in the freedom of their deliberation'.[161] Von Halem most of all meant the National Assembly's being pressured by the royal troops in the early summer of 1789. Excesses by the 'rabble' were to be traced back to the actions by the state power and could not solely be blamed on the revolutionaries.

In a letter to his father-in-law, Christian Gottlob Heyne, of 12 July 1791, the widely travelled writer and democrat Georg Forster (1754–91) argued more fundamentally in favour of the revolution. The imperfection to be expected of a new order should not lead to taking in one's stride every 'atrociousness' of the old one. As all human things are imperfect, one could not expect anything perfect from a new France. Furthermore, mistakes could be corrected; the 'good institutions' obviously predominated and 'when evil comes to light, and a terrible destruction as the recent despotism and aristocratism really threatens, who will it be ascribed to but to bitter necessity, the unavoidable law of nature, might it be impossible to abolish an extreme without having to go to another extreme? No mistake, no error, no abuse of which the National Assembly can be accused, of which the curse does not fall back on prior despotism'.[162] Whoever had in this manner made the transfer from one extreme to another into a natural law could not be too surprised by the reign of terror of the Jacobins. But in Forster's letters, the bad actions of the 'ultra-revolutionaries'[163] also darkened the picture of the descriptions of the revolution in the second half of 1793. Many observers who had up to then watched the revolutionary events with basic approval now revised their views. The French Revolution appeared to fall into a permanent extreme.

The President of the United States of America, George Washington (1732–99), had clearly recognized this danger when he emphasized the necessity of cool reason in a letter to the Marquis de Lafayette on 10 June 1792 in finding a load-bearing, constitutional political solution: 'The just medium cannot be expected to be found in a moment, the first vibrations always go to the extremes, and cool reason, which can alone establish a permanent and equal government, is as little to be expected in the tumults of popular commotion, as an attention to the liberties of the people is to be found in the dark Divan of a despotic tyrant'.[164] Tyranny and an unrestrained crowd of people offered the same kind of unfavourable conditions for ensuring political freedom.

The Jacobins' reign of terror remained the epitome of the politically extreme in the nineteenth century. From their official proclamation on 5 September 1793 until the fall of Robespierre on 27 July 1794, it had claimed hundreds of thousands of victims. After the Austrian, British Hanoverian and Spanish restoration armies had been forced back successfully, the terror within had developed even more strongly, raging even more unrestrainedly against all real and assumed enemies of the Republic.[165] Most of all in the capital and in the centres of revolutionary fighting such as Lyon, Lille, Nantes and Marseille nobody could feel safe any more. Fear and terror spread. Where the guillotine could not kill those condemned by the revolutionary tribunals, mass shootings were carried out, or the victims were loaded on to boats which were then sunk in rivers such as the Rhône and the Loire. The suppression of the 'white' opposition in the Vendée was especially bloody. A distinctive part of the population was eradicated. The horrors and the atrocities penetrated deeply into the consciousness of the contemporaries.

The excesses and the extremes of the revolution soon became the subject of fundamental examination. One of the earliest contributions of this kind came from the daughter of the Geneva banker and last Minister of Finance of Louis XIV, Jacques Necker. In the beginning, Anne-Louise de Staël (1766–1817) had belonged to the followers of the revolution, but had turned away in horror from the conditions in Paris which were becoming more and more dangerous. She had withdrawn to her country estate Coppet near Geneva and undertaken journeys before returning to the capital in 1795, where the moderate 'Directoire' was now ruling. Here, she now examined the previous reign of terror, described the different trends and the dynamics of its development, the direction of the political wing, the psychology of its polarization, its controversies, but also certain parallels:

> Those who get excited for or against the same old errors are gullible souls, and their uncontrolled tendency toward violence provokes in them the need to orient themselves on the extreme of all ideas, so to correspond to their own judgment and character. [ ... ] It was often said in the course of the revolution that the aristocrats and the Jacobins spoke the same language, were equally absolute in their opinions and, according to the situation at hand, employed an equally intolerant leadership style. This remark must be counted as the simple consequence of one and the same principle. Passions let people become similar as fever causes different temperaments to be thrown into the same condition.[166]

The liberal Benjamin Constant (1767–1830), who was friends with Madame de Staël for many years, characterized the swinging of the pendulum from one extreme to the other in a similar way, if one – as happened in the revolution during the reign of the Jacobins – left the path of the law and employed despotic measures.[167] According to his understanding, the demagogy of the Jacobins had opened the door to Napoleon's 'despotism'. In the one as well as in the other case, the dogma of the 'sovereignty of the people' appeared to be an 'instrument of tyranny', and power was concentrated, not controlled and balanced. In both extremes, a tyrannical will came to the fore: 'The extremities found themselves in agreement as in the background, in the two extremes there was the will to tyrannize'.[168]

Another advocate of the mixed constitution, John Adams, in hindsight viewed the tendency to eliminate outstanding personages and their dependants that had emanated in the French Revolution in order to supposedly protect the general welfare as an authentic expression of autocracy. With the escalation of the revolutionary events, the head of one outstanding personage after another had dropped into the basket under the guillotine. And after Mirabeau, Marat, Brissot, Danton, Robespierre and many others had been eliminated, the remaining personages had only been able to save their heads by fleeing into the arms of one singular outstanding person, those of the conqueror Napoleon.[169] A liberal solution could therefore not consist of the elimination of the political variety but only in suitably balancing it. For Adams, the appearance of party leaders with their appendage was an expression of natural human plurality.

In this way, the mesotês doctrine and the mixed constitution theory were able to pave the way to a positive understanding of the party system which had been banned for a long time. The parallelization of the extremes structurally corresponded to a psychological interpretation figure of religion as it connected to the rich in a traditional formula of 'fanaticism'. This term had been solely limited to religious objects; however, in the French Revolution, it was extended to political trends – and as such used merely for those groupings that fought religious furore with an eagerness likening them to their opponents.[170]

# 4   Extreme ideologies in the political laboratory of the nineteenth century

## 1 Revitalization and expansion of right–left geography

The connection of the Aristotelian mesotês categories to 'right' and 'left', the new political terms of direction carried out during the first 'constitutional' phase of the French Revolution, was only slowly revived at the end of the Napoleonic era. At the beginning of the Restoration period, the paralysis of political life still continued. The representatives of the Chamber of 1814 coming from the Empire 'were so strongly accustomed to bowing to the emperor's will that differing opinions were not outwardly recognizable in elections, although these took place openly'.[1] However, after the turmoil of the Hundred Days, this changed rapidly. The new political geography that developed in the first year of the Revolution found its mirror image in the parliamentarian seating order (Figure 4.1).

Already before 1820, there was a differentiation between the 'extrême droite', the 'droite modérée' and the 'centre droite' and the 'centre gauche', the 'gauche modérée' and the 'extrême gauche'.[2] The wing terms 'extrême droite' and 'extrême gauche' found entry into dictionaries such as those of the 1830s.[3] They have remained firmly anchored in the political language until today as neutral terms, as pejorative foreign terms (of the oppositional camp)[4] and even – yet more rarely – as positive self-designations.[5] Apart from this, the term 'extrémités' continued to exist. The French parliamentary minutes of the nineteenth century are full of 'rumeurs aux extrémités', 'murmures aux extrémités' and 'exclamations négatives aux extrémités'.[6]

With the expansion of constitutionalism, the French terminology spread out to other European states. The right–left differentiation, on the other hand, could be connected to the inherited terms 'extreme' and 'moderate'. It finally found a home in England and the United States of America, where it was applied to the long-established two-party systems reaching back to the time of the French Revolution. However, the French terminology with its broad range was mostly used in its simpler forms, as there was not the same need for such a subtle formation of categories as in countries with complex party and coalition formations.[7]

Germany and Italy with their multiparty systems more closely resembled the French country of origin in this respect. In Italy, the French terminology was

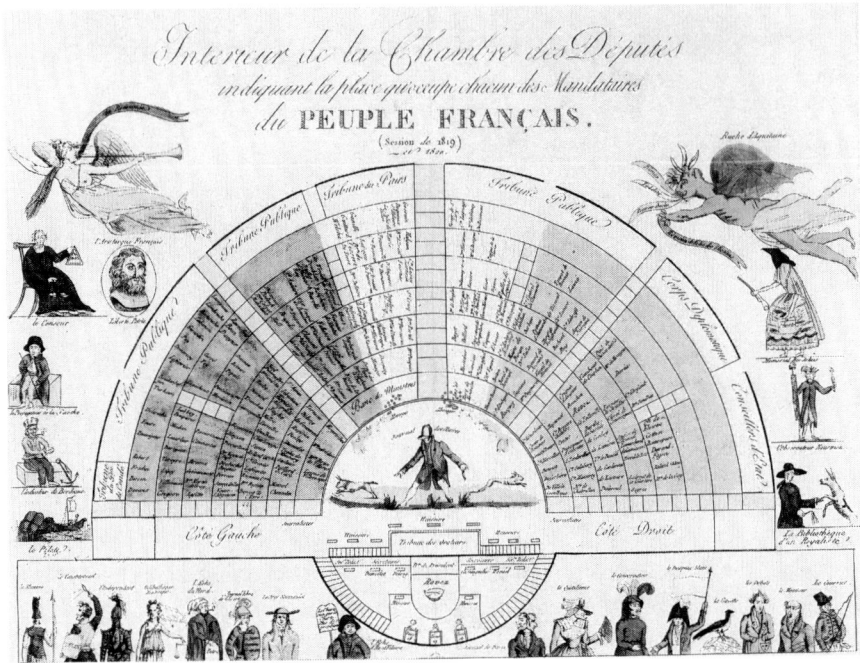

*Figure 4.1* 'Right' and 'left' in the parliamentarian seating order of the Restoration period
Source: Bibliothèque nationale de France.

used in the Chamber of Deputies of the kingdom of Sardinia–Piedmont (from the 1850s on).[8] In Germany, the new political geography was established not just with the formation of the central party[9] whose designation, after all, preconditioned the existence of a 'left' and a 'right'. Moreover, it had already been a firm element in the political parliamentarian seating order of the Saint Paul's Cathedral Parliament in 1848/49. In Gottfried Eisenmann's depiction and documentation regarding the 'parties of the German Empire Assembly', the 'Milani Party' as the 'outermost right' was placed in opposition to the 'outermost left'. In-between them, he placed the 'Casino' as the 'right in a closer sense', the 'Landsberg' as the 'right center' and the 'Wuerttemberg Court' as the 'left center'.[10] The liberals of different persuasions, who constituted the overwhelming majority, understood themselves as the 'mean' between the extremes of absolutism and 'radicalism'.

The parliamentarian right–left subdivision had been employed for the first time in the liberal south-west. When the representatives from Baden 'separately took their seats in the half-circle of the hall according to their different political directions' during the opening of the Federal State Parliament of 1843, this constituted a 'premiere' in the history of the German Federal State Parliament. In this *political seating order* from 'left' to 'right', shaped after the Paris Chamber of Deputies, the factions of the Chamber, which were in the process of becoming established, also showed themselves outwardly for the first time, and 'even the Chamber reports spoke of interference calls now already coming from the *"right"* – whereby they meant government-friendly groups – or from the *"left"*, the liberal–radical opposition'.[11] Thus, the somewhat lengthy process of faction and camp formation had come to a temporary conclusion. In 1822, still, a liberal representative from Baden had complained that 'there was no right and no left side; today, this one speaks out against the government, tomorrow that one, today, a friend against his best friend, depending on their individual viewpoints'.[12] This, however, did not prevent the liberals from setting up boundaries against the 'ultras to the left and to the right'.[13]

## 2 Juste milieu theories in France, England and Germany

The commandment to seek a 'juste milieu' between the extremes was firmly anchored in the Aristotelian tradition long before it became the maxim of the government. The anonymously published text by Abbé Jerôme Besoigne, in which he pleaded for moderation in the intense fights for the influence of the Jansenists at the Faculty of Arts in Paris and decried the 'vices of the extreme', offers an example from the first half of the eighteenth century. It consisted of 'carrying the things to the extreme and in committing one excess in order to avoid another'.[14]

The idea of the 'juste milieu', the 'golden mean' or the 'proper middle' was subject of intense struggles for direction in the post-Napoleonic era. The extremes were called revolution and reaction, between which a practicable path had to be found. The reign of the Jacobins had also demonstrated the terrors of the revolution to those who were convinced of the necessity of a fundamental change in the ancien régime. This applied likewise to the group of 'doctrinaires' that had formed around the liberal Pierre-Paul Royer-Collard (1763–1845) in Paris as of 1817 – presumably a foreign term from the ultra-conservative side, which contained a stab at their predilection for principles, theories and doctrines.[15] Soon afterwards, François Guizot (1787–1874), who was to shape the intellectual profile after 1820, joined them. Royer-Collard had been a member of the Convent in 1793, escaping the terror only by a margin; Guizot's father's life had ended under the guillotine.[16] With this background, they defended and romanticized the charter of 1814, which Louis XVIII had consented to, and saw the task of the Restoration period in ending the revolution, creating a stable constitutional order and avoiding a return to the ancien régime.[17] Looking back, they acknowledged the constitutional political designs of the Chamber of a Hundred Days, which had likewise kept its distance from the 'partis extrêmes', paying homage to neither 'imperial despotism' nor 'revolutionary violence'.[18] They pleaded for a middle of the road 'moderation' between those who damned the principles of the revolution, lock, stock and barrel and those whose principles they defended. With the rejection of the term 'sovereignty' in the sense of any concentration of state power – be it in the hands of an individual or in the midst of a large crowd – they connected with the plea for a mixed system, consisting of democratic and monarchic elements: the constitutional monarchy.[19] In it, they saw a realistic, reform-oriented middle road between the extremes. Yet, Guizot simultaneously opposed suppressing extreme positions. If one gave the old Jacobins enough slack, they would hang themselves by their own rope: 'Retranchez les ultrà, répetè-t-on chaque jour, et vous n'aurez plus d'ultrà-libéraux à redouter. [ ... ] Laissez là les hommes décriés, les vieux jacobins, et les ultrà obtiendront bien moins de crédit'.[20]

As Vincent E. Starzinger has shown, the concepts of the 'doctrinaires' also found acceptance in the British Isles, although the local conditions there were decidedly different from those of the French. He found surprising analogies between the juste milieu and those of the 'Whiggism' of the Reform Bill era.[21] As an evaluation of the moderately liberal *Edinburgh Review* shows, the ideas of the 'doctrinaires' enjoyed great approval there. Francis Jeffrey (1773–1850), the founder of the reform-oriented magazine, which was to become the model for many others, defined the Whigs as a 'middle party between the two extremes of high monarchical principles [ ... ] and extremely popular principles'.[22] Against the background of the arguments for the parliamentary form, one of the leading representatives, Henry Brougham (1778–1868), reached for the means of placing the *high Tory principles* at the same level as the positions of the ultras in France. Simultaneously, he critically examined the theories of the 'radicals' around Jeremy Bentham who pleaded for concentrating the political forces in a chamber on a utilitarian basis in order to reach an 'identity of interests' between those ruling and those being ruled.[23] In contrast, Brougham emphasized the importance of 'checks and balances' in a mixed constitution. To him, the deeper meaning of the 'checks' consisted of balancing the extremes against each other: 'The efficacy of the checks always consists in the general reluctance of all parties to risk the consequences of driving matters to extremities'.[24]

The July Revolution in France was instrumental in the formation of Earl Grey's Whig government in which Brougham, as Lord Chancellor, was counted among the driving forces of the Reform Act of 1832 and the Abolition of Slavery Act of 1833. In Paris, Guizot now reached high government positions. The decision of the 'doctrinaires' to avoid extremes became the rule of the 'citizen kingdom'. Louis-Philippe explained his governmental course as follows: 'We are seeking to keep ourselves to the proper middle – equally distanced from the excesses of the people's power as well as that of royal power'. To the 'friends of liberty',[25] he promised to dam the revolutionary chaos, simultaneously decidedly working against any miscarriage of justice.

The larger the rift between constitutional theory and practice became, the more intense the controversies regarding the legitimacy of the juste milieu grew. Followers again brought up Montesquieu's responsibility of the lawmaker in respect of the principle of moderation, defending the regime as the only possible way 'between the two extremes'[26] – the excesses of the people's power as well as those of the absolute monarchy. The young publisher Adolphe Thiers (1797–1877), who had kept in contact with Louis-Philippe in the days of the revolution, thereafter having been promoted to minister and playing a great role in French politics in the following decades, admonished them to use their common sense, as one had had to expect from the start that the new government would disappoint the expectations of the 'extremes of all categories'.[27] Even more moderate liberals who abhorred every kind of extreme soon distanced themselves from Louis-Philippe's governmental practices. In a letter to the Baden liberal Karl von Rotteck (1775–1840), the Marquis de Lafayette wrote that the juste milieu was neither just nor did it keep to the middle.[28]

On the other side of the River Rhine, the political developments in France had been watched very closely. The readers of well-informed papers such as the *Augsburger Allgemeine Zeitung* were informed in detailed fashion about the political directions of the Paris Chamber of Deputies, that of the 'right side (of the ultras)' as well as that of the 'left side'.[29] Here as well as there, this corresponded to the introspection of the bourgeoisie to seeking one's political path between the extremes of the conservative or even absolutist hanging on to the past, on the one hand, and the Utopian egalitarian belief in the future, on the other hand. The history of the European revolutions offered numerous examples of how the takeover of power by one extreme furthered that of the next one.

In his text *Teutschland und die Revolution*, Rhinish publisher Joseph Görres (1776–1848) in 1819 described the typical course of revolutionary changes as ups and downs of extreme tendencies. In France,

> Girondists, Jacobins and Cordeliers had chased each other away and in the Netherlands the Geuse had soon joined the iconoclasts, as the rage of the previous level always appears to the following one as cold half-heartedness; until at last the complete gamut of human evil has been run through step by step, everything existing has fallen, everything solid been broken, everything high been dragged down and all property has changed hands. When, however, nature exhausts itself in anarchist anger in such a way, the reign of unity comes about again as the necessary opposite, which in the beginning is able to easily overtake the tired forces, but then, as life, which in its interior is excited, has awakened great contradictions and the most intense centrifugal directions, gripping the masses sharply and strongly by and by amounts to the highest despotism and then again runs through another set of steps of evil until finally, having run full-circle, an outer and an inner catastrophe leads the extremes toward the middle again.[30]

In contrast to his later years and in spite of first attempts towards a conservatively romantic turn,[31] Görres was a supporter of liberal reforms – and simultaneously a decisive opponent of a revolution à la française, it being

connected to incalculable risks. To guide the state through the extremes pre-
supposed the clear-sightedness for what was politically possible, the concilia-
tion among the different social forces, and their institutional balancing and
control. Instead, the extreme directions tended towards driving the political
principle – for example, that of equality, of liberty or of order and security –
to the utmost consequence, ignoring the differences in social interests and
destroying the historically grown in favour of an imagined ideal condition.

Later, the Kassel liberal Friedrich Murhard (1778–1853) cited Görres. It
generally made no difference to the peoples whether '*they were despotized
monarchically or democratically*':

> For whether the despotism of a pure democracy without fear and worries –
> as the punishment when many sins never reach the guilty – and without
> shyness and shame – as the crowd, judging good and evil according to its
> own measure and not sparing itself with applause, neither lets itself be
> held back by any feeling of shame nor any fear of opinion – encouraged
> by wild demagogues and seduced by useless sycophants – bloodthirstily
> carries out every violence, or whether despotism, beginning with the
> *unlimited wilfulness of an individual* – as is the case in the pure or absolute
> monarchy – by employing *from above to below* the evil tools of tyranny,
> must – as in having the same meaning in success – basically also be
> understood as equally evil.

When the 'ultra-monarchists, as sworn and irreconcilable enemies of the
demagogues, sought to depict democratism in the most spiteful light', this
happened 'only too often to merely position another extreme, namely its
opposite, in its place'.[32] Not only reform-oriented thinkers such as Görres
and Murhard but also restoratively inclined thinkers sought to benefit politically from the horrors of the extremes. Friedrich Ancillon (1767–1837),[33] who
sought close annexation to Metternich's line in the Prussian Foreign Ministry,
published a collection of essays, *Zur Vermittlung der Extreme in den Meinungen*
in 1828, in which the Prussian status quo, itself strongly influenced by (enlightened) absolutism, was steeped in the mild light of a reticently reformed political
reconciliation programme.[34]

The recognition which the Leipzig liberal state professor Karl Ludwig
Pölitz (1772–1838) gave to Ancillon's thought in a necrologue ('moderata
durant'[35]) resulted from his intellectual agreement with the reform system
that Ancillon propagated, whose basic insight was 'that in most cases the
truth is found in the middle between the two extremes',[36] with revolution on
the one side and reaction on the other. This mildness of judgement was
hardly still to be found among the representatives of moderate liberalism after
1830. The July events in Paris had produced new reform-oriented vigour. A
second constitutional wave reached northern and eastern Germany.[37] The
time between 1830 and 1848 could be compared with an intellectual labora-
tory in which the early forms of the great ideological trends took shape,

whose struggles ran throughout the entire nineteenth century and whose ruling practices shaped the twentieth century to a large degree.

Ancillon, chiefly on account of his political behaviour,[38] was seen as an unrestrained opportunist. He had, first of all, made a name for himself (above all in his *Tableau des révolutions du système politique de l'Europe*) as an advocate of 'the liberal system which had initially been shaped by the Reformation and the English Revolution, then been defended by Kant, Pütter and Häberlin as well as Montesquieu, finally being accepted by the Princes and the peoples in the War for Freedom'. He later established a career in Prussia as a representative of the 'reaction party', thereby betraying his one-time principles. In his work on the *Vermittlung der Extreme in den Meinungen*, he subscribed to a juste milieu that toyed with the truth as it pleased,[39] according to Karl Theodor Welcker's (1790–1869) evaluation in the *Staatslexikon*.

By the same token, the great topic of the moderate liberals consisted of mediating between the opposite principles of 'divine law and the sovereignty of the people', as the 'extreme parts of the German fatherland'[40] demanded without compromise. They saw most of all destructive forces in the extremes, regardless of how much they differed in their motives and goals. Looking back, it was possible to characterize the time from the end of Napoleonic rule in the way the Marburg liberal Sylvester Jordan (1792–1861), who originated from Tyrol, did it:

> As anyone knows, since the War of Freedom (1812–15), the two extreme parties, the reactionaries and the revolutionists [ ... ] have been embattled as they had also already actively participated in that war in order to execute their plans and desires. Since then, the reaction party has attempted to bring back the 'good old days' by way of destroying everything new that had been acquired during the time of the French rule and by cleaning out and refurbishing the past into the present, which was called *restoring*; the revolution party on the other hand was no less busy to convert the older state forms and institutions in Germany which were still left over from that time through violent destruction into a brand-new, ideal El Dorado. In order to forestall any misconceptions at this point, one cannot but remark that, basically, the extreme parties are both simultaneously revolutionary and reactive. The reactionaries are destructive in reference to the new that has come about and have tried to stop it from spreading, whereas the revolutionaries are destructive in respect to the old that is still left, being only reluctantly active in the restoration of the historic, so that they differ merely in their reasons, directions and purposes.[41]

Only those who were able to connect the principles, finding their expression in them in such a way that they mutually inhibited each other and came to a moderate balance, could escape the maelstrom of destructive energies produced by the extremes. Therefore, the moderate liberals were all supporters of a mixed constitution, although there were diverging opinions on the kind of mixture it should be. Karl von Rotteck (1775–1840), the leader of moderate liberalism during the Vormärz, favoured a mixture of monarchy and democracy with the emphasis on democratic elements. In contrast, the northern German liberal Friedrich Christoph Dahlmann (1785–1860), the Württembergian Paul Achatius Pfizer (1801–67) and the Hessian Karl Theodor Welcker were oriented towards the English constitution with its connection to monarchic, aristocratic and democratic elements.[42] For the present, the constitutional monarchy was seen as a suitable compromise. Nevertheless, this in no way excluded republican solutions (in mixed forms) for the future.[43]

Karl von Rotteck had used the foreword to the first volume of the *Staatslexikon* to programmatically distance himself from Louis-Philippe's *juste milieu* and, yet, to still define an appropriate middle between the extremes of absolutism and republican, directly democratic 'radicalism'.[44] Therewith, he gave a summary of the political programme of the Vormärz liberals:

> In the pages presented here we have given the spirit and the character of the *real state doctrine*, according to which the task or direction of our state lexicon is said to follow the *'proper middle'* between the opposing extremes. However, we thereby do not want to say that we subscribe to the system known by the ominous name of 'juste milieu'. No! A middle between straight and bent, between truth and lie, between justice and injustice we do *not* want; for such a one would indeed be bent, untrue and unjust. The middle which we are seeking is the one drawn between two opposing curves, as such the *straight* line, the line between two opposing lies, as such the *truth*, the middle between opposing injustices, as such justice *itself*. [ … ] Our proper middle is a government system which first of all honestly aspires to keeping peace with foreign nations [ … ]; then, in reference to the latter, counteracts revolutions, yet not through terror and not through deception or Machiavellian art and not through the suppression of the intellectual and moral power of the people, but through *befriending the people's spirit*, through *respecting the people's voice* and among those of the *people's representatives*, through *openness*, through *steadfast holding on to the constitution* and all the rights guaranteed to the citizens, in fact, on all logically acquired ones. It is also a government system which seeks to win the reasonable *public opinion* and recognizes a reliable support in the *agreement* with it against the enmity of criminal supplicants and bad parties, a system which does not only avoid *publicity* but loves, furthers, and honors it as a palladium of all rights and liberties.

Thereby, all that 'which is sacred and protects the *honesty of the people's representation* is to be supported, therefore also the *freedom of elections*. However, everything which can only be carried out by *force* against the majority of a reasonable people is to be refrained from'.[45] Herewith, Rotteck formulated programmatic guidelines about whose importance there prevailed widespread unity among moderate liberals.

Under the above-mentioned conditions, the proper middle was definitely compatible with a census voting right. As Rotteck explained to the readers of the *Staatslexikon*, there were supporters of the unlimited right to vote at both poles of the political spectrum. There were to be found 'followers of absolutism (as in particular the speakers of the Carlists in current France), who demanded the general right to vote for the reason that they counted on the political dependency of the majority of the people of the lower classes and hoped to be able to direct their votes according to their own interests by way of ruse, bewitchment or bribery. Whatever the *Carlists* desire in France cannot be any good; but herein lies again proof that the extremes touch each other; for the exalted *Republicans* used one and the same language here as the Carlists'.[46] The structural common ground of the extremes mentioned by Rotteck served the purpose of a middle line, which claimed political realism in the evaluation of the consequences of legal measures. From his viewpoint, whoever made programmatic demands merely on the basis of a principle without considering the consequences – be it of traditional legitimacy or be it of absolute equality – was taking incalculable risks.

The moderately liberal critique of the 'juste milieu' was aimed more towards its practice than towards the theory on which it was based. The representatives of 'radical', (directly) democratic positions went even further. Wilhelm Schulz (1797–1860), a Darmstadt democrat, poured out biting mockery in the *Noth- und Hilfsbuechlein für vorsichtige Esser und Trinker* (1844): 'At last a wise middle was chosen for the reconciliation of the hostile views. This juste milieu is the mule, the legitimate offspring of the horse and the donkey, which does not quite possess the father's mobility, yet has fully inherited his natural wit'.[47] And: 'The police's nose sniffs out the smell of the state body regardless whether monarchic, aristocratic and democratic elements are mixed constitutionally'.[48] The mocker himself, who was to be classified among the 'democrats' of the moderate wing and had worked closely together with the publishers of the *Staatslexikon*, Rotteck and Welcker,[49] fell back upon the image of the 'extreme parties' in his description of the events of the French Revolution.[50]

The critique in retrospect by Heinrich Bernhard Oppenheim (1819–80) was of fundamental nature:

> One constructs the constitutional monarchy as a dialectic point between the extremes. But would the middle not lie elsewhere if only the extremes were moved? – It is said as Odilon said to Louis-Philippe: 'We are also juste milieu if only the middle was moved somewhat more to the left'. – 'With your permission', answered the polite monarch, 'let us leave it as it is!' – As if it depended on the middle at which point it would like to be! The central state's wisdom changes according to the changed parties, soon it is called constitutional, soon democratic, and soon rural guild

monarchy [ ... ] If it only depended on a 'mediation of the extremes', with Ancillon, the more definitive parties would have been right to increase their 'demands' to the utmost extreme in order to gain a bit more of the centre for themselves. But it is just these mediators who reproach democracy for having spoiled everything due to its unbridled passion and the inappropriateness of its demands.[51]

If this argumentation aimed at the relativity of the purpose of the position by way of the extremes seen in concrete historic situations, the Hegelian leftist Arnold Ruge (1802–80) came to another conclusion. He attached a forward-urging role to the extremes in the fights of the parties in so far as these were carried out on the basis of 'a principle': 'and there then the most common experience should already prove that one extreme always calls forth the other by necessity, that development and life only exist at all where there are still opposites to be balanced, where struggle and conscious effort are called for. [ ... ] Political and religious interest is found only where unbalanced opinions oppose each other. Only there will a form of freedom be appreciated and protected where it is derived as precipitation from the fermentation of the parties'.[52] According to Ruge, the 'necessary extremes' are an indispensable part of the 'gravitation of the world system' and of history, which was kept in 'constant progress'[53] by the collision of the opposites. This view was based on Hegel's understanding of history, which comprehended the 'spirit' as the 'unity' and the 'middle' of the 'extremes' and the interaction of the 'extremes'[54] as finding its expression in 'state power' and 'noble consciousness'. However, in the moderate liberals' Aristotelian understanding, the extremes were degenerations, not necessary components of political plurality. On the other hand, Ruge's Hegelian party theory attached the central role of a driving force of historic progress to them.

## 3 Ultraism and extremism

During the Vormärz quarrels, the structural agreement of the extremes established by Rotteck found its foremost expression in the term 'ultraism'. More than any other, the Leipzig philosopher Wilhelm Traugott Krug had dealt with its content through extensive political publications. Krug,[55] born in 1770 at Radis near Wittenberg as the son of a farmer, had arrived at the University of Leipzig in 1809 from Königsberg, where he had taught as the successor to Immanuel Kant. In Leipzig, he published tirelessly. From the perspective of a liberal Protestantism,[56] he expressed a committed opinion on many of the topics of his time. Thus, he was the first in Germany who, after the uprising of Ypsilanti, joined sides with the Greek freedom movement against foreign domination by the Turks.[57] As a pioneer of a moderate liberalism, he became known beyond the borders of Saxony. He wrote numerous reviews, from time to time led the editorial department of the magazine *Hermes*, founded by him and the publisher Friedrich Arnold Brockhaus in 1818, and contributed to the *Jahrbücher der Geschichte und Staatskunst* (1828–38) founded by his equally committed Leipzig publishing colleague Pölitz. Krug's *Collected Writings*, published in 1834, encompass twelve volumes. Not included therein are the autobiography and the six volumes of the *General Dictionary of the Philosophical Sciences* he conceived by himself. He developed his system based on the rationalism of the Enlightenment and Kant's *Critique of Reason*, mediating between idealism and the realism/materialism of a 'transcendental synthetism' in the *Fundamentalphilosophie* (1803, third edition 1827), the *Rechtslehre* (1817), the *Tugendlehre* (Aretology, 1818) and the *Religionslehre* (1819).[58] Beyond numerous political writings, he expounded on his understanding of the state in the *Rechtslehre* (Dikaeologie, 1817) and the Dikaeopolitik or new restoration of state science by means of the *Rechtsgesetz* (1824).[59] Krug was the vice-chancellor of Leipzig University in the years 1813 and 1830. The university reform of 1830, with the elimination of the national classification of the teaching staff and the student body which had existed since 1409, carried his mark.[60] His thoughtful and courageous actions during the troubles in September 1830 won him the respect of the Leipzig citizenry.[61] He had represented the university already in 1820/21 at the meeting of the guilds.[62] He took publishing influence upon the considerations regarding the Saxon constitution in 1831. The university sent him to the First Chamber of the new Federal State Parliament in which he was particularly engaged in allowing women into the debates of the parliament, freedom of the press[63] and the legal equality of the Jews.

In respect of the Aretology, Krug joined Kant's critique of the Aristotelian ethics of virtue as a 'mediocrity of action'.[64] Yet, this did not keep him from strongly defending the liberal path of constitutional reform as the proper middle between the extremes. Krug dealt intensively with the extreme ideologies of his time. He strongly criticized 'right-wing', 'reactionary' ultraism for the first time in 1817. The year before, the introductory part of the *Restaurazion der Staats-Wissenschaft* by Carl Ludwig Haller (1768–1854), which was divided into six volumes, had been published.[65] This patrician from Bern had developed therein a patrimonial theory, taking as his model the feudalism of the Middle Ages, which understood a monarch simply as the bearer of a basic rule spanning the entire federal association. This – apparently – 'natural' and original form of order served as the backdrop for an anti-modernistic counter-programme to the 'wrong' theories of the Enlightenment with its concept of 'bourgeois society', the naturally legal constitutional theories as well as the principles of the people's sovereignty, the representation, the division of power, in fact any form of 'artificial', as driven by human hands, 'legality'.[66]

When Adam Müller (1779–1829), the imperialist Austrian senior civil servant and general consul in Leipzig,[67] elaborately praised the work in the *Deutsche Staatsanzeigen*, the medium for Metternich's politics that he published, Krug took up his pen to describe the historical political mechanisms that had paved the way for modern constitutionalism. Thus, he was being ironical about the fact that the restorers were not of one mind concerning the origin of the 'evil' and therefore argued about how far back the wheel of history needed to be turned. Accordingly, Müller criticized Haller for the flawed development that did not lie 200 years back but 300 instead and had in fact come about 'through the ill-fated Reformation in the sixteenth century': 'therefore, one needed not only to restore politics but the Church as well and, following from this, of course, the hierarchy, intensively and extensively, as well as placing politarchy back on to the foundation on which it had stood before the sixteenth century – whereby unfortunately a small detail has been overlooked, namely, how one was to begin this without decapitating several million people in order to replace their heads by completely new ones from the restoring state and church Factory'. In comparison to such fantastic plans, to Krug, the 'French restorers' appeared a great deal less 'demanding', as they were satisfied with restoring the conditions of the time before the Revolution. At times, they deserved to 'rather be called citras than ultras'.[68]

His *Geschichtliche Darstellung des Liberalismus alter und neuer Zeit* (1823) sought to show that the principles of liberalism and constitutionalism had not only been developed in the course of the Enlightenment but reached as far back as Antiquity. Thereby, he criticized the ultraism of the restorers, simultaneously warning against similar dangers on the left wing of the political spectrum. For, 'in a time of extremes',[69] liberalism would structurally approach its ideological antipode because of exceeding its own principles. Although basically justified, it would overshoot its goal 'if it did not want to admit anything positive, thus at times itself breaking through all the barriers of wilfulness, suddenly wanting to restore everything. It will then, however, become revolutionary and rightfully be called ultra-liberalism, Jacobinism, sansculotism, radicalism, and carbonarism'.[70] 'Anti-liberalism', on the other hand, rightfully demanded 'that one treat what exists with respect and care, that one did not preach non-belief instead of superstition and unrestraint instead of unfailing obedience. He would be wrong, however, who only held fast to what exists for the mere reason that it exists and to the old only due to its being old with such persistence that he will not permit the necessary changes and obviously needed improvements, if he thus sought to lock mankind in unresolvable shackles, so perpetuating the slavery of blind faith and action'. In this way, anti-liberalism would change into a 'sort of ultraism, as it would throw itself onto the other utmost and can as such rightfully be called ultra-royalism, illiberalism, servilism, obscurantism or imperfectibilism'.[71]

Liberal as well as anti-liberal ultraism shared a tendency towards the use of violence: 'as the extremes always touch each other, the degenerations of Liberalism and its opposite also show a certain similarity in that they both want to validate themselves through violent measures and as such themselves document their reprehensibility [ ... ] Therefore we often see the tragedy in history that revolutions and counter-revolutions take turns and the latter again and again destroys that which the former has created'.[72] Krug predicted that, in the long run, liberalism with its principles would become overbearing, whereas anti-liberalism would always continue to exist. Liberalism would be advised not to fundamentally dispute the right of anti-liberalisms to exist. For, 'without antagonism, there is no true life in the world'. Nature had taken care 'that there would be an antithesis to the thesis. Hence, there will always be people who counteract the Liberals, partially in order to call them to action, so they would not themselves fall asleep but also partially keep a tight reign on them, so that they would not go out of bounds and give their power a destructive direction'.[73] This is how Krug reasoned for the principal legitimacy of political pluralism.

Krug said that it was not 'true' liberalism that was to have a tendency towards the destruction of the antagonists but ultraistically exaggerated liberalism. Republican tendencies, antagonistic towards the monarchy, as they had erupted at the Hambach Festival, offered the reason for general reckoning with ultra-liberalism. According to his own admission, Krug had written his paper, in which he warned against the 'disaster' that would be inescapable if one continued 'to move toward the extreme',[74] for the most part even prior to the decisions by the German Confederation (Deutscher Bund) of 28 June 1832.[75] A 'false' or 'ultra-liberalism' would in this sense make 'despotism its principle'[76] and would prove injurious to current law, endanger peace, propagate an 'absolute' freedom of the press, which, by necessity, would lead to the 'audacity of the press',[77] would not put its hopes on reforms but on the revolution and would thus miss its 'aim of moderation'. This, Krug countered with the old German proverb:

Zu wenig und zu viel
Ist aller Narren Ziel.

Too little and too much
Is all fools' goal.

As Aristotle had already realized, 'attaining the proper middle'[78] was, without doubt, difficult. Yet, one would always have to attempt to reach it. What this concretely meant, Krug explained by using republicanism as it had been represented at the Hambach Festival as his example. By no means was he a fundamental opponent of republican principles. Yet, whoever lived in a monarchic state would have to first try to improve that which existed through reform instead of throwing out the status quo lock, stock and barrel. For, in this way, everything worth saving would also be jeopardized and an incalculable risk taken: 'in order to then abandon the certainty that we already possess for an uncertainty which we are first to acquire among great sacrifices of blood, sweat and tears: I defend the existing, the monarchic state form and resist all those who throw it over and want to change it into a Republican one'.[79]

Turning away from the Aristotelian middle road appeared in Krug in the form not only of political ultraism but also of moral ultraism. This was either 'too strict or too lenient in its demands'.[80] In the paper about the *Kampf zwischen den Konservativen und Destruktiven*, he returned to the *Nichomachean Ethics*: 'For all evil moves in extremes, as Aristotle has already mentioned in his ethics. [ ... ] The natural feeling for what is right and proper, the respect for the laws of logic will by and by become weaker and weaker in whoever subscribes to one of these two extremes. In the end he will even talk himself into thinking that "everything was good which served his cause"'.[81] Here, he called the two political extreme positions boundless 'conservatives' and 'destructives'. They both tended towards 'political absolutism'.[82] Yet, the proper middle between them consisted of the 'reformatives' or – as the 'Englishman' called them – the 'reformers'.[83] These did not shrink from destroying anything antiquated through 'gradual improvement', at the same time keeping in mind saving everything that 'due to its inert goodness and overt usability'[84] was worth saving.

Krug did not apply the image of the middle and the extremes to the level of the doctrine of state reform, although pleading for a mixed constitution. This he called 'syncracy' – the opposite of 'autocracy', which was to be rejected in all its forms. The syncratic monarchy was to be preferred over the syncratic 'polyarchy'.[85] Whether monarchic or 'polyarchic': in a syncracy, the highest power of state was carried out in a legally bound and controlled form by a number of individuals under participation of the people. Krug paid great respect to the representation of the guilds, a tradition from the Middle Ages, in the manner in which it had retained its importance in Saxony throughout the time of absolutism. Nevertheless, he thought a drastic reform necessary, among other things also on account of the sobering experiences he had had with the awkward currier system of the guilds' assembly as a university representative. In the selection of the representatives, he wanted to eliminate outdated privileges (e.g. those of the aristocracy and the Christian churches), yet in no way permit complete political equality for all social groups. It conformed to widely accepted liberal thinking to protect an individual against the grasp of the state by anchoring basic rights and defence rights, but to limit the active bourgeois rights to mature and economically independent men and therefore exclude women as well as all those 'who served a lord for their wages and keep or even lived of alms [ ... ] as long as they persist in this condition'.[86]

The 'syncratic monarchy' propagated by Krug had at its disposal a one-chamber people's representation of a newly formed guild assembly.[87] The census voting right was to produce a 'dynamic' (in no way 'mathematical') people's representation according to the 'value and rank of certain classes of citizens'[88] (here, the idea was also to include independent merchants, scholars and farmers beside the clergy and a reformed 'lords and knights' guild). The parliament was in no way thought to be solely an advisory organ. Without its agreement, laws could not be accepted nor could budgets be agreed upon.[89] In addition, publicity of the debates was the highest commandment. Hereby, political opposition was natural, nevertheless damaging in party-relevant organized form.[90] Thus far, Krug shared the sceptical views regarding the parties of many liberals of his age[91] (strangely contrasting with the demand for the freedom to associate).

In the logics of the Krugian terminology, 'ultraistic' associations strove towards 'autocracy'. In a later supplement to his many volumed *Allgemeines Handwörterbuch der philosophischen Wissenschaften* (1838),[92] he spoke of 'extremists': 'Extremists are called those who do not want to accept a proper middle but are only pleased with themselves in the extreme. More commonly they are called ultraists'.[93] Whether Krug coined this term or whether he took it from the political discussions of his time cannot be concluded from this short remark. It was not a common expression in the political language of the Vormärz. Apparently, Krug did not use the extremism '-ism' formation in any other publication. As in the time of the Wars of Religion, the polarization and the idealization of public debates, the intensity of the argument with the political 'extremes' and the growing tendency to perceive these as a structural unity invited such a word formation, even though by the ultraism formula, there was already an isomorphic term in use.

## 4 'Extrematic parties'

'Ultraism' remained a key political term for a time. Still, no other German language source using the terms 'extremists' or 'extremism' could be found for the entire nineteenth century. After the political turning of the tides of the 1848/49 Revolution, ultraism seems to have lost some importance. It remains to be seen whether the relative calming down of the political arguments played a role: in any event, one now again spoke more frequently simply of the 'extreme parties', which not only in Germany but also in Switzerland pointedly expressed the political differences.[94]

Another '-ism' formation was introduced by Friedrich Rohmer in his *Party Doctrine* (1844). Here, not only the 'extreme' parties were spoken of but also, on equal footing, the 'extrematic' ones. Rohmer saw the different ages of man and the connected prevailing attitudes (of mind) as the natural foundation of the party. Radicalism was equal to childhood, absolutism to old age. The two 'sensible' forms were liberalism as the expression of the younger man's age and conservatism as that of the more mature man. Rohmer saw radicalism as the product of the equally barren extremes. The two differing strivings were both right and wrong at the same time:

> when the French Revolution toppled the despotism of the absolutist times, it was right against it, as mankind needed revenge; simultaneously it was also wrong, as it only planted new despotism in place of the old. When the absolutist party in Germany complains about the destructive tendencies of the radicals, for example the Hambachiads in the earlier time and the present boyishness of literature, it was right toward radicalism but wrong in itself for without them, the Hambachiads would have been laughable and the nonsense of the press less effective.[95]

According to Rohmer, the extremes interrelated with each other: 'One extreme constantly calls forth the other. Radicalism in Germany creates the wrong federal resolutions, they in turn cause radicalism and so forth'. Radicalism exploits absolutism, and absolutism gives way to it. A true union between them appeared impossible and, if at all, only as a 'union against a third party'.[96] There could be no balance. The 'struggle of the extremes is by its very nature a never-ending one and can only be decided through the intervention of the masculine principles'. A 'perfect condition' is only reached 'when the extreme parties, merely indirectly, stand in the course of it as satellites, whereas the organic battle is carried out between the masculine ones themselves. Therein lie the determining ideas of mankind; from its friction oozes the blessing. A relentless war of the middle levels against the extremes would tear apart mankind and lies outside nature'.[97]

The 'phases of time development' determined whether the 'masculine' or the extreme parties would become overbearing. In 'prospering times', the 'masculine' ones dominated; in 'extrematic ones', that necessity of a mediation by the extremes would create itself, that need of a thorough yet reconciling principle which our time is so full of.[98] The parties compared with the boy's age and the very old age corresponded to specific characters: 'In reality, the extrematic parties consist of extrematic persons', and these bundle unfavourable traits within themselves, which with conservatives and liberals occur at best in mixed form: 'a radical, an absolutist of that kind, falls victim to all the mistakes of his level and shows only them, without replacing them by a counterweight of great quality'.[99]

Rohmer's *Party* book belongs to the first of its kind in the German language. It was therefore intensively discussed, its terminology leaving traces behind. Presumably, historian Heinrich von Sybel was influenced by Rohmer when he spoke of 'extrematic' and 'extremistic' parties in his essay about the 'political parties of the Rhine Province' in the year 1847.[100] With these formulas, Sybel brought the followers of the respective opposite wings, that of feudalism on the utmost right and that of communism on the utmost left, to a common ground. In all their dissimilarity, they resembled each other in the doctrinaire form of their activities, which, beyond the borders of the European states, made their followers appear more similar than the confusing, richly varied camp of the 'constitutionals' adapted to the most different conditions.

They also had in common that they did not permit a mediating position between themselves and the opposite viewpoint: 'As the historic political papers do not leave room for a third between strict Catholicism and pure atheism, so, here there remains only the choice between Communist practices and those of the Middle Ages. Either the bloodthirsty egalitaires or Rhinish autonomy'.[101] Critical discussion with a representative of the utmost right led Sybel to the following insight:

> When one was only able to escape the dissolution of the feudal state by falling prey to the despotism of a Cabetist community, one could give in

to the temptation of granting the speaker an inner justification of his viewpoint. Only that one always remembered that an equally strong justification was also owed the Cabetists. For each of them constitutes one of the two extremes in whose respective cancellation the truth can then be found. The feudal one exaggerates the freedom of the individual in the same manner as the Cabetist exaggerates omnipotence in its entirety. However, the true task of all politics is the balance between both powers, namely a justification of the power of state, which suffices for the activities of national matters without destroying the individual legal sphere. The more an individual state form approaches this balance, the less it makes a claim unto the consequence according to the extreme, as the more perfect it must be considered.[102]

State theorist Johann Caspar Bluntschli (1808–81) who, from time to time, had cooperated with Rohmer in the framework of his Liberal Conservative Party in Zürich at the beginning of the 1840s, 'which was basically preparing to fight the extremes of radicalism and absolutism',[103] spoke of the 'extreme' but not of the 'extremetic' or 'extrematic' parties. With his respected and highly publicized handbooks, Bluntschli later on contributed to the circulation of Rohmer's party doctrine. He adopted Rohmer's party psychology with its evaluation of the 'extreme' parties as the forces of political demise:

> For leading the state only the masculine parties, only the Liberals and the Conservatives, are qualified but not the two extreme parties, the Radicals and the Absolutists. The delusion that radicalism was simply decisive, consistent Liberalism is opposed by the doctrine in the same manner as the assumption that Conservatism in its highest potency would become absolutism. Moreover, it insists on the *differentiation* between the two parties of the growing development, boyish radicalism and youthfully masculine Liberalism and, by the same token, between the two parties of the declining development, Conservatism and absolutism, and demands the *subjugation* of the Radicals to the Liberals and of the Absolutists to the Conservatives.

Rohmer's psychological insights confirmed Bluntschli's political convictions: 'Only when the Liberals and the Conservatives have the leadership, the spirit rules over the masses and strength of character over excitability'.[104]

## 5 Extremists and civil war

Only a few years after the publication of Sybel's paper, the extremism formula turned up in an American publication for the first time. However, in the American states, which were completely determined by the cultural influences of Europe at this time, the term 'ultraism' prevailed.

In the 1830s, strategic arguments had led to violent discussions in the anti-slavery movement, foremost in the markedly puritanical New England states.

The contrast between the northern states in which slavery, only of subjugated economic importance anyway, had been abandoned and the largely agrarian southern states with their cotton plantations, became more pronounced.[105] From the viewpoint of their distinct opponents, slavery contradicted Christian principles and the liberty rights anchored in the Bill of Rights. What was to be done in the light of the abominable conditions in the south? Was it permitted to follow one's own aims by using force if necessary? Or was this not to be justified under any circumstances? Particularly, the consistent pacifists were seen as ultras: 'Non-resistance was in some ways the most "ultra" of all the nineteenth-century "ultraisms"'.[106]

At the beginning of the 1830s, when William Lloyd Garrison (1805–79) founded the publicist flagship of the anti-slavery movement in Boston, the commandment of non-violence was unapproachable; yet, this did not exclude steadfastness concerning one's principles and unwillingness to compromise in the fight for one's own aims. Thus, Garrison makes the renunciation of any 'moderation' a virtue in a programmatic basic contribution on the occasion of the publication of the first issue of the *Liberator*: 'I will be as harsh as truth and as uncompromising as justice. On this subject, I do not wish to think, or speak, or write, with moderation. No, no! Tell a man whose house is on fire, to give a moderate alarm; tell him to moderately rescue his wife from the hands of the ravisher; tell the mother to gradually extricate her babe from the fire into which it has fallen; – but urge me not to use moderation in a cause like the present'.[107]

Garrison's position forbade any concession to the supporters of a step-by-step, gradual overcoming of slavery. In the *Liberator*, it said: 'there is no more mischievous and unfounded than the *gradual abolition of slaveholding*'.[108] Whoever cited the Aristotelian–Thomistic commandment to moderation was seen as 'lukewarm' and halfhearted: 'speaking of emancipation, Mr. D. said, "no *extreme* which has reference to this subject will do – *the middle course is the only safe one*". Now here, we say, is a fatal heresy. There is no neutral ground between right and wrong – liberty and oppression – truth and error. The slaveholders are either guilty, they are without excuse – if not guilty, why allude to them at all? [ ... ] There is no middle road in this business'.[109]

This stance caused Garrison and his followers to be labelled 'zealots, fanatics, political incendiaries'.[110]

In addition, one placed the 'anti-slavery fanatics'[111] at the same level as unconditional supporters of slavery. Once more, in the centre of the argumentation stood the lack of understanding of the advocates for the immediate, unconditional abolition of slavery. On the one hand, the economic consequences for the slaveholders and the plantation management were not taken into consideration; on the other hand, freeing them without any period of transition would throw the affected slaves into social deprivation.[112] Therefore, many fundamental slavery opponents pleaded for a 'gradual abolition'.

The radical abolitionists, on the other hand, had to accept the accusation that, by their unrealistic demands, they were strengthening the position of the supporters of slavery who were equally blind to reality: 'Here, indeed, extremes have met. The ultra abolitionist and the ultra slaveholder are riding the same hobby'.[113] Thus, as no other term, 'ultraism' seemed to be suited 'to designate the tendency to extremes at the present day'.[114] Its followers, however, praised themselves for their loyalty to principles. It has become the fashion to denounce 'ultraism' as a 'dangerous monster'. Still, the ultraists are finding themselves in the best company: 'Columbus was an ultraist. [ … ] Our pilgrim Ancestors were ultraists. [ … ] Franklin was an ultraist. [ … ] We like ultraists. They should be treated with respect. They are *pioneers*'.[115]

The tense atmosphere during the two decades before the beginning of the American Civil War caused a radicalization of the political language. Uncompromising supporters of slavery as well as opponents took to violent means in growing measure. Election announcements became the stage for violent clashes of the political camps, and often led to mutual shouting matches and physical violence. The well-known lawyer and former presidential candidate Daniel Webster (1782–1852) seems to have been the first to have spoken of 'extremists' in this context. He referred to the violence of the verbal clashes and the endangerment of the concordance of the Union when he complained in a Senate speech in 1850: 'There are outrageous reproaches in the North. Sir, the extremists of both parts of the country are violent; they mistake loud and violent talk for eloquence and for reason'.[116] Webster was against expanding slavery, at the same time however defending the rightful return of slaves who had escaped to the northern states.

The fronts' becoming more and more entrenched concerning the slavery question was described by the landscape architect Frederick Law Olmsted (1822–1903) in his travel reports from the slavery states, which found a wide readership in the United States and England. Owing to their inability to compromise and the spread of respective images of the enemy, the 'extremists' in both camps contributed considerably to the undermining of the foundation of trust between the north and the south: 'Very little candid, truthful, and unprejudiced public discussion has yet been had on this vexed subject of slavery. The extremists of the South esteem their opponents as madmen, or robbers; and invariably misrepresent, misunderstand, and, consequently, entirely fail to meet their arguments. The extremists of the North esteem the slaveholders as robbers and tyrants, wilfully and malevolently oppressive and cruel'.[117] Nonetheless, the moderates with their attempts to suppress extreme agitation had also added to this climate. For only the possibility of free, uninhibited discussion would be able to restore lost trust.

What those willing to compromise had feared for a long time ensued in 1860/61. After the election as president of slavery opponent Abraham Lincoln, South Carolina, as the first of the southern states, officially resigned from the Union.[118] By June 1861, all the other states had gradually joined it. In the Congress debates during the winter of 1860/61, the political polarization was openly expressed. For the political language of this turbulent time, the memories and speeches of the Democratic representative Samuel S. Cox (1824–89) constitute an excellent source.

Cox, representing the district of Columbus, Ohio, had been elected to Congress in 1860,[119] when leading representatives of the south presented and explained their secession plans right at the beginning of the parliamentary session. Cox belonged to those endeavouring a compromise, thus fighting for the preservation of the Union. Nevertheless, all the efforts were ruined by the 'calamities which were pressed by extremists, North and South'.[120] On the one side were the ultra-abolitionists, on the other the 'heresies of the ultra Calhoun School',[121] hence the followers of John C. Calhoun who had died in 1850. With biblical arguments, he had tried to legitimize the subordinate relationship of slave and master as a patriarchal protection community. Here, too, the interaction of the extremes, which produced 'immoderation and violence',[122] undermined the establishment of a compromise, leading Cox to presume a possible silent conspiracy: 'Extremes thus meet. Extremes north have aided, if not conspired with, extremes south, in the work of disintegration'.[123]

The slavery ideologists of the north and the south were not the only ones seen as extremists, but also the 'peace Democrats' who, because of their mark of recognition, a copper penny, were soon called 'copperheads'.[124] They formed themselves within the Democratic party of the north during the secession crisis in 1860/61, met the beginning of the Civil War partly with scepticism, partly with rejection, declared the preservation of the Union the foremost goal and were willing to make important concessions to the south on the slavery question. Lincoln's opponent Clement Vallandigham was seen as their most important spokesman. He had supported his cause with 'silvery tongue' and 'Jesuitical pen', as the *New York Times* wrote in a review after the end of the Civil War.[125]

In this respect, 'extremism' experienced a shift in importance. For Vallandigham could hardly be accused of inability to compromise. Rather, the formula says little about his stance towards the constitutional contents of the state constitution. The ultra-abolitionists vehemently claimed its basic laws. The supporters of slavery, on the other hand, could be seen as the opponents of the universal equality of man but were not per se opponents of freedom-preserving institutions.

From the Civil War on, the term extremism established itself as a solid component of the political language. Soon, it was also extended to other topics of disputes/debates. To mention but one example, in the 1880s, the puritanical supporters of temperance and prohibitionists as well as their decided opponents were seen as 'extremists'. 'Liquor dealers' and 'prohibitionists' opposed having to obtain a licence to deal in alcoholic beverages: 'They appear on the same side in the committee room, and on some points they urge the same arguments – that high license has been a failure where already tried. That beer is responsible for most of the drunkenness, and so forth. It is just this extremism, which makes any effective control of the traffic in liquors so nearly hopeless in this country'. The prohibitionists compared themselves with the founders of the Republican party: 'They are more like the extreme Abolitionists who would not vote for a Free Soil or a Republican candidate, and who denounced those two parties hardly less vigorously than they did the advocates of the extremism of slavery'.[126] With their eagerness, they tremendously served the cause.

## 6 Extremism in the British crown colony of India

In the British Empire, towards the end of the nineteenth century, the traditional distinction between 'moderate' and 'extreme' enjoyed widespread acceptance. The distinction between 'extreme left' and 'extreme right' was just as well known, particularly in press reports about the developments in France.[127] However, in this context, there was no mention of 'extremists' or 'extremism'.[128] It appears that this terminology found its way into political publications only at the beginning of the twentieth century with reports about India.

The attentive reader of the London *Times* could occasionally find reports about acts of violence by Sikh 'fanatics'.[129] However, the coming about of the new designation was also closely linked to Hindu nationalism becoming stronger and to the person of Bal Ganghadhar Tilak (1856–1920). Tilak derived from the highly respected caste of the Chitpavan Brahmans and had already become acquainted with the Hindu traditions of the Deccan Highlands as a child through the tales his grandfather had told him.[130] British rule in India seemed to him – in contrast to a great number of his contemporaries – illegitimate in every shape and form. Typically, he declined a position with the government after he had completed his law studies. Instead, he worked in education, participated in the foundation of the Deccan Education Society and the Fergusson College. He opposed the 'moderate' majority of the Indian National Congress, founded in 1885, which in its beginnings was foremost aiming at administrative reforms.

When two British officers were murdered in Poona in 1897, Tilak was accused of having stirred up hate against the government through the Hindu nationalist magazine *Kesari* ('The Lion') whose co-founder he was. Tilak seems to have been mentioned as an extremist (in quotation marks) for the first time in a police report from the year 1895: 'Another bone of contention between the parties was the holding of the Social Conference in the National Congress Mandup. Tilak took a prominent part and on behalf of the "extremists" urged that the principles of the social reformers, who mostly belong to the "Moderate" party, are antagonistic to the teachings of the Hindu religion and not acceptable to the masses'.[131]

The Hindu nationalist movement represented by Tilak distinguished itself in four points from the positions of the 'moderates'.[132] First of all, it emphasized the size and greatness of the teachings of Indian history and culture, which constituted the foundation for designing the present. Second, it counteracted the 'begging' of the National Congress, which would not lead to the envisaged aim. Instead, one was to trust in one's own strength, claim one's inalienable rights and be willing to take upon oneself great suffering and sacrifices. Third, the declared aim was self-government (Swaraj) which, fourth, was to be reached through winning over the broad masses of the people. A famine was the opportune occasion for Tilak to phrase his complaints towards the government. From then on, he was blacklisted by the British as 'Enemy No. 1'.

A further escalation of the conflict as well as the propagation of the extremism formula in the British and the Indian pro-British press (as a foreign term) began as of 1905. In the light of the separation of Bengal executed by Lord Curzon, a highly controversial subject among the population and the Indian elites, Tilak joined the activist powers in the National Congress who aimed at independence and called for a boycott against British goods.[133] From 1906 to 1908, the power struggle raged between the 'moderates' and the 'extremists'. Most of all, the press of the English mother country and circles close to the British Indian government characterized the radical independence fighters as 'extremists'. This term not only referred to the absoluteness of their aims (to shake off British rule) but also to the tendency towards employing brutal methods.

Tilak's political commitment ended for a time in 1908, when he was sentenced to imprisonment and exiled to Mandalay in Upper Burma for having been the ringleader of a revolutionary movement.[134] There he wrote his great work, a two-volume commentary on the Bhagavad Gita. After his release in 1914, he participated more moderately in the political life of India where he is honoured today as one of the fathers of independence.

# 5   Extremism at the beginning of the 'age of extremes'

## 1 Revolution in Russia

'Extrémisme' appears only once – as an adjective – in the time before 1917: in the *Trésor de la langue française*. In a letter from the year 1915, the lyricist and philosopher Paul Valéry (1871–1945) admitted: 'Ma nature est extrémiste, changeante!' (My nature is extreme, changeable!).[1] This was to be understood in the psychological and not the political sense. Two years later, the term all at once became the keyword of political publications.

The terms 'extrémiste' and 'extrémisme' found their widest distribution with the Russian February Revolution in 1917 (in March according to the Gregorian calendar): The Parisian press used it[2] foremost for the qualification of the revolutionary 'maximalists' ('Bolshevists', 'Leninists'), who fought uncompromisingly against the provisional government and tended towards an immediate end to the war.[3] Their ideas were derived from the radical Zimmerwaldian left and the strategic concept of Wladimir Iljitsch Uljanov called Lenin (1870–1924), who, at the beginning of the revolution, still lived in humble conditions in his Swiss exile but was soon to play an important role after returning to Russia.

Possibly, a number of French journalists were under the influence of the language of British news agencies during the introduction of these new formulas. There, they had been in use for a long time.[4] However, the formula had already been used by the organ of the moderate French left for some time before this. Salomon Grumbach (1884–1952), a social democrat journalist from Alsace who had gone to Switzerland after the beginning of the war in order to escape conscription,[5] had – under the pseudonym 'HOMO' – copied down the conflicts and the violent polemics in the months before the conference between the rather moderate ones and the ultra-left wing in his report about the Second Zimmerwaldian Conference at Kienthal (24–29 April 1916). The group around Robert Grimm (1881–1951), the representative of the Social Democratic Party of Switzerland, was traded as 'extrémistes' (in the today rather unusual spelling).[6] It had supposedly expressed its desire for a division of the International in Kienthal. On account of these arguments, the results of the conference had been meagre. This would probably also explain 'why the extremists have determined the vote regarding the declaration of principles which, incidentally, is well suited to drawing a clear line of separation between democratic and "absolutist" Socialists'.[7]

After the outbreak of the revolution in Saint Petersburg, Paris newspapers gave priority to the question of whether the new forces would be able to stabilize the conditions of the interior while energetically continuing the war. In the light of the longing for peace prevalent at all levels of Russian society, the balance of power and the behaviour of activist groupings were observed with great concern. On 21 March, *L'Humanité* reported with a certain satisfaction, 'Under the pressure of the moderate elements, the extremists have consented to taking up the tram service once again'[8] and to remove the damages that had been caused. The majority of workers were willing to return to normal.

Early on, liberal observers saw the Bolsheviks as the advocates of dangerous extremistic positions. George Buchanan (1854–1924), the English ambassador in Saint Petersburg, considered the designations 'Bolsheviks' (majority socialists) and 'Mensheviks' (minority socialists), which derived from the party meeting of the Russian socialists in London (1903), as misleading. Instead, it was more suitable to differentiate between 'extremists' and 'moderates'.[9]

Acknowledging the Bolsheviks as a threat was often not so much connected to the ideological profile of this direction but to their attitude in reference to the question of war. It gave rise to various suspicions. On 28 March, *L'Humanité* presented the former chief editor of *Pravda*, Tchernomasov, as the *agent provocateur* of the Tsarist secret police Ochrana.[10] Hereby, the Socialist Party newspaper referred to a report by the writer Jean Schopfer (1868–1931), the correspondent of the *Petit Parisien* in Petrograd, who wrote under the pseudonym 'Claude Anet'.[11] Anet described rumours according to which Tchernomasov was said to have received money from secret funds. Hereby, he characterized *Pravda* as a 'journal des extrémistes'.[12] Lenin himself referred to this article in his last contribution written before his departure and presumably introduced the expression to the Russian language.[13] In the *Petit Parisien*, the former Tsarist informer Tchernomasov was called the 'former editor of the extremist Social-Democratic newspaper *Pravda*'. This showed 'how malicious and contemptible the fighting methods of the Gutshov–Miljukov government were'.[14] Although Lenin could only recognize a 'purely liberal un-Marxist characterization'[15] in the appeal of the Soviet of the worker deputies who had spoken of a government consisting of 'moderate elements', nevertheless, he later vehemently rejected the designation of his movement as an expression of political 'extremism'.[16]

Lenin's arrival in Saint Petersburg was seen as the 'most dangerous test' confronting the Russian Revolution.[17] French ambassador Maurice Paléologue (1858–1944), a diplomat of the 'old salon school',[18] was filled with profound scepticism in view of the revolution and its consequences. To recently arrived socialist representatives Marcel Cachin, Ernest Lafont and Marius Moutet, dispatched by the Foreign Committee and the SFIO faction of the French National Assembly, he painted the dangers of a strengthening of the extreme trends in glaring colours:

In its very being the Russian revolution is anarchic and destructive. If left to its own devices, it can only lead to the terrible demagogy of the rabble and the soldateska, to a rift between all national bonds, to the complete collapse of Russia. With the excess particular to the Russian character, it will quickly fall to the extreme; it is sentenced to degenerate to devastation and barbary, to horror and absurdity. You have no idea of the brunt of the forces that will be set free [ ... ]. The support which you are offering to the extremists will accelerate the final catastrophe.[19]

The three socialist deputies – in contrast to the ambassador's fears – did not show the least tendency towards supporting the Leninists. After the outbreak of the war, they had supported a conditional cooperation with a government of national defence and later fought uncompromisingly against the Zimmerwaldians. Therefore, they had a hard time in Saint Petersburg. The leadership of the Russian Social Democrats, but most of all the ultra-revolutionary forces represented therein, displayed profound suspicion towards them. They were suspected of wanting to thwart the revolutionary cause.[20] A well-informed observer of the situation in Saint Petersburg, the correspondent of the English newspaper *Daily Chronicle*, realized that not only among the 'Bolsheviks' but also in the Menshevik camp and the social revolutionaries were there numerous party members in support of an immediate peace agreement. The left wing of the social revolutionaries appeared to him as equally 'extremist' as Lenin's party, because he, too, tended towards the violent foundation of a 'dictatorship of the proletariat'.[21]

The French delegation thus found itself in a difficult situation. Cachin (1869–1958), who was to become one of the founders of the French Communist Party two years later, at this time considered Lenin's thesis of the necessity for pushing the revolution ahead mercilessly in order to force the German Reich to its knees 'perfidious'.[22] He was hoping that the Saint Petersburg workers – 'well-fed and highly paid' – would not follow the extremists under these conditions.[23] Towards the end of his stay in Russia, he had the impression that his own mission had not been without effect. The moderate forces appeared to him to have been strengthened. The Bolshevist danger was being overestimated: 'Now, Lenin is burned out. The same will apply to all extreme theories'.[24]

Paléologue, who had to step down as an ambassador by the end of April – chiefly because of his scepticism towards the revolution and lack of popularity with the new powers in Saint Petersburg[25] – judged the situation differently. To him, Lenin's influence appeared far greater. Lenin was assembling under his command 'all the fanatics of the revolution'.[26] His picture of the leader of the Bolsheviks was an unflattering one:

Utopist and fanatic, prophet and metaphysicist, lacking any understanding of the impossible and the absurd, closed to every feeling of fairness and compassion, violent and Machiavellian, crazy with conceit, Lenin devotes his bold and cold will, his cutting logic, and his exceptional ability of command and obedience to his Messianic dreams. [ ... ] He demands the revolutionary dictatorship of the workers' and farmers' masses; he preaches that the proletariat does not have a homeland and with all his wilful energy calls forth the defeat of the Russian armies. When one confronts his chimeras with some contradictions gained from reality, he replies with a boastful remark: 'The worse for reality!' [ ... ] This person is even the more dangerous as he is described as virtuous, sober, and ascetic. The way I envision him is that he combines within himself the character traits of a Savonarola and Marat, Blanqui and Bakunin.[27]

In France, public interest in Lenin grew rapidly in May 1917. In the magazine *Demain*, the forum of 'literary defeatism'[28] by the Zimmerwaldians working in their Geneva exile, the organ's initiator and later co-founder of the Third International, Henri Guilbeaux (1885–1938), complained that not only were attributes such as 'extremist', 'fanatic', 'demagogic' and 'anarchist' used for the designation of the Russian revolutionaries and 'the supporters of the German peace' in the bourgeois newspapers but also in the 'so-called Socialist ones'.[29] Looking back later, he mocked the 'pantouflards jusqu'auboutistes',[30] the 'henpecked husbands' who were fiercely determined, who in the cosy café du commerce bravely fought for the continuation of the war at any cost. Alexander Lozovsky (name at birth: Solomon Abromovitch Dridzo, 1878–1952), the later secretary general of the Red Union International in Moscow, then an emigrant in Paris active in the Union and publisher of a Russian-speaking pro-communist newspaper, defended Lenin in the *Journal du Peuple* – under the pseudonym of S. Drudzo – and opposed the qualification of the Russian revolutionary as an 'extreme extremist'.[31] He, nevertheless, confirmed the fears of Lenin's opponents by the following statement in the May issue of the metal workers' magazine: 'We are for the revolution to the last, i.e. the revolution which goes to the extreme limits of what is humanly possible'.[32] After reading the 'Drudzo' article in the *Journal du Peuple*, the winner of the Nobel Prize for literature, Romain Rolland (1866–1944), wrote down some biographical information about the 'leader of 'Bolshevism' and the extremist tendency of Russian Marxism[33] in his diary.

Whereas the formulas 'extrémiste' and 'extrémisme' were used by the liberal press in order to negatively label political opponents of a different persuasion, the thus attacked sought to read a neutral or even positive meaning into it. In May 1916, *Le Populaire* had been founded in Paris, the newspaper of that socialist minority that rejected the 'jusqu'au-boutisme' of the 'union sacrée' and stood for a peace with neither victors nor losers. There, a representative of the Socialist Party Association of the Seine, Louis-Oscar Frossard (1889–1946), who later became a supporter of the annexation to the Comintern,[34] devoid of any illusions called Lenin 'the leader of the extremists'[35] and a power every government would have to reckon with in the future. The numerous commentaries by press agencies who held a hostile attitude towards the Bolsheviks and their announcements proved that these were mistaking their desires for reality. The Russian revolutionary Michail Kalinin (1875–1946), who was later to become head of state of the Soviet Union, went one step further. In *Demain*, he wrote in June 1917 that the attribute 'extrémiste'[36] meant that kind of socialism that had remained unshakingly loyal to its own principles.

The forces of the 'union sacrée' continued to fear a separate peace. In the process of his mission in Saint Petersburg, Defence Minister Albert Thomas (1878–1932) travelled throughout the country and held numerous speeches in which he sought to convince his listeners of the necessity of a continuation of the war. Many 'disliked his impulsive manner, his nervous irritation and his outward appearance with his bushy red beard, the shaggy hair and the mocking eyes behind his gleaming spectacles'.[37] From time to time, there were hostile reactions. Claude Anet reported in detail about his stay in Kiev. Thomas had given five speeches there. His being a patriot had been interpreted as a crime by the internationalist circles of New Russia. He wanted the allies to force German imperialism to its knees. 'Here, these idiots become angry when one speaks to them of war. They cannot tolerate the thought that someone might want to harm Germany, the homeland of Socialism, the cradle of Marxism'. In a meeting, Thomas had been treated rudely by 'two extremists'.[38]

The Belgian socialist Émile Vandervelde (1866–1938) judged the situation more optimistically. Accompanied by Louis de Brouckère and Henri de Man, he started on a journey to Russia at the beginning of May. Delegates assured him that it was wrong if many people in France believed that the Russians were thinking about a separate peace. It was not only rejected by the moderates. This attitude was also to be encountered among the 'Zimmerwaldians' and even among the 'extremists',[39] or at least among those who were not paid by the Germans.

This opinion was to prove hardly realistic. The desire for an immediate peace treaty was widespread among the population suffering from their sacrifices. The Bolshevists benefited from this. Looking back, Claude Anet criticized Kerensky's attitude towards the Bolshevist danger. Kerensky had not been able to bear the idea of taking action against his revolutionary brothers. He should have made use of the July victory. But what had happened? 'The extremists who had been arrested on account of an armed uprising should actually have been executed yet were by and by released'.[40] It was General Kornilov's putsch that accelerated the disintegration of the February regime, provoked an uprising of the Soviets, freed the Bolshevists and decisively strengthened them again.[41]

The worst fears had finally become reality in November (October according to the Russian calendar): 'Lenin and Trotzky, the terrorist dictatorship of two men who feel capable of leading Saint Petersburg and Russia. [ ... ] It is sheer madness! [ ... ] The arrogance of the two maximalist pro-consuls knows no limit. [ ... ] We sent the best France had to offer: Cachin, Moutet, Lafont,

Ch. Dumas, Albert Thomas [ ... ] What have these great masters been able to achieve? Despite their intelligence, their good will and their efforts one has to say: nothing'.[42] British ambassador Buchanan's judgement was hardly more favourable: 'The Government is now in the hands of a small clique of extremists who are bent on imposing their will on the country by terrorist methods'.[43]

In Germany, the formulas 'extremism' and 'extremist' did not enter the journalists' language until the revolutionary year 1917, when they were borrowed from the reports of the English, French, Italian and Dutch correspondents.[44] Here, as on the other side of the Rhine, the Russian revolutionary Lenin was seen as the embodiment of the 'extreme element'. Yet, in contrast to France, one was hoping to benefit from his stirring things up, especially militarily.[45] After the goal of a quick peace had been missed, the policy of the Foreign Office was aimed at splitting up the member states of the 'entente' and reaching a separate peace with one of the allies. The plans to strengthen the revolutionary and 'pacifist' trends in Russia went back to the year 1915. After the option of coming to an understanding with the Tsar had proved unrealistic and the revolution had broken out in Russia, a strategic course correction was effected that was now aimed at the stimulation of the extreme forces.[46] The influence of the 'peace-friends of utmost leftists'[47] was deemed considerable. In the focus of the debate was the question of how these were to be supported as effectively as possible. German Chancellor Theobald von Bethmann-Hollweg (1856–1921) made a personal effort for the Zimmerwaldians with Lenin at their head to receive the necessary visas for the famous passage through Germany in supposedly 'sealed railroad cars'.[48]

The hope that Lenin's extremism would cause a fundamental change in the political framework conditions, making possible a reasonable peace treaty for Germany, also enflamed the imagination of part of the left wing. Also, the circles around the socialist, agent, successful speculator and entrepreneur Alexander Helphand (1867–1924), who had initiated and organized the revolutionizing politics of the Foreign Office thought likewise. With the help of the ministry, he had initiated the magazine *Die Glocke* in 1915, which, ideologically, moved along the lines of the Sozialistische Partei Deutschlands (SPD) faction in the Reichstag, subscribing to a strong national socialism and with Heinrich Cunow, Eduard David, Kurt Haenisch, Paul Lensch and August Winnig among its contributors.[49]

What writer Otto Flake (1880–1963), who was at the political department in Brussels[50] at this time doing his military service, spoke of several weeks after the October Revolution had all the makings of an apotheosis of extremism. First of all, he swept the idea of the solution of a compromise off the table: 'A mediator? Oh, the fight has long since outgrown this stage; a mediator appeals to last feelings that have remained; a mediator reconciles – there is nothing to reconcile, there is something to be called to a halt by someone who knows the truth and shouts it into the world: You have let yourselves in so deeply that you have destroyed the order in which you used to live'.[51] Where then was the path out of the orgies of violence? Flake saw it in a positively interpreted 'fanaticism': 'This peace will only be born of pure will, fanaticism, the order and the commandment, and from a mindset to which the collapse of society is irrelevant; unless it even accelerates it and finally relentlessly brings it about'. The Holy Land of fanaticism was Russia, the 'land of the extreme, the radical and the utmost'. In this country, there was someone in charge 'who thought two things through – war and arch-Christian thinking: he connects them by forcing the one into being through the other'. By this, he meant Lenin, and Flake knew full well that the Russian revolutionary was no Christian 'in the religious sense'.[52] However, Lenin saw himself as a socialist, and from Flake's viewpoint, he functioned as the bearer of a Messianic mission:

> The imagination of the peoples is waiting for the name that will fertilize it like an egg cell awaits fertilization. [ ... ] Only a Socialist can attempt something similar, and it robs it of little that the Socialists of all countries assure that they do not accept his extremism or do not consider it useful for their peoples: this extremism has carried out its task if peace were to come about through it, the centre of the utmost pressure. Kerensky, too, was a Socialist; he wanted to save and hold together, which is why he failed: the utmost only comes from the utmost.[53]

In hoping for peace through 'radicalization', Flake met up with the strategic considerations of the German government, but his hoping for socialism separated him from it.

In the years immediately following World War I, the Bolshevists in France remained 'the' embodiment of extremism. In 1930, still, the great French encyclopaedia *Larousse du Xxème siècle* treated 'extremism' and 'maximalism' as synonyms.[54] With the internal socialist struggles, the term had played a certain role in the dissociation from the methods and the political understanding of the Bolshevists. A number of those who had initially welcomed the revolutionary project with enthusiasm and had hoped for a worldwide change in the direction of more social justice had soon distanced themselves from Moscovite communism. The growing attempts to subjugate the workers' movements of the European countries to the directives of the Communist International founded in 1919 by the self-ordained 'Centre of World Revolution' had brought about this change of mind.

One of the critical voices belonged to the leading metal union member Alphonse Merrheim (1871–1923). In 1921, the former Zimmerwaldian turned against the 'demagogic maelstrom of the extreme right as well as that of the extreme left'[55] in the union paper 'L'information ouvrière et sociale': 'We protest against the extremists of politics and of the union movement, as they have neither principles nor programmes but only hate toward the activists against whom they never become tired to conduct their venom and their accusations of betrayal'.[56] At the Confédération générale du travail (CGT) congress in Orleans, Merrheim took a clear anti-Bolshevist position: Lenin wanted to carry the dictatorship into the world in order to stabilize his auto-cratic regime in Russia. He had suffocated the intellectual life of his country, deceived the spirit of the union movement by his thirty-one conditions and declared war on revolutionary syndicalism.[57] In the preface to Max Hoschil-ler's book, *Le mirage du soviétisme* (1921), he denounced some of the workers around Lenin for their personality cult and compared their behaviour with the enthusiasm that had once been bestowed on the right-wing populist General Boulanger: 'In the mysticism of Lenin's devotees I have found the same feelings which made the French working classes line up behind the feather bush and the tail of General Boulanger's black steed approximately twenty years ago'.[58] Merrheim was defeated in the conflict over the attitude to the Bolshevist revolution as it had been carried out openly at the CGT congresses in the years 1920 and 1921.[59] Nevertheless, he remained the speaker of a strong anti-Bolshevist minority within the unions until his early death.

Someone who possessed excellent knowledge of the workers' movement and the history of social movements in the nineteenth century was the lawyer and historian of ideas Maxime Leroy (1873–1957), who had worked out the CGT statutes with Merrheim and Victor Griffuelhes, belonged to the editorial staff of the Charte of Amiens (1906), had given legal advice to the Clem-enceau government in labour arguments and had been a member of the Académie des Sciences morales et politiques.[60] He made Merrheim's parallel-ization for the first time the subject of systematic discussion in his book *Les techniques nouvelles du syndicalisme* (1921). One of the chapters, titled 'L'ex-trémisme', began with the remark that extremism had become one of the most en vogue words of the political vocabulary since the Russian Revolu-tion.[61] Bolshevism was the main subject of the author's theoretical conclu-sions. Leroy termed Lenin and his supporters 'abstract spirits' who had an unlimited belief in the general validity and the feasibility of their ideas. He compared 'red' extremism with the 'white' extremism of the ultra-monarchists. Like them, Lenin's followers were overlooking how social divergences were a result of a 'variety of interests, milieus, religions and regions'. From this diver-sity came 'thousands of moral and logical reasons'. The 'extremist ideology' wanted to make a 'tabula rasa'[62] of all this and replace natural plurality with a unity dictated by logics. This resulted in the death of liberty: 'The too logi-cal spirits are authoritarian, and there is only a short way from authoritar-ianism to cruelty which all those authoritarian believers pursue light-heartedly'.[63] According to Leroy, pure logics applied to politics led directly to terror. The extremist 'creed' was of a religious nature, which showed itself by the frequent use of terms such as 'schism', 'betrayal' and 'dissidence'.[64] When Lenin emphasized the necessity for compromise in his work about 'left-wing radicalism', this was – contrary to the protestations of its apologetics – a trick but not a pledge for approaching another, even though just as legitimate, posi-tion. Typically, Lenin was making concessions to his irreconcilable opponents while mercilessly fighting against the least deviation in the socialist camp.

Every means that seemed suitable for reaching his goal was seen as justified. This proved Lenin's moral inferiority.[65]

Lenin himself did not at all see himself as an extremist. Without using the word, he denounced the 'childhood illness'[66] of his opponents in the communist tendencies of Western Europe. Leroy characterized Lenin as a 'pocket-sized Talleyrand'. From this viewpoint, he could – in contradiction to his earlier statements – say: 'No extremism whatsoever: Lenin relinquishes extremism to general contempt'.[67] The writer H.G. Wells (1866–1946) who, during his stay in Moscow, had a long interview with Lenin, took Lenin's 'anti-dogmatism' at face value. He had developed wonderfully in recent times and written equally profound and subtle analyses 'against the extravaganzas of his own extremists'.[68] At the same time, Wells also realized that there was a strange synthesis between the undeniably strategic flexibility and an immovable Marxist dogmatism: 'Until today, the entire Bolshevist government seems to harmonize its actions with its convictions, which its followers accept with an absolutely religious fanaticism'.[69]

## 2 Extremism and Italian fascism

Those political tendencies and groupings that had embodied the 'extreme right' during the nineteenth century were rarely called 'extremists' after World War I. Merrheim and Leroy had drawn that parallel, but the ultra-monarchists serving as the object of point-by-point comparisons were not given the focus of attention. The main danger to freedom was Bolshevism. This picture began to change after former socialist Benito Mussolini (1883–1945) had arrived at the control centres of power after his spectacular March on Rome in autumn 1922. Fascism, until then little noticed as a political phenomenon, now moved more and more into the focus of attention. In spite of the open ideological borrowings from revolutionary syndicalism and socialism, it soon became the incarnation of the new extreme right. Thus, the anti-fascist Italian opposition borrowed the extremism formula.

As in Germany, the neologisms 'estremismo' and 'estremisti' had reached the political language via the influence of French and English news agencies. In the big conservative Milan newspaper *Corriere della Sera*, for example, 'estremisti' (between quotation marks) appeared for the first time on 1 April 1917 in an article based on information from the *Daily Telegraph* correspondent in Saint Petersburg.[70] Later, the Lenin people were regularly mentioned as the embodiment of that kind of extremism that favoured a separate peace and, therefore, of autocratic Prussian militarism.[71] The correspondent of the socialist daily newspaper *Avanti*, who had reported with great goodwill about the 'pacifist' forces in Russia by March 1917, complained about the 'rowdy tone' of journals such as those on *Le Temps* (the most popular French daily newspaper of the time), *The Times* and *Corriere della Sera*, which blacklisted those whom they called 'extremists', 'demagogues' and 'anarchists' in the most impertinent fashion. When reading the various telegrams in Italian,

French and English newspapers, one realized that the government and the leading circles of the liberals and the conservatives were doing everything humanly possible to gain the support of the other social classes and the armed forces against the so-called 'extremist'[72] tendencies among the workers' committee in Saint Petersburg.

Whereas in the following months the Socialist Party newspaper obviously avoided using the term 'extremisti' for Lenin and his followers, who were approved of, *Il Popolo d'Italia*, Mussolini's interventionist organ, denounced the 'estremisti russi' as 'agenti della Germania'.[73] Later, the future 'Duce' interpreted the July troubles supported by the Leninists as the 'infamous betrayal manoeuvre of the extremists in the service of Germany'.[74] When a delegation of the all-Russian Soviet visited Italy in August 1917, they were enthusiastically welcomed in a provincial town by Lenin followers with calls of 'Hail Lenin!' Mussolini commented on this – in the light of the situation in Russia – naive reaction by the remark that 'extremism' was the 'prevailing condition of the soul of the Socialist supporters'.[75] A few months later, after the coup d'état by Lenin and Trotzky, he spoke of the formation of 'a stable extreme regime'.[76] The German–Austrian offensive against Italy (peaking in the Italian debacle of Caporetto) had been furthered by the 'Russian military inactivity': 'the power takeover by the Russian extremists may mean a separate peace'.[77]

The 'estremismo' formula did not become a key word of the 'fasci italiani di combattimento' founded in a hall on the Piazza San Sepolcro in Milan on 23 March 1919. Nonetheless, the fascists of the first hour sometimes employed it as a fighting term against the extreme left. In a proclamation by the central committee of the 'fasci di combattimento' addressed at the 'pro-letariato italiano' (27 April 1920), it said: 'Workers! [ ... ] Let the general strike of Turin wanted by the swindlers of Socialist extremism, which ended after twenty days with the greatest defeat of the proletariat, be a warning to you'.[78]

In Italy – as in France – during the first few years after World War I, the words 'extremism'/'extremismo' and 'extremist'/'extremista' remained closely connected to the utmost left wing of the political spectrum. In comparisons between communism and fascism, the former at times stood for 'extremists of the left', the latter for 'fanatics of the right'[79] without a common terminological denominator. At the Paris Peace Conference at the beginning of 1920, the British Prime Minister David Lloyd George (1863–1945) had warned against driving the masses of the people into the 'arms of the extremists'.[80] He was speaking of the Bolshevists who had begun with the foundation of the Comintern in March 1919, decidedly aiming at world revolution. Lloyd George commented on his particular concern about the situation in Germany, where the extreme left had practised the revolution, and council governments had taken over power in Munich and Bremen from time to time. A transition of Germany to 'Spartacism' might evoke a threat to the Western democracies. The risks were also obvious in Italy, where large parts of the socialist workers' movement favoured the Bolshevist revolution project. The 'massimalisti' (maximalists), who favoured the Russian Revolution, had left their mark on the party conference of the socialists in October 1919. As the only one in Europe, the Socialist Party of Italy announced its annexation to the Third International and passed a new party statute with the demand for a violent conquest of power and the foundation of a 'dictatorship of the entire proletariat'.[81] The revolutionary socialist union Confederazione Generale del Lavoro (CGL) made a tremendous acquisition of members in the years 1919/ 1920. In 1919, there were 1,663 strikes in industry and 1,881 in 1920; furthermore, there were 208 strikes by the union-organized country workers in 1921 and another 189 in 1920. From September to November 1919, there was a wave of land occupation in central and southern Italy. The following year, a number of factories were occupied. The socialists were convinced that it was only a matter of time until a revolution would break out similar to that in Russia.[82] In the light of the situation, large parts of the conservative and liberal bourgeoisie were fixated on the danger from the left but tended to overestimate it by far. The extremism formula remained reserved for Bolshevism for several years. Still in 1923, an Italian dictionary defined the 'Franco-Italian neologisms "estremismo" and "estremisti" as synonyms for dogmatic socialists, intransigenti, thus people absolutely opposing war'.[83]

Yet even before the dictionary was published, many observers who feared for their freedom and possessions had expanded their concern to Italian fascism as a new danger additionally triggered by the communist threat. In the early stages of the 'fasci' founded by Mussolini, the tendency still existed among liberal circles in Italy to view fascism, with its nebulous ideology and its chameleon-like changing appearance, as a transitional phenomenon triggered by philo-Bolshevism. There was a tendency to not completely deny it some positive effects as a counterweight, this attitude being responsible for adding a certain respectability to fascism. The assaults and bloody deeds of the paramilitary 'squadri d'azione', which quickly rose in number and intensity in the years 1920–22, were judged much too mildly by many observers while they simultaneously tended to dramatize the violence of the extreme left. When the fascists ravaged the headquarters of the socialists and the unions in Livorno, Genoa and other big cities, destroyed factories, set fire to the building of the newspaper *Avanti* in Milan and chased away the local socialist government after the badly organized general strike in August 1922, which cost the left party a large number of votes, the conservative and liberal press reacted reticently, partially even favourably.[84] The attitude of resistance towards the fascists grew only after they had begun to exert systematic pressure on many municipalities, removed elected representatives from their positions and took over the city councils. After the efficiently planned propaganda coup of the 'March on Rome', many early silent sufferers and defenders on the liberal side began to realize the movement's unlimited demand for power.

Political opponents of fascism borrowed – aside from the neologisms 'totalitario' and 'totalitarismo'[85] – the extremism formula to stigmatize it as

an anti-constitutional movement and to place it at one level with Bolshevism.[86] By his analysis of fascism, one of the pioneers of the totalitarianism concept[87] made an important contribution to the development of the
term 'extremism'. This was the Catholic priest Luigi Sturzo, who was born in
the Sicilian town of Caltagirone in 1871. He had been the mayor of his home
town for many years when he founded the People's Party ('partito popolare')
after the model of the German Zentrum Party at the turn of 1918/19. Its
foundation became possible after Pope Pius IX had practically abolished the
ban on Catholics and particularly clerics participating in party politics, the
'non expedit', formulated after the triumph of the Italian national movement
with its strictly laeicistic attitude. Already in the parliamentary elections of 16
November 1919, the People's Party, with 20.6 per cent of the votes and 100
seats, had taken office in the representatives chamber, and thus Sturzo became
one of the leading political figures in Italy for several years.[88] After the
'March on Rome', the role of Mussolini's most important opponent was his
for a short while.

From the beginning, Sturzo had no illusions about the fascists and criticized the naivety of the so-called 'Klerikofascisti'. Simultaneously, he warned
against egalitarian–Utopian social experiments, which also had followers on
the left wing of his unusually wide-ranging party. When Sturzo explained the
principles of his 'centrismo', his central course, in the party newspaper *Il Popolo
Nuovo* on 26 August 1923, this determined an interior as well as an exterior
direction. The text sheds light on Sturzo's anti-extremist/anti-totalitarian
understanding of freedom.

The political programme of 'centrismo' was 'temperato e non estremo',[89] as
it was founded on Christian ethics and fundamentally refuted the possibility
of a condition of perfection and an absolute good on earth. Neither socialists
nor fascists shared this world view:

> The Socialists are saying: evil derives from the bourgeois condition of
> society; one must remove it, then a new order will come about: they are
> extremists, since they reach such an absolute opinion. The Fascists are
> saying: the nation will only prosper if it is 'fascisized' in its foundations,
> its thinking and its social life: they are tending toward an absolutum and
> are also like those 'extremists'. Even if we, out of sheer laziness, call the
> ones extremists of the left and the others extremists of the right, and this
> in reference to bourgeois society, so the 'monopolistic', 'absolutist',
> 'extremist' tendency is still the nature of their movement.[90]

Sturzo was far from ignoring the ideological differences of the extreme
movements. Yet the 'habit' of placing them according to their predominant
social carrier groups at the two opposing wings of the political spectrum, in
his opinion still obscured the fact of their essentially common ground. This
was that both tendencies, so different in their content, claimed their own
world view to be absolute and denied the legitimacy of any other. They expanded

the political sphere to all areas of life, no longer allowing anything private, and wanted to determine people's entire life according to the maxims of their doctrines. With the historically grown and the different social forces, there could therefore be no substantial compromise. The complete variety of cultural forms of expression appeared as weeds in need of elimination; the only thing that had a right to exist was whatever corresponded to the unalterable principles of a comprehensive world view.

Sturzo rejected the strivings for the big self-contained political condition that penetrated all areas of life and was shaped according to an ideal, a kind of ideal state, for two reasons. First of all, it contradicted Christian faith to seek perfection here on earth. Second, history showed that such an endeavour was doomed to failure. Sturzo then introduced an important differentiation. He called striving for the absolute here on earth an 'estremismo programmatico e finalistico'. Extremism was therefore already established in its programmatic aim. It was to be distinguished from the 'estremismo di metodo' arising from this aim.[91] Here, he meant the instrumental investment that would have to be effected in order to reach such a high aim. Striving for ideal conditions appeared to him to be the expression of hubris and the authorization for action rich in sacrifice to be derived from it as a blazing political danger. Therefore, Sturzo pleaded for fundamentally renouncing revolutions and for outlawing violence as a legitimate political means.[92]

The anti-extremist Sturzo had to lay down his political leadership office in the same year by order of the Vatican. Pius XI disapproved of the priest's political commitment; the relationship between the Vatican and the People's Party had cooled considerably after Mussolini's takeover of power, also for strategic reasons.[93] In October 1924, Sturzo left Italy. After many years in exile in London and New York, he was to return to his homeland in 1946 as the then grand old man of Catholic Italian anti-fascism. In exile, he had belonged to the leading advocates of the totalitarian concept in which fascism and Bolshevism were placed at one level of comparison. Several monographs had come out of the reflection about the foundations of Church and state. Aside from Jacques Maritain, Sturzo is seen today as one of the most important representatives of Christian personalism.[94] His accomplishments in the realm of political and sociological theory have received much recognition,[95] yet his contribution to the development of the concept of extremism seems to have gone unnoticed. This is actually not so surprising, as the reflections of 1923 were not taken up again in his systematic later works. Instead, 'totalitarianism' served as a key word in the analysis of ideological extreme movements.[96]

## 3 Extremes in the political language of the Weimar Republic

At the time of the Weimar Republic, the extremism formula did not spread in Germany as much as in France, Italy and the Anglo-Saxon countries. In the press reports of German daily newspapers about the Russian Revolution, it typically showed up when some information from foreign correspondents was used.[97] The term also occurs in the translations of French books by experts on Germany such as Henri Lichtenberger[98] or the Russian emigrants living in Paris.[99] When experts on France reported about the politics of the neighbouring country, they occasionally resorted to its use of the language, transforming it into German. Accordingly, Eugen Quendt differentiated between the 'moderate' and the 'extremist' direction oriented on Moscow in a report about the Socialist Congress of Tours (December 1920).[100]

In the early press reports regarding Italian fascism, the term 'estremisti', which was popular in Italy, was also sometimes translated into German. The results of the Italian parliamentary elections of May 1921 were summarized by the *Frankfurter Zeitung* in the following manner: 'The extremists of the right as well as of the left, Fascists as well as Communists, have experienced a decisive defeat'.[101] The term for Lenin's 'revolutionary totalism',[102] coined by Alfons Paquet, the Russia correspondent of the *Frankfurter Zeitung*, did not meet with a great response. This is how Paquet described the Bolshevists' attempt at founding a new empire of 'democratic republics' in Europe and Asia. The neologism bore a similarity to the term 'totalitarianism' later coined in Italy, which served to designate a new type of regime that could not suitably be expressed by the ancient Greek state form terminology of 'tyrannis' and 'despotism'.

The majority of German authors spoke of the 'extremes' or used the term 'radicalism' for designating the right as well as the left of the political spectrum.[103] This terminology was not common in France and the other Romance countries, as there the older meaning of the radicalism formula being connected to nineteenth-century liberalism had asserted itself.[104]

The term 'extremism' was occasionally used in the academic use of the language as an analytical category, besides 'radicalism'. This is shown in a contribution by the Catholic theologian Franz Keller (1873–1944), who held the Chair for Moral Theology at the Theological Department of Freiburg University. The article in the *Staatslexikon* (1931) drew a clear dividing line between radicalism and extremism. Certainly, radicalism as a 'spiritual attitude' reaching all the way to the roots of things was compatible with the striving for a step-by-step change in the existing state. 'Extremism', on the other hand,

is similar to radicalism only in so far as, like the latter, it also demands radical change of the existing conditions but, in contrast to radicalism, it ends with these foundation-toppling demands. For translating them into practice, extremism only offers the alternative 'all or nothing' and, since it is impossible to immediately reach the goal completely, it feels relieved of the arduous step-by-step changing of the conditions. Extremism is the flight from the burdensome responsibility of creative activity, it is a widespread illness in all the practical areas of life. Therefore, extremism is to be rejected wherever it shows up, as it destroys without rebuilding. It is particularly harmful in the areas of politics, economic and social ethics, where it pairs up with rigorism.[105]

Yet this academic differentiation was in no way gained from the prevailing use of the language of the time. The attribute 'radical' was usually applied to regime-critical to -hostile wings and immediately placed at the ends of the political spectrum. A parliamentary speech about France's policy towards Germany and its effect on German politics by Gustav Stresemann (1878–1929) on 22 November 1923 gives an illustrative example:

> The French Prime Minister has recently drawn the attention of the German Government to the development of the conditions in Germany and expressed his concern about radical tendencies spreading in Germany, namely, as it seems to have been called, about radical tendencies of a nationalist kind. It would be foolish to try to deny that the development in Germany is drifting toward the extreme. Aside from the phenomena in public life, the recent elections have also shown this, which makes one realize that people everywhere are turning toward this extreme. Yet the kind and the cause of this development are also completely clear. If the French Prime Minister and French politics had the sincere wish to ensure the stability of conditions in Germany on the basis of a constitutional democracy, they would foremost be able to take care of the matter, making a development toward the extreme and to radicalism in Germany unnecessary. (Very true! In the centre.) Which, after all, are lastly the foundations of these developments? The misery of their circumstances drives people to the extreme. Communism derives its strongest support from social misery, and right-wing radicalism draws its strongest support from the politics of constant national humiliation the present German Reich and, so far, every German government has been exposed to, irregardless of its political attitude.[106]

Hereby, radicalism and extremes went hand-in-hand. At the same time, the communists' hostile attitude towards the Republic was placed on an equal footing with that of the 'right-wing radicals'.

The liberal-left *Vossische Zeitung* had addressed the interaction of the wings in an early contribution on the topic (17 October 1922) under the heading 'Fascists and communists': 'The Communists have once again proved themselves to be the best helpmates and friends of the right-wing radicals'.[107] It mentioned communist 'meeting crashers' who systematically forced their way into the party meeting halls of their political opponents. The author for one included the 'German nationals' with the right-wing radicals, who benefited from 'indignation over the brutalities'. The former had introduced an application to the Reichstag for the intensification of the right of assembly and taken advantage of the situation to settle an account with the German government. 'Behind this parliamentarian action' the author saw the work of those groups 'who see their master in Italian Fascism. They demand that the German National People's Party should leave the parliaments if they rejected the announced agitation applications and "gather all those forces in the country who are aware of their Germanness and willing to sacrifice everything for people and fatherland"'. Obviously 'fear of the Communists was to be used to first of all undermine the position of the government, thus to prepare the ground for further Fascist experiments'. The author referred to the events in Italy and emphasized the 'soulmateship' of German and Italian 'fascists': 'The German Fascists are rather servile toward their Italian masters in the same manner as the Communists are toward their Bolshevist lords and masters'.

That not only the followers of the Nationalsozialistische Deutsche Arbeiterpartei (NSDAP) but also those of the 'German National People's Party' (DNVP) favoured Mussolini's course in Italy became obvious from the Reichstag speech by the German national representative Oskar Hergt (1869–1967) on 20 November 1923. Hergt pleaded for dispelling the concern of foreign countries regarding stability in Germany by creating an authoritarian government: 'The German people is – if it could ever tolerate a parliamentarian government at all – in no way ready for this today'.[108] In the light of the kind of government the DNVP had in mind, the fear of foreign countries of such an 'overly extreme radicalism' will diminish, as the DNVP would steer clear 'of such a most extreme radicalism'.[109] In spite of the unintentional play on words with the terms 'extreme' and 'radical', this may hardly have contributed to ease the concerns of outside observers.

The crisis year 1923, with attempted coups and revolts from the left and the right, was followed by a period of relative stabilization, with the forces hostile towards the Republic losing some of their resonance. This changed again with the world economic crisis of 1929/30. Again the 'radicals' and the 'extremes' stood in the focus of attention. However, the political language of the forces who carried the Republic hardly changed compared with the crisis-prone years when the Weimar Republic was still in its infancy.[110]

The growth of the political wings increased the violence of public arguments. Those warning against radicalism clashed with those recruiting for radicalism. From an undoubtedly loyal perspective towards the Republic, the Prussian Minister of the Interior, Karl Severing (1875–1952), explained the political condition of Germany to Austrian readers. The aftermath of losing the war and the world economic crisis established the 'breeding ground for radicalism'. Communists and National Socialists did not gain members 'due to their programmes', for these are Utopian and confused, it is much more the expression of the mood of desolation that pushes for something different without questioning whether this 'something different' is also 'something better'. Although this mood is shaping the 'spiritual state of mind of broad circles of the German people' and these victims of crisis 'had almost unanimously fallen prey to the radical parties', the Prussian politician sought to dispel the concern of foreign countries about his country's slipping into chaos. Of course, the 'agitation of the radical parties [ ... ] had brought on considerable tension'. However, 'the rough propaganda of Communists and National Socialists [ ... ] with their forms of threats and coercion set up in such a way to intimidate their opponents and the indifferent masses, faking a strength which does not correspond to the power of the party apparatus and the followers in the voting masses'. The respective governments were strongly determined to put a stop to the 'political morals going to the bad'. A civil war was in no way to be expected. The great majority did not want 'any catastrophes but peaceful restoration'. Germany's condition would remain difficult for some time to come; however, the German people had not lost their 'self-confidence, their craftiness and their faith in a better future'.[111]

Thomas Mann (1875–1955) defended the Weimar state against the political 'obscuredom' of 'radicalism' in another way. Of course, one had to at least admit that the communists were fulfilling the function of a social 'conscience corrective', whereas the 'swastikadom' could merely be seen as an 'uprising of resentment'. Both movements, however, were matched in their being mere 'surrogates of a truly pious religious worldview'. No matter how one felt about them: '"they do not exhaust the possibilities of the meaning of life". To find it, to set it as the goal in new wording, is the task of intellectual Europe'.[112]

The romantic restorative conservatives had looked after this task in a manner that hardly corresponded to Mann's and Severing's political intentions. From this perspective, one could work out the parallels between Bolshevism and fascism and in them find the 'same will to world development and of actual progress' at work. Wilhelm Schramm (1898–1984) pleaded for including the will, which was directed against the individualism of the 'liberalist parliamentarian development'.[113] Yet Germany, which was 'divided into a Fascist and a Communist denomination', 'could not find its unity under either extreme'[114] but only under a new type of 'synthesis', the realization of a Christian "middle"'.[115] The 'world revolution' was inescapable but had to be steered on to a constructive course by 'radical politics':

> A general change of mind is necessary to completely eliminate and overcome the worldview of liberality and its false individualism that was perhaps appropriate yesterday. For this, a general, universal and orderly worldview must first of all be created intellectually – a 'theory', a comprehensive doctrine which gives clear principles of order. In Germany, some inner colonization must go hand in hand with a radical 'inner mission' building a new community which all attempts have been aiming at from the romantic period (most of all Fichte's 'Geschlossener Handelsstaat') via Socialism and Communism to today's National Socialism.[116]

'Radical politics' was thought of as a 'radical synthesis between individualism and Socialism', which 'would overcome both in the true radicalism of moderation and the middle'.[117] The political order of the future consisted of a Christian state of classes, a community of believers filled with the spirit of the commandment of brotherliness.

In a social democracy[118] shaken by ideological crises and inner party conflicts, the 'radicalism of moderation and the middle' was countered by the pledge for a 'positive radicalism'. August Rathmann (1895–1995), the editor of the *Neue Blätter für den Sozialismus*, the social democratic yet in its intellectual profile very independent organ, pleaded for taking advantage of 'the science based on a Marxist economy analysis'[119] to force back the 'influence of the liberal spirit and the economy'[120] and 'to contemplate aiming at a new order of life' with 'a positively radical attitude'.[121] Apparently, this did not refer to the overcoming of parliamentarian democracy but a fundamental transformation of economy and society. The 'protest movement of National Socialism'[122] equally directed towards individualism and materialism was doomed to fail, as its 'negative radicalism' only offered make-believe solutions but no effective prescriptions for 'healing' the world.[123] The author's hope was deceptive in that he thought that the 'profound shaking up in National Socialism of the most extensive masses of people who had hardly ever been touched by politics before' would offer 'a great opportunity to Socialist politics of the coming years'.[124] Instead, those who had in mind giving the 'ailing corpus of the people' a radical dose of another persuasion[125] came to power.

## 4 Extremes in Hitler's writings and speeches of the 'Kampfzeit'

The National Socialists understood themselves as the advocates of a positive radicalism, in fact, of a positive extreme. This can be shown on the basis of Adolf Hitler's (1889–1945) political language. In the course of the restoration of his party after the failed putsch attempt of November 1923, he developed from a 'drummer' into an irreproachable 'leader' of the National Socialist movement. The reports handed down from earlier times show a clear line from the year 1924 on. Hitler had read a great deal during his imprisonment at Landsberg, written the first volume of *Mein Kampf* and thereby secured, rationalized and systematized his own political ideas. He essentially held on to the thus gained 'Weltanschauung' without fail to the very end.[126]

One particularly convincing passage is found in the last chapter of the first volume of *Mein Kampf*, where Hitler describes the nature of the National Socialist movement. The essential task is the 'nationalization of the masses'. It could

> never take place through half measures, through the weak emphasis of a so-called objectivity viewpoint but through a ruthless and fanatical, one-sided adjustment to the chosen goal. This then means that one cannot make a people 'national' in the sense of our present bourgeoisie, meaning with so and so many restrictions, but only nationalist with all the vehemence that is inherent in the extreme. Poison is broken by antidote, and only the meaninglessness of a bourgeois mind can see the middle line as the path to Heaven.[127]

Hence, the National Socialist doctrine was seen as an extreme and as the antidote that was to heal the ailing 'corpus of the people'. If Hitler had finished the thought, he would probably have recoiled from it, as it is well known that an antidote only works in small, exactly measured amounts. Instead, it was his intention to convert as many Germans as possible to National Socialism, which – to remain with this image – would have meant killing them all with an overdose.

In the second volume of *Mein Kampf*, written in 1925/26, Hitler determined the political extreme in a way that avoided the contradiction of this metaphor. In a kind of National Socialist doctrine of virtue, he differentiated between three 'big classes'. The first consisted of the 'extreme of the best of mankind [ ... ], good in the sense of all virtues, particularly outstanding through courage and willingness to sacrifice'.[128] Opposite it stood 'the extreme of the worst ejection of humanity, evil in the sense of the presence of all egotistical impulses and vices'. Thus, virtue was located at one of the extremes. The middle, on the other hand, was represented by a social 'class' that 'neither showed glowing heroism nor the most common criminal attitude'. Hitler linked this social ethical typology to a scheme of historical development:

> The times of the rise of the corpus of a people stand out, yes, exist only through the absolute leadership of the most extreme part. The times of a normal, balanced development or a stable condition are marked by and exist through the noticeable predominance of the elements of the middle, whereby both of the extremes balance each other, respectively, or rather cancel each other out. The times of the fall of the corpus of a people are determined by the predominance of the worst elements.[129]

The last-cited passage of the text is emphasized by italics as a particularly important aphorism in terms of content. Here, National Socialism is not an antidote but an extreme that personifies virtue and looms over the lukewarm, half and weak-willed middle, therefore being the strongest contradiction to the other extreme, the incarnation of vices. The middle 'would only then make its appearance felt when the two extremes link themselves to one another in mutual struggle'. If one of the extremes wins, the middle will subjugate itself or will at least not put up resistance: 'for the mass of the middle itself will never fight'. Hitler's hate for the bourgeoisie found its expression in the 'hate for the principle of the middle'.[130]

In Hitler's eyes, World War I had disturbed the balance of the three classes he described 'insofar as that one – while respecting all of the sacrifices of the middle – still must realize that it had led to an almost complete bleeding to death of the extreme of best humanness'.[131] The weakening of the one extreme allowed the opposite to shoot up: 'Now the elements of meanness, malice and cowardice, in short, the mass of the extreme of evil, weighed more heavily than in earlier times'. Unreasonable laws and the renunciation of applying the law of war had, among others, caused the extreme of evil to survive the war safe and sound. 'The well-preserved scum of the corpus of our people then made the revolution, and it could only make it for the extreme of the best elements no longer stood opposite it: – It was no longer alive'. Not the German people but 'the trash of its deserters, pimps, etc. that shun the light'[132] had accordingly produced the Weimar Republic. 'The international Jew'[133] acted as organizer and pulled the strings. The revolution had been made

> by a minority of the worst elements [ ... ], with all of the Marxist parties immediately rallying behind them. The revolution itself supposedly is of moderate nature, which incurs it the hostility of the fanatical extremists. These then begin to fire off machine guns and hand grenades, occupy state buildings, in short, threaten the moderate revolution. In order to ban the terror of such further development, an armistice is signed between the bearers of the new condition and the followers of the old one, to now be able to carry on the fight against the extremists together. The result is that this way the enemies of the Republic have stopped fighting against the Republic as such and assist in forcing those to the ground who, themselves, even though from entirely different premises, are also enemies of this Republic.[134]

The unequal alliance of the Republicans and the right-wing opponents of the Republic triggered a neutralization of the extremes: 'Gradually, the Spartakist barricade fighters and the nationalist fanatics and idealists bleed to death, respectively, and to just that extent to which the extremes annihilated each other, the mass of the middle won, as always'. So the 'corruption residue'[135] of the Weimar Republic could become reinforced and the regime gain stability. However, with the National Socialist movement, the positive extreme which had, to a large degree, been destroyed in World War I, had risen anew to lead the German people out of the Jewish–Marxist party quagmire.

This terminology and the interpretation of history frequently returned in the speeches of the 'Kampfzeit'. At an NSDAP meeting in Plauen/Vogtland, Hitler recommended to his movement to take the 'path of the extreme'. 'World history' had 'not come about through half-measures'. [ ... ] Our movement is to draw people who are willing to stand up for their ideal ruthlessly to the end'.[136] Later, it was said that the shaping of a new 'corpus of the people' called for the 'working out of a new national thought which was able to concentrate the extremes, a new form of national thought in which someday also the large army of the international proletariat would see its salvation and spiritual well-being'.[137] This was aimed at the workforce that was to be won over for National Socialism. Yet there was also a certain common ground with parts of the workers' movement. They had recognized the reprehensibility of the system that had come about after World War I: 'Seven years after 1918 we can say that we have been on the decline piece by piece. This is a sign that there is something amiss in Germany. Only the two extremes from the left and the right are saying that there must be a stand made against it'.[138] Beyond that, ideological elements of the opposite extreme could be brought to fruition in a new kind of connection. The task of the National Socialist movement consisted of bringing together the two 'worlds of thought': that of the national bourgeoisie and of 'international Marxism. National Socialism seeks to unite these two extremes'.[139] Hence, National Socialism also meant breaking with the traditional political right. Therefore, Hitler declared war equally on 'today's camps of the right and the left'.[140]

The new ideological synthesis between right and left which National Socialism claimed to personify was, however, not to be mistaken for the middle path. As he had already done in *Mein Kampf*, in a speech in February 1928, Hitler explicitly turned against the 'so highly praised middle path between the right and the left. [ ... ]. World history was not made by middle paths but by determined battle. History did not know semi-truths'.[141]

According to Hitler's understanding, National Socialism with its 'Weltanschauung' had a decisive advantage in the competition against all political competitors. Accordingly, in a speech on 4 November 1925, he attacked the 'comedy-like behaviour' of the parties that were loyal to the Republic. They remained blocked from bringing forth 'mass-suggestive, eruptive evolutions from the souls of the people',[142] as their programme, after all, was 'moderately bourgeois and radically subdued'. National Socialism, on the other hand, personified a 'new Weltanschauung', a new kind of connection of socialist and nationalist elements. Socialists fought '"fanatically for the rights of man"', and "nationalists stimulated to the utmost" the fanatical will and the divine faith of the people, just as in the anti-Napoleon Wars of Freedom'.[143]

The National Socialist movement received a boost from the world economic crisis. Now, concrete considerations were legally given to the possibilities of a takeover of power. In one of his contributions to the *Illustrierter Beobachter*, Hitler discussed the problem of the inner heterogeneity of the Austrian home guard and drew consequences from it for the National Socialist movement. In the light of the instrumentalization of the home guard by the 'bourgeois parties', he admonished his fellow party members: 'And never forget that any dissolution of Marxism must, parallel to it, bring about the dissolution of the bourgeois party world! We are not a part of the party life of the nation but we must force ourselves to the extreme confession that the nation is our movement!'[144] The 'extreme confession' included the identity of movement and nation, which left no room for the development of other parties.

The party system stood for the 'extreme of despair', National Socialism for the positive 'extreme of faith'. Beyond that, there was a negative 'extreme of faith',[145] – Marxism. Marxism and National Socialism were the 'two extremes between whom everything that is located in the middle will be crushed. [ ... ] Everything that lies in-between will either be obliterated or will have to move toward the one or the other extreme'.[146]

Hitler consistently kept to this line until the takeover of power. In a programmatic essay for the magazine *Deutschlands Erneuerung*, he once more summarized the essential points of his world view. According to it, the November

Revolution was to be ascribed to 'our people being penetrated by a doctrine' which 'in its final effects has also become the cause of our unspeakable present misery – Marxism. The most essential basic feature of this doctrine invented by some Jews, which accommodates the more evil traits of man, is the denial of the value of the personality. Marxism sets the masses, its 'factory ware' as Schopenhauer called the majorities, in place of the aristocratic principle as it was. 'The individual is replaced by the number'.[147] The destruction of the personality would lead to the gradual poisoning of the corpus of the people, a process that has come a long way in Germany: 'International Jewry, the racial tuberculosis of the peoples, slowly but surely destroys the basic pillars of our people, its race and its culture. In the most different varieties, as Social Democracy, U.S.P.D. and K.P.D. until far into the ranks of the so-called "bourgeoisie", the Marxist doctrine rules politics, culture and the economy'. All the attempts made by the national conservative circles towards the end of the Weimar Republic to avert the pernicious development had only given evidence to their helplessness. Anyway, it was an 'insane' undertaking to 'fight against an epidemic that can only be exterminated by the strongest extreme by means of state power. Marxist internationalism is only to be broken by a fanatically extreme nationalism of the highest social ethics and morals'.[148]

Thus, with National Socialism, the saving extreme had arrived on the political stage, whose intervention alone could prevent the threat of destruction. A negative extreme could only be fought successfully by a positive one. This extreme had taken over the reigns of power on 30 January 1933.

# 6 Extreme terms in the political language of German ideocracies

## 1 About the political language in ideocracies

However large the differences were, the two autocracies in Germany, the National Socialist (NS) regime and the Sozialistische Einheitspartei Deutschlands (SED) regime, can be differentiated from other forms of non-democratic systems as ideocracies. Presumably, the conservative historian Heinrich Leo (1799–1878) from Halle coined this expression in his *Naturlehre des Staates* for those regimes which, similar to the theocracies already known from Antiquity, placed themselves completely in the service of a fanatic doctrine of salvation.[1] In the nineteenth century, Johann Caspar Bluntschli contributed to the circulation of the term[2] which was to play a certain role in the discussions concerning the systems of the twentieth century seen as 'totalitarian'.[3] In recent times, authors such as Peter Bernholz, Jaroslav Piekalkievicz and Alfred Wayne Penn have revived it in order to reduce the ruling entities oriented along a 'monistic' ideology to a common denominator.[4]

The political language of ideocracies is oriented along the guidelines of a state ideology with a great range in its message as well as an exclusive claim to interpretation and explanation. Official communication is marked by a system of language regulations with more or less exactly defined terms. The ideology and propaganda centre constantly endeavours to 'drum' the formulas and versions of the state's ideology into people's heads as it were, defending the unity and the purity of the ideological interpretations against 'falsifications' and 'deviations'. Whoever publicly expresses undesirable opinions is threatened with draconian punishment. Radio, press as well as book and magazine publishing are subject to strict control.

Concerning the history of terms of the political extremes, the contents connected to them receive a respective place in the dogma systems and definitions of ideocracies. Nonetheless, here too, important differences between the NS regime and the SED regime must be taken into account from the start.[5] The NS system was much more strongly focused on the 'Weltanschauung' of the 'Fuehrer'. The SED regime was based on an ideological system, which (especially after the death of the revolutionary cult figures Lenin and Stalin) far exceeded the degree of formalization of the NS ideology, particularly as it did not even come close to reaching the unity and the uniformity of the Marxism–Leninism of Moscow coinage in its comparably short time of politically practical effectiveness.

For the NS system, the following history of reception is foremost oriented at the almost completely handed down and carefully edited speeches and notes of its chief propagandist, Joseph Goebbels, who had been in closest contact with Hitler throughout the entire period. As far as the political language and propaganda of the SED regime are concerned, the dogma structure of Marxism–Leninism is fundamental. Foremost, the official ideological compendia as well as the respective current interpretations and attempts at legitimation of the SED theory organ *Einheit* constitute meaningful sources.

## 2 NS regime

In the 1937 edition of Meyer's *Lexicon*, it said under the entry 'extremism': 'Views and actions of radical politicians (extremists); National Socialism was called e. by its opponents, in order to disparage it'.[6] In as far as the National Socialists as well as their 'Fuehrer' felt themselves to be the incarnation of a positive extreme,[7] they could only understand this label as a title of honour. What is more, they hardly ever missed an opportunity to document their own will to radicalism and utmost political determination. What could be shown for the 'Kampfzeit' by Hitler's writings and speeches, for the time after the 'Machtergreifung' was documented especially in the speeches by Joseph Goebbels (1897–1945), the chief propagandist of the 'Third Reich'. In contrast to Hitler's speeches, these are thoroughly documented and can also be appropriately supplemented with the now completely edited *Goebbels Diaries*.

In the 'Angriff', Goebbels interpreted the result of the Reichstag election of 5 March 1933 as a sweeping empowerment for the radical programme of the NS movement:

> In all his speeches before 5 March, the Reich-Chancellor has repeatedly emphasized that he does not want to present illusions to the people, that he rejects lying and swindling, that he needs four years to put Germany back on its feet, within and without, that it is necessary to work and to act in these four years and also not to shrink from radical cuts into abscesses of public life. None could have any doubts that this government was determined to eradicate every kind of Marxism in Germany root and branch, that it had the intention to restructure the entire state and economics apparatus, to cleanse the administration and to clean the atmosphere of the stench of pestilence of party-political corruption. All this had been said clearly, openly and unequivocally. And for this the German people have given Hitler and his men free reign.[8]

When students in Berlin set fire to a woodpile in front of the university shortly before midnight on 10 May 1933 to ostentatiously burn books with 'subversive' content removed from the libraries that had been written by 'Jews', 'Marxists' or other 'un-German' authors, the propaganda minister, who had arrived on the scene, acknowledged the incident as a symbolic act signalling that the 'age of an exaggerated Jewish intellectualism' had now come to an end. It had not been possible to dream on 30 January that 'Germany could be cleaned up as quickly and as radically as this'.[9]

Radicality and unconditionality stood for proof of the quality of a movement that wanted to make its 'Weltanschauung' into the foundation of the state without having it watered down:

> If someone objects: You are *radical!* – then we can only answer: Have we ever claimed that we were *not* radical? (amusement). When we are told: You are against the *Jews!* – then we can only answer: Well, had you assumed that we were *for* the Jews? (amusement). When we are told: You are too rigorous! You are too direct! You don't even make compromises! – then we can only answer: We have never left any doubts about this during our time of opposition. And I believe that this is why the German people have given us their allegiance. The people *want* it this way. The people are *fed up* with compromises! The people want to make *clear ship!*[10]

After the regime had been established, the priorities changed. Too 'radical' demands might now unsettle the population and undermine the credibility of the system. Inner party arguments raised the question of what deserved pre-eminence: the just conquered departmental structure of the state or the party? From the Nationalsozialistische Deutsche Arbeiterpartei (NSDAP) leadership's point of view, ministers as well as peasant leader (Reichsbauernführer) Richard Walter Darré appeared renitent by defending the autonomy of their departments against the interventions of the party.[11] Party representatives, on the other hand, insisted on their pre-eminence. In summer and autumn 1934, the conflict peaked. Goebbels emphasized the predominance of the party with Hitler, however, deeming the functionality of the state's institutional structure equally important in the sense of an efficient government and administration. On 24 October 1934, he noted in his diary: '"The party is in command of the state". The sentence will soon fall into oblivion. If it now turns into the opposite extreme, it will be the fault of the extremists'.[12] The advocates of an extreme position concerning the issue of the relationship between party and state at times stood for 'extremists'. Apart from that, one also spoke of the 'hopeless extremism'[13] of a misguided sectarian such as Ludendorff.

Conflicts of this kind also occurred in later years. On the occasion of the so-called 'clerics trials' in August 1937, Goebbels voiced his disappointment about Roland Freisler's behaviour, as the latter was too much oriented towards legal norms: 'He used to be a true radical. And today? A jurist like all the others'.[14] He blamed the German minister of the interior, Wilhelm Frick, for too much radicalism. The latter had made an 'unwise speech about minority issues': 'He sometimes gets a radical complex. This then permits him to be a bureaucrat for another year'.[15] One could then also overdo radicalism: Göring does 'not let himself be influenced by the hyper-radicals in the party'.[16] Later, one spoke of the 'sledge hammer methods of many hyper-radicals'.[17]

A certain moderation of programmatic statements did not contradict the basic radicality of NS 'ideology':

> You don't know the people well if you believe that you will have the people on your side in the long run with such radical demands. This was possible when we were still in opposition and had no power. Then, the people ran after us, since they said to themselves: The Nazis don't just *talk*, instead, when they have the power, they'll *do* something! However, if you make demands today and *cannot* fulfil them, and therefore you *will* not be able to fulfil them, then you will make the people restless and insecure in the long run. And your own party comrades as well. It is by no means necessary to make our own party comrades *more radical* than they *already* are! Now it is right to gradually draw the millions of people who still have no contact with the party towards our radical goals.[18]

An example of this was offered by the laws for the Jews: 'It is also not suffi-cient if our *party comrades* understand the laws for the Jews which were adopted yesterday, but the *people* must understand them. For we do not want to be a *party* government, we want to be a *people's* government'.[19] Demands by propaganda that was too radical could have further undesirable reactions. In the eyes of the propaganda minister, the Fuehrer's speech on 15 September 1935 was an example of the skilful reserve of radicality. In a circle of intimates, he recalled it as follows:

> We are hoping that – um, with these laws for the Jews, the possibility now exists to come to a tolerable relationship between the German and the Jewish people and – [amusement]. That's what I call *diplomacy*! That is *accomplishment*! However, had one said immediately afterwards: So, these are *today's* laws for the Jews; but don't you believe that that's everything, in the next month – there is *absolutely nothing* to be changed about it – next month come the next ones and in such a manner until you are sitting again in the ghetto, *dirt-poor* – well, then you shouldn't be surprised if the Jews mobilize the whole world against us. If you, however, give them a chance, a *low* life opportunity, then the Jews will say to themselves: Hah, if they now again start hate tirades abroad, things will get even worse; so then, children, let's be quiet, *perhaps* things will work out! [amusement, applause][20]

In this respect, there were occasional compromises which, in themselves, appeared to be false promises, but were in the long run supposed to lead to conditions that made compromises unnecessary. Hence, the propagandists who –

in an all too dutiful manner – publicly criticized compromising behaviour of the sort mentioned were admonished 'for you may be convinced: in the *long run* it will not be tolerated that *those* people who have been condemned to now and then make a compromise as it cannot *be done* otherwise, – that these people are then publicly attacked on account of it'.[21]

Yet it was not compromise orientation that was defined as a guideline for the propagandists of the movement but utmost radicality. The propaganda of National Socialism was to be oriented at the extreme, as its 'ideology' was revolutionary, and the penetrating and groundbreaking has the greatest effect on the people: 'This is why propaganda does not only have to be aggressive but also revolutionary. It must use *those* means that have a penetrating effect. And the extreme always has the most penetrating effect on the people. We cannot limit ourselves to parliamentize about things in sated comfort'.[22]

National Socialism and Bolshevism were seen as equally extreme. The positive extreme had the world historical task of annihilating its negative antithesis: 'A reconciliation of the two extremes cannot come about. Bolshevism must be destroyed if Europe is to regain its health'.[23]

Extremism was also needed in dealing with the Jews. In April 1938, Goebbels cynically wrote in his diary: 'We will take away from Berlin the character of a Jewish paradise. Jewish shops will be marked as such. In any event, we are now taking action more radically. The Fuehrer wants to gradually deport all of them. Have to negotiate with Poland and Romania. Madagascar would be the most suitable for them'.[24]

After the 'Reichskristallnacht', Goebbels reported to the Fuehrer. 'He agrees with everything. His views are totally radical and aggressive. The action itself went excellently. 17 dead. But no German property damaged'.[25] A few days later, they met for a conference at Göring's in order to assess the results and to discuss the 'Jewish issue':

> Hot arguments for the solution. I support a radical point of view. Funk is somewhat soft and lenient. Result: A contribution of one billion will be imposed on the Jews. They will be entirely eliminated from economic life without delay. [ … ] A whole number of other measures is planned. In any event, tabula rasa will now be made. I work splendidly together with Göring. He also goes at it harshly. The radical opinion has won out.[26]

With the creation of the Rome–Berlin axis, the relationship with the previously frequently criticized Italian allies improved. In his daily dictation, Goebbels praised Mussolini's 'very clever and radical action against profiteering and smuggling'[27] and characterized Roberto Farinacci, who was in Germany at that time, as a 'Fascist of the first hour, a radical polemicist, completely ungnawed by liberal trains of thinking'.[28] The blunt language of the 'Kampfzeit' also returned in public. The anti-Bolshevist propaganda, which had stopped following the Hitler–Stalin pact, was heard anew. In a speech in Linz, Goebbels damned what had been practised previously: If

England made a pact with Bolshevism, it would itself be the inferior, as the bourgeois forces were defeated if they cooperated with the Marxist powers:

> The radicals always devour the less radical, that's an old story. That was the same with us [amusement]. Never has a weakling devoured a strong one, it has always been the opposite: not the jackals devour the lions, but the lion devour the jackals. [ ... ] And if today the English camp of the plutocrats signs an agreement with Bolshevism in an attempt to save English world power through this unnatural bed-fellowship, this is a useless attempt on a useless object.[29]

In the face of the millions of (mostly Russian) prisoners of war, radicalism was called for as well: 'As it stands, we cannot feed the approximately three-and-a-half million prisoners that are in our hands, anyway. The population is definitely inclined toward a radical course of action against them'.[30] In contrast to this, when it came to dealing with the Catholic Church, Goebbels, for opportunistic reasons, pleaded for an adjournment until after the war. Bormann, too, had begun – so he writes in his diary on 18 August 1941 – 'to gradually realize that he is proceeding too radically in some respects and that radicalism can create more disadvantages than advantages in this realm, at least at the present'.[31]

This was different concerning the 'Jewish issue'. Here, after the attack on the Soviet Union, the time for a 'radical solution to the problem' had come.[32] The population, too, seemed ready to accept such politics.[33] Some months afterwards, he wrote once more: 'Now the situation has come to bring the Jewish issue to its final solution. Later generations will no longer have the energy and also not the instinctual awareness. Therefore, we are doing well in this case to proceed radically and consistently'.[34] That this solution amounted to mass destruction was indicated in the diary a little later:

> The Jews will be undergoing a punishment which is barbaric to be sure, but which they completely deserve. The prophesy that the Fuehrer has given them to think about due to their bringing about a new world war, is beginning to fulfil itself in the most terrible way. One cannot fall prey to sentimentality in these things. The Jews would destroy us if we did not fight them off. It is a fight of life and death between the Aryan race and the Jewish bacillus. No other government and no other regime could summon the power to generally solve this issue. Here, too, the Fuehrer is the perseverant pioneer and spokesman of a radical solution.[35]

In the ideology of the National Socialist, Jewry and Bolshevism represented an inseparable union. The pitiless fight against Jewry had its basic justification among others in the cruelty of Bolshevism: 'Bolshevism is a doctrine from the devil, and whoever has once suffered under its scourge, never again wants to have anything to do with it. The suffering that the Russian people have had to endure under Bolshevism is indescribable. This Jewish terrorism must be eradicated once and for all in the whole of Europe. This is our historic task'.[36]

In view of the alarming developments at the eastern front in 1942, Goebbels incessantly warned against a 'radicalization of our conduct of war'.[37] The Stalingrad catastrophe achieved a 'booming increase that could in no way be beaten',[38] in the language that was rich in superlatives aiming at monumentality, anyway. Now it was even more important than before to goad the population and to outwardly document the determination to mobilize all forces and energies for the war effort. Goebbels had vigorously interceded with Hitler and the leading circles of party and state for a 'total war' as of winter 1941/42, when the thrust of the German units had been brought to a standstill in the icy cold of the Russian winter. After the fall of the Sixth Army, the worst was to be feared at the eastern front. 'Total war' had already been the slogan of the speech at the Sportpalast on 30 January 1943, the tenth anniversary of the seizure of power. Goebbels countered the Allied camp's hopes for a breakdown in the near future with the statement of a '*total* readiness of our people for the concentration of all its forces'. From the nation, the 'call for the *most total* war effort'[39] hails to the outside. He praised the '*fanatical* will to fight', paid his respects to the entire population for its '*fanatical* determination'.[40]

Even more effective propagandistically was the speech at the Sportpalast on 18 February 1943, where, as is generally known, the question concerning the approval of the 'total war' was among the ten final questions posed to the crowd whipped into a frenzy in the densely packed hall: '*Do you want the total war?* [passionate cries: "Yes!" Strong applause]. Do you want it [cries: "Yes, we want it!"], if necessary *more total and more radical than we can imagine it at all today*? [passionate cries: "Yes!" Applause.]'[41] In the back ground of the speaker's platform decorated with flags with the swastika, the only banner in the rather soberly designed hall read: 'Total war – shortest war'.[42] Through the mobilization of all forces, the taking into service of the entire society, including women and adolescents, the turnabout of the war was to be achieved. The speech was spiked with exaggerated, positively associated superlatives: To overcome the 'most fatal threat'[43] of Bolshevism and 'international Jewry' allied with it, the most extreme efforts appeared to be inevitable: 'Today, the most radical is just radical enough, the most total is just total enough to lead to victory! [cries of bravo, applause]'.[44] With a revealing slip of the tongue enthusiastically welcomed by the audience, extinction was announced to 'Jewry', the 'incarnation of evil', the 'demon of destruction', 'the carrier of an international, culture-destroying chaos':[45] 'In any event, Germany does not have the intention to bow to this Jewish threat but rather that of taking action against it *in good time*, if necessary the *most complete and most radical extermination* of Jewry! [strong applause, wild cries, laughter.]'[46] In the later distributed printed versions of the speech, it only spoke of the 'most radical elimination'. In the original sound version, the 'more radical' slip of the tongue can be heard, whose wording foreign correspondents repeated[47] and which corresponded to what was happening in the East: the murderous trade of the 'Einsatztruppen' and the killing machinery of the extermination camps.

In contrast to its 'weakly' adversary, National Socialism possessed the utmost determined radicality, which appeared to be a virtue and enabled it to put a stop to the doings of the Jews aiming at an 'international, Bolshevistically veiled capitalist tyranny'[48] and to avert the fall of the occident. The speech did not bring about the hoped for change in the population's mood. Yet, the 'defiance and the determination which had been evoked by Goebbels' speech at the Sportpalast, supported by additional draconian repression, contributed to the ruling out of any prospect of a breakdown on the home front. This again was to lead to the fact that the fall of the regime was to drag on another two years while prolonged fighting, 'with one's back to the wall against a more and more invincible superior power, carried death and destruction to the extreme'.[49]

In the last phase of the war, marked by defeats and retreat battles, hate remained concentrated on 'the Jew' who, after all, was responsible for all the evils of the world. Because of his rejection of fanaticism and radicality, he was also the antipode of National Socialism. Only the 'well-fed citizen sees the fanatic as a bothersome, eccentric dreamer, radicalist and revolutionary'. In the 'Angriff' from 23 February 1943, the Reichsorganisationsleiter (Head of National Organisation), Robert Ley, accused 'the Jew' of 'giving a bad name to fanaticism. The Jew loves compromise, as in haggling over opinions, he can act as a Jewish broker. The Jew lives off tolerance, as without it he would have long since been exterminated. The Jew is lazy and cowardly as well as criminal and cowardly, which is why he hates the fanatic who denounces these traits as undignified and deplorable'.[50] The Germans should become fanatics and radicals to conquer 'international Jewry' in the 'final battle' ('Endkampf').

Unvarnished 'racial hygiene' and eliminatory radicality more than ever before marked the NS propaganda of the last few years of the war:

> The complete elimination of Jewry from Europe is not a question of *morals* but a question of the *security of the countries*! [applause] The Jew will always act in the manner that complies with his nature and his racial instincts; he *cannot* do anything else. As the potato bug destroys the potato fields – yes, *must* destroy, so the Jew destroys the countries and the peoples! There is but *one* remedy against it, namely: *the radical disposal of the danger*! [cries of bravo, applause][51]

Finally, in a proclamation on the occasion of the founding day of the party on 24 February 1945, Hitler accused the 'cowardly bourgeois compromise parties' of not having generated resolute resistance to 'Jewish–Bolshevist annihilation'. 'Individual areas in the East of our Reich already have to experience first-hand what Bolshevism means. What this Jewish pest is doing to women, children and men is the most gruesome fate that a human brain is capable of conceiving'. In view of such a threat, there exists 'but one commandment: to rally yet the last strength that a gracious God lets man find within himself to defend his life in difficult times with the utmost fanaticism and dogged steadfastness. What thereby becomes weak, falls, must and will perish'.[52]

In the light of approaching defeat, the terms became more and more mixed up. A physically as well as psychologically exhausted Goebbels wrote in his diary on 8 April 1945 that he had now, for the first time, stepped out of the 'moderate reserve' and had spoken a 'radical language' in editorial articles: 'It no longer makes any sense to beat around the bush. One must call things by their names, even at the risk of the foreign countries making use of it for themselves for the time being'.[53] The 'radical language' referred to the insight into the inevitability of defeat and, among others, found its expression in a call to partisan fighting ('Werewolf'), which was yet to claim the lives of thousands in the last few weeks of the war.

The NS reversal of values in the name of an imperialist racial ideology corresponded to the reinterpretation of terms. This constituted a definite rejection of the norms and categories of the Aristotelian tradition of freedom. A short time after the end of the war, the Dresden scholar of Romance languages and literature, Victor Klemperer, diagnosed the interpretation reversal that the fanaticism term had experienced under National Socialism:

> that National Socialism is founded on fanaticism and carries on the education to fanaticism by every means possible, so fanatical has been a superlativistically acknowledging byword throughout the entire era of the Third Reich. It meant the exaggeration of the terms brave, dedicated, persistent, to be more exact: a gloriously melted together, complete statement of all these virtues, and even the slightest pejorative side effect fell by the wayside in the usual LTI usage of the word (lingua tertii imperii).[54]

What goes for 'fanaticism' also goes for the categories of the radical and the extreme. Radicalism and political will determined to the utmost were seen as marks of quality, whereas willingness to compromise, moderation and middle stood for the expression of an overcome, decadent world. Praising the extreme marked the depth of the cultural break that took place under the National Socialists during the twelve years of their reign.

## 3 SED regime

The SED regime was neither able to assume the official or officious language use of the 'capitalist', 'bourgeois' and 'reactionary' Weimar Republic nor the characteristic style of NS propaganda. The fascination with the extreme could have drawn food for thought from Marx's critique of Hegel's state doctrine. Hegel's reconciliation doctrine, in which he interpreted the classes as the mediating element between the extremes of the government and the people, implied the error to Marx 'that the determination of true contrasts, their becoming extremes, which is nothing else but their self-knowledge as well as the spark that ignites the decision to fight, is thought to be something possibly to be prevented or harmful'.[55] However, the superior language conventions of the Aristotelian tradition and the extremism of the NS regime apparently prevented the SED from conferring a constructive role on the extremes in their political language and propaganda.

Moreover, the SED propaganda was marked less by the struggles of the past than by a new political constellation: the East–West conflict and the considerations of the other German state in the West. This did not find its expression alone in the first issue of the theoretical publication *Einheit* of February 1946 nor when titled *Monthly Journal for the Preparation of the Socialist Unified Party*, from which the traces of lacking unity discernible in the foundation year quickly disappeared.[56] The political ideological front-line position against the West German state was based on the way the Kommunistische Partei Deutschlands (KPD)/SED saw itself reaching the historically possible maximum of democracy under the conditions of 'building up socialism' with the 'dictatorship of the proletariat' and, hence, the reign of the broad masses of the people. In contrast, the 'bourgeois democracy' of the 'West' founded itself on the 'power of the monopolies'; hence, smaller minorities which, by applying clever manipulation methods and with the help of different parties, were successful in asserting their own interests against those of the large majority of the population. All the parties in West Germany, except for the KPD, which was oriented towards East Berlin and Moscow and, at best, the left-wing Sozialistische Partei Deutschlands (SPD) basis, were, from this view, seen as 'anti-democratic'. From this viewpoint, the KPD's bad performance in the first election for the Bundestag in August 1949 amounted to 'a strengthening of the position of the anti-democratic German monopolist forces, which were at the point of successfully establishing their power under the supreme authority of American imperialism'.[57]

According to the SED view, East Germany and West Germany stood opposite each other, almost like heaven and hell. Walter Ulbricht (1893–1973) sketched this manichaeic propaganda image at the second SED party conference as follows:

> After being freed by the Soviet Army, in East Germany the lessons were learned from the catastrophe into which Hitler-Fascism had propelled Germany. The democratic and peace-loving powers carried on a politicy of peace, of reconstruction of economy, of peace and of friendship with other peoples. In West Germany, in contrast, the reign of the monopolist lords and the Fascist bureaucrats was re-established with the help of the American, English and French occupational forces, Hitler's politics of revenge taken up again, hate against other peoples stirred up and a policy of preparations for war carried out.[58]

From the viewpoint of the SED, the events in East Berlin and many other places in the German Democratic Republic (GDR) on 16/17 June 1953 were the result of the Western imperialists and saboteurs stirring things up, and not at all an uprising of the people. A rebellion with mass participation was an impossibility in the 'workers and peasants' state. In the demonology of the SED propagandists, the suppression of 17 June 1953 was a historic continuity of the heroic fight against the NS regime: 'The events of 17 June have proved: The means and methods of the Fascist provocateurs were the same as those of the SA and SS bandits. The Fascist putsch did not in the least have anything in common with a strike or an uprising of the people'.[59]

With the 'Fascist putsch attempt', the Adenauer government, as the servant/bailiff of American capital interests, had made the attempt to frustrate the 'peaceful cooperation of the Germans amongst themselves', to deceive the West German population about the conditions in the other part of Germany, and to create an excuse 'for carrying out provocations and the further intensification of terror against all patriotic and democratic forces in West Germany'.[60]

This referred foremost to the West German KPD, against which in October 1951 – parallel to the application against the extreme right-wing Sozialistische Reichspartei (SRP) – an application for a ban had been made to the Federal Constitutional Court on the suspicion of 'unconstitutionality'. It was presented as a determined defender of the 'democratic rights and liberties established in the basic law of the West German population'. Not that it was 'unconstitutional', but the politics of the Adenauer government which carried on 'armament and preparation for war'.[61]

Logically, the characterization of the KPD, the SED's 'brother party' in the West, as a party political form of 'radicalism' was rejected. A commentator on the KPD ban angrily stated in the SED theory organ *Einheit* in 1965: 'What the Bonn and Karlsruhe reaction here calls "radicalism" fit to be banned is nothing else but the epitome of the position of democracy as such'.[62] Propagandistically clever, the SPD was taken into the same boat as the 'democrats', and the presumption voiced that 'all the political forces oriented against Adenauer politics'[63] were now threatened by a ban. The author characterized the 'bourgeois parties' as some kind of cartel of interests that gave 'the authoritarian reign of the monopolists, bankers and large estate-holders, thus, the dictatorship of a disappearing small minority, the advantage of the deceptive front of a democratic regime carried by the will of the people'.[64] Within their leading ranks, 'more and more prominent Nazi personages and old Fascists'[65] were to be found; with the build-up of the new 'Wehrmacht under the leadership of the old Hitler generals and officers, shock troops of the Fascist reaction against the social and political movements of the working class'[66] were coming into being. In this way, the accusation of 'radicalism' was implicitly reversed and used against the political system of the Federal Republic.

Notwithstanding, the SED propagandists hardly used the radicalism formula in this sense. Instead, they reached back to pejorative designations such as 'reactionary', 'counter-revolutionary' or even 'fascist'.

Interior enemies of the same cloth, such as the 'Harich group' which, with the help of 'imperialist sabotage centres' such as the 'Eastern Office of the SPD', had intended the 'liquidation of the state power of the GDR', were 'counter-revolutionary'.[67] In this way, they had become collaborators of the 'Bonn ultras' who, after the stabilization of their power, went on to prepare a military aggression:

> The Nazi generality has worked out military plans for the violent conquest of the Socialist German Democratic Republic to thus create a starting point for the implementation of their ambitious goals of imperialist aggression against Germany's eastern neighbours. In the summer of 1961 the preparations for the civil war of the Bonn ultras reached their peak and were thwarted by the German Democratic Republic – supported by the entire Socialist camp under the leadership of the Soviet Union – through the erection of the anti-Fascist protective wall.[68]

The SED propaganda against the 'Bonn ultras' peaked in the weeks after the Berlin Wall had been built. According to Ulbricht, the governing mayor of Berlin, Willy Brandt, had landed 'in the ditch of the Fascist ultras'.[69] Brandt had sharply commented on the events in Berlin, had spoken of the 'dividing wall of a concentration camp'[70] which now ran through the middle of Berlin. For the SED, the Bonn state, in cooperation with the 'Brandt–Wehner clique',[71] had been changed into the 'clerical militarist dictatorship of the most aggressive and most reactionary groups of the West German monopolist capital'. The Adenauer–Strauss party was continuing[72] 'Hitler's politics' and had 'decisively contributed to the restoration of Bonn neo-Nazism'.[73]

Already in July 1947, the SED theory publication *Einheit* had published a harsh critique of a book by Herbert Gross, in which the Düsseldorf *Handelsblatt* publisher had expressed himself against a state-controlled economy, citing the Soviet type of planned economy as a deterrent example. The author saw a close relationship to the *Guidelines of Christian social politics* written by Konrad Adenauer, which in Gross' view were directed towards a restoration of capitalism and imperialism and therefore – true to Georgi Dimitroff's formula, according to which fascism stood for an 'open, terrorist dictatorship of the most reactionary, chauvinist and most imperialist elements of the finance capital'[74] – deserved the designation 'neofascism'.[75]

All of the 'bourgeois forces', including the 'right-wing SPD leaders' who worked into the hands of monopolist capitalism, were grasped with the economy-centred neofascism formula. The term permitted only slight differences between the Christian Democratic Union/Christian Social Union (CDU/CSU) and the right-wing extremist National Democratic Party (NPD) founded in 1964:

> The openly nationalist development in West Germany is also expressed by the creation and work of the directly neo-fascist National Democratic

Party (NPD) [!]. For all the attention to the fact that it proclaims nationalism especially loudly and aggressively and that its influence has dangerously increased in a number of cities and districts of the Federal Republic, it would nonetheless be wrong to overlook that the main responsible body of the new nationalist wave is none other than the ruling party of the Federal Republic, the CDU/CSU. Hereby, there exists a certain 'division of labour' between it and the NPD, in which the latter announces open nationalism a couple of ticks more strongly, so that the CDU/CSU can raise it by a tick to impress the masses.[76]

In the light of the NPD election successes in the second half of the 1960s, this version experienced a further escalation: 'The present main strength of West German neo-Nazism and West German fascisation is the CDU/CSU (especially the forces around F.J. Strauß), whose subsidiary and special kind of offspring is the NPD'.[77] 'Neofascism' and 'neo-Nazism' appeared as synonyms.

In the course of the new policy towards the East, whose essential features had already become apparent during the grand coalition, the critique of the 'right-wing SPD leaders' and 'social democratism' – it continued to be seen as a 'position of the reaction, the negation of democracy, the imperialist counter-revolution'[78] – took on milder forms, whereas the hostile attitude towards the soon to become oppositional CDU/CSU remained steady, from time to time even experiencing an increase. One commentator even thinks that the CDU's sixteenth Federal Party Rally (3–7 November 1968 in Berlin) had been held 'in the style of Fascist party rallies'.[79] After the social–liberal coalition had been formed, this view intensified. If 'certain circles of the West German monopolist bourgeoisie currently support a Social–Liberal variant of the execution of power in the form of the Brandt/Scheel government', this, 'of course, does not mean that the reactionary trend [ ... ] has lost its political importance. As long as the imperialist system exists, the foundation of an extremely adventurous, reactionary and aggressive regime with all its cruelties and suffering will remain a serious danger to the working people'.[80] Ulbricht saw the 'appearance of the neo-Nazis and the extremely reactionary forces of the CDU/CSU'[81] in close relationship.

In the Honecker era and in the course of the attempts towards a relaxation in the 1970s, enemy definitions and stigmatizing terminology grew softer, however, without any basic changes. Most of all, the public provocations from openly appearing neo-NS groupings offered permanent opportunity to warn against the dangers of 'neofascism'. In view of the Oktoberfest assassination attempt in Munich (September 1980), it said:

> On the one hand, relieving the bourgeois parliamentarian ruling form of the monopolist bourgeoisie through the establishment of the openly terrorist dictatorship of the reactionary and aggressive elements of the monopolist capital is not exactly imminent; nevertheless, the historic experience strongly teaches how disastrous it is to play down the right-wing

extremist dangers to the survival of bourgeois democracy while simultaneously maligning and pursuing Communists and other left-wing forces who consistently fight against Fascism and war but for democracy and social progress.[82]

The formulas 'neofascism' and 'right-wing radicalism' remained for the most part economically determined and aligned with the interpretations and the language rulings of the Comintern. During the first half of the 1980s, GDR fascism researchers still undauntedly insisted on the validity of Dimitroff's 'classical' definition of fascism.[83] When the designations 'right-wing radicalism', 'ultra-right-wing' or 'right-wing extremism'[84] were used, this occurred as a rule in the interest of a varying stylistic design or in leaning towards foreign terminologies without filling these with one's own Communist–Leninist content. When reaching back to the term 'radicalism' as the 'terminology for extreme ("right-wing" as well as "left-wing") political trends', so the information regarding the difference of the 'class character' and the different attitudes towards 'societal progress'[85] were not allowed to be missing.

The SED language possessed numerous pejorative terms for a left-wing that deviated from the Marxist–Leninist 'general line': Whereas 'right-wing' deviations were labelled as e.g. 'revisionism', 'opportunism', 'social democratism', 'reconciliationism', left-wing deviations received attributes such as 'ultra-left-wing', 'anarchist', 'Trotskyist', 'Maoist', etc. Thus, the connected tendencies were expressed by the term 'left-wing radicalism'.

This term had its own ideological basis in Lenin's paper about 'left-wing radicalism' as an 'infantile disorder'.[86] According to this version, with 'left-wing radicalism', unbridled revolutionary passion was connected to the inability of strategically thought-out politics corresponding to the respective realities. By it, among others, Marxist opinions were expressed which Lenin – for example in his arguments with Mach and Pannekoek – had fought against. Lenin's paper was seen especially as a 'Handbook of Marxist–Leninist strategy and tactics'. In the initial years after the October Revolution, 'left-wing radicalism' – connected to 'doctrinarism, dogmatism and sectarianism' – had become the main hindrance to the inner consolidation of the young communist parties' development into 'proletarian mass parties'. Based on the experience 'in the fight with petit-bourgeois, half-anarchist revolutionarism', Lenin revealed the class character of 'extreme revolutionarism' and exposed its inability for 'endurance, organizability, discipline and steadfastness'.[87] In addition, he emphasized the necessity of a tightly organized, unitedly acting party of professional revolutionaries and instructed in the art of tactical compromises in the class struggle.

'Left-wing radicals' were thus Marxist critics of Lenin who stepped on the basic insight of Marxist–Leninist strategy and tactics.[88] The reproach of 'left-wing radicalism' was meant for anarchists and anarchic syndicalists as well as for Trotskyites and Maoists. In the 1970s and 1980s, there existed a differentiation between the 'non-proletarian forces' of left-wing radicalism and 'left-wing opportunistic' phenomena in the working class and the work-ers' movement.[89] To the latter group also belonged unorthodox Marxists who interpreted Lenin in a 'distorting way' or doubted the Marxist nature of his doctrines.[90] Instead of 'left-wing radicalism', one often spoke of 'ultra-left-wingers'[91] and occasionally also of 'left-wing extremism'[92] without any dif-ferences in meaning coming to the fore. 'Left-wing radicalism', 'left-wing extremism' and 'gauchism' (in France) were seen as 'synonyms'.[93] These forms of 'petit-bourgeois "left-wing" revolutionarism',[94] whose being left-wing appeared questionable and necessitated question marks, was attested by frequent 'vacillation from one extreme to the other'.[95]

'Left-wing radicalism' was to be rejected according to the Marxist–Leninist view, yet not in the manner in which 'right-wing radicalism' or 'neofascism' was to be condemned. Thus, the secretary of the central committee of the (illegal) KPD, Josef Schleifstein, who as a Marxist–Leninist expert had had a lightning career in the GDR and had moved to the Federal Republic[96] to build up the new Deutsche Kommunistische Partei (DKP), praised the 'fan-tastic fighting spirit' of the 'politically active forces' among the young stu-dents on the occasion of a conference in Frankfurt (Main) in the 'revolutionary May' of 1968. Further, he tried to win support for cooperation and joint activities while at the same time criticizing their 'left-wing radicalism' from a superior vantage point of serene Marxist–Leninist dialectics:

> This especially goes for left-wing radical and anarchist theories which reject participation in parliamentary elections and parliamentarian activ-ities, it also goes for the absoluteering of certain fighting methods of the so-called direct action, for the attitude toward issues concerning organization and tradition, for purely mechanistic opinions of the anti-authoritarian and anti-institutionalism. Marxism does not approach the issues of the ways of fighting as well as any other societal phenomena in a doctrinarian manner but historically concretely and dialectically.[97]

Therefore, communists oriented at East Berlin basically had to differentiate between 'the ideologists and leaders of the left-wing radical sects who consciously took the path of a pseudo-revolutionary anti-Communism and adventurous-ness and the misled sympathizers' who 'had fallen into such groups due to political inexperience, however wanted to actively fight against the imperialist system. Nowadays, too, it is still necessary to make the revolutionary poten-tials of these simple members of left-wing radical sects productive for the joint fight for peace and Socialism'.[98]

Soon thereafter, the 'newly constituted' DKP presented itself as a force working in this direction, wanting to make use of the political potential of the students' protest movement. In view of the limits to their mobilization ability already evident in 1969 (the election alliance 'Action for Democratic Progress' initiated by the DKP had reached a mere 0.6 per cent of the votes in the

Bundestag elections), a concerned *Einheit* reader asked whether the Marxist–Leninist hopes for the further growth of left-wing protest were not exaggerated. Helmut Hesselbarth replied that the students' movement was the result of 'the contradictions caused and reinforced by state monopolist capitalism which express themselves in the university realm in a specific way. As long as contradictions exist and increase, with great certainty the students' movement will also continue to exist'. Nevertheless,

> ultra-left-wing radicalism has more and more proved its inability to lead student energies into a real and not Utopian fight for an anti-imperialist, democratic renewal of the university. On the contrary, it has driven these energies away from this fight. This has led to disappointment among the protesting students, to the loss of influence of left-wing radicalism and to the inner crisis of the SDS. [ ... ] In view of these tendencies it becomes increasingly pressing that real Marxist theory, strategy and tactics gain influence within the students' movement.[99]

On the basis of its 'illusory' politics, 'left-wing radicalism' was not only condemned to failure; it also played into the hands of 'big capital':

> Only a short overview of the experience with the class struggles of the 1960s makes clear that the upper classes rely especially on right-wing and 'left-wing' opportunism in the fight against societal progress. Representatives of Social Democratism and revisionism as well as of Maoism and other forms of 'left-wing' radicalism acting upon Socialist slogans are to achieve what the directly anti-socialist ideologists of the upper classes have so far been unable to carry out. Even Trotskyism, historically long since exposed as a counter-revolutionary form of 'left-wing' opportunism, is being polished up and used as an instrument of anti-Communism.[100]

Ten years later, nothing much had changed in this situation. Therefore, at the tenth SED party rally, an intensified occupation with left-wing radicalism was urged: 'From an offensive position, the slanderous attacks of bourgeois, revisionist and ultra-left-wing ideology against true Socialism, against its peace politics and against the further development of the Communist world movement must be rejected and disproved with convincing arguments'.[101] Among others, young social scientists of the Academy for Social Science at the Central Committee of the SED and at university faculties dedicated themselves to this task.[102]

Left-wing radicals functioned as an instrument of anti-communism; right-wing radicals, on the other hand, formed its ideological spearhead. The actual danger therefore came from right-wing radicalism or left-wing radicalism; both formulas stood next to each other in the 1980s. 'Right-wing radicalism' was a central category in the propagandistic fight against the supporting political forces of the Federal Republic of Germany ('BRD'), most of all the CDU/CSU. There was only a slight difference between the Union parties and the 'neo-Nazism' and 'neofascism' of the NPD. 'Despite the talk about being the party of the "middle", the CDU/CSU operated in the political realm of the right wing or rather of extremely militant anti-Communism', and so, coming to a boiling point, one could formulate: 'The CDU/CSU itself strongly embodies neo-Nazism'. It thus maintains a 'positive relationship' to the NPD 'in the manner that it had e.g. existed and could exist with the Central Party and the Nazis. Nowadays, not only has one party, as it were, slipped to the right but the entire party system, to which the politics of the Social Democrat leader has essentially contributed'.[103]

In the 1970s, this picture became more differentiated. Ludwig Elm at Jena University intensively examined 'the traditions and tendencies of Conservatism in the Federal Republic of Germany'.[104] In a volume published by him, the results of this research were summarized in the following way at the beginning of the 1980s:

> After a period of the creation of various small post-Nazi organizations, a symptomatic activation of Fascism occurred in the Federal Republic of Germany with the NPD. It was called forth by the more strongly revengeful politics of the CDU/CSU government of that time which, additionally, was also connected to the breakdown of the 'economic miracle' in this country. The activation of the neo-Fascist forces in the FRG, the 'Hitler-wave' which is spreading throughout Germany, partially evoking an openly displayed Nazism nostalgia, compels one to a retrospective and gives rise to serious concerns. The crowd of extreme right-wing sympathizers has drawn markedly younger blood, its activities have gained strength, become more aggressive than in the previous years, and is gaining a considerable degree of latitude. Simultaneously, official political circles simplify the danger hidden in neo-Fascism and claim that allegedly there is not the least danger to inner security.[105]

Even in this more differentiated form, the reader gained the impression of a gradual drift of the West German system into the direction of fascism.

Arno Winkler painted an even more glaring picture of the political situation: 'The dangerous activities of the neo-Fascist forces in the Federal Republic of Germany have snowballed in the last few years. The whole world is being alarmed by more and more new facts proving that the neo-Fascist tendencies in the societal life of the Federal Republic of Germany are growing stronger. Neo-Fascist organizations are mushrooming all over the place'.[106] The official reports of the West German Federal Office for the Protection of the Constitution were accused of: 'depicting right-wing extremism and neo-Nazism merely as a "brown bogeyman"' and of falsely depicting 'left-wing extremism' (between quotation marks) as 'the main danger to the existence of the Federal Republic'.[107]

Such propaganda images found wide distribution via magazines and publishing companies (foremost Pahl-Rugenstein in Cologne) in the realm of the

DKP, also in West Germany. The 'brother party' could not gain approval from the West German voter, but was however able to develop strongly influential activities due to its alimentation from East Berlin (even for the year 1990, DM 67.9 million in transfer funds were still earmarked[108]). A considerable number of intellectuals and professors on the state's payroll followed the ideological wake of East Berlin. The papers by the Marburg political scientist Reinhard Kühnl, whose understanding of fascism showed a strong resemblance to that of the SED, enjoyed special attention and appreciation. His paper about 'The political forces represented by F.J. Strauß and their relationship to Fascism' earned him much praise in the SED organ *Einheit*:

> For conducting the evidence that it is definitely legal to connect Strauß and Hitler, Kühnl chooses the method to, on the one hand, consistently compare F. J. Strauß' attitude and politics to the right-wing extremist forces of the 1920s and 1930s – as they had been united e.g. in the Harzburg Front – and, on the other hand, to the neo-Fascist forces such as the NPD or the 'German People's Union' in the Federal Republic of Germany.[109]

The 'Harzburg Front' also motivated the Munich publicist, long-standing communist and former concentration camp prisoner Kurt Hirsch, who connected the struggle against right-wing extremism with violent attacks against the Union parties.[110] The 'Press Service Democratic Initiative' (PDI) initiated by him also served this purpose. Information about the activities of actual or supposed 'right-wing radicals' (in the most alarmist tone and with an inquisitorial attitude) always went hand in hand with attacks against the CDU and the CSU, and sometimes also against 'right-wing' social democrats.[111] At the beginning of the 1990s, information reached the public, according to which Kurt Hirsch had been carried as an unofficial staff member by the East German Secret Service HVA Department X ('desinformation'). As was confirmed later, the East German Ministry for State Security had Hirsch (IM 'Helm') transport 'Elaborations by Department X concerning the extreme right-wing scene through various book projects to the West German public'.[112]

With the breakdown of 'real existing socialism', this form of influence had come to an end in the same way[113] as the specific form of confrontation with the 'capitalist system of the Federal Republic of Germany'. In the SED propaganda, the way one sees oneself, being the expression of a 'positive extreme' characteristic for National Socialism, had not played a role. According to the East Berlin view, the political extremes existed on the other side of the 'anti-faschistischer Schutzwall' ('anti-fascist protective wall'; the Berlin Wall). Nevertheless, in the course of four decades, the right-wing extremism accusation weakened; the recipients changed. The following course can be identified in somewhat simplified form: In the 1950s and 1960s, the right-wing extremism accusation ('right-wing radicalism', 'neofascism', 'neo-Nazism') was no less made against the SPD than against the CDU and the CSU. In the 1970s, the attacks against the ruling social democracy decreased in line with the relaxation of politics, whereas the now oppositional Union remained the preferred target. In the 1980s, the picture changed the most. The CDU and the CSU again came to governmental power at the federal level, helped East Berlin with the negotiations for credits of billions, whereas the SPD negotiated with the SED about an ideology paper in the interest of 'joint security'.[114] Foremost, the 'new political thinking' announced in Moscow led to greater inhibition in the use of propaganda formulas,[115] even though these did not change essentially. One had always used a milder tone towards 'left-wing radicals' anyway. Here, the signs now stood entirely on dialogue and cooperation[116] in as much as the respective groupings did not act on GDR territory as 'hostile negative forces'.[117] How far goodwill could go in practice was found out only after the end of the SED state: RAF (Red Army Faction) terrorists, criminally indicted in Western Germany, yet in the meantime weary of fighting, had found a sort of political asylum in the 'state of workers and peasants'.[118]

# 7 Extremism as an element of the official/ semi-official language of the Federal Republic of Germany

## 1 Extremism and the anti-totalitarian basic consensus

In the western zones of Germany occupied by the victorious forces, the reconstruction of liberal democratic structures began at the municipal level accompanied by the constitutional debates of the states.[1] Here, as two years later, in the constitutional debates for the foundation of a western state which was conceived as provisional, the question of the protection of democracy was of central importance. The new German democracy was not to suffer the fate of the old one. The traumatic experience of National Socialism and the events in the Soviet-occupied zone, which accompanied the negotiations, allowed for an anti-totalitarian consensus to spread among all the parties, which only the representatives of the Kommunistische Partei Deutschlands (KPD) withdrew from. Speaking of a 'consensus' is only possible with the exclusion of the communist minority, which, in the first few postwar years, benefited from the vitality of 'anti-fascism'.[2] It was therefore represented in many state parliaments and state governments (mostly all-party coalitions) but had lost influence – particularly because of its connection to East Berlin and Moscow and the events in the Soviet-occupied zone – already at the beginning of the banning proceedings (1951).[3]

General terms for those forces against whom protection was necessary was for the most part avoided on account of the legal coinage of the negotiation language of the time. At best, it was discussed that the emerging German constitution (Grundgesetz) should not have a hand in 'its own total elimination or destruction', 'especially for a revolutionary, anti-democratic movement to turn the here normed legal democratic state order into its opposite by seemingly "legal" means'.[4] This is what justified the inclusion of an 'eternity guarantee' into the German constitution (Grundgesetz) (later Art. 79,3 GG).

Which revolutionary, anti-democratic endeavours they had in mind is shown, for example, by Sozialdemokratische Partei Deutschlands (SPD) representative Rudolf Katz in the organization committee of the parliamentary council, who pleaded for the possibility of banning parties that had an unconstitutional attitude:

We cannot afford to forget that a 12-year-dictatorship lies behind us, and the ghosts of such parties are still spooking around among certain groups of the people in a very lively manner. We must expect that shortly hidden dictatorship-parties of the Communists and the National Socialists will show up on the scene; in certain forms they are perhaps already here today. Therefore I find it necessary to have a regulation that allows for immediate action against such parties.[5]

In the debates on regulating the 'legal state of emergency', Johannes Brockmann warned against a 'radicalization': 'Extreme party directions tend toward making the government's work impossible'. Respective legal constitutional regulations should serve 'to put a stop to the parties' flight from responsibility'.[6] The fear that 'radical developments might occur'[7] was an ever present one.

The 'militant democracy' anchored in the German constitution (Grundgesetz) was founded on the democracy protection thinking which found its expression in this remark. It was also to find its expression at the official level. When the Western military governors permitted the foundation of an inland intelligence service in the so-called 'police letter' to the president of the parliamentary council of the future federal government in April 1949, they spoke of a 'place for the collection and distribution of information concerning subversive activities directed against the Federal Government'.[8] They were foremost concerned about the growing danger of communist infiltration. In the parliamentarian debates regarding the constitutional protection law, other forms of 'counter-propaganda by anti-democratic forces'[9] were being thought about. When the KPD representative Fisch declared it was futile to protect a state that had come about 'on command of foreign imperialist lords',[10] the SPD representative Otto Heinrich Greve, who had belonged to the parliamentary council, replied:

> Ladies and Gentlemen! Protection of the constitution means protection of democracy. We should not be surprised that Mr. Fisch and his comrades have a different opinion in this field than the majority of this house. [ ... ] Yes, Mr. Fisch, you asked what we wished to protect. By the constitution and by this democracy we wish to protect ourselves against you and your opponents on the political right, Mr. Fisch![11]

The 'necessary means against all the enemies of democracy',[12] from the right and the left, are to be used. The speakers of the government parties and their SPD opposition both agreed about this as well as about the necessity of anchoring liberal democracy in the thinking of the broad population.

This corresponded to the stability trauma of the founder generation of the West German state, when the first elected Bundestag called into being a 'Committee for the Protection of the Constitution' immediately after the constituency, which – under the auspices of SPD representative Walter Menzel – took up its work and was to make a contribution by observing 'subversive and hostile tendencies toward the state',[13] so that a relapse into the mistakes made by Weimar would be avoided. There was the determination to counteract endeavours that were hostile to the constitution by means of the criminal law and the repressive instruments anchored in the German constitution (Grundgesetz), if necessary.

The determined willingness to protect oneself against the left and the right found its expression in a decree by the Federal Minister of the Interior of 19 September 1950, regarding 'political activities by the members of public service against the democratic basic order':

> The decision by the Federal Government makes it clear that the participation of civil servants, employees and workers in the direct and indirect federal service with endeavours and organizations directed against the liberal democratic basic order is not compatible with loyal duty to the Federal Republic. This applies likewise to any left-wing and right-wing radical endeavours or organizations.[14]

In a guideline by the Hessian Minister of the Interior from 19 October 1950, addressing the same set of problems, membership of 'the KPD or a totalitarian, right-wing radical organization or one of its camouflage organizations' was called a violation of loyal duty.

By law of 27 September 1950, the Federal Office for the Protection of the Constitution was put into effect. Its task was to 'collect and evaluate information, news and other documents concerning efforts that had the aim to abolish, change and disturb the constitutional order in the Federation and the Länder or illegally impair the conduct of the office of the members of constitutional institutions of the Federation and the Länder'.[15] After a difficult starting phase (John affair), systematic observation activities developed, foremost aimed at 'right-wing' and 'left-wing radicalism', as it was called in the prevailing use of the language harking back to Weimar times. The content of these terms was oriented to the violation of the norms of the 'liberal democratic basic order', thus at 'hostility toward the constitution' and 'adversity to the constitution' in reference to the core of indispensable values and rules protected by the German constitution (Grundgesetz).

These criteria were sharpened by the verdicts of the Federal Constitutional Court, forbidding the Sozialistische Reichspartei (SRP) and the KPD. The court was able to reach back to the work of the legal committee of the German Bundestag, which had connected the criminal delict of 'endangering the state' with the attempt to eliminate the 'liberal democratic basic order' and formulated five principles concerning content.[16] On this basis, the court's decision on the SRP ban determined 'liberal democratic basic order' as an order 'which under exemption of any violence and despotism constituted a legal state jurisdiction order on the basis of the self-determination of the people according to the will of the respective majority as well as liberty and equality'. Their basic principles 'at least' included:

The respect for the human rights concretisized by the German constitution (Grundgesetz), most of all the individual's right to life and free development, the people's sovereignty, the division of powers, the government's responsibility, the legality of the administration, the independence of the courts, the multi-party system and the equality of opportunities for all political parties with the right to constitutional education from carrying out an opposition.[17]

The key term to be examined by the court was the 'unconstitutionality of the party', not the term 'radicalism'. Still, 'the court reached back to this term in its characterization of the SRP's "hostile attitude toward democracy"'. Already 'a superficial look at the leadership, the organic structure, the program and the SRP's behaviour in public gave rise to the presumption that theirs seemed to be an attempt at taking up radical right-wing ideas in the manner that had last manifested themselves in National Socialism. Hearing the evidence confirmed this impression'.[18]

In the KPD banning verdict four years later, the attribute 'left-wing radical' was not used in any way. Yet, here too, the category of t 'unconstitutionality' was the legal criterion derived from the term 'liberal democratic basic order' of the German constitution (Grundgesetz), whose creators had made a 'constitutional decision' in favour of 'combative democracy',[19] had learned their lesson from the 'coming about of "totalitarian" parties after World War I'[20] and had arranged the 'possibility for the elimination of political parties that were hostile toward the constitution'.[21]

In the time that followed, the radicalism term did not find entry into legal constitutional terminology, although it was to be found there in the sense of 'hostile to the constitution' and 'adverse' efforts against the 'liberal democratic basic order'. The legal language calls for more specific descriptions of evidence and avoids general terms of this kind. Also, the much older American constitutional law knows 'extremism' only in the sense of concrete evidence and thereby additionally restricted to the attempt of a violent elimination of the constitutional order. Instead of 'extremism', there is talk of 'subversion', 'insurrection' and 'sedition'.[22] Here too, the boundary between remarks/actions that conform to the constitution or are hostile towards the constitution is not always easy to draw, as is shown by the verdict by Court Justice Oliver Wendell Holmes, which goes back to the case of the socialist Charles Schenck (1919), in which Holmes made an interpretation of extreme statements in the sense of their being hostile to the constitution dependent on the existence of a 'clear and present danger'.[23]

The German founding fathers took another path by anchoring a 'defensive', 'ready to defend' and 'militant democracy' against the background of the Weimar experience. This made possible the observation of endeavours 'hostile to the constitution', independent of their relevance to criminal law ('the bringing forward of the protection of the constitution').[24] This was meant to put a stop to 'legality tactics' by political extremists in the manner in which the National Socialists had successfully exercised at the beginning of the 1930s.

## 2 Extremism in the early constitution protection reports

The Federal State Office for the Protection of the Constitution in Cologne, founded in November 1950, carried out its work in the first few years according to the following guidelines passed by the Federal Ministry of the Interior:

> (a) determination of Communist and right-wing radical infiltration of the authorities, especially those of the Federal Republic of Germany, (b) clarification of the intentions of the Communist Party and its aid organisations as well as the new foundation of camouflage organisations, (c) clarification of the illegal activities of the Communist Party, (d) surveillance of Eastern secret news services within the Federal Republic of Germany, [ ... ] (g) surveillance of the legal and illegal activities of right-wing radical organisations, particularly those which are prohibited.[25]

Nonetheless, in the first few years, constitution protection reports were not made public. In many instances, the traditional understanding of the classical 'secret service' still predominated, according to which it was foremost expected to inform the government and to collect material for the preparation of executive measures (in particular the banning of clubs and parties hostile to the constitution). Not until a wave of indignation evoked by the anti-Semitic smudge wave of 1959/60, so soon after the war, had put justification pressure on the German Federal State at home and abroad did the first publications to inform the general public appear. In 1960, a report about the anti-Semitic incidents was published by the Federal Government in both German and English.[26]

The Federal State Office for the Protection of the Constitution published a first report about 'right-wing radicalism in the Federal Republic'.[27] In particular, it dealt with the observation of and protection against 'radical right-wing and anti-Semitic tendencies' in the year 1961. In the following year, another report of this kind appeared, as those of the previous year had 'received great resonance in the country and abroad':

> This report contributed to sharpen the watchfulness of the democratic powers toward radical right-wing endeavours, at the same time being able to correct wrong ideas about the extent and the influence of these forces. Its effect on the right radical forces themselves have shown that the signs of decay in these groups were being accelerated considerably when their numeric weakness and their organisational estrangement became known.[28]

Similar reports of this kind also appeared in the following years.[29] They spoke of the 'carriers of radical right-wing endeavours', recorded the 'development of organized right-wing radicalism',[30] examined 'non-organized' forms of 'extreme right-wing beliefs'[31] (among others, authors, journalists and pamphletists), documented the 'development of the editions of the radical right-wing press organs',[32] analysed the manner of argumentation of 'radical right-wing statements',[33] e.g. 'the extreme right-wing agitation concerning Communism'[34] and devoted a separate chapter to the 'effects of international Fascism in the Federal Republic'.[35] Legal violations by members of 'radical right-wing organisations'[36] were depicted, as well as measures by the state 'against supporters of nationalist and anti-Semitic endeavours'.[37] In this, the authorities conveyed the positive results of their activities:

> The self-cleansing and reconstruction work in the Federal Republic has, year by year, knocked the bottom out from under the radical right-wing splinter parties and associations. This is a lasting development. Compromised by setbacks and election defeats, also fragmented and estranged from each other, these groups have become a merely peripheral phenomenon of political life in the Federal Republic of Germany. In this condition and under the present circumstances they do not constitute an actual danger to the liberal democratic basic order. Of course, they will have to be under further intensive surveillance, particularly since they are partially trying to camouflage themselves, but partially also show growing anti-democratic tendencies, becoming groups of remaining fanatic sectarians due to the loss of moderately thinking followers.[38]

These fields of examination and diagnoses show the linguistic range of variations in dealing with the endeavours from the right that are hostile to the constitution. 'Right-wing radicalism' remained the terminus technicus. At first, it was only vaguely outlined. Finally, the report for the year 1965 paid more attention to it. 'Right-wing radicalism' is

> no legal term. The word belongs to the colloquial political language of our days. There, it is used to designate various forms of exaggerated nationalism. Each further interpretation of the term compels us to determine a political location. This becomes especially clear when looking at the ideologic and tactical political foundations, from whence the anti-democratic forces from the left and the right agitate the topic of right-wing radicalism.

In order to elude this dilemma, the collective expression 'radicalism' was defined in the following. In 'states with a liberal democratic constitution', it comprised such 'endeavours [ ... ] which tried to attack the fundamental principles and institutions of law and state order, to eliminate it or to at least put it in question'.[39] In the following report, whose main topic dealt with the Nationaldemokratische Partei Deutschlands (NPD) that had been successful in the Federal state parliament elections, the efforts to explain the term were intensified. The NPD had declared that the term 'radical right-wing' was incorrect. 'To counter this objection, it shall therefore first of all be explained from which features of the term the state protection authorities are starting out'.[40] After referring to the definition problems seen in science, a catalogue of ideological characteristics followed, among them also 'pronounced nationalism and hostility toward strangers connected to this', 'an irrational, nationalist philosophy and vocabulary usually connected to anti-Semitism', 'uncompromising in political disputes, intolerance and defamation toward people who espouse differing opinions, elitism',[41] etc.

With the last point, a feature was mentioned that was equally typical of 'communist activities'. A first report concerning this topic appeared in 1965.[42] The main emphasis was put on the activities of the illegally operating KPD, which had been prohibited in 1965, the Sozialistische Einheitspartei Deutschlands (SED), Freie Deutsche Jugend (FDJ) and Sozialistische Einheitspartei Westberlins (SEW) as well as any other 'Soviet-zone organisations'. Close attention was paid to the influence of communist associations on the 'guest workers' living in the Federal Republic and organizations influenced by communism, among them the Deutsche Friedens-Union (German Peace Union), the Bund der Deutschen (Association of the German People), several organizations of the Friedensbewegung (Peace Movement) and the Vereinigung der Verfolgten des Naziregimes (Association of the Victims of Persecution by the Nazi Regime). However, neither here nor in the final 'overall evaluation' was there any mentioning of 'radical left-wing endeavours'. This also applied to the reports for the years 1965–67.[43] The central focal point remained the GDR's 'real existing socialism'. Therefore, there was apparently no need for a term at a higher level of abstraction.

Aside from 'radical right-wing', the attribute 'extreme right-wing' had also been used from the beginning of public reporting – with growing tendency. In the report for the year 1967, it was said for the first time that the terms 'radical right-wing' and 'extreme right-wing' were 'essentially synonymous'.[44] This indicated a terminological change. In the same year, the communism report appeared under the title 'Left-wing radicalism in the Federal Republic',[45] and the attributes 'radical left-wing' and 'extreme left-wing' were used just as unsystematically as for the other wing of the political spectrum. The reader was left in the dark about what the definitional characteristics of the terms were.

The report for the year 1968 carried the confusion to the hilt. The two main chapters bore the title 'Extreme right-wing endeavours' as well as 'Communist and other extreme left-wing endeavours'. Nevertheless, in the subparagraphs, the 'unchanged radical right-wing nature of the NPD', 'Extreme right-wing tendencies with immigration from the East', 'Crimes with a radical right-wing background' or 'SED contacts to foreign radical left-wing organizations'[46] were discussed without any convincing reason for the different designations.

### 3 Radicalism or extremism?

It took several years before the terminology was standardized. In the scientific, journalistic and political analysis of the NPD and the Außerparlamentarische

Opposition (extra-parliamentary opposition; APO), the extremism term had gradually gained increasing weight. However, the essential reason for changing it to the official language may have been a political one. After the formation of the liberal–social coalition, which 'wanted to risk more democracy', it no longer seemed opportune to the government to locate every form of fundamental left-wing critique regarding the status quo at the legal constitutional fringes by calling it radicalism. The use of the term extremism made it possible within the framework of the constitution to terminologically separate hostility to the constitution from a legitimate radical critique of the status quo. Behind this was the consideration that, in spite of all the necessary boundaries, the attempt had to be made to integrate the students' protest movement politically.

This political intention left its mark on the discussion about applying the principle of loyal duty to the members of public service, whose unaltered validity the head of the government of the Federation and the Länder had called to mind in a resolution from 28 January 1972.[47] Opponents spoke of the 'decree against radicals', followers of a 'decision against extremists'. The one formula implied a political witch hunt, the other emphasized its legal constitutional correctness.[48] As opposed to the students' protest movement inspired by anarchist and Marxist ideas, the motive of boundaries and exclusion dominated on the side of the Union. Here, the older diction was held on to longer. This attitude became obvious, for example, in a speech by the CDU representative Alfred Dregger in the Hessian parliament on 9 March 1972: 'Three things will be absolutely essential if we want to fight the radical parties and organizations by ourselves without banning them: 1. the solidarity of the democrats, 2. uncompromising boundaries between the democrats and the radicals, and 3. decisive action by the democrats in the fight against the radicals'. Dregger urged equidistance towards the political wings: 'These three preconditions were available when it became necessary to remove the NPD from the parliaments again. This was successful. It would be terrible if these preconditions were not available in fighting the radical left. For this, there were and are symptoms'.[49] From Dregger's point of view, the differentiation between radicals and extremists may have seemed like splitting hairs, signalling an insidious abandonment of the equidistance commandment. Nevertheless, the front-lines in the terminological argument of 1972/73 were uneven; concerning 'radicals' and 'extremists', there was a hopeless mess, and the use of one or the other slogan did not always point to the membership of this or that political camp.[50]

Not until 1973 did an official clarification of the language take place at the federal level. The Federal Ministry of the Interior changed the terminology when dealing with endeavours being 'hostile to the constitution' at the beginning of the 1970s. In the constitution protection report for the year 1973, the term 'radical' was replaced by the term 'extremist'. The Minister of the Interior, Werner Maihofer, a Free Democratic Party (FDP) politician and respected philosopher of law, explained this as follows:

The term 'extremist' takes [ ... ] into account the fact that political activities or organisations are not already hostile to the constitution if they have a certain aim that goes all the way to the roots of a question, although it might be 'radical' according to the common use of the word. They are 'extremist' and therefore hostile to the constitution in the legal sense only if they are directed toward the [ ... ] foundations of our liberal democratic basic order.[51]

In a similar way, Maihofer also marked the terminological difference in a contribution at the German Bundestag during a debate on 15 November 1974 about loyal duty concerning the members of the public service. Within the liberal democracy of the German constitution (Grundgesetz) also, a 'radical critique of our existing societal policy and valid state constitution' was not per se 'to be equated with hostility to the constitution':

In every generation, particularly in a liberal order and for the sake of just this freedom, there must be a new radical thinking over of the performance fulfilment and the timeliness of societal conditions. Even if I, as a liberal, would e.g. fight such radical thinking about a 'socialization of the means of production' with every political passion, this does not make such a radical, who publicly thinks about what, according to Article 15 of our constitution, could be decided by a simple majority of the Bundestag, an extremist or an enemy of the constitution.

The boundary between radicalism and extremism is only then exceeded if that legal constitutional 'core issue' is violated which the Federal Constitutional Court had outlined by the term of the liberal democratic basic order: 'Whoever fights against these basic values is not only a radical but an extremist. He leaves the foundations of our German constitution (Grundgesetz)'.[52]

In a lexicon contribution published a little later, Maihofer defined the term extremism as follows:

We describe as political extremism [ ... ] any unconstitutional efforts made in the fight against our 'liberal democratic basic order', be it by political parties (Art. 21 GG), be it by political organizations (Art. 9 GG) or be it through unorganized political activities of individuals or groups (Art. 18 GG). Hereby, extremist efforts need not necessarily be directed toward the entire constitution nor against any individual regulations of our German constitution (Grundgesetz) but against the core content of our state constitution which we call 'liberal democratic basic order'.[53]

For the content of this term, the dispensation of justice by the Federal Constitutional Court was referred to. In this way, an official terminology had been outlined that was to prove durable for the coming decades.

The constitutional protection reports of the Federal State (and the Länder in as far as they published their own reports) subdivided 'extremism' into 'right-wing and left-wing extremism'. Added to this were the activities of 'foreign extremists' ('security-endangering efforts by foreigners'[54]). From time to time, 'terrorism' – mostly on account of the challenge of the spectacular hostage kidnappings by the Red Army Faction – received its own chapter.[55] In the 1970s and the early 1980s, 'extreme right-wing' endeavours were followed by 'extreme left-wing' endeavours; starting with the report for the year 1982, this was reversed. After the change of government in 1998, the whole thing happened again. After the formation of the great coalition in 2005, the Federal Minister of the Interior, Wolfgang Schäuble, kept to the order his predecessor Otto Schily had introduced.[56]

The symbolism of the order of the chapters did not change anything about terminology. The categorical differentiation of extremism and radicalism carried out at the beginning of the 1970s was kept. In a brochure by the Constitutional Protection Agency from the year 1999, it said unequivocally:

> Those endeavours which are directed against the core content of our constitution – the liberal democratic basic order – are called 'extremist'. Often, there is some confusion about the term extremism. It is wrong to frequently place it on an equal footing with radicalism. Thus, critics of capitalism who espouse fundamental doubts in the structure of our economic and societal order, wanting to change it from the bottom up, are not extremists by a long shot. Radical political beliefs have their legitimate place in our pluralist societal order.[57]

After the setting up of constitutional protection authorities in the Eastern countries that had joined the Federal Republic, the terminology valid in the Federal Republic was adopted there as well. In the first public constitutional protection report for the state of Saxony, it said, for example:

> The Regional Office for Constitutional Protection of Saxony observes right-wing, left-wing and extremist endeavours, spying activities and continuing structures and activities of the information and protection services of the former GDR. [ ... ] An effort is only then right-wing or left-wing extremist if it tries to disturb or eliminate the liberal democratic basic order or if there are at least indications in that direction.[58]

The report published in the year 2006 supplemented the usual chapters 'Extremist right-wing endeavours', 'Extremist left-wing endeavours', 'Security-endangering and extremist efforts by foreigners' by separate texts concerning 'Islamistic/islamistic-terrorist efforts and suspicion cases', and added the earlier, separately treated 'Politically motivated crimes' to the fields of 'right-wing extremism' and 'left-wing extremism'. A terminological uncertainty came to the fore in the formulation already used in the year 2004: 'Fundamentalism and extremism as well as hostility to and violence toward strangers are a continuous challenge to the legal social state'.[59] The term 'fundamentalism' was taken into account especially after the attacks on 11 September 2001, which led to a general awareness of the dangers of Islamic terrorism. The expansion of the report by an Islamism chapter may also be due to the fact that 'fundamentalism' is not only to be found among extremists 'from abroad'.

## 4 The German terminology in the international context

On account of the great attention which constitutional protection reports attract in Germany – surely also an effect of its double dictatorship past reaching into the present – their terminology has essentially marked the public use of language. This practice, with the system of the 'moving forward' of democracy protection in the framework of the concept of the 'militant democracy', became popular after the end of 'real existing socialism', most of all in the Czech Republic, where constitutional protection reports are being published ('Informace o problematice extremismu na uzemi ceske republiky'), in which a differentiation is made between right-wing (Pravicovy extremismus) and extreme left-wing groupings (Levicovy extremismus).[60]

Another path was taken by Austria and Switzerland, in that state/constitution protection was not 'moved forward' there, thus concentrating itself on criminally relevant endeavours, especially those oriented towards violence. The terminology in the reports published for the last several years is only slightly different from that of Germany. Here too, there is a differentiation made between 'right-wing extremism' and 'left-wing extremism'. In Austria, this additionally includes 'extremism and terrorism with a reference to abroad'. The Swiss state protection report generally speaks of 'violent extremism and terrorism'.[61]

The report from the Dutch General Intelligence and Security Service (AIVD) is also oriented to the violence criterion; however – in contrast to the German-speaking countries – at the same time, it is marked by very little terminological consistency. So, 'Politiek gewelddadig activisme' mentions 'Extreem rechts [right-wing]' yet not 'Extreem links [left-wing]'. Instead, the 'Links activisme'[62] is dealt with.

Reports of this kind exist neither in France nor in the United Kingdom. Therefore, both countries lack a developed official terminology with reference to efforts hostile to the constitution. In France, data from the Renseignements Généraux with a reference to extremism reach the public only through the annual reports by the 'Commission nationale consultative des droits de l'homme', which has been active on behalf of the government since 1986. They are solely concerned with acts of 'racism', 'xenophobia' and 'anti-Semitism'.[63] In less integrated immigration communities in Britain, the examination of Islamism has led to a recollection of the basic values of the constitutional order. In an official announcement of October 2005 with the title 'Preventing extremism together', it said: 'Addressing the problem of extremist activity within communities in the UK has never been more important. Whether it is people planning terrorist attacks or attempting to subvert British values of democracy, tolerance and free speech, the Government is committed to tackling extremism head-on'.[64] But, although the British government has talked of violent 'extremism' in the context of Islam since 2001, at times it has sought to delete the word 'extremism' in this context from public discourse, clearly in an attempt to encourage accommodation with 'mainstream' Muslims, and the term 'radicalization' is also common in the United Kingdom in the context of conversion to Islamism.

The official American language practice, especially that of the Federal Bureau of Investigation (FBI)'s Inland News Service, is also oriented towards the violence criterion; however, it does not use the term extremism as a systematic category. Instead, the term 'domestic terrorism'[65] is used. The range of news reporting reaches from Al-Qaeda to the Ku Klux Klan and on to 'animal rights and environmental extremism'.[66] 'Extremism' functions as a descriptive, not as a terminologically analytical, category. Similarly, this also goes for the reports of those 'watchdog' organizations which, under their own leadership, examine the political foreground of extremist crimes and hereby – which is typical of the USA[67] – work closely with government authorities. Let us just mention the Anti-Defamation League supported by Jewish organizations, which constantly reports about 'Extremism in America', particularly about extreme right-wing and Islamist groupings.[68]

Thus, the terminology and the observation systematics of German constitutional protection authorities constitute something special in the democratic world, even if, at the international level, it does not stand out in every respect. Likewise, this does not apply to the measures of the 'liberal democratic basic order' at which the official term extremism is oriented. Differences are to be found especially in view of the observation radius of groupings seen as 'extremist'. This is drawn tighter and tighter in the states orienting themselves to the violence criterion, even if the exact boundary of the orientation towards violence, as e.g. in the debate about 'fighting words' and 'hate speeches',[69] is not always easy to delineate.

# 8 Lines of development of the extremism concept in the twentieth century

## 1 Extremism and early totalitarianism discussion

As shown in Chapter 6, the first attempts to systematically conceptualize the term extremism go back to the first decade after the Russian Revolution – to a time when the new type of radical challenge to the liberal constitutional order established in wide areas of Europe in the nineteenth century became obvious. To this, Maxime Leroy and Luigi Sturzo offered the first contributions from a – in the broadest sense – liberal perspective. In their critique, both of them reached back to interpretations of the anti-democratic/anti-liberal movements and ideologies that had become an established part of the political interpretation culture from the end of the eighteenth century on.

The intellectual familiarity with a perspective that included the wing positions of the pluralist political spectrum in its analogies and isomorphies might, however, have contributed to the fact that Leroy's and Sturzo's ideas did not play an essential role in the debates of the following decades. Although Luigi Sturzo achieved great influence with the totalitarianism term he developed, his extrapolations on extremism, however, remained largely ignored. Nevertheless, in the course of the international totalitarian debate, which had been becoming more intense since the 1930s, quite a few authors reached back to the older, structurally similar extremism concept.

Former communists such as Franz Borkenau (1900–57), who changed into a supporter of the totalitarianism concept under the impression of the Hitler–Stalin pact, belonged to them. In his much read book *The Totalitarian Enemy* of the year 1949, he sharply criticized the 'antagonistic fanaticisms'[1] which, due to their fundamental common ground, he believed should be characterized as 'brown Bolshevism' and 'red Fascism'.[2] Here, however, the attribute 'extremist' was used in a relativizing form. This is how Borkenau characterized the supporters of any extreme position. Accordingly, there were 'extremists' in the Nationalsozialistische Deutsche Arbeiterpartei (NSDAP) as well as among the 'liberal bourgeoisie'.[3] He rather moved along Aristotelian trains of thought when he referred to the English tradition of liberty: 'Traditional English liberty always consisted of checking extremes. For no extreme is compatible with liberty'.[4] From this perspective, National Socialism (NS) was marked by 'extreme forms of mob rule' slipping into 'extreme forms of autocratic tyranny'.[5] In this way, Borkenau sought to understand the specific mass basis of the NS movement in contrast to traditional forms of 'autocracy' such as the Tudor regime. Bolshevism, on the other hand, had distanced itself under Stalin from its internationalist, Messianic origins and developed into an 'extremely nationalist' regime, the 'most extreme form of totalitarianism'.[6]

In those years, one could also subject the ruling system of 'Bolshevist extremists'[7] to a fundamental critique from the point of view of the 'ultra-left-wing'. The Council's communist Otto Rühle (1874–1943), a companion of Trotsky in his Mexican exile, did not interpret 'totalitarianism' under Stalin as the foremost result of 'nationalist' deviation but as a product of Lenin's, which had deceived the Council's movement that was 'anti-centralist, anti-parliamentarian and anti-unionist'[8] in its core, and then instead erected a 'dictatorship over the proletariat'.[9] Rühle's paper led the way to a Council's communist critique of totalitarianism.

As far as the liberal democratic circle of ideas is concerned, publications from the 1930s by the German–Jewish state jurist Karl Loewenstein (1891–1973) meanwhile gained greater importance. Loewenstein had lost his teaching licence as a result of the 'law for the re-establishment of professional civil service'. After his immigration to the USA, at the Political Science Department of Amherst College (Massachusetts),[10] he dealt with the question of by which legal measures the European democracies had defended themselves against the onslaught of 'extremist' subversive movements after the end of World War I possibly more successfully than the unfortunate Weimar Republic. His study on *Militant Democracies and Fundamental Rights* (1937) included in its name the formula, whose German translation was later to express the second German democracy's understanding of the constitution.[11] In 1938, a continuation to this investigation was published in the *Columbia Law Review* under the title 'Legislative Control of Political Extremism in European Democracies'. It was possible to publish it in the French language the following year through the assistance of the *Revue du droit public*.[12] A summary in the German language had appeared in the *Neue Zürcher Zeitung* in April 1937. There, the reader found out how the European democracies had reacted to the 'attitude toward fighting off international Communism as well as Fascism' by their state security legislation. There was 'no country in the diminished group of European democracies [ ... ] which did not have political movements that were to be seen as subversive from the point of view of ruling democratic state opinion'.[13] The 'subversion' in the sense of fundamental democratic principles substantiated the classification of the respective movements as 'extremist'. By a 'development towards a militant democracy', many European countries had successfully limited the range of activities of 'extremist parties'.[14] Yet constitutional protection laws had also been developed in Latin America. During World War II, Loewenstein acted as a legal adviser to an inter-American committee (Emergency Committee for Political Defence) in Montevideo (Uruguay) in order to coordinate 'the necessary laws of all of the 21 American republics in the interest of a unified defence against totalitarian endeavours'.[15] The result of this work was a two-volume documentation on state protection laws, which, among others, dealt with the legal measures for the containment of the 'Doctrinas extremistas, revolucionarias o disolventes'.[16] Anarchist, communist, National Socialist and fascist ideas were considered 'doctrinas extremistas'. As the documentation showed, the state protection laws were much more concerned with left-wing extremism ('las doctrinas del extremismo izquierdista'[17]) than with right-wing extremism. The 'propaganda extremista' had become the terminus technicus of state protection laws in countries such as Bolivia and Peru.[18] Other countries stopped the immigration of people who supported 'extremist doctrines',[19] took away the residence permits of foreigners who appeared suspicious or placed legal sanctions on the formation of extremist associations of foreigners ('associaciones de extranjeros con fines políticos extremistas'[20]).

After 1945, Loewenstein belonged to the founders of West German political science, and his terminology may not have remained without influence. Nevertheless, he pragmatically adapted himself to the respective language culture in which he published. In a contribution on 'Communism and the American Constitution' at the beginning of the 1950s, he pointed out his earlier publications on state and constitutional protection in the following words: 'The author has dedicated a good measure of his scientific efforts and practical work to political radicalism'.[21]

Hannah Arendt's (1906–75) essay *Ideology and Terror* (1953), a commemorative publication for Karl Jaspers,[22] which was included in the new edition of her *Elemente und Ursprünge Totaler Herrschaft* in 1958, appeared a short time later. There, 'extremism' is closely connected to the mindset of totalitarian ideologies. These claim 'the total explanation of the past, the total knowledge of the present, and the reliable prediction of the future',[23] thus making themselves independent of all experience and founding that circular thinking deduced from premises seen as absolute, which leads to the 'tyranny of logicality'.[24] 'The famous extremism of totalitarian movements, far from having anything to do with true radicalism, consists indeed in this "thinking everything to the worst", in this deducing process which always arrives at the worst possible conclusions'.[25]

At the end of the 1930s, the term extremism had found entrance into revolution research. In his comparative considerations regarding the patterns of the course of revolutions (1938) – most of all in England, the USA, France and Russia – the Harvard historian Crane Brinton (1898–1968) focused on the fight between 'moderates' and 'extremists'. According to Brinton, the American Revolution stood out in as much as 'it was missing the victory of the extremists over the moderates'.[26] Normally, the first revolution period was determined by the moderates and the following 'critical one'[27] by the extremists.

After some time, which was short in Russia but somewhat longer in England and France, it came to a power struggle between the moderates and the extremists, which in many ways resembled the struggle of the earlier government and the revolutionaries. The moderates suffered defeat. They had to emigrate, they were arrested and executed, at best they were able to go underground somewhere and were forgotten. Now, the extremists grasped the power.[28]

Brinton used the expressions 'extremists' and 'radicals' synonymously, e.g. when he established the move to the left during revolutions: 'After every crisis the victors tend to split up into a right wing, which is in power, and into an opposing left wing. Up to a certain stage, every crisis ends with the victory of the radical opposition'.[29] The moderates are mostly better or at least more normal human beings than their radical opponents, but they suffer their demise not due to greater idealism but due to their more highly developed realism, as they proceed more upon their 'common sense'.[30] In the crisis, a 'man with a healthy dose of fanatical idealism becomes the leader'. The extremists feel 'intensive, durable and uncomfortable hatred for groups of their compatriots', and they violently force all moderates out of the revolution-promoting organizations. 'The discipline, monomania and centralization of leadership, which are among the marks of the victorious extremists, are first developed in the revolutionary groups of the illegal government and then perfected'.[31] The 'fanaticism' of the extremists is the same as the religious one. The Bolshevists and the Jacobins were as convinced as the Calvinists that they alone were right, and that their programme was the only possible one. All radicals were willing to commit themselves to sacrifice silence and security, to subdue themselves to discipline and to have their personality absorbed by the group.[32] At its peak, determined by the extremists, the revolution displays an 'ascetic puritanical feature'.[33] Hence, the 'strongly believing, victorious extremists are crusaders, fanatics, and ascetics, who want to create Heaven on Earth'.[34] The 'eschatologies of these revolutionary religions' also resemble each other:

> In the English revolution, the extremes as well as the moderate Christian eschatologies made their influence felt. Year by year, the millenists expected the return of Christ. The government of the Saints was imminent. The Jacobins had a less concrete image of Heaven. In any event, it was to be represented on earth in the form of Robespierre's Republic of Virtues. [ ... ] The Russian Heaven is the classless society which will come as soon as the hellfire of proletarian dictatorship has gradually liquidated the earthly misery of the class struggle.[35]

Millenarism is one of the most important engines of terror. Especially the 'true to their convictions, decent extremists'[36] fall prey to it. People are overtaxed with the attempt to in no time achieve a 'life without vices'. Thus, change comes about: 'Political propaganda, which carries the traits of obsession, seems to have a point of saturation that, once it is exceeded, works against its originators'.[37] The 'extremist attempts'[38] to change the 'habits, feelings and inclinations' of the people fail. At last, a tyrant takes over power, and when it comes to a decline in moral standards, the churches gain influence again. In Brinton's typology, Lenin was the arch-extremist, and Stalin merely his tyrannic, Machiavellian beneficiary.

Presumably, Brinton's musings influenced Richard Löwenthal (1908–91) who spent time on a research grant at the Russian Research Centre of Harvard University in the years 1959/1960, and there wrote his later repeatedly reprinted, much read contribution on *Totalitarian and Democratic Revolution*. Other than Brinton, however, he emphasized the special quality of the 'totalitarian' revolution in Russia in comparison with the democratic revolutions in the West. According to this, the Russian Revolution had taken a similar course as the democratic ones in the West until the beginning of the 1920s. First, a 'double rulership' had come about with new institutions of 'revolutionary democracy' that opposed the provisional government. Then, 'with the help of these new institutions, there followed the fall of the moderates by the extremists'. These, 'without any consideration of traditional ideas and inherited rights, strove to carry out the revolutionary programme by help of methods of dictatorship'. However, after the centralized ruling apparatus had been created and the outbreak of embittered conflicts 'under the auspices of the extremist dictatorship party',[39] the revolution took another path. The 'thermidor' and the fall of the extremists did not take place, yet their desire for 'making the revolution permanent'[40] remained unbroken. In contrast to Hannah Arendt, who had defined totalitarianism as the 'extremes of horror', Löwenthal held the opinion that the Soviet Union after Stalin also displayed 'the decisive characteristics of the totalitarian power structure and dynamics'.[41]

In the context of the dominating totalitarian discourse, 'extremism' for the most part remained a subordinate terminological category by which certain traits of totalitarian actors and their role in revolutionary transformation processes could be described. When 'extremism' as a scientific concept extracted itself from the totalitarianism discussion and gained an independent role, there were several reasons for this. The fixation – from time to time – on the autocracy type seen as 'totalitarian' accompanied by growing critique of the totalitarianism concept[42] gradually dissolved itself from the 1960s on and led the attention of research more strongly again towards the multitude of the, globally, by far more prevalent non-constitutional political systems. Hence, anti-liberal/anti-democratic groupings, parties and movements at the edges of the pluralist power structure of democratic constitutional states could hardly be classified as 'totalitarian', particularly as it proved to be difficult to conclude the to be expected ruling practices in case of a seizure of power from the kind of – additionally often veiled by 'mimicry' – system critique/system hostility. The research originating from the characteristics of the dictatorships of the Iberian peninsula and Latin America led to a systematic differentiation of an 'authoritarian' and a 'totalitarian' regime type.[43]

## 2 The import of the term extremism into West German humanities and social sciences

'Extremism' and 'totalitarianism' were ingredients of the vocabulary of political emigrants whose works frequently attracted much attention in postwar Germany. In general, theory import from the USA played an important role in spreading the term extremism to West German humanities and social sciences. An early contribution was made by the psychologist Peter R. Hofstätter (1913–94) with his influential *Einführung in die Sozialpsychologie* (1954). There, 'extremists' or 'radicals' – both terms were used synonymously – were people who held opinions that deviated greatly from the average attitude profile of a reference group. Hofstätter adopted the empirically quantified research results of Anglo-Saxon colleagues and crystallized the connection between extreme points of view and strength of conviction: 'Where the distribution of opinions of a group in reference to a topic vary widely, the convictional strength of the representatives of middle of the road views are relatively small, that of the representatives of extreme points of view, though relatively high'.[44] 'It is the "radicals" who are quite sure of their issue, and there is rarely a "moderate one" who is as definitely convinced of his view as the extremists'.[45] Extremism appeared as the inability to see reality in all its rich facets and to weigh one's judgement. In another place, it was seen as nonconformist resistance in the light of the uniform pressure of one's own group of reference.[46]

Already in the mid-1920s, the terms and concepts used by and imported into the German language by Hofstätter had found entrance into American political psychology and opinion research. At a cooperation conference of the American Political Science Association and the American Psychological Association in Washington, Floyd H. Allport and D.A. Hartman presented research results on the measurement of motivations for 'atypical opinions' in December 1924, which inspired a number of studies in the following decades. In general, there was agreement on what made a 'radical view' ('radical' in contrast to 'reactionary'); nevertheless, did there also exist a 'radical personality type'? For the identification of the personality type, the authors developed standardized questionnaires and attitude scales, which made it possible to gauge the opinion range in view of controversial topics such as the attitude towards the League of Nations, the suitability of the presidential candidate Coolidge, the control of the Supreme Court, the lifting of the Prohibition or the banning of the Ku Klux Klan. The extremes of the opinion scales discovered in this way were marked as 'radical' or 'reactionary', according to the usual right-wing/left-wing spectrum. Those holding positions strongly deviating from the average of the opinions of the investigated groups were seen as 'extremists'.[47] In in-depth interviews with a number of 'radicals' and 'reactionaries', the authors found corresponding personality traits (e.g. 'lacking agreement with the conventional moral code'[48]), but also noticeable differences between the extreme groups. The 'reactionaries' were characterized as rather 'tough-minded' and 'extroverted'; the 'radicals', however, as mostly 'tender-minded' and 'introverted'. These personality attributes derived from philosophy[49] and psychoanalysis played an important role in empirical socio-psychological research on 'radicalism' and 'extremism' in the following decades.

Hans Jürgen Eysenck's work (1916–97) at London University was influential. There, the connection between 'radicalism', the 'extreme left-wing', 'tender-mindedness' and introversion were put in question.[50] 'Fascists' and 'communists' showed themselves to be equally 'tough-minded' in Eysenck's investigations, meaning that both were not willing to raise questions concerning their own position, therefore tending to force their own viewpoint on to others. A one-dimensional depiction of the attitudinal range which positioned 'fascists' and 'communists' at the extreme end of a scale did not do justice to this common ground. Therefore, Eysenck suggested imagining this attitudinal range as two-dimensional (see Figure 8.1).

One of the axes extended itself between the poles of 'radical' and 'conservative', 'radical' also marking the 'extreme left-wing', and 'conservative', in contrast, marking the 'extreme right-wing'. He called the poles of the other axis 'authoritarian' and 'democratic'. Thus, 'communists' and 'fascists' differed only by their placement on the right-wing/left-wing axis but not in their distance to the 'authoritarianism'[51] pole of the second dimension. Hence, in Eysenck's terminology, there existed an 'authoritarian' as well as a 'democratic' extreme left-wing and right-wing. The term 'radicalism' remained reserved for the extreme left-wing.

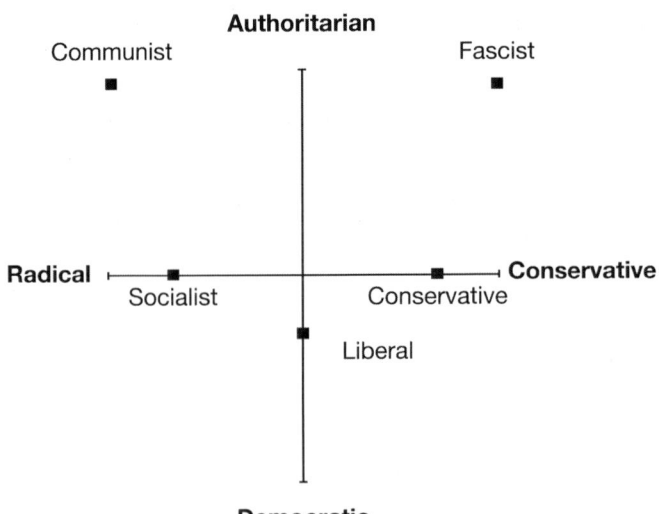

*Figure 8.1* Two-dimensional depiction of the political attitudinal range according to Eysenck
Source: Eysenck (1954: 110).

Eysenck's positioning of 'communists' and 'fascists' corresponded not by word but by meaning to the interpretation pattern of the totalitarianism concept that became general intellectual property in the USA, Great Britain and Germany in the 1950s. The analogizing view of the political extremes was its permanent component.

This, however, did not apply to the studies that had come about under the leadership of the emigrated Frankfurt social scientists Theodor W. Adorno (1903–69) and Max Horkheimer (1895–1973). In their determination of the *Authoritarian Personality*, the examination of the conscious contents and the personality traits of fascists/National Socialists was the decisive factor. If one spoke of the 'super-ego of the extremists', this had to do with the violent anti-Semite who imposes his merciless death sentence on 'the Jews' as a collective on account of 'stereotypical accusations'.[52] 'Anti-democratic' thinking was hardly sought among communists. They were rather taken under one's protective wing in the 'irrational' equating of fascists and communists by anti-communists. Accordingly, this resulted in 'correlations between anti-Semitism and anti-Communism'[53] among the American test persons.

This slant was astutely criticized by the Chicago sociologist Edward A. Shils (1910–95). He outlined the development of the British and the American intellectual culture in its dealing with Bolshevism whose totalitarian traits had also not been recognized due to the generally accepted right-wing/left-wing dichotomy. Only gradually had the analogies between fascism and Bolshevism been realized which, for a long time, had been understood as two completely separate worlds: their mutual hostility against bourgeois liberty rights and political democracy, contempt for parliamentarian institutions, individualism and private entrepreneurship, their Manichaean ideology, their leanings towards conspiring and to conspiracy theories: 'all of these showed that the two extremes had much in common'.[54]

After the beginning of military action against Nazi Germany, many Americans became aware of a problem that had hardly been noticed during times of peace: the lack of loyalty of certain political groupings. John Roy Carlson, for example, had shocked his readership with a report about the activities of the *Nazi Underworld of America*. Had it been possible for German secret agents, in connection with their American helpmates, to infiltrate security-relevant zones? And what was going on with the other extreme, respectively? For sceptical contemporaries, it appeared clear: 'Still the political ethics of American Communists are about as low as anything ever observed in these parts, including the Ku Klux Klan'.[55] During the war, a discussion about the defence capability of democracy had been carried on. Had the West not remained passive far too long during the rise of the extremist movements in the 1920s and 1930s? Numerous authors had participated in the debate on the necessity of a 'militant democracy', which had essentially been set in motion by Karl Loewenstein.[56] After the end of the war, the falling apart of the anti-Hitler coalition supported the sometimes suppressed insight that the danger came not only from the extreme right-wing but also from the extreme left-wing.

To scientific observers such as Shils, the analogies between the antagonists were obvious. Therefore, by being limited to the right-wing, they only proved in numerous commendable and inspiring studies on the *Authoritarian Personality* how tenacious prejudices are. Hence, Shils, on the basis of many characteristics used in the 'F-scale', which had been used for the identification of attitudes typical of fascism, was able to show the overlapping with characteristics typical of Bolshevism, such as the demand for unconditional obedience to the party or for keeping the Marxist–Leninist doctrine pure. Adorno and his staff later took up this critique at the Frankfurt Institut für Sozialforschung and developed scales to identify 'left-wing radicals with an authoritarian character'.[57]

In his critique on the socio-psychological studies of the Adorno School, Shils named another weak spot: The authors of the *Authoritarian Personality* had assumed a too direct connection between the existence of authoritarian character traits and the creation of authoritarian movements. As shown by nativist circles in the USA, extreme authoritarian attitudes were often paired with the inability to obey strict organizational discipline. Furthermore, the liberal democratic society offered space for a multitude of social roles in which different personality types could find fulfilment.[58]

In a highly noteworthy book published two years later on *The Torment of Secrecy*, Shils dealt with a special aspect of the social and political design of pluralist societies.[59] Against the background of Senator McCarthy's and the Senate Committee's activities for the exposure of 'un-American activities', he subtly analysed the precarious balance of the (general) public, privacy and secrecy and the threat to it from political 'extremism' – the key word of the analysis. Shils revealed the preconditions for the security hysteria and the communism phobia that had spread throughout the United States after the end of World War II. The efforts to preserve the technical knowhow for constructing the nuclear bomb was the essential reason for the increase in the importance of state secrecy as well as for the intensive espionage activities of the Soviet Union, which knew how to make use of the security leaks of a society accustomed to far-reaching publicity in the political realm. At the same time, there existed a left-wing 'intelligentsia' that had developed during the 1930s, which painted a rosy picture of Soviet communism and whose illusions had only temporarily been disrupted by the Hitler–Stalin pact. The irrationality of the perception of 'communist extremism'[60] exceeded the irrationality of the 'extremistic anti-communists'[61] who saw communist dangers looming everywhere. Through their points of view, they were able to connect to the xenophobic public opinions of American 'nativists' whose 'hyperpatriotism' stemmed from the identity problems of immigrants, who, due to the assimilation pressure they themselves were subject to, reacted by intensified disassociation efforts towards new immigrants. Shils described the explosive mixture of xenophobia, isolationism, 'extremist, paranoid anti-Semitism',[62] 'extremist anti-revolutionism',[63] populism and Christian fundamentalism as it was especially to be found in the mid-West.

To Shils, the interaction of extremisms endangered the openness of the pluralist society. 'Extremism' and 'pluralism' stood in an antithetical relationship to each other: 'Pluralism' seemed 'conservative' in comparison to 'revolutionary extremism', yet liberal in comparison to 'reactionary extremism'.[64] Pluralism offered a position that was closest in itself only in contrast to the 'extremes of the estrangement of social order and orderly change'. In reality, though, it was based on conflict and diversity, change and critique, allowing for a variety of interests, opinions and viewpoints. Nevertheless, these had to be represented with a certain moderation. Liberals and 'radicals' had assumed that 'revolutionaries and communists' were their allies, whereas conservatives believed that it was possible to form alliances with 'fascists, Nazis, nativist–fundamentalists and McCarthyists'.[65] The overcome right-wing/left-wing scheme tempted such erroneous assumptions. In reality, the political division line took another course: Actually, pluralism was based on the conviction that the representatives of legitimate political alternative ideas had more in common among themselves than with the concepts of 'apocalyptical politicians'.[66] Shils reached the following conclusion: 'the really crucial dividing line in politics is between pluralistic moderation and monomaniac extremism'.[67]

Seymour M. Lipset later brought the antithesis of 'pluralism' and 'extremism' around to a terminological system. In *The Politics of Unreason* (1970), a work on the development of right-wing extremism in the USA written jointly with Earl Raab, extremism was defined as a violation of the rules and regulations of liberal democracy: 'extremism means going beyond the limits of the normative procedures which define the democratic political process'.[68] The core of this process was formed by a pluralism of ideas, interests and viewpoints. Extremism, on the other hand, was 'monistic',[69] took the Manichaean world view as absolute and did not allow any other opinions beside it. It subscribed to 'simplism',[70] propagated simple solutions for highly complex problems and saw mysterious forces at work everywhere conspiring against the forces of good (Figure 8.2).

Lipset's formula of the *extremism of the middle* caused lively discussions and many misunderstandings. It was based on a Marxist-inspired ('basis' and 'top structure') theory on the connection between the socio-economic technological structures of modern societies and the establishment of certain political ideological trends.[71] The upper, middle and lower classes could thus produce liberal as well as extremist ideologies. Conservatism was the liberal ideology of the upper classes, and traditional authoritarianism was the extremist one. The liberal ideology of the lower classes was found in (democratic) socialism, and their extremist variants were found in the communism and Peronism camp. Liberalism, lastly, stood for the expression of the ideology of the middle classes, and fascism stood for its extremist degeneration.[72] Lipset sought to support this theory with data about the supporters and the electorate of the different political camps. For German National Socialism, it was most of all Jürgen W. Falter who, by sociological election analyses, later

|  | lower class | middle class | upper class |
|---|---|---|---|
| e<br>x<br>t<br>r<br>e<br>m<br>e | Communism<br><br>Peronism | Fascism | Traditional<br><br>Authoritarianism |
| m<br>o<br>d<br>e<br>r<br>a<br>t<br>e | Socialism | Liberalism | Conservatism |

*Figure 8.2* Relationship between socio-economic layering and political ideology according to Seymour M. Lipset

established proof of broader distribution layers and a less expressive 'middle class belly' of the NS movement.[73]

The works by Lipset and other American social scientists exerted a strong influence upon the West German disciplines, particularly as the election successes of the Nationaldemokratische Partei Deutschlands (NPD) and the students' movement at the left wing of the political spectrum caused a sensation in the second half of the 1960s. With the theory import from the USA as well as with the spreading of the term extremism, the methodically progressive Cologne social sciences under the auspices of Erwin K. Scheuch (1928–2003) played an essential role.

In the contribution written in collaboration with Hans D. Klingemann on the *Theorie des Rechtsradikalismus in westlichen Industriegesellschaften*, Scheuch sought to attribute the coming about of 'right-wing radicalism' to structural similarities of modern industrial societies. Hereby, various socio-psychological as well as sociological explanation attempts (such as Eysenck's 'authoritarian personality' as well as Talcott Parson's system theory) were integrated. 'Right-wing radicalism' was the central term, yet the term extremism was employed synonymously, and the category of 'left-wing radicalism' introduced simultaneously. 'Extremism' (synonymous with 'radicalism') saw the 'basic rejection of the present form of society and its political organisation as intolerable, yes, as evil by reference to an alternative and more efficient type of the organisation of society'.[74] The authors attributed the development of mass movements to the fundamental changes in social relationships (suppression of 'primary' and 'secondary' relationships) in industrial society and, on this basis, explained the differences between left-wing and right-wing variants of the phenomena. The attractiveness of 'particularly totalitarian and extremist mass movements' was most of all founded on 'their promise to simultaneously increase the efficiency of the type of society characterized by secondary relationships ( = "modern" society) and to restore and enlarge the society determined by primary relationships ( = "traditional" society)'. The 'right-wing' and the 'left-wing' variants were differentiated in the following way: 'These extremist political movements we call "left-wing", when the present society is being combated by reference to a future ideal situation whose essential acting institution is to remain the movement of likeminded people. Furthermore, a novel explanation scheme for the causes of the present conditions is being offered (e.g. exploitation by owners of means of production)'.[75] However, such movements were considered 'right-wing' 'if they fought against the present by help of an (improved) re-establishment of past organisational forms and values and offered explanation patterns from the past (e.g. biologistic thinking)'.[76]

### 3 Extremism or radicalism?

The theory of 'right-wing radicalism' connected itself to a definition of 'right-wing extremism', whereby the terms appeared exchangeable.[77] 'Right-wing radicalism',[78] the key term at first preferred by the Cologne Institute for Comparative Social Research, soon gave way to 'right-wing extremism'. In an essay from the year 1970, Scheuch presented the NPD as a 'right-wing party' (in the text also simultaneously as a 'right-wing extremist' one),[79] discussed the differences and common grounds of 'right-wing' and 'left-wing extremism'[80] in a volume on 'new rightists (right-wingers) and old leftists (left-wingers)' and entitled his extensive, rich in materials and ideas contribution of principles for the anniversary edition of the 25-year existence of the second German democracy published by Richard Löwenthal and Hans-Peter Schwarz as follows: *Political Extremism in the Federal Republic of Germany.* The key term 'radicalism' was replaced by 'extremism'.

In a footnote, Scheuch distanced himself from a fundamental Marxist critique on the extremism term and emphasized the importance of comparative research since the 1930s:

> 'Political extremism' and especially 'totalitarianism' were supposed to terminologically depict the common grounds of the Communist, Fascist and National Socialist regimes of that time, common grounds in view of the deviation from the model of a parliamentarian democracy. In the meantime, the terminology can be grasped apart from the historical

reference of those days. 'Extremism', or better yet 'political extremism', means the rejection of the moral concept of a liberal and democratic political order.[81]

Scheuch referred to a dissertation Thomas A. Herz[82] had written at his institute and to a study by Lipset/Raab with the juxtaposition of 'pluralism' and 'monism'.[83] In this way, 'political extremism' was classified as a creative product of highly differentiated societies and the definitional connection to a – multidimensioned, politically disputed – democracy term avoided: 'Simplified, extremism means an understanding of the political order and the actions aimed at it as a cancellation of the condition by which politics are made to become a conflict among groups, values and interests. The existence of a highly differentiated society is conditional for an understanding of extremism such as this. The differentiality causes those political – and also generally social – conditions which are understood as antithetical to extremism'.[84] Leaving it unsaid, Scheuch in turn resumed the 'theory of right-wing radicalism in modern industrial societies' and the socio-historical process of the suppression of 'primary relationships' by 'secondary relationships' or rather of 'communal' relationships by 'societal' ones.

Not even the staff members of the Cologne Institute for Comparative Social Research unanimously followed Scheuch's tacitly carried out replacement of the key term 'radicalism' by 'extremism'. By terminologically differentiating between the two terms, Scheuch's (then) staff members Hans D. Klingemann and Franz U. Pappi held on to the radicalism term and simultaneously introduced the extremism term in a theoretically and methodically demanding election study on the parliamentary election in Hessia in 1970. By a comparison of voters' attitudes, they had noticed that, in comparison to the NPD, the Deutsche Kommunistische Partei (DKP) voters agreed with 'democracy' in the sense of the expansion of democratic rights ('democratization') but – like the NPD – simultaneously tended to agree with 'undemocratic' methods (such as the use of violence as a means of politics). Therefore, they differentiated between a 'norm-oriented' (methods-oriented) and a value-oriented (goal-oriented) concept of democracy. 'Radicalism' was defined as the rejection of democratic methods and 'extremism' as the negation of democratic values.[85] According to this understanding of the terms, the DKP was radical but not extremist, whereas the NPD, in contrast, was radical as well as extremist.

This understanding of the terms was later adopted by the Mannheim social scientist Max Kaase in a theoretically and methodically supported Infratest study on political protest in the Federal Republic of Germany.[86] Kaase summarized it at the beginning of the 1980s as follows:

> The goal and value dimension is operationalized via the left-wing/right-wing classification and defined as political extremism. According to this understanding, left-wing radicalism includes a radical–democratic, egalitarian

understanding of politics, whereas right-wing radicalism corresponds to an anti-democratic, anti-egalitarian position. [ ... ] In contrast, the middle or norm dimension applies to the agreement or rather rejection of institutionalized political processes and is called political radicalism at its anti-institutional pole. To this particularly belongs the use of violence against individuals and objects in the political process. [ ... ] However, much to the disadvantage of terminologic precision, this terminological differentiation had so far not been able to assert itself.

One reason therefore was the popular constitutional law interpretation of extremism in the sense of political activities 'against the constituents of the constitution', whereas 'radicalism' was seen as the 'pursuance of radical political aims within the framework of the given constitution'.[87] This was the terminology which, among others, the Federal Minister of the Interior, Werner Mayhofer, had supported, making it the basis for the work of constitution protection authorities.[88]

Nevertheless, the difference in using the terms expressed by Kaase applied not only to the terminology of state law. Also in the socio-scientific discussion, the terms were grasped from the perspective of different disciplines, attempts and approaches. In a plural scientific landscape with a matter of such complexity which, in addition, was politically disputed, this might also have been different. The state of the discussion towards the end of the 1970s is mirrored in a collective volume by the Bonn historian of contemporary history, Manfred Funke, which found wide distribution in an edition by the Federal Agency for Civic Education. In his terminological definitions, Funke worked out the structural characteristics of extremist ideology as well as the absolute claim to the truth and 'assurance of salvation',[89] the intolerance towards those having other opinions, the contempt for compromises and the overt or covert willingness to violence. Simultaneously, he emphasized the time restriction of the phenomenon: 'Extremism, as a to be defined specific measurement of the highly unstable distance between a norm and the desire to destroy it, appears as a verbal placement directly to the rating subject and is therefore not to be classified as removed from time and space'.[90] This is not an appearance 'with an unchangeable core character and removable attributes' but a bundle of characteristics. The extremist is in the 'process of centrifugal distancing from the middle of that gravity which orders and designs the actual social system'.[91]

In the same volume, this relativity of 'middle' and 'extremes' in different historic political constellations moved within a tension area of terminological definition by the political scientist and 'futurologist' Ossip K. Flechtheim from Berlin. He differentiated 'radicalism' from 'extremism' in a positive way. He saw the essential difference particularly in the question of what is politically possible:

In contrast to extremism, humane and democratic radicalism always remains aware also in its Socialist version that although it may be necessary to replace the existing societal order by a radically new one, but that also this new society can only be new in some important aspects, however, in others it must remain attached to the tradition of history. This new formation of society may be better, more humane and more democratic than the old order – but it too will not be a perfect realm of freedom and happiness. Whereas the extremist believes in an absolute and total break with all the class societies of the past and in a future society without classes and rulership which must therefore be fought for with every means possible – sparing no costs and without regard to sacrifices – the self-critically rational radical believes that also tomorrow's better society will still be under the sign of final human inadequacy and natural limitation.[92]

The bolder radicalism develops its visions, the 'more humane these means need' to be. Also, herein it differs 'from right-wing as well as left-wing extremism. According to its nature, the latter is extreme, illusionary and blind to reality, subjective and dogmatic, but also elitist and authoritarian'.[93] Therefore, in comparison to the extremes, the 'middle' deserved preference as, already since Aristotle, the 'middle' has been a reminder of the priority of cool logics opposite blind emotion, rational hypothesis opposite dogmatic thesis, sober compromise opposite wild, destructive battle.[94]

Flechtheim's terminological differentiation was no more successful in research than that of Klingemann/Pappi and Kaase. Nonetheless, the differentiation between the value and methods dimension of a (liberal) democracy was occasionally taken up. The terminology of the Antwerp political scientist Cas Mudde turns the Klingemann/Pappi differentiation of extremism and radicalism into its opposite: 'Radicalism is reserved for those groupings that accept democratic methods (such as free elections) yet negate democratic values (such as pluralism)'.[95] 'Extremism', on the other hand, embraced both: the negation of democratic methods and values. This terminology then resembles that of those authors who speak of 'radicalism' if a grouping moves in the realm of extremism but does not completely fulfil its definitional characteristics. Many 'right-wing populist' parties are thus classified as 'radical' yet not 'extremist'.[96] The political scientist Hans-Gerd Jaschke from Berlin criticized in this terminology how 'radicalism' was made into the 'non-binding catch-all term [ ... ] for all the trends to the right wing of established Conservatism'.[97] Yet the reversal undertook by Hans-Uwe Otto and Roland Merten in a study about right-wing extreme violence[98] did not convince: 'Violent equalling right-wing radical, without violence "only" right-wing extreme, "right-wing radicalism" as superlative form of "right-wing extremism"?'[99] What Jaschke finds fault with is found in the application to the opposite political wing in the French political scientists Jean Chiche and Dominique Reynié, who differentiate between a 'tough' 'extreme left-wing' and a 'soft' 'radical left-wing'. All these differentiations are the result of the circumstance that the superlative 'extremism' causes problems when it comes to making gradations within a range of subversive phenomena.

The author who, at the end of the 1980s, suggested relinquishing the term radicalism in scientific analyses also did not escape this problem.[100] Owing to the positive connotation of solving the problem by 'getting to the roots' of a false development and in view of the prevailing use of language in Romance countries going back to the liberal and democratic trends of the nineteenth century, misunderstandings were unavoidable if the language was used for describing anti-liberal/anti-democratic trends. Instead, it was recommended to restrict oneself in this context to the key term 'extremism' and to define its content as an antithesis to the democratic constitutional state. With the definition of political extremism, it was possible to differentiate between a definitio ex negativo and a definitio ex positivo.[101] The first form of the definition of the term was based on a minimum definition of the democratic constitutional state, hence grasped 'extremism' by rejecting fundamental values and rules of the game (most of all human rights, securing basic rights, pluralism, division of powers). In contrast, the second form defined the intellectual physiognomy of extremisms by working out typical thought structures such as 'offensive and defensive claims to absolutism', 'dogmatism', 'utopism and the categorical renunciation of Utopia', 'friend–foe stereotyping', 'conspiracy theories', 'fanaticism and activism'.

The analysis grid gained in such a way formed the foundation of a complete representation of political extremism in the Federal Republic of Germany jointly worked out with Eckhard Jesse, originally in three volumes first published in 1989 and later published numerous times in updated versions, also sold by the Bundeszentrale für politische Bildung.[102] In the same year, a *Jahrbuch Extremismus & Demokratie* was founded which since then has devoted itself to the documentation and analysis of current developments in right-wing and left-wing extremism in Germany and other countries.[103]

## 4 Extremism, authoritarianism and dogmatism

The social scientific extremism/radicalism discussion of the 1970s and 1980s drew from the reservoir of (predominantly psychological) authoritarianism research in manifold ways. The discussions set in motion by the Adorno School were continued by a number of empirical studies.

Hereby, 'authoritarianism' denoted a personality type characterized by specific attitudes which explained the susceptibility for autocratic solutions.[104] Milton Rokeach's concept of 'dogmatism' built on the work by the Berkeley group, but moved away from its psycho-analytical orientation. Instead, the author reached back to attempts by Gestalt psychology.[105] In the centre of his theory stood the differentiation between the 'open' and 'closed mind'.[106] Individuals with 'closed' dogmatic orientation systems tended to uncritically adopt the opinions of authorities and in certain situations proved themselves to be incapable of perceiving the characteristics required for suitable action.

For a long time, 'authoritarianism' and 'dogmatism' were researched foremost only on the 'right-wing' side of the political spectrum. The assumption of a correlation of 'authoritarianism' and 'dogmatism', which sounds banal in the ideological–historical sense, was generally cut out.[107] Only after the end of 'true socialism' was this issue dealt with more intensively. Hence, Gerda Lederer and Angela Kindervater came to the conclusion that school classes investigated in East Germany and Russia at the beginning of the 1990s showed higher measurements for authoritarianism than in West Germany.[108] For Russia, there were also found to be positive correlations between pro-communist attitudes and authoritarianism.[109] Against this background, Jeff Greenberg and Eva Jonas developed attempts to comparatively investigate the 'ideological rigidity' of extreme right-wing as well as extreme left-wing orientations.[110] In this, they deviate from that terminology preferred by the Canadian psychologist Bob Altemeyer. Accordingly, every form of blind devotion towards authorities stands for 'right-wing' authoritarianism – regardless of whether these are to be classified from an economic and social political perspective as 'right-wing' or 'left-wing'. According to Altemeyer, the supporters of the Tiananmen Massacre in Peking are seen as right-wing radicals as well as Russian hardliners who want to win back the old monopolist position for the Communist Party.[111]

## 5 Extremism and fundamentalism

Long before 11 September 2001, political religious 'fundamentalism' came more strongly into focus. The fundamentalism term stems from American Protestantism of the 1920s and connects to religious revival movements that derive an exclusive political design claim from unshakeable 'fundamentals' often codified in 'sacred writings', lay claim to man in his entire existence and subjugate him to a rigid system of rules.[112] The term spread from the Islamic Revolution in Iran in 1979 and was applied to political religious phenomena of all cultural circles. The demand for the union of state and religion is seen as the central characteristic of fundamentalism.

Nevertheless, the term was extended to the secular forms of the 'rebellion against modernity'.[113] Thomas Meyer developed an extensive typology of fundamentalisms at the end of the 1980s, whose realm of definitions covered phenomena that other authors had brought together under the terms 'extremism' and 'radicalism'. Christian J. Jäggi and David J. Krieger also included secular ideologies in their presentation. Consequently, they admitted the categories of a 'Marxist' and a 'green', that is to say radical ecological fundamentalism.[114] Such an extension of the terminology takes place 'if, from the perspective of an analysis of scientific or philosophical ideology, "fundamentalism" is seen as certain general structural peculiarities of ideologies which can be shown independent of the often so different contents of ideological thought structures'.[115] This perspective marks, for example, the ideology critique of 'critical rationalism' founded by Karl Popper as it is, among others, currently represented by Hans Albert and Kurt Salamun.[116] The hereby used terminological labels vary from 'fundamentalist' to 'totalitarian' and on to 'extremist' and 'anti-democratic'. According to Salamun, the necessary conditions for this characterization of conviction systems as 'fundamentalist' are: 'An absolute and exclusive claim to the truth', 'an elitarian–authoritarian conviction ideal', 'monistic striving for totalitarianism' and 'a strong tendency toward alternative radicalism'.[117]

In contrast to this use of words, Hans-Gerd Jaschke reserves the fundamentalism term predominantly for those extremes that do not apply to the inherited right-wing/left-wing differentiation.[118] And the fundamentalism project of the American Academy of Arts and Sciences under the direction of Martin E. Marty and R. Scott Appleby has limited the term to those trends to whom an otherworldly life is not unknown. With regard to the critique of the use of the fundamentalism formula, they note: 'Asked for alternatives, the scholars mention adjectives such as "neo-traditionalist", "extremist", "radically reformist" and "ultra-orthodox" to describe belief and behaviour patterns that television and radio channels and politicians simply call fundamentalism'.[119]

In contrast to Appleby/Scott, some authors see 'fundamentalism' as a form of right-wing radicalism or 'fascism'. In a contribution from the year 1923, the liberal Protestant theologian, Theodor Karl Eduard Bornhausen, must have been the first to describe the connection of right-wing ideologemes with religious contents by, among others, using the example of the Ku Klux Klan.[120] However, few authors go as far as Walter Laqueur, who generally awarded fundamentalisms to the extreme right or even subordinated them to the category of 'clerical fascism'.[121] It might then be less controversial, on the other hand, if certain forms of the extreme right, which resemble religions, are labelled 'fundamentalist', such as Stefan Breuer's study on the George circle.[122]

## 6 Right-wing and left-wing extremism

Aside from 'fundamentalism', the classical differentiation, according to the right-wing and left-wing terms of direction, asserted itself. Nonetheless, this differentiation found itself confronted by a fundamental critique on the way it was presented in West Germany, especially in the aftermath of the 1968 movement. Whereas the analytical usefulness of the term 'right-wing extremism' (nevertheless under different labels) was and is uncontested, the existence of 'left-wing extremism' was seen as doubtful. For:

> Leftists want the expansion of individual autonomy, the progress of the emancipation of social groups or classes from rationally no longer legitimizable rulership, new expanded forms of participation for everyone in the political formation of the will and decision making processes – all this by using an, optimally speaking, rationally to be known instrument; rightists want the organization of the individual into enduring natural communities, the bonding of the social groups to a hierarchically layered societal order, the stabilization of decision-making structures which are defined by institutions prescribed by individuals and society – all this with an instrument that gives priority to ultra-rational references.[123]

Helga Grebing's definition of the left-wing made 'real socialism' appear as a merely irrelevant form of deviation that caused no legitimation problems whatsoever to the 'progressive' project.

This understanding of the term differed from the Marxist–Leninist one represented by the SED and its Western allies by explicitly ignoring 'left-wing radicalism' in the sense of a strategic (actionistic, revolutionary enthusiastic) deviation from the 'real socialist' orthodoxy.[124] When it came to like-minded Italians,[125] the 'infantile disorder' denounced by Lenin now and then simply stood for 'extremism', while circumventing the radicalism formula which has a different connotation in the Romance context.

Rather, while following Grebing, the Berlin political scientist Richard Stöss withdrew the fundamentum in re from 'left-wing extremism'. In a – rich in ideas and material – examination of the structure and development of the West German party system, parties such as the NPD stood for being 'anti-democratic'. On the other hand, parties such as the DKP, which oriented themselves towards Moscow and East Berlin, stood for being 'anti-capitalist'. As the 'preconditions for the existence and success of anti-capitalist and anti-democratic parties [ ... ] obviously were very different' and their being based on contrary ruling concepts, the collective expression 'extremist parties from the left and the right' proved to be of 'little use'.[126] From this perspective, it seemed consistent when Stöss placed paramount importance on the problem of democracy compatibility in his work on right-wing extremism while, in the case of the (left-wing) Party of Democratic Socialism (PDS), he declared 'the question of subversiveness to the constitution' to be 'secondary'.[127]

Wolfgang Wippermann used different arguments from Helga Grebing and Richard Stöss. The extremism concept suggests a

> similarity between right-wing and left-wing extremism [ ... ]. which does not exist in reality but only in the books of so-called 'extremism researchers'. In fact, this way the weak spots of the totalitarianism theory comparing and far-reachingly identifying Fascism and Communism were only being reproduced and at the same time increased, particularly since actual comparisons between right-wing and left-wing extremism, still made by totalitarianism theoreticians, are being ignored. Instead, right-wing and left-wing extremism are only defined and identified by their alleged common rejection of democracy.[128]

Wippermann thus raised questions about the 'similarity' of the two forms found in comparative analyses, but implicitly allowed for the possibility of a scientifically productive comparison.

Critiques of this kind benefited from the difficulty of a sensitive boundary between the dichotomic terms of direction. For their terminological precisioning, the Torino law philosopher Norberto Bobbio (1909–2004) offered a highly esteemed suggestion in the mid-1990s. There, the political extremes are given a fundamental role. The opposing pair expressed the contrary attitude towards the ideal of equality – nevertheless, not in the sense of some completely reject-ing it and others applying it to all questions of life without any compromise. Such a view would be too simple, just for the reason that, in the light of the kind of the goods to be distributed, the mode of distribution and the size of the circle of recipients, the equality term allowed for very different inter-pretations.[129] According to Bobbio, leftists or 'egalitarians' are all those 'who, without failing to recognize that all men are as equal as they are unequal, give more importance to what makes them equal rather than unequal when it comes to judging on them and transferring rights and duties upon them'; rightists or 'non-egalitarians', on the other hand, are all those 'who, starting out from the same premise and having the same goal in mind, give more importance to what makes them unequal rather than equal'.[130] The left-wing sometimes tended to interpret inequalities as the result of alterable social conditions and to insist on their removal, whereas the right-wing was more frequently willing 'to accept what is natural and this second nature that expresses itself by customs, traditions and past potential'.[131]

According to Bobbio, the different relationship to the equality principle offers the key to the differentiation between the political 'right-wing' and 'left-wing'. The comparatives he used ('bigger' and 'rather') already point out that the placement of group A and group B is in this sense only possible in a relative way and not in an absolute one: In evaluating the assignment of rights and responsibilities, group A emphasizes what appears to make people equal to each other more strongly than group B – or vice versa. The place-ment of the right–left axis is all the more difficult, the more similar the respective groups are in ideologically programmatic respects. In a political system in which the decisive powers are crowded in the middle, labels in the sense of the terms of direction must seem particularly questionable. On the other hand, the presumption is suggesting that Bobbio's criterion is easier and applied more convincingly for the differentiation of political ideas and actors in the centrifugal rim areas of the political power fields of pluralist societies.

Bobbio did not deal with the issue of the differentiation of left-wing and right-wing extremism separately, yet he paid strong attention to the opposite pair of 'extreme' and 'moderate'. This differentiation followed a different principle from that of 'right' and 'left'. The ideal the terms 'extreme' and 'moderate' were based on was historically of at least as much importance as the terms 'right' and 'left'. If the terms were oriented at the principle of equality, the antithesis of 'extreme' and 'moderate' applied to the principle of liberty and thus to the differentiation 'between liberal doctrines and move-ments on the one hand and authoritarian doctrines and movements on the other hand'.[132] According to Bobbio, an authoritarian left-wing and right-wing must sometimes be differentiated from a liberal left-wing and right-wing. Bobbio's differentiation reminds us of the two-dimensional depiction of the political realm in Hans Jürgen Eysenck at the beginning of the 1950s and leads to a quadrupling of the intellectual political realm (Figure 8.3).

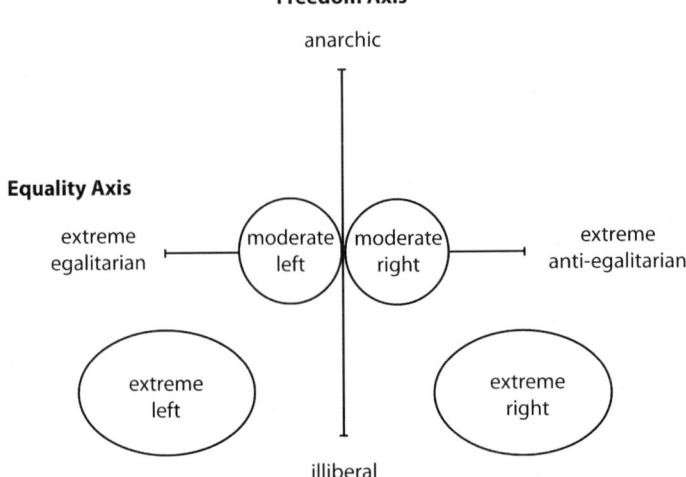

*Figure 8.3* Two-dimensional depiction of the political realm according to Norberto Bobbio

The four areas of the coordinate system are described by Bobbio in the following manner:

1 the 'extreme left-wing' encompasses all those 'egalitarian and at the same time authoritarian movements whose most important example had been the Jacobins';[133]
2 the 'left middle' (one could also speak of the moderate left-wing) is determined by 'egalitarian and at the same time liberal doctrines and movements',[134] as they mark social democracy, for example;
3 the 'right-wing middle'[135] (or moderate right-wing) includes democratic conservative parties which are liberal but anti-egalitarian;
4 the 'extreme right-wing',[136] finally, constitutes the collective pool of anti-liberal anti-egalitarianism; the best known historic examples are fascism and National Socialism.

Bobbio's short definition formula of the 'extreme right-wing' is: 'anti-liberal anti-egalitarianism', that of the 'extreme left-wing' is 'anti-liberal egalitarianism'. Accordingly, the extreme right-wing is marked by the negation of 'liberty' as well as the 'equality principle', and the extreme left-wing only by the negation of the liberty principle. The common denominator is thus the negation of the 'liberty principle'.

## 7 Extremism of the middle?

According to the Platonic–Aristotelian terminology, the middle lies between the two extremes; furthermore, the extremes and the middle also constitute an antithesis. An 'extremism of the middle' thus appears to be a paradox. Still, the term had already spread in the 1990s, in part in critical polemic intention. Generally, the term did not serve as an analytical category, as proved by its colourful content.

If the 'extremism of the middle' is understood socio-structurally, as Seymour M. Lipset did, meaning the 'extremism of the middle class', it is in no way in the necessary contrast to the Aristotelian tradition. Of course, in the interests of political stability and security of liberty, the philosopher recommended a society centred on the middle class, as a deprivation of the middle one seemed less possible to him than that of the lower and the upper classes. This, however, did not fundamentally exclude such a development. If this happened, though, a change in the constitution would be the logical consequence. Applied to our times, this would mean: If the broad middle levels of society fall to the political extreme, this will inevitably lead to a transformation of the system.

Lipset's thesis of fascism as the extremism of the middle (meaning the middle class) had in the general sense already been advocated in the 1930s. Lipset referred to the American national economist David J. Saposs. In an essay about 'The Role of the Middle Class in Social Development', he had juxtaposed the ideologies of socialism and fascism and claimed: 'Fascism being the extreme expression of middle-classism or populism, it also is the exact counterpart of Communism, which may be described as the extreme expression of Socialism'.[137] In a similar way, the German sociologist Theodor Geiger had given 'the panic of the middle class'[138] as the cause for the NSDAP's enormous gain in votes after the Reichstag elections of September 1930. On the basis of its social situation, parts of the old and the new middle class had become susceptible to extreme ideological trends.

Lipset's thesis of the 'extremism of the middle' was provided with considerable limitations by historical and social science research. According to the historian Heinrich August Winkler, the voters' move from liberalism to National Socialism did not take place as immediately as Lipset had thought.[139] And election research raised questions about the close connection claimed between the middle-class vote and the rise of the NSDAP.[140] These studies, however, were not able to prevent the expression of the 'extremism of the middle' from making a career of its own in political publishing, especially in the face of the wave of subversive violence at the beginning of the 1990s.

Nevertheless, even authors who did not want to deny this expression's insightful functions pointed out its ambiguity. Wolfgang Kraushaar distinguished between four variants of meaning. 'Extremism of the middle' applied to:

1  the 'marking of the social origin' of subversive perpetrators;
2  the 'naming of an assumed' complicity between perpetrators and politicians, especially between right-wing radicals pulling the strings and state authorities;
3  the 'characterization of modern right-wing conservative parties'; and
4  the 'analysis of reactionalized right-wing conservative ideologies'.[141]

The common ground in this critique consists of the following facts: Authors who consider themselves left-wing make the 'middle of the society' responsible for the 'right-wing' becoming stronger. Most of the polemic contributions have undeniable and simultaneously banal facts on their side: Developments at the wings of the political spectrum (measured as the distance of the political positions of the mainstream and the constitutional political basic consent) take place in a dynamic interrelation with system-shaping trends and predominant social forces. The importance of the problems outlined by the term 'extremism of the middle' is therefore not to be denied. Whoever accepts this may yet simultaneously question the form in which the problems are labelled as it takes the already regrettable confusion of the terms to extremes.

Typically, the expressed critique frequently brought up by the far left produced an echo on the right-wing. At the beginning of the 1990s, the former fraternity man and author of the *Junge Freiheit*, Hans-Ulrich Kopp, castigated 'liberal extremism' for defining the guidelines of German politics. 'Liberal extremism' was leading to a multicultural society, in this way undermining the 'identity of the German people', courted 'asocial and criminal minorities', pushed the 'majority of the decent people to the edge', dealt with foreign politics under contempt of international norms and cooperated unrestrainedly with 'maximum demands by unfriendly neighbouring states, while the East German compatriot associations and ethnic German minorities were simply passed over'.[142] Kopp received much applause from the 'national revolutionaries' for stating his opinions. Jürgen Riehl rapidly established in the extreme right-wing organ *Right and Truth*: From 'the "democratic" system saviours' point of view, all demands for revolutionary alteration are extreme'.[143] Speaking of 'liberal extremism' has since made the rounds and found its way into the political propaganda of the outer right-wing parties. The repressive side of the German federal society (e.g. when dealing with 'right-wing' breaks of taboos[144]) as well as its permissive traits (the 'bloody deed of Erfurt' as a consequence of the alleged loss of values due to the '68ers' – Verausländerungsextremisten ['alienization extremists'][145, 146]) can be labelled in this manner.

# 9  Political extremism
## Final results, classification of terms and outlook

## 1 Final results of the history of terms

The idea of the political extreme is rooted in the ancient Greek ethics of moderation. In every action situation, there is a mean (mesotês) between too much (huperbolê) and too little (elleipsis), the excessive and the moderate. An elaborate system of terminological categories is found in Plato's writings of the middle and late periods. Plato connected the ethics of moderation to the constitutional doctrine. His form of government continuum spread out between the extremes of despoteia/tyrannis and anomic/lawless democracy (in the sense of the rule of the rabble). Oligarchy, basileia (kingdom), aristocracy and legal democracy were located between the extremes. The mean (meson), at the same time guaranteeing moderation (metrion) and virtuousness (arete), was reached through a mixture (meikte) and the balancing of constitutional elements which, by themselves, are harmful (kakon) and extreme (akron). The ontological phenomenological dimension of the differentiation of the forms of government was in this way connected to the normative axiological dimension of the mesotês doctrine.

Aristotle freed the Platonic terms from their theological, ontological framework, embedded them into a comprehensive scientific system and gave them a politically realistic calibre. In his *Nichomachean Ethics*, he established virtue or moral competence (arete) as the mean (meson) or the centre (mesotês) between too much (huperbolê) and too little (elleipsis), which were meant to be the farthest ends or extremes (akron, eschatôn) of an action continuum. In his *Politics*, he connected the ethical mesotês doctrine with the concept of the mixed constitution. The interests of the upper and the lower classes were to be balanced in a society carried by the middle classes (mesoi) and to be balanced by the means of an artful composition of politically institutional organizational elements from different constitutional forms. Under the condition of the humanly possible, Aristotle recommended 'polity', a mixture of 'oligarchic' and 'democratic' elements, as the relatively best form of government, in which the maxim of the avoidance of extremes was to lead to a constitution while at the same time guaranteeing stability such as the liberty of the citizens.

Aristotelism, with its connection of the ethical mesotês doctrine and the theory of the mixed political constitution, has shaped the history of the political ideas of the constitutional state – not least through the mediation of scholasticism and humanism. The republicanism of the northern Italian city-states and later the United States of America was able to connect to this as much as the monarchic constitutionalism of Great Britain. The extremes were the carriers of human aberrant behaviour as well as the maxims and social forces they were based on. Extremes stood for depluralization and the concentration on violence; the mean stood for pluralism and the control of violence. Two major forms of the extreme were to be differentiated: depluralization and the unleashing of violence could be caused by the despotic tyranny of an individual just as much as through the anarchic rioting of the masses. Already, Plato had based his two-dimensional conceptuality on these two types of extremes. Aristotle took up this differentiation. It was not only the rulership of the Jacobins which later on documented its unchanged relevance.

The ontologically axiological two-dimensionality of the Platonic–Aristotelian mesotês and mixed constitutional doctrine offered logical possibilities for connection to the new political taxonomy that developed in the aftermath of the French Revolution. It kept its differentiation of 'extreme' and moderate/ 'mean' forms and connected these with the new respective terms of the 'right' and 'left' direction of the parliamentarian seating plan. Now, so to speak, the two traditional extremes obtained their seat at the wings of the political continuum. With the expansion in the right–left differentiation, the old terms were also transported further, even though they frequently severed the connection to the mixed constitutional discourse that partially lost its importance as the central medium of the exegesis of constitutionalism in the nineteenth century.

The '-ism' of 'extremism' found entrance into the political language several times without at first establishing itself, however, as an enduring terminological category of its own. This applies to its appearance during the age of religious wars as well as to its introduction into the terminology of the German Vormärz. In both cases, this concerned times of political polarization when the traditional words and expressions did not seem to suffice to describe a phenomenon perceived as a danger threatening one's existence. This also applied to the Russian Revolution of 1917, as a result of which the term 'extremism' was established permanently – at first in the Western states – in the political language. In France and England, 'extremism' became a catch-phrase[1] which, initially, expressed the fear of the threatening separate peace more than the fear of the consequences of the political radicality of the Bolsheviks. For a time, 'extremism' remained limited to the 'extreme left', yet was extended to the new formation of the 'extreme right' – fascism – after the 'March on Rome'.

In this way, the term regained the comparative perspective of the Platonic–Aristotelian categories. Spiritual isomorphies of the extremes had already been worked out by liberal observers such as Madame de Staël and Benjamin Constant during the first few years following the French Revolution. In the nineteenth century, it had become customary to parallel the extremes of the political spectrum from the vantage point of constitutionalism and, aside from the obvious differences, to work out the analogies and structural similarities. Again and again, the inseparably connected comparative dimension to the extremism term, introduced into scientific discussion at the beginning of the 1920s, sparked controversies.

Whoever recalls the history of the terminology of the political 'extreme' and of 'extremism' is able to name a whole array of structural characteristics. 'Extreme' and 'extremism' determine something which is the *farthest out*. There is nothing beyond the extreme; extremes cannot be increased, they embody something that cannot be surpassed or exceeded. Saying 'A is more extreme than B' or 'C is the most extreme value' thus contradicts the logic contained in the term.

Extremes can be thought of spatially as the ends of a distance, but just as well as the boundary of a circular surface or even as the surface of a sphere. Whether in one-, two- or three-dimensional examination: in all these cases, a centre can be established that lies at an equal distance from the extreme points. Ergo, the principle of equidistance is inherent in the picture of the mean and the extremes.

The extremes of a distance are the points that are the farthest removed from each other. The relationship of the two extremes to each other as well as that to the centre between the extremes can be thought of as different. The extremes then form the antitheses; at the same time, the centre finds itself in an antithetical relationship. Nonetheless, one of the antithetical relationships is expressed more steeply. In the Aristotelian tradition, the centre is at the same time a point of balance between too much and too little. In it, traits that are fully expressed by the extremes come to the fore in a milder form. The centre, often the metaphor for equilibrium and scales, embodies the principle of *moderation*. In the doctrine of virtues, the centre stands for morally appropriate behaviour that neither exaggerates nor understates; it neither extends far beyond that which is imperative nor remains far behind. Virtuous behaviour is the condition for a telos which the individual is capable of reaching, both with and within the society of the state: a moderate and virtuous life allows for eudaimonia, the unfolding of human happiness.

In politics, Aristotle transferred the image of the centre and the extremes to the doctrine of the forms of government. The centre corresponds to politeia which, according to the experience gained from the condition of the humanly possible, is the best constitution. It creates a solid foundation for the successful striving for virtuousness and bliss; in it, the fundamental principles and components of various forms of government, especially oligarchy and democracy, are mixed in such a way that the middle classes dominate, the togetherness of a multitude of social forces is made possible, the exchange of interests is institutionally coordinated, and power is controlled effectively.

With his description and recommendation of politeia, the mixed constitution, Aristotle, in his critical further development of Plato's late work, measurably contributed to the founding of the constitutional state tradition of the occident.[2] The image of the centre and the extremes was closely connected to it for centuries. The extremes corresponded to negative constitutional terms such as 'tyranny' and 'despoteia', which have a pejorative connotation and express a defence mechanism as the quintessence of that what must be absolutely rejected.[3]

Negative constitutional terms are generally borrowed terms, meaning that they serve as labels for political opinions, forms of action and actors from which one disassociates oneself most carefully. They are therefore also always a means employed in political arguments, namely aggressive vocabulary which, in the framework of a 'naming'[4] strategy, serve the derogative characterization of political opponents. They are stigma words,[5] used to mark political legitimacy boundaries, to judge others unworthy and to designate dangers. The flaunting of the extreme is a part of normalization discourses,[6] in which the majority society permanently reflects its normality and middle. In normalization discourses, cultural power struggles find their expression in the severe criticizing of unpopular opponents. Not always are the values of the system-necessitated political minimum consensus actually violated.

The use of the stigma word 'extremism' on the part of a political majority culture creates what Reinhard Koselleck called an 'asymmetric' language situation.[7] Those being labelled cannot accept the label they are addressed with, distance themselves from the borrowed term, doubt the load-bearing capacity of its content, stress its denunciatory nature and deny its scientific causality. Now and then, there are even legal battles fought over the use of political stigma words. For instance, the French Front National (FN) of the national populist Jean-Marie Le Pen brought a lawsuit against the press classifying it as 'extreme right', as the expression suggests violence.[8]

In contrast, as in the case of the FN, once in a while those being negatively labelled choose another strategy, turning the meaning of the label in the opposite direction. A negative borrowed term then becomes a positive self-designation. Here, an example from the months following the end of World War I can be cited: The publishers of a 'thoroughly French extremist weekly newspaper' (*Hebdomadaire extrémiste bien français*) delightedly informed their readers that 'extremism' was fortunately more powerful in France than in the homeland of the unfortunate Liebknecht: 'Heureusement que notre extrémisme est plus puissant qu'au pays de l'infortuné Liebknecht'.[9] Another language strategy of the stigmatized consists of turning the tables on to the labellers by using the negative borrowed term on them. With this in mind, the term 'extremism of the middle' is sometimes courted.[10] However, the strategy of the restoration of symmetry in the language situation has an opportunity for success only if the labelled or the labellers have societal power of definition at their disposal.

## 2 Heterogeneous extremism terms

As the – often sketchy, but by no means claiming completeness – overview of the terminological development within the extremism debates of the twentieth century has shown, the authors not only differed in their ways of using the expressions they favoured, respectively, but also in how they limited their subject area's contents. Therefore, several extremism terms stand side by side.

A definition attempt already found in the early conceptual forms of Leroy and Sturzo consists of defining 'extremism' through a number of structural characteristics of the ideological systems they are based on. The core is formed by a political absolutism and monopolist claim that does not permit opposite ideologies beside it, therefore not offering leeway for a pluralist range of interests and opinions. In this vein, Lipset/Raab emphasized the 'monism' of extremisms. The American social philosopher Robert Nozick worked out eight (possible) characteristics of extremism, which do not refer to the contents but to the form of the respective doctrines: the (1) emphasis of a 'certain objectivity' and 'impersonal validity'; (2) the essential function of an 'enemy who is absolutely evil'; (3) the inability to compromise; (4) readiness to use 'extreme measures'; (5) insistence on an immediate and complete realization of one's own goals; (6) organized action; (7) a tendency to consistently push forward an extreme position; and (8) the specific personality structure it is based on.[11] In a similar way, this author named elements of a 'definitio ex positivo'.[12] This kind of definition is closely connected to a definition of terms which understands 'extremism' in the sense of rejecting the minimum conditions of democratic constitutional states (or 'liberal democracies' to use the term with the, for the most part, same meaning usual in the USA). In as far as pluralism and institutional controls of power constitute the heart of the constitutional state, such a 'definitio ex negativo' is just the other side of the coin.

A closer definition builds on this basic understanding, yet restricts 'extremism' to a certain analysis level. As mentioned, Hans D. Klingemann and Franz U. Pappi proposed relating 'extremism' to the rejection of democratic values, but to call the negation of democratic methods 'radicalism'. This analytical division already formed the basis for Luigi Sturzo's differentiation between methods and programme extremism. Nonetheless, for Sturzo, 'extremism' encompassed both dimensions. In contrast to this, Cas Mudde resolves both dimensions terminologically, however just the other way round, as suggested by Klingemann and Pappi: whereas 'extremism' rejects the 'belief in the people's sovereignty' (for example in the form of the electoral system according to the one man, one vote principle), 'radicalism' accepts 'democratic ways of proceeding' but questions the liberal foundation of procedural democracy, particularly the 'positive value of pluralism'. For him, the perfect example is populism, which divides society into two 'homogeneous and antagonist groups': 'the pure people' and 'the corrupt elite'.[13] Yet another variant of definition was suggested by Paul Lucardie. His argument is based

on the model of mixed constitution: slightly provokingly, he speaks of 'democratic extremism', meaning political trends – such as certain kinds of anarchism – which take the principle of democratic equality to the extremes
and thus undermine the liberal/constitutional components of representative
democracy.[14]

Fundamentally different from such analytical differentiations is a relativistic use of words which allows for the differentiation of 'moderate' and 'extremist' positions for any number of trends. Crane Brinton's revolution theory is
an example of this. The same applies to Giovanni Sartori's doctrine of parties,
which defines anti-system parties by the size of their distance to a fluctuating
ideological political middle.[15] However, such an attitude does not necessarily
go hand in hand with a rejecting attitude towards the basic principles of the
political system. In this sense, the definition of 'extremism' is also relativistic
for somebody occupying an outside position in the communication process.[16]
According to such a definition, liberal regime opponents in dictatorships must
as a rule be seen as 'extremists'. Then, the relativistic extremism term contradicts a 'liberal democracy' oriented to an understanding of minimum conditions. This is also true for a definition of extremism focusing on eccentricity,
without the content of the 'centre' being determined: 'extremism is defined as
moving away from the centre towards the extreme rather than towards an
equilibrium position'.[17]

Other definitions of the term are not relativist but value-oriented; however,
they do not accept the fundamental values of the democratic constitutional
state which is rooted in Aristotelianism and aims at securing plurality and
control of power. This does not apply to the much quoted statement by
Republican presidential candidate Barry Goldwater: 'Extremism in the
defense of liberty is no vice, moderation in the pursuit of justice is no virtue'.
For, the plausibility of this statement results from topically emptying out the
concept of extremism which means hardly anything more than 'decisiveness'.
In contrast to this, Goldwater was far from praising the extreme in the sense
of uncompromisingly insisting on one's own point of view while consequently
delegitimating everybody else: precisely this was typical of historic national
socialism, which made fanaticism a virtue at the same time. However, praising
the extreme is also found with the ideological antipode, if in a normatively
different way. Karl Marx, when criticizing Hegel's 'doctrine of reconciliation',
had emphasized 'the decisiveness of real contradictions, their development
towards being extremes which is nothing else than both their self-knowledge
and them being ignited to become the decisive fight'[18] as a productive element
of the historic process which, beyond capitalism, goes as far as socialism and
communism and there comes to its end. The terminology of 'left-wing radicalism'/'left-wing extremism', which was developed by Lenin and continued by
the Soviet communist regimes and their Western offsprings,[19] was only at first
sight different from this interpretation. For, these terms included an only strategically reasoned criticism of 'revolutionary adventurism' but no fundamental
dissent on value or goal at all. Thus, 'left-wing extremism' was much less

pejorative than 'right-wing extremism', the latter including all those forces not willing to share the prospect of a future classless society which transcended the constitutional state as the shell of bourgeois–capitalist situations.

Still today, radical–egalitarian projects, which sometimes definitely show a distance to the practice of Soviet communist rule, guide a kind of fundamental criticism of the liberal–Aristotelian concept of extremism which aims at 'capitalism'. They find a theoretical extreme of the modern age by the idea that 'the ruling form of capitalist rationalization must be accepted because possible alternatives would go beyond the limits of the socially possible and democratically acceptable'.[20] Wolfgang Wippermann may be supposed to see things in a similar way, although his way of arguing is different. He defends communism against the wholesale accusation that it negates the fundamental values and rules of democratic constitutional states. Authors, he states, who use the evening-out terminology of 'right-wing' and 'left-wing extremism' spread a 'legend of extremism' and are 'rather similar to exorcists than to scholars'.[21] It was no coincidence that this criticism was published (among others) in a publication of the 'Antideutsche (anti-Germans)', a sectarian wing of the 'autonomous'/'post-autonomous' left-wing for which there is no real parallel in any other European country and which can probably be understood only as an eccentric product of the development of a society that is traumatized by Auschwitz. From this milieu, there even developed an 'Initiative gegen jeden Extremismusbegriff (Initiative against any kind of extremism concept)' (INEX), which declares war on this formula because it is said to play down the 'Nazi problem' and to prevent any 'fight against racist, anti-Semitic, sexist and authoritarian attitudes'.[22]

## 3 An attempt at definition

The history of the terminology of the 'extremes' and of 'extremism' proves their variability and dependency on context, which in the most extreme case can go as far as the expression of a 'golden middle' which, previously, had been fought against as being extreme. The contents connected to the image of the centre and the extremes have frequently been subject to change and, for that reason alone, encompass contradictory ideas and world views as the political opponents sometimes make use of the term coined for them, filling it with different meaning.

In the Aristotelian tradition, enormously effective for the historical shaping of the constitutional state, the image of the centre and the extremes, however, does not express such a change at will. The quintessence of the extreme arises from a consensus about what must absolutely be rejected. The consensus in the negation narrows the range of possibilities of choice thought legitimate, yet allows for numerous ways towards an aim that is considered good. The content of the consensus about what must absolutely be rejected can be reduced to four points: (1) *Pluralism* instead of monism: The state unites a number of people and human groups whose interests and world views are different yet, nevertheless, at the same time legitimate. It can, neither in its institutional design nor in its communication and decision-making processes, be formed solely according to the maxims of an individual or a group; (2) *Orientation towards a common good* instead of an egotistic execution of interests: A legitimate order must be obliged to the idea of a 'bonum commune'. Under the condition of a plurality of equals, different interests and world views are to be taken into consideration. A thus understood 'bonum commune' therefore does not contain a comprehensive a priori common good;[23] (3) *Legal state* instead of despotic state: A political order must be composed of rules that are to be adhered to by everyone, and also by those ruling at the moment. Without a system for the control of power (division of power, limitation of power, distribution of competencies), this cannot be guaranteed on a permanent basis. And, finally, (4) S*elf-determination* instead of outside determination: Decisions are only acceptable if there exists at least a fair possibility of participation in their establishment. The political system must make participation in power possible, meaning there must be processes intended for the controlled execution of conflicts and a formation of the will – and decision-making process organized under plurality conditions according to the respective resulting majorities.

As the history of terminology shows, those who want to speak of 'extremes' and 'extremism' in the framework of a scientific terminology must decontextualize the terms to a certain degree, to free them from their changing historical contents – unless relativity has been established as the central content. This, however, would contradict the tradition of the history of terminology as opposing poles of a political 'middle', which causes the spreading of violence and the social balancing of interests through the 'mixture' of constitutional elements. Most of the key terms of historical political language are used in different contexts, monopolized by various political directions and instrumentalized for political arguments. Nonetheless, hardly anyone would come to the conclusion that the word 'democracy' should be abandoned just because it has a great deal of historical terminological meaning. If new terms would have to be invented for all the misused words, this would – for the uninitiated – result in a puzzling artificial language that would serve more as a barrier to communication than as a means of communication. Therefore, one cannot forgo defining terms of colourfully sparkling, historically political content in such a way that popular understanding is taken into account as much as possible, yet, simultaneously, gains high selectivity.

In the light of the outstanding importance of the Aristotelian heritage concerning the history of occidental constitutionalism, determining 'extremism' as the *antithesis of the constitutional state* seems to suggest itself. A dichotomy, extremism/constitutional state, completes the terminology pair of autocracy/constitutional state that Karl Loewenstein developed terminologically in his constitutional doctrine.[24] The central differentiation criterion formulates the question referring to the division and the control of power. According to this, extremism would be the – voluntary and involuntary –

*striving for 'autocracy'* (or 'dictatorship') in the sense of the concentration and the lack of control of governmental authority.

The constitutional state and extremism cannot be determined only on the basis of the institutional structure of the state, but also on the structure and the organization of the power process. The well-known minimum definition of the constitutional state by Robert A. Dahl establishes it as a 'polyarchy', a system in which a competition for influence, power and positions is carried out by peaceful means.[25] Such a system assumes the existence of several competing parties and interest groups (pluralism), the legitimacy of political opposition, institutional mechanisms for the regulation of the interaction of majorities and minorities (such as elections and parliaments) and the validity of an array of fundamental vested rights of the citizens against the infringements of rights by governmental authority as well as also for the participation in political matters (such as the freedom of opinion, freedom of unification, and freedom to meet). Without a functioning, power-controlling institutional structure, there is no formation of will and decision-making process, and competition cannot be carried out peacefully. *Extremism thus aims at 'monism' and 'monocracy'* in the sense of the enforcement of a bundled claim to power which – if at all possible – eliminates any competition, does not tolerate variety and opposition, at least seeking to render it harmless, stops political change, obstructs and suppresses the autonomous commitment of groups and individuals, at least if it stands in the way of the ambitions of the rulers. The idea of the citizen therefore belongs to the world of the constitutional state. Apart from the powerful, there are only subordinates (underlings) in the sphere of the activities of political extremes.

Extremism as the antithesis of the constitutional state can be more closely determined beyond the institutional and procedural political level by the structure of the societal communication process. Whereas the constitutional state corresponds to the 'forum type', in which questions of state are consequently included among public matters to be discussed in an exchange of different opinions on a 'marketplace of political ideas', in debate and discussion, argumentatively, discursively, transparently, accessible and visible to everyone, *extremism aims at the 'palace type'*,[26] where shunning publicity in matters of state is the rule, entitlement to have one's say and discussion are undesirable, and the strategy of ruling depends on the most careful preservation of the 'arcana imperii' accessible only to small, select circles behind the unbugged walls of the control centre.

The tendency of the extremisms towards the 'palace', on the other hand, can be traced to commonalities in their ideal morphology. The push towards monocracy/power concentration and monism is called forth through an exclusive *demand for truth, interpretation and organization*, which pleads 'higher insights', 'incontestable authorities' and/or knowledge of the 'laws of history' (historicism),[27] immunizes itself from criticism, therefore leaning towards dogmatism. The insight and interpretation monopoly forbids the acceptance of competing designs and gives grounds for the 'inability of coexistence'.[28] The plurality of opinions, interests and life designs, in this light, prevents absolutely to be striven for unity, concord and harmony. Extremist ideologies develop a political power uniformity programme. Whatever does not fit to one's own political design is interpreted away, declared illegitimate and exterminated, if necessary. Extremist ideologies unfold a bipolar Manichean world view that assigns the spiritually deviant to the 'kingdom of evil' and thus justifies a clear friend–foe differentiation. In the social psychology realm, such thinking can be interpreted as a consequence of ambiguity intolerance,[29] refusal to accept the heterogeneity and ambiguity of the world, the complexity of life circumstances and the conflictuality of society as facts and to constructively put them into practice.[30]

With their striving for the concentration of powers, monistic standardization and the conclusion of the formation of opinion- and decision-making processes, extremisms not only undermine the *liberty of the citizens*: They also undermine the *equality of the citizens* in the sense of ancient Greek isonomia and isêgoria, meaning equality under the law, the right to equality and the right to free speech and to stating one's position in matters concerning the general public.[31] Accordingly, extremism aims – at least in its effect (not necessarily in its intentions) – at the *hierarchization* of those governing and the governed, the rulers and those ruled over, political 'initiates' and the ignorant.

## 4  Forms of political extremism

From the different aspects of a definition for the term 'extremism' orienting itself at the antithesis to the constitutional state, the criteria for a sensible organization of the realm of definitions can be gained. A first possibility results from the interpretation of the modern constitutional state as regimen mixtum. The 'extreme democratic' thrusting element that strives for the total equality of citizens and the permanent and direct civil execution of power is limited to the elementary rights of liberty on account of 'monarchic' and 'aristocratic' *checks and balances*, for instance in the interest of a quick governmental decision, qualified discussion in parliaments or judicial protection from infringement upon one's rights by the people's will on to the elementary rights of liberty. In particular, the mixed constitution creates equilibrium between civil liberties and civil equality.

The warning against the extreme democracy of a mob of people stirred up by demagogues has been a permanent topos of the history of ideas since Plato and Aristotle. The modern constitutional state is in need of the monarchic and aristocratic counterbalance no less than the ancient state was. For within it, the principle of equality, in contrast to constitutionalism of old, gained validity even more strongly in the aftermath of the revolutions in America and France. The group of full citizens was step-by-step expanded to all grown-up citizens. The ethos of the fundamental equality of human beings having sprung from the ancient sources (especially the stoa), channelled by Christianity, humanism and the Enlightenment, has gradually overcome the natural categorical inequality of women, slaves and strangers, basing the constitutional state on a broad foundation of the people. The democratic constitutional state forms a tense synthesis of monarchic, aristocratic and democratic elements. It has, therefore, often been described as a complexio oppositorum.[32] Alois Riklin – in a critical connection to Dolf Sternberger – has newly called attention to the importance of the tradition of the mixed constitution to the unfolding of occidental constitutionalism.[33]

The insight into the mixed nature of the constitutional state makes it possible to differentiate forms of political extremism according to their respective main thrust direction. Is the democratic element being overextended to a degree that would endanger civil liberties? Or is the liberty of certain citizens to be held high at the expense of civil equality? According to the dimensions of civil equality and civil liberty, one can distinguish an *anti-democratic* from an *anti-constitutional* thrust direction. The former undermines civil equality – for instance in the form of the axiom of human fundamental equality – which in the form of the human rights idea constitutes the ethical foundation of the constitutional state of the present. The latter aims at the power-controlled set of regulations that is to ensure civil liberty.

Carl J. Friedrich described the creation of the modern constitutional state as a process of the merging of democracy (in the sense of equality and the people's sovereignty) and constitutionalism (a plurality-ensuring, power-controlled institutional structure).[34] However, for an analytical differentiation, there arises a problem in respect to the definition of extremism. Is the combination of anti-constitutionalism and anti-democratism a necessary requirement when speaking of extremism? Or would one of the two dimensions suffice? Theoretically, the two dimensions can be combined into three typical ideal forms. Hereby, one needs to differentiate between *democratic anti-constitutionalism, constitutional anti-democratism* and *anti-constitutional anti-democratism* (or rather anti-democratic anti-constitutionalism; type 4, democratic constitutionalism, constitutes the antithesis of the other three).[35] The first form would represent an ideology/movement that answers to the ethos of fundamental equality of human beings, but rejects the power-controlling design of the constitutional state. This might apply to all the communist and anarchist doctrines in as far as one were to take seriously their radically egalitarian manner of seeing themselves. The second form would apply to Aristotle's politeia, a constitutional state on the basis of slavery – a pattern that is still found in many of the North American republics of the founding days and marked the domestic policy arguments of the USA until well into the twentieth century. Regarding the present, one might think of the followers of an apartheid on a constitutional basis (as in the South Africa of the past). The third form is found in Hitler's and the other leading National Socialists' world view: radical negation of the ethos of the fundamental equality of human beings in favour of national racism connected to the propagation of the total leader state, which eliminates the system of the assurance of civil liberty in a process of Gleichschaltung (forcing into line).[36]

If one were to reserve the term 'extremism' for the combination of both dimensions, one would exempt ideologies/movements that aim at the elimination of the constitutional state or the exclusion of parts of the population from the realms of the assurance of essential basic rights. For a historical view of the hatching of democratic constitutional states (the process of democratizing the constitutional state) and their political antipodes, it is most important to separate both dimensions. Their differentiation is also of great importance for the analysis of the present. Yet it would contradict the current understanding to the greatest possible extent if one were to reserve the term 'extremism' for the combination of enmity between democracy and constitutionalism.

However, a definition of extremism that only calls for one of the two dimensions has its price. In the strictest sense, as soon as only one of the two dimensions is available, it is no longer restricted to an exclusively antithetical relationship, so that anti-democratism is connected to constitutional orientations or – in the reverse – anti-constitutionalism to democratic values. If such ideological relationships pass themselves off as 'extremism', it is no longer restricted to the farthest reaching or unsurpassable. Moreover, the respective conviction systems on the 'freedom axis' between the assumed centre and the extremes move a bit closer towards the direction of the middle. In this way, a political space is created in which one must differentiate between 'extreme' and 'more extreme' (or 'softer' and 'harder') forms – actually a contradictio in adjecto.

Still, whoever holds fast to the definition of extremism of only one of the afore-mentioned two dimensions must be aware of the problematic situation and pay his dues to it when it comes to the analysis of political ideologies. What is more, the dimensions of 'anti-democratism' and 'anti-constitutionalism' can be subdivided again. In this way, in 'anti-constitutionalism', further partial domains such as anti-parliamentarianism, anti-liberalism (in the sense of the restriction and the suspension of liberal rights) or anti-pluralism (such as anti-party effects and interest group prudishness) can be named. With anti-democratism, one would, for instance, have to differentiate between anti-egalitarianism with regard to individual liberal rights (e.g. discrimination against population groups) and the relationship to the people's sovereignty. A definition of extremism should in any case be drawn up in such a way that the negation of at least one dimension is required, without which a democratic constitutional state would not be worth its name. This includes the ethos of the fundamental equality of human beings as a basic value as well as the political pluralism of parties and associations, the thereto connected autonomy of civil commitment, the legitimacy of political opposition, the periodic conducting of elections (in which the traditional principles of democratic voting law exist) as well as a number of indispensable basic rights (such as freedom of opinion, freedom of association, freedom to meet) and their guarantee through a power-balancing institutional structure (among others, legitimacy of the government, parliamentarian control, independence of justice).

The differentiation between the two dimensions, anti-democracism and anti-constitutionalism, has a great deal in common with Norberto Bobbio's two-dimensional subdivision of the political realm. The differentiation between extremism/autocracy and the constitutional state orients itself on the principle of (individual) freedom, whereas the one between 'right' and 'left' is oriented on the principle of equality. Both dimensions are not thought to be parallel but axes crossing each other.[37] Accordingly, aside from a temperate constitutional state oriented right and left, there is also an extreme autocratic right and left that favours autocratic leadership forms.

Bobbio's two-dimensional division of the political realm can be connected to the above-introduced dimensions of 'anti-democratism' and 'anti-institutionalism'. In this way, a spiritual, politically traditional connection comes to the fore, and the 'axis of freedom' with a catalogue of values and institutional processing regulations experiences concretization. As shown in Figure 9.1, the political realm can be grasped two-dimensionally by differentiating between a constitutionalism and a democracy axis. The extreme poles of constitutionalism are termed 'anarchic' and 'totalitarian'. 'Anarchic' anti-constitutionalism negates every form of state order, whereas the 'totalitarian' one develops a claim to omnipotence that penetrates all societal realms, disintegrating the separation of the public and the private realm. The extreme poles of the axis of democracy are called 'extreme egalitarian' and 'anti-egalitarian'. Hereby, 'democracy' foremost grasps the equality dimension. Following Bobbio's plausible classification on the equality axis, it is identical to the traditional right–left dimension.

On the constitutional axis, the focus is on the control of power and plurality assurance, i.e. civil liberty, whereas on the democracy axis, the subject is

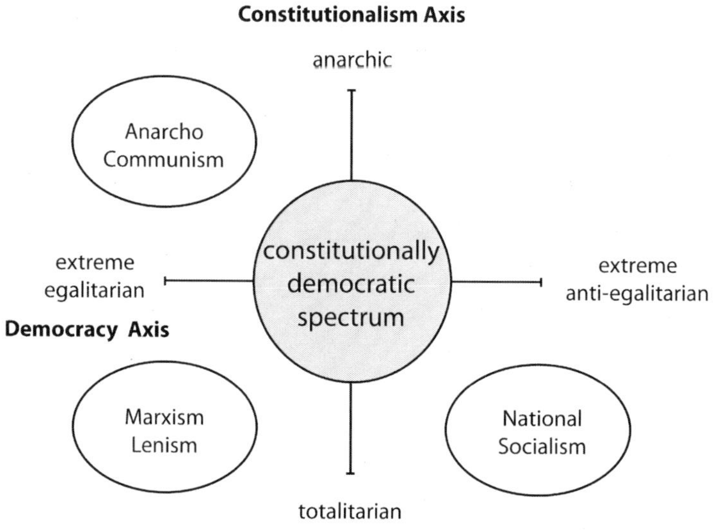

**Constitutionalism Axis**

anarchic

Anarcho Communism

extreme egalitarian

**Democracy Axis**

constitutionally democratic spectrum

extreme anti-egalitarian

Marxism Lenism

National Socialism

totalitarian

*Figure 9.1* Forms of political extremism in the two-dimensional political space (anti-democratism/anti-constitutionalism)

the relationship to the principles of civil equality and the sovereignty of the people. The extreme right and left tending towards autocratic solutions are similar in their anti-constitutionalism but differ in their classification on the democracy axis. According to the way they are seen, Marxism–Leninism can be described according to this scheme as 'democratic anti-constitutionalism', and National Socialism as 'anti-democratic anti-constitutionalism'. Nevertheless, these are only rough classifications. The different ideological variants (Leninism and Stalinism distinguish themselves from each other just as Hitler's and Rosenberg's National Socialisms do) would have to be described more exactly, individually, whereby the terminological clusters, 'anti-democratism' and 'anti-constitutionalism', would be broken down into their individual components in the already described manner. In this depiction, anarchism takes up its own individual position. In the form of anarcho-communism, it connects an 'extreme egalitarian' with an anarchic–subversive orientation. Besides, there is no lack of an ideological connection between anti-egalitarianism and anarchism; only practically speaking has it remained almost meaningless, therefore not having found acceptance for the diagram.

Religious political fundamentalism,[38] which has gained political importance at the edges of all the world religions, in particular in the Islamic cultural circle during the last few decades, nevertheless clearly shows that the two dimensions, anti-constitutionalism and anti-democratism, in no way suffice to adequately comprehend the spectrum of political extremisms at the level of their own ideological and programmatic self-knowledge. The relationship to the egalitarian principle is obvious, and therefore the classification on the

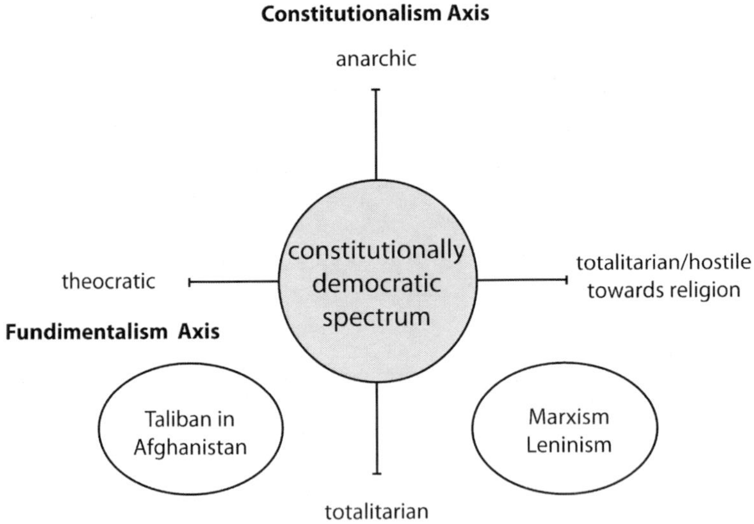

*Figure 9.2* Forms of political extremism in the two-dimensional political sphere (constitutionalism/fundamentalism)

equality axis is not crucial for these forms. Another line of conflict, namely the one that is determined by the question regarding the relationship of religion and state, appears to be more important.[39] To explain these facts more clearly, one can think of the political sphere as being two-dimensional, whereby the democracy axis is replaced by an axis of religion (see Figure 9.2).

The extreme poles of this axis can be termed enmity towards religion and theocracy. As far as enmity towards religion is concerned, this would address ideologies that condemn every form of belief in a thereafter as an intellectual attack on reason and meet the followers of such a belief with intolerance. An example of the connection of enmity towards religion and totalitarian anti-constitutionalism is found in Lenin's and Stalin's communism with its systematic killing of priests, the destruction or desecration of houses of God, the 'movement of the godless' and other excesses. Typically, the enmity towards religion springs from a state ideology which, like the state religion of theocracy, claims absoluteness (of superior rationality). Here, too, extremes touch. The essential difference lies in the radical worldliness of the enmity towards religion ideology, which is in stark contrast to the otherworldliness of a fundamentalist political theology. In respect of rule, theocracy may approach enmity of religion totalitarianism to the same extent to which the claim of God's reign on earth is faithfully put into effect. The reign of the Taliban in Afghanistan comes close to this relationship.

To explain the independence of the three dimensions of political extremisms in the abstract political realm, a three-dimensional depiction with a constitutionalism, a democracy and a fundamentalism axis suggests itself (see Figure 9.3).

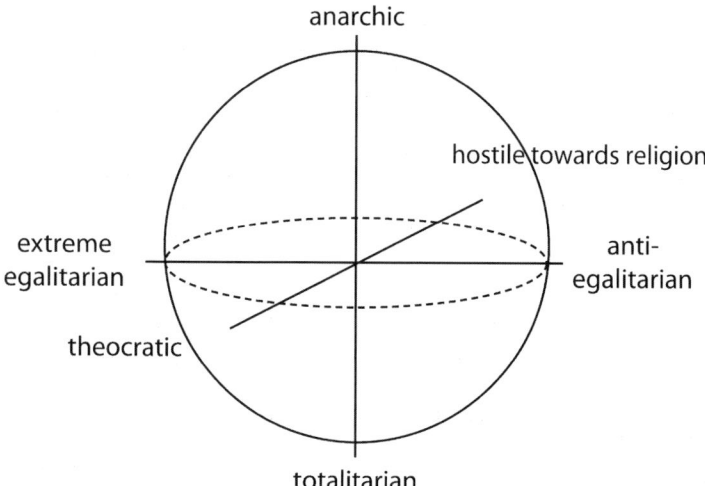

*Figure 9.3* Forms of political extremism in the three-dimensional sphere (constitutionalism/democracy/fundamentalism)

The more unconditional certain organizations are in their ideological pro-grammatic self-interpretation in striving towards the extreme poles in their abstract political realm, the more pronounced may be their tendency – by summoning every possible means – to impose their proposed absolute aims in their claim for exclusive truth, interpretation and design. The conviction of the superiority of their own insight and prognosis capability, in combination with the claim of preventing a catastrophe and 'to put the world to rights again' and/or to create a new world, leads from intellectual self-empowerment to self-sacrificial action.[40] Their high aims, seen as sacrosanct, allow for the use of violence and, in the extreme case even, for mass murder to appear legitimate.

Nevertheless, it would be inappropriate to see the use of violence or illegal methods as defining characteristics of political extremisms. The question about the use of violence and the breaking of norms can – independent of the respective ideological programmatic orientation – be answered differently from the perspective of different strategic considerations. The political beha-viour of the Nationalsozialistische Deutsche Arbeiterpartei (NSDAP) at the beginning of the 1930s shows that extremist ideology and the practice of violence do not necessarily go hand-in-hand. The legality tactics took advan-tage of the widespread relativistic understanding of democracy in the Weimar state. Thus, Goebbels could announce frankly: 'We are entering the Reichstag to supply ourselves from the weapons arsenal of democracy with their own weapons. We are becoming representatives of the Reichstag to immobilize Weimar convictions with their own support. If democracy is so stupid as to give us free tickets and diets for this bad turn, it is its own business. To us, every legal means is welcome to revolutionize today's conditions'.[41]

The moulding of ideology does not allow for any compelling logic with respect to strategic behaviour. Is it possible, then, in a stringent manner, to make any assumptions from the ideological programmatic structure on to the type of autocracy that is to be expected after a takeover of power? Here, one must exercise caution, as the processes of the transformation and the estab-lishment of autocracy depend to a large degree on the respective political conditions of power, the institutional requirements and the socio-economic as well as the cultural framework conditions. At the same time, one can deduce basic political intentions and forms of legitimation from the ideology of a political movement that give a direction to the moulding of the regime to be expected. Therefore, the communist education dictatorship following the ideology of Marxism–Leninism is structured in the same way as the charis-matic leader dictatorship in the doctrines of fascism and National Socialism. In a similar way, one can assume theocratic traits for establishing a successful autocracy with political religious fundamentalism.

Can evidence also be found to answer the question about the 'authoritarian' or 'totalitarian' moulding of autocracy? From the degree of moulding and the configuration of the structural characteristics of extremist ideologies, conclu-sions should be possible on the degree of the to be expected depluralization and 'thorough domination' of a society. The experience of the totalitarian regimes of the twentieth century suggests that a utopian piety heightens the probability of totalitarian rulership practice, as utopia is able to deliver a foundation for the justification of a rigorous transformation, Gleichschaltung (forcing into line) and 'cleansing' of society.

## 5 Prospects

A definition of extremism in the sense of the rejection of basic values and rules of the game in the democratic constitutional state in no way amounts to the same thing as seeing extremism as a consequence of negations and reactions. A look at history tells us that constitutional states came into existence only several thousand years after the first high cultures had come into being on the shores of the big rivers Euphrates, Tigris and Nile. Someone thinking along the lines of the concentration of powers, monism and monocracy can thus claim 'older rights' and, in addition, point to the worldwide predominance of non-constitutional forms of state over a period of many centuries. Therefore, it was not at all absurd when one of the most extravagant intellectual endeavours in the age of the radical revolutionary changes in America and France sought to establish proof of the 'natural state' of founding father patrimonialism and the merely residual importance of republicanism.[42]

Autocracies are older than constitutional states; they have accompanied their development and sustained themselves on a global scale until well into the present, regardless of all the waves of democratization.[43] Thereby, the ideocracies or world view dictatorships with their totalitarian traits are meanwhile only rather an exception, whereas those forms which, in many points, correspond to the Aristotelian description of tyranny to a large degree make up the majority. Among present-day autocracies, there are several – such as the theocratic system in Iran or 'sultanism'[44] – that partially carry archaic traits. After the most beautiful dreams of the flowering transitology of the 1990s have dissipated, comparative system research has, in addition, adopted new 'hybrid' regimes which connect the typical characteristics of autocracy with those of the constitutional state.[45]

Aside from vital autocracies, there is no lack of intellectual trends that delegitimize the constitutional state and point to new adventurous ways. This is why radical globalization critics, in their leanings towards Marx and Lenin, see the expansion of liberal democracy and the market economy as a kind of theoretical imperialism.[46] Anarchism, historically not burdened by oppression regimes, is developing new attractiveness.[47] Leading thinkers of a so-called 'new right' are unmasking fascism, communism and liberalism as equally totalitarian.[48] And after the 'third universal theory', introduced by Muammar Al-Gaddafi in the 1980s, has mercifully disappeared into oblivion, the 'milestones' of the Egyptian Muslim brother Sayyid Qutb are being viewed as a political revelation in Islamist circles.[49] Islamism is obstructing liberal development in terrorist as well as in non-terrorist variants.[50] The factor of religion has also unexpectedly furthered the formation of political ideologies in other cultural circles which aim at 'integral' rulership methods that force back every other design claim as illegitimate.[51]

It would hardly be meaningful if one were to restrict the term in such a way that extremism were to be seen as a reaction to twentieth-century totalitarianism. For good reasons, a world historical view can reach the final conclusion that autocratic systems and extremist efforts aimed at their establishment are just as strongly anthropologically anchored as those trains of thought and world views that further constitutional national solutions. The tendency, popular in old, consolidated democracies (such as the United Kingdom), to see extremisms as marginal minorities may be correct for some bizarre species; this nevertheless shows a certain arrogance, which quickly dissipates as soon as one calls forth the memory of the historical political conditionality of the 'experiment of freedom'.[52]

However, also to take seriously the challenge of political extremisms in the future does not mean one should make a case for alarmism and exorcism. When a certain justification can be ascribed to the formula of the 'extremism of the middle', frequently used in polemic contexts, it is in vain that the political middle – in the sense of the system-carrying trends of democratic constitutional states – and extremisms (as long as they are not completely marginal such as a 'lunatic fringe') mostly stand in an interrelationship to each other. According to experience, in a certain way, they belong to the 'normal household' of open societies. The succession of extremisms often points to weaknesses and oversights by the political majority culture. Criticisms from the extremist vantage point may frequently be exaggerated but sometimes also contain a grain of truth. Extremism – like prison – is in some respect a mirror image of social development and allows for conclusions about the condition of the majority society. The mesotês doctrine permits the insight that the centre contains something of the extremes. They overexpand those principles which, in temperate and balanced form, are of use. Above all, political extremisms that act in the framework of legality can, in such a way – like poisons that, in small dosages, develop healing effects – give an impetus to course corrections, point to neglected problem areas and, lastly – aside from their disintegrating effects – bring about integrative effects. The friends of the constitutional state should therefore refrain from a Manichean crusade mentality which, as a result of the resolution of merciless fighting against extremism, has led to the behavioural patterns of the antipodes. For a middle that wants to drive its aims to the last consequence itself becomes extreme.

# Notes

## 1 Introduction

1 Cf. Hobsbawm, *Age of Extremes*.
2 Cf. Reimann, 'Der Erste Weltkrieg'.
3 Cf. Ludendorff, *Der totale Krieg*.
4 Cf. Schwarz, *Das Gesicht des Jahrhunderts*.
5 In 'A State Against its People', Werth shows, on a broad foundation of sources, that Stalin's excesses were only a continuation and an acceleration of those of Lenin: Werth, 'Ein Staat gegen sein Volk'.
6 Compare this term with Arendt, *The Origins of Totalitarianism*, pp. 423–25.
7 Lenin, How to organize competition (24–27 December 1917), p. 413. Compare for interpretation most of all: Colas, 'Säubernde und gesäuberte Einheitspartei'.
8 See only Eliasberg, *Der Ruhrkrieg*; Koch-Baumgarten, *Aufstand der Avantgarde*; Petracchi, *La Russia rivoluzionaria*.
9 Cf. only Gentile, *Storia del Partito Fascista*, p. 63; Payne, *A History of Fascism*, p. 89.
10 Cf. Schumann, *Politische Gewalt in der Weimarer Republik*; Wirsching, *Vom Weltkrieg zum Bürgerkrieg?*, pp. 478–81.
11 Cited according to Reichardt, *Faschistische Kampfbünde*, p. 619.
12 Cf. Griffin, *The Nature of Fascism*, p. 26. For the discussion initiated by Ernst Nolte (*Der Faschismus in seiner Epoche*, p. 51), see Eatwell, 'Zur Natur des "generischen" Faschismus', with further literature data.
13 Hobsbawm blends out the interactions of the extremes when he gives to the 'October Revolution' the credit for keeping the world from the permanent establishment of authoritarian and fascist systems (Hobsbawm, *The Age of Extremes*, p. 7). One does not have to imply a necessity of consequences between the excesses of national socialism and Stalinism to arrive at the insight which Hobsbawm formulates in another place as follows: 'The rise of the radical right after the First World War was undoubtedly a response to the danger, indeed to the reality, of social revolution and working-class power in general, to the October revolution and Leninism in particular. Without these, there would have been no fascism'. Hobsbawm, *Age of Extremes*, p. 124. Ernst Nolte's claim of a 'causal nexus' between 'gulag' and 'Auschwitz' was interpreted as a necessity of consequences in the 'Historikerstreit'. Compare Nolte, 'Vergangenheit, die nicht vergehen will', p. 46, and the controversial points of view documented in the same volume. See also Nolte, Der europäische Bürgerkrieg, p. 548. Regarding the controversy concerning the interactions and interrelationships of the extremes from a greater distance, see Furet/Nolte, *'Feindliche Nähe'*; Kailitz, *Die politischer Deutungskultur*; Nipperdey/Doering-Manteuffel/Thamer (eds), *Weltbürgerkrieg der Ideologien*.

14 Cf. with these characteristics among others, Bracher, *Die totalitäre Erfahrung*.
15 Cf. Benz, *Der Holocaust*.
16 Goebbels, 'Rede auf der Kundgebung des Gaues Berlin der NSDAP (Berlin, Sportpalast, 18 February 1943)', p. 187.
17 Himmler, 'Rede des Reichsführers-SS bei der SS-Gruppenführertagung in Posen, 4 October 1943 (Document 1919-PS)', p. 145.
18 Cf. Kershaw, *Hitler, 1936–45*; ditto, *The 'Hitler Myth'*.
19 Cf. Bracher, *Zeit der Ideologien*.
20 Cf. Schulz, Art. 'Communismus' (1846).
21 Talmon, *The Origins of Totalitarian Democracy*, p. 47.
22 Ibid., p. 249.
23 Cf. Buonarroti, *Babeuf und die Verschwörung für die Gleichheit* (1828).
24 Cf. Cabet, *Voyage in Icarie*. The first version was published in 1839 under a pseudonym as a travel report.
25 See most of all Bluntschli/Seiler, *Die Kommunisten in der Schweiz* (1843).
26 Cf. only Grün, *Die soziale Bewegung in Frankreich und Belgien* (1845).
27 Cf. the self-description in Engels, 'Die Entwicklung des Sozialismus von der Utopie zur Wissenschaft' (1880).
28 Cf. Popper, *The Open Society and its Enemies*, vol. I, pp. 86–168.
29 Cf. Talmon, *Political Messianism*, pp. 177–200.
30 Cf. Arendt, *The Origins of Totalitarianism*, parts I ('Antisemitism') and II ('Imperialism').
31 Cf. Bluche, *Le bonapartisme*; Hammer/Hartmann (eds), *Le bonapartisme*; Rémond, *Les droites en France*, pp. 99–121.
32 Cf. Sternhell, *Maurice Barrès et le nationalisme français*.
33 Cf. Puschner/Schmitz/Ulbricht (eds), *Handbuch der 'Völkischen Bewegung'*.
34 Cf. Gasman, *The Scientific Origins of National Socialism*, p. XIX; Schwartz, *Sozialistische Eugenik*; Weikart, *Socialist Darwinism*.
35 Cf. Sternhell, *La droite révolutionnaire*.
36 Cf. Bauer, 'Der dritte Totalitarismus'; Tibi, *Der neue Totalitarismus*.
37 Cf. Kepel, *Das Schwarzbuch des Dschihad*. Hereto critically: Tibi, 'Vom klassischen Djihad zum terroristischen Djihadismus'.
38 Cf. Fukuyama, *The End of History*.
39 Cf. only Hardt/Negri, *Empire*; Holloway, *Change the World*. See hereto Moreau/Steinborn, 'Die Bewegung der Altermondialisten'.
40 A new reader concerning the role of political ideologies for a good reason contains a chapter on anarchism with a contribution by Noam Chomsky, 'Powers and Prospects'. See also Ward, *Anarchism*.
41 Cf. only Benoist, *Demokratie*, p. 32; ditto, *Communisme et nazisme*, pp. 133–40.
42 Cf. only Rüstow, *Ortsbestimmung der Gegenwart*.
43 Cf. Nieke, 'Extremismus', p. 883.
44 Funke, Art. 'Extremismus', p. 133.
45 Ibid., p. 133 f.
46 Krug, *Allgemeines Handwörterbuch*, Band 5 als Supplement. Erste Abteilung, p. 394.
47 Cf. Wende, Art. 'Radikalismus', pp. 113–33; Williams, *Keywords*, pp. 209–11.
48 Maccoby, *English Radicalism*, p. 15.
49 Cf. Young, 'Introduction', p. 9 f.
50 Baal, *Histoire du radicalisme*, p. 3. See also Avril, 'Radicalisme'.
51 Numerous examples are found in Button, *The Radicalism Handbook*.
52 Cf. most of all the excellent history of terms and ideas by Colas, *Civil Society and Fanaticism*.
53 Zedler, *Großes vollständiges Universal-Lexicon aller Wissenschaften und Künste*, vol. 9, p. 212.
54 Cf. Schwenn, Art. 'Kybele'.

55 Zedler, *Großes vollständiges Universal-Lexicon aller Wissenschaften und Künste*, p. 212.
56 Backes, *Politischer Extremismus in demokratischen Verfassungsstaaten*, p. 55.
57 Ibid.
58 Cf. Gralher, 'Mitte – Mischung – Mäßigung'.
59 Aalders, *Die Theorie der gemischten Verfassung im Altertum*; Blythe, *Ideal Government and the Mixed Constitution*; Höchli, *Der Florentiner Republikanismus*; Krämer, *Arete bei Platon und Aristoteles*; Nippel, *Mischverfassungstheorie*; Riklin, *Machtteilung*.
60 Cf. Koselleck, 'Einleitung'. See hereto Richter, 'Appreciating a Contemporary Classic'.
61 Cf. Pocock, *The Machiavellian Moment*, p. 361 ff. See hereto Richter, *The History of Political and Social Concepts*, pp. 124–42.

## 2 Extremes, mean, moderation and constitutional mixture in Antiquity and the Middle Ages

1 Pol, IV 1295b 34.
2 So in a summary of an extensive poetic and philosophical source: Kalchreuter, *Die Mesotes*, p. 44.
3 Ibid.
4 Cf. Wolf, *Griechisches Rechtsdenken*, vol. I, pp. 207–10.
5 Solon, 'Elegiac poetry', p. 113.
6 Cf. Jaeger, *Padeia*, p. 204.
7 Herodotus, *Histories*, I 32.
8 Cf. Laue, *Maß und Mitte*, p. 45. The printed paper of the same title (Münster/ Osnabrück, 1960) only offers a listing of contents. In the following, there is only a reference to the long typed version.
9 Cf. ibid., pp. 46 et seq.
10 Polykleitus, Kanon Vors, 40 A 3. Cited according to ibid., p. 47.
11 Isokrates, 'Rede an Nikokles', p. 26 (II, 33).
12 In detail as to this circle of questions: Müri, 'Der Maßgedanke', pp. 183–201; Laue, *Maß und Mitte*, pp. 101–12.
13 Hippokrates, 'Die Regulierung der Lebensweise', p. 231 (First Book, VI 471 et seq.). See further notes in Kalchreuter, *Die Mesotes*, pp. 35–38.
14 Sophokles, 'Oedipus auf Kolonos', pp. 170 et seq. (1212–23).
15 Cited according to Laue, *Maß und Mitte*, p. 19.
16 Cf. ibid., pp. 5 et seq.
17 So in Müri, 'Der Maßgedanke', p. 185. Also see Laue, *Maß und Mitte*, p. 210.
18 Cf. this question with Stark, *Aristotelesstudien*, pp. 96 et seq.
19 Aeschylus, 'Eumenides', 525–30.
20 Ibid., 696 et seq. Cf. Laue, *Maß und Mitte*, p. 32.
21 Thukydides, *Geschichte des Peloponnesischen Krieges*, VIII 97.2. Cf. Müri, Maßgedanke, p. 194; Laue, *Maß und Mitte*, p. 32.
22 Plato, 'Politeia', VIII 563e–64a (emphasis in the original).
23 Cf. Krämer, Arete bei Platon und Aristoteles, most of all pp. 244–379.
24 Cf. Plato, 'Politeia', IV 430d–32a.
25 Plato, 'Politeia', VIII–IX 545c–76b.
26 Today, the authenticity of the seventh autobiographical letter ascribed to Plato is generally answered in the affirmative. Cf. the question of authenticity: Fritz, *Platon in Sizilien*; Trampedach, *Platon*. Thinking the content of the letter is fiction: Annas, 'Platon', p. 373.
27 Plato, 'Politikos', 284e. Cf. this place in detail for the interpretation: Raeder, *Platons philosophische Entwicklung*, p. 349; Laue, *Maß und Mitte*, p. 25.
28 Plato, 'Politikos', 303b.
29 Cf. Plato, 'Politikos', 291a, f., 297c, 300c, f., 303b, f. See also: Krämer, *Arete bei Platon und Aristoteles*, pp. 201–20.

30 Cf. Herodotus, *Histories*, III 80–83. See hereto in detail: Bleicken, 'Zur Entstehung der Verfassungstypologie', pp. 149–72; Romilly, 'Le classement des constitutions d'Herodote à Aristote', pp. 80–99.

31 Cf. Plato, 'Politikos', 294b–97d.

32 Cf. Plato, 'Nomoi', III 691d.

33 Plato, 'Nomoi', III 691e.

34 Plato, 'Nomoi', III 692a–b.

35 So Krämer, *Arete bei Platon und Aristoteles*, pp. 207 et seq.

36 Plato, 'Nomoi', III 693d.

37 Ibid.

38 Plato, 'Nomoi', III 701e.

39 Plato, 'Nomoi', VI 756e.

40 Cf. Krämer, *Arete bei Platon und Aristoteles*, pp. 208 et seq.

41 Ibid., p. 211.

42 Cf. Plato, 'Nomoi', III 691d54.

43 Cf. Plato, 'Nomoi', VI 752d–55b.

44 Cf. Plato, 'Nomoi', XII 961a–61c.

45 Cf. Plato, 'Nomoi', XII 945b–48b.

46 Cf. Plato, 'Nomoi', VI 756c–58.

47 Eighth Letter 354e–55a. Cf. also Plato, 'Nomoi', IV 716d. The importance of the eighth letter is emphasized by Krämer, *Arete bei Platon und Aristoteles*, p. 213.

48 Cf. Annas, 'Platon', p. 393.

49 Cf. Plato, 'Nomoi', V 728c–29a.

50 Cf. Plato, 'Nomoi', VI 729c–d.

51 Cf. Plato, 'Nomoi', VI 756d.

52 Cf. Plato, 'Nomoi', VI 764c–66b, 788–89b, 804c–6c.

53 Jaeger, *Paideia*, p. 840. The 'eugenic breeding choice' for the removal of 'racial degeneration' constitutes a cornerstone of Popper's argument, who interprets Plato as the ancestor of totalitarianism due to his ideal state concept: Popper, *Die offene Gesellschaft und ihre Feinde*, vol. I, p. 27. A large-scale 'salvation of Plato's honour' founded especially on the late work is derived from Levinson, *In Defense of Plato*. A balanced acknowledgement on the basis of the state of up-to-date research is offered by Hüttinger, 'Platon', pp. 15–32.

54 Cf. only Plato, 'Nomoi', V 740d, 742a–b, VI 779e, VII 795e–97a, XII 950d–51c.

55 Cf. Plato, 'Nomoi', X 909a–d.

56 For the controversy about the continuity/discontinuity between the doctrines of Plato and Aristotle, see most of all Bien, *Die Grundlegung*, pp. 18–57. As the founder of 'politologics', Aristotle is honoured in a brilliant essay by Sternberger, *Drei Wurzeln der Politik*, pp. 87–156.

57 Aristotle, *Metaphysik*, 1055b 2.

58 Ibid., 1055a 4.

59 Ibid., 1055a 6–7.

60 Cf. also ibid., 1057a 19–1057b 32.

61 Aristotle, *Prior and Posterior Analytics*, 25b 23–40. Cf. also for the previous: Weber, 'Extreme', col. 1199.

62 Aristotle, *Topik*, IV 123b 10–20. Cf. also Krämer, *Arete bei Platon und Aristoteles*, p. 344.

63 Aristotle, *Nicomachean Ethics*, X 9, 1181b 15 (in the following abbr. as EN).

64 EN, II 1103b 29.

65 Cf. EN, V 1131b 13. Cf. Laue, Maß und Mitte, p. 45; Gralher, 'Mitte – Mischung – Mäßigung', p. 91 f.

66 Cf. EN, II 1106a 30–36. For checking Greek diction, the following edition was consulted here and in all other places: Aristotle, *Opera omnia*, vols I and II.

67 Cf. EN, V 1129a 3–1133b 30.

68 EN, V 1133b 41–1134a 2.
69 So Ernst A. Schmidt, Comment 29 to EN Book V.
70 Cf. EN, II 1103a 14–16.
71 Cf. EN, II 1104a 13 f. See hereto in detail Wehrli, 'Ethik und Medizin', pp. 36–62.
72 EN, II 1104a 21–24: 'τῆς ὑπερβολῆς καὶ τῆς ἐλλείψεος, ὑπὸ δὲ τῆς μεσότετος σώζεται'.
73 EN, II 1106b 35–37.
74 EN, II 1108a 14–16.
75 EN, II 1180b 25–28.
76 EN, II 1108b 29–1109a 2.
77 So the often repeated wrong judgement by Immanuel Kant: *Metaphysik der Sitten*, p. 283 (II. Tugendlehre, 405). Fitting critique by Höffe, 'Ausblick', p. 281. For the discussion about the philosophical essence of the mesotês doctrine, see also Wolf, 'Über den Sinn'; Urmson, 'Aristotle's Doctrine of the Mean'.
78 EN, II 1107a 7–9; Aristotle, *Opera omnia*, vol. II, p. 20. Cf. Hartmann, 'Die Wertdimensionen', p. 193; Schilling, *Das Ethos der Mesotes*, pp. 6–10.
79 Cf. Kohoutek, Die Differenzierung des anthropinon agathon, p. 56; Schilling, *Das Ethos der Mesotes*, p. 23.
80 EN, V 1131a 14–26.
81 EN, V 1133b 38–1134a 16.
82 So Flashar, 'Aristoteles', p. 340.
83 Ibid., p. 341.
84 EN, X 1181b 23.
85 Cf. EN, VIII 1160b 5 et seq.
86 Pol, IV 1295a 35–37.
87 Pol, II 1261a 23.
88 Cf. Pol, II 1261 9 et seq. Cf. For the importance of the differentiation: Arendt, Vita activa, pp. 31–38; Spahn, Oikos und Polis, pp. 529–64.
89 Cf. Pol, III 1275a 22f.; 1275b 18–21.
90 Pol, III 1275b 6–9.
91 Pol, III 1279a 17–22.
92 Pol, III 1279b 4 f.
93 Pol, IV 1293b 33.
94 Cf. Pol, IV 1294a 35.
95 Pol, IV 1294a 37–1294b 1.
96 Pol, IV 1294b 2–5.
97 Pol, IV 1294b 7–14.
98 Pol, IV 1294b 15–18.
99 Cf. Pol, IV 1294b 19–39.
100 Pol, IV 1295a 25–31.
101 Pol, IV 1295a 35–1295b 1.
102 Pol, IV 1195b 6–14.
103 Pol, IV 1295b 9–23.
104 Pol, IV 1295b 29–31.
105 Pol, IV 1295b 39–1296a 1 f. Cf. for the tyrannis doctrine: Mandt, 'Das klassische Verständnis: Tyrannis und Despotie'.
106 Pol, IV 1296a 10–17.
107 Cf. Pol, IV 1296a 19–21.
108 Pol, IV 1296a 29 f.
109 Pol, IV 1296b 37–1297a 7.
110 Pol, IV 1297b 35–1299a 2.
111 Pol, 1299A 3–1300b 11.
112 Pol, V 1309b 19–29.
113 Cf. Pol, V 1309b 33–34.
114 Cf. Pol, V 1312b 33–41.

115 Pol, V 1313b 33–41.
116 Cf. Pol, VI 1319b 3.
117 Cf. Pol, VI 1319b 29.
118 Pol, VII 1323a 14–1324a 4.
119 Cf. Pol, VII 1326b 15.
120 Pol, VII 1326b 39.
121 Pol, VII 1327b 29.
122 Cf. Pol, VII 1327b 36.
123 Cf. Pol, VII1327b 31.
124 Pol, VII 1328a 16.
125 Cf. Pol, VII 1330b 26 f.
126 Pol, VIII 1340b 1–5.
127 Cf. Pol, VIII 1342a 34.
128 Pol, VIII 1342b 14–17.
129 Pol, VIII 1342b 31–34.
130 Cf. Riklin, 'Aristoteles und die Mischverfassung', p. 342.
131 Cf. hereto also Ryffel, ΜΕΤΑΒΟΛΗ ΠΟΛΙΤΕΙΩΝ pp. 160–70.
132 Cf. Aalders, *Die Theorie der gemischten Verfassung*, p. 61; Höchli, *Der Florentiner Republikanismus*, p. 105; Kluxen, 'Die Herkunft', p. 133; Löwenstein, 'Verfassungslehre', p. 34; Nippel, *Mischverfassungstheorie*, pp. 57 et seq.; Panagopoulos, *Essays on the History*, p. 13; Vile, *Constitutionalism*, pp. 22 et seq.
133 Cf. Polybios, *Geschichte*, VI 3 et seq.
134 Cf. Fritz, *The Theory of the Mixed Constitution in Antiquity*, pp. 184–219; Graeber, *Die Lehre von der Mischverfassung*; Nippel, *Mischverfassungstheorie*, pp. 142–53. See also Taeger, *Die Archaeologie des Polybios*, pp. 128–33. Partially outdated: Zillig, *Die Theorie von der gemischten Verfassung*.
135 Cf. also places found in the *Polybios-Lexikon* for the 'akra' and 'eschata' (and additional word-related terms), which hardly have anything to do with political subjects: Berlin-Brandenburgische Akademie der Wissenschaften (ed.), *Polybios-Lexikon*, vol. 1, del. 1, col. 41–46, vol. 2, del. 2, col. 1003 et seq.
136 Polybios, *Geschichte*, VI 51 5 et seq. Cf. Hereto also Aalders, *Die Theorie der gemischten Verfassung*, p. 97.
137 Cf. Wehrli/Wöhrle/Zhmud, 'Der Peripatos bis zum Beginn der römischen Kaiserzeit', p. 498.
138 Theophrastus, *Characters*.
139 Cf. Wehrli/Wöhrle/Zhmud, 'Der Peripatos bis zum Beginn der römischen Kaiserzeit', p. 530.
140 Cf. ibid., p. 535.
141 Cf. for the complicated, only partially reconstructable history of tradition: Moraux, *Aristotelismus*, p. 18.
142 Cf. Düring, *Aristoteles*, pp. 250–312.
143 Wehrli/Wöhrle/Zhmud, 'Der Peripatos bis zum Beginn der römischen Kaiserzeit', p. 593.
144 See hereto Moraux, *Der Aristotelismus bei den Griechen*, vol. 1.
145 Cf. Dieter, 'Zum Begriff der Moderatio bei Cicero'; Gigon, 'Cicero und Aristoteles'.
146 Cf. Klingeis, 'Das aristotelische Tugendprinzip der richtigen Mitte in der Scholastik', pp. 33–49, 142–72, 269–88, VIII (1921), pp. 1–14; 83–112, here VII, 35.
147 'Numquam enim iratus qui accedet ad poenam mediocritatem illam tenebit, quae est inter nimium et parum quae placet Peripateticis et recte place, modo ne laudarent iracundiam et dicerent utiliter a natura datam'. Cicero, *De officiis*, p. 78 (I 89).
148 Cf. Aalders, *Die Theorie der gemischten Verfassung*, p. 109.
149 Cicero, *De re publica*, II 39–59. Cf. Nippel, *Mischverfassungstheorie*, pp. 154 et seq.; ibid., 'Cicero', p. 59.
150 Cicero, *De re publica*, I 68.

151 Ibid., I 69.
152 Ibid., I 69.
153 Cf. Gawlick/Görler, 'Cicero', p. 1040.
154 Q. Horatius Flaccus, *Oden und Epoden*, pp. 104 et seq. (II, 10).
155 Q. Horatius Flaccus, *Satiren – Briefe, Sermones – Epistulae*, pp. 18 et seq. (I, 2 24, 28).
156 Ibid., p. 208 (I, 18, 9).
157 Lefèvre, *Horaz*, p. 210.
158 Dionysius of Halikarnassus, Roman Antiquities, p. 306 (VII, 55,2). Cf. the remark by Nippel, *Mischverfassungstheorie*, p. 25.
159 Dionysius of Halikarnassus, *The Roman Antiquities*, VII 56 et seq. Cf. Aalders, *Die Theorie der gemischten Verfassung*, p. 119.
160 Aalders, *Die Theorie der gemischten Verfassung*, p. 120.
161 Plutarch, *Lives*, vol. II, p. 450 (XV, 2).
162 Plutarch, *Vitae Parallelae*, p. 172 (92.16). See hereto also the remarks in Nippel, *Mischverfassungstheorie*, p. 22 and Aalders, *Die Theorie der gemischten Verfassung*, pp. 124–26.
163 Cf. Flashar, 'Aristoteles', p. 449.
164 Isidori Hispalensis Episcopi Etymologiarum sive Originum, vol. I, II ix 1.
165 Cf. Grabmann, *Die Geschichte der scholastischen Methode*, p. 93.
166 Cf. Hermann, *Der Begriff der Mäßigung*.
167 Adelard of Bath, De eodem et diverso, L.c. 15, 31. Cf. Hermann, *Der Begriff der Mäßigung*, p. 36.
168 John of Salesbury, Etheticus, v. 751 f (M. 199, 981). Cited according to Hermann, *Der Begriff der Mäßigung*, p. 45 with additional reference.
169 Thus, the Persian philosopher Avicenna (Abu 'Ali al-Husayn Ibn Sina; 980–1035) mentions a 'Politics' by Aristotle, but does not delve into its content. Cf. Butterworth, 'Die politischen Lehren', p. 146.
170 Cf. Flasch, *Das philosophische Denken im Mittelalter*, p. 48. See also Grabmann, *Die Geschichte der scholastischen Methode*, pp. 148–77.
171 Cf. also with the following: Flüeler, *Rezeption und Interpretation*, pp. 2 et seq.; Grabmann, *Die mittelalterlichen Kommentare*.
172 Cf. the issue of dating and authorship of the complicated evidence in: Flüeler, *Rezeption und Interpretation*, p. 15.
173 Borst, 'Religiöse und geistige Bewegungen im Hochmittelalter', p. 544.
174 Ibid., pp. 544 et seq.
175 Cited according to Honnefelder, 'Die philosophiegeschichtliche Bedeutung Alberts des Großen', p. 256.
176 Cf. Flasch, *Das philosophische Denken im Mittelalter*, pp. 317 et seq.
177 Cf. ibid., p. 317.
178 Ibid.
179 Alberti Magni ratisbonensis episcopi, ordinis praedicatorum, Opera Omnia, volumen septimum Ethicorum Lib. X, p. 179 (Lib. II, Tract. II, Caput V).
180 Ibid. Cf. with this place also Schilling, *Das Ethos der Mesotes*, p. 5.
181 Cf. Pol. IV 1294b, 14–18.
182 Alberti Magni ratisbonensis episcopi, ordinis praedicatorum, Opera Omnia, volumen octavum Politicorum Lib. VIII, p. 366 (Lib. IV, Cap. 7; emphasis in the original).
183 Cf. Pol. IV 1295b 1 et seq.
184 Alberti magni ratisbonensis episcopi, ordinis praedicatorum, Opera Omnia, volumen octavum Politicorum Lib. VIII, p. 377 (Lib. IV, Cap. 9).
185 Ibid.
186 Ibid., p. 379.
187 Ibid., p. 378.

188 Ibid., p. 380.
189 Cf. also with the following: Chenu, *Das Werk des Hl. Thomas von Aquin*; Grabmann, *Thomas von Aquin*; Schilling, *Die Staats- und Soziallehre des hl. Thomas von Aquin*.
190 Cf. Thomas von Aquin, *Opera omnia*, vol. 4, p. 159 (053 CTC Ib2 Ic7 no. 9).
191 Thomas von Aquin, *Über die Herrschaft der Fürsten*, p. 53 (I, xiv); 'finis esse multitudinis congregatae vivere secundum virtutem'; ibid., *De regimine principum ad regem Cypri*, p. 17 (I xiv).
192 Ibid., p. 23 (II iv).
193 Ibid., p. 70 (Germ.), p. 23 (Lat. II iv).
194 Ibid., p. 22 (Germ.), p. 7 (Lat. I vi). Cf. most of all with: Blythe, *Ideal Government*, pp. 49–59; Matz, 'Nachwort', p. 84. See also: Goertz, 'Staat und Widerstandsrecht'; Turchetti, *Tyrannie*, pp. 267–74.
195 Thomas von Aquin, *Summe der Theologie*, pp. 505 et seq. (105. Examination, first article).
196 Cf. hereto also: Tierney, 'Aristotle, Aquinas, and the Ideal Constitution', p. 2.
197 Cf. Ptolemy of Lucca, *On the Government of Rulers*. The extremes play no role in this work.
198 Cf. this question with Blythe, *Ideal Government*, pp. 70 et seq.; Lambertini, 'A proposito della "construzione"', pp. 315–70; Turchetti, *Tyrannie*, pp. 274–76.
199 Egidio Colonna, *De Regimine Principum*, p. 475 (II. Pars, Lib. III, Cap. IX).
200 Ibid., p. 469 (II. Pars, Lib. III, Cap. VII).
201 Cf. Ubl, *Engelbert von Admont*, p. 70.
202 Cf. Blythe, *Ideal Government*, pp. 118–38.
203 Cf. Ubl, *Engelbert von Admont*, p. 15.
204 Cf. Kucher, 'Der Bildungsgang'; Baum, 'Engelbert von Admont'; Schmidinger, *Romana Regia Potestas*; Ubl, *Engelbert von Admont*.
205 Cf. Engelbert von Admont, *De regimine principum*, p. 18 (Tractatus I, Cap. VI).
206 Cf. Ibid., Tractatus I, Cap. VI–IX.
207 Cf. ibid., p. 8 (Tractatus I, Cap. I; emphasis in the original).
208 Cf. ibid., p. 194 (Tractatus VII, Cap. III).
209 Cf. Ubl, 'Einleitung', pp. 1–91; ibid., 'Zur Entstehung der Fürstenspiegel', pp. 499–548.
210 Cf. Ubl, *Die Schriften des Alexander von Roes und des Engelbert von Admont*, Speculum vertutum IV, Cap. VI, 10 et seq.
211 Ibid., IV, Cap. VII ('De comparatione et distantia medii ad extrema et extremorum ad invicem'), 15 et seq.
212 Cf. e.g. ibid., V, Cap. III; VIII, Cap. VII; IX, Cap. IX; X, Cap. II; X, Cap. XII.
213 Cf. Blythe, *Ideal Government*, p. 203, note 1.
214 Cf. Gautier-Dalché, 'Oresme et son temps', pp. 7–80; Quillet, 'Nicole Oresme Traducteur d'Aristote', pp. 81–91; Quillet (ed.) *Autour de Nicole Oresme*; Mittelstraß, 'Oresme', pp. 1089–91; Piron, *Nicolas Oresme*.
215 Cf. Shahar, 'Nicolas Oresme', pp. 203–9.
216 Oresme, *Le livre de éthique d'Aristote*, p. 544: 'Extremes ou extremites sont les bouz des fins, les termes de choses. Mais en special en matiere moral, extremes sont les habiz et operacions qui sont hors le moien de vertu en trop et en super-abondance ou en peu et en deffaute. Et pour ce dit l'en que la vertu est moienne et que les vices sont extremes'. Cf. in the text and the commentaries most of all the passages on pp. 169–72. A critique of the edition written by Menut is found in Knops, *Etudes sur la traduction française de la Morale à Nicomache d'Aristote par Nicole Oresme*. Oresme does not seem to be the first to use the word. Cf. Meißner, 'Maistre Nicolas Oresme', pp. 51–66; Taylor, 'Les neologismes chez Nicolas Oresme', pp. 727–36.
217 Cf. Oresme, 'Le livre de politiques', especially pp. 182, 185, 190. See hereto also Grignaschi, 'Nicolas Oresme', pp. 95–125.

218 Oresme, 'Le livre de politiques', p. 166 (IV, chap. 2).
219 Ibid., p. 167 (IV, chap. 2).
220 Ibid., p. 180 (IV, chap. 12). See also: Blythe, *Ideal Government*, p. 227.
221 Cf. Oresme, 'Le livre de politiques', p. 190 (IV, chap. 17).
222 Ibid., p. 274 (VI, chap. 6).
223 Cf. Blythe, *Ideal Government*, p. 207. See also: Dempf, *Sacrum Imperium*, p. 538; Düring, *Von Aristoteles bis Leibniz*, p. 307.

## 3 Extremes and the tradition of the mixed constitution from early humanism to the age of democratic revolutions

1 See the synopsis at: Düring, *Von Aristoteles bis Leibniz*, pp. 250–312 and the essay worth reading from Maier, 'Zur Lehrgeschichte der politischen Wissenschaft', pp. 15–52.
2 Cf. Flasch, *Das philosophische Denken im Mittelalter*, pp. 335 et seq.
3 Cf. especially Ullmann, *Medieval Foundations*.
4 Bielefeldt, 'Von der päpstlichen Universalherrschaft zur autonomen Bürgerrepublik', p. 99.
5 Cf. Miethke, 'Der Weltanspruch des Papstes', p. 397.
6 'tunc enim solum politie diriguntur ablique – democratie scilicet, oligarchie atque tyrampnides – que in servitutem cogunt genus humanum, ut patet discurrenti per omnes, et politizant reges, aristocratici quos optimates vocant, et populi libertatis zelatores; quia com Monarcha maxime diligat homines, ut iam tactum est, vult omnes homines bonos fieri: quod esse non potest apud oblique politizantes'. Dante Alighieri, *Monarchia*, p. 97 (I, xii 9).
7 'Si ergo homo medium quoddam est corruptibilium et incorruptibilium, cum omne medium sapiat naturam extremorum, necesse est hominem sapere utranque naturam'. Ibid., pp. 243 et seq. (III xv 5).
8 Cf. hereto the commentary by Ruedi Imbach at: Dante Aligheri, *Monarchia*, pp. 330–34; and Ley, 'Dante Aligheri', pp. 95–106.
9 For the importance of 'civic humanism' cf. especially: Baron, *The Crisis of the Early Italian Renaissance*, pp. 191–269. For the critics of the concept, see Skinner, *The Foundations of Modern Political Thought*, vol. 1, pp. 71–84.
10 Cf. ibid., pp. 64–75; Pocock, *The Machiavellian Moment*, pp. 89–91; Schmitt, *Aristotle and the Renaissance*, pp. 67 et seq.
11 Bruni, *Politicorum Libri Commentarii*, p. 62 ('Annotationes ad Cap. Decimum').
12 Cf. ibid., p. 62 ('De optima republica/partibus ciuitatis/mediocritate/excessu atque defectu. Cap. XI').
13 Cf. Münkler, *Machiavelli*, pp. 374–80.
14 Cf. for life and works Höchli, *Der Florentiner Republikanismus*, pp. 388–400; Landi, 'Nota critica', p. 551–88; Skinner, *The Foundations of Modern Political Thought*, vol. 1, p. 153.
15 Brucioli, *Dialogo* VI, 112 (411). The classification of virtue as 'mediocrità' between depraved extremes can be seen as a central motive within the dialogues. Cf. e.g. ibid., *Dialogo* XI, 283 (162); ibid., *Dialogo* XII, 289 (44 et seq., 51 f., 65, 68, 71); ibid., *Dialogo* XXII, 421 (42, 54), 429 (281).
16 Cf. detailed Höchli, *Der Florentiner Republikanismus*, pp. 398 et seq.
17 Cf. Albertini, *Das florentinische Staatsbewusstsein*, p. 83.
18 Giannotti, *Die Republik Florenz*, p. 141 (III 82 f.).
19 Cf., p. 144 (IV 85).
20 Cf. Riklin, 'Donato Giannotti – ein verkannter Staatsdenker der Florentiner Renaissance', 53–62; ibid., *Machtteilung*, pp. 141–81.
21 Cf. concerning the editions Höchli, 'Zur Übersetzung', p. 119; ibid., *Der Florentiner Republikanismus*, pp. 703–72.

22 Cf. the analysis by Riklin, 'Donato Giannotti – ein verkannter Staatsdenker der Florentiner Renaissance', pp. 55–62.

23 Ciconia, *De republica veneta fragmenta*, p. 468. Cf. also the reference at: Riklin, 'Die venezianische Mischverfassung', p. 265.

24 Cf. Riklin, 'Die venezianische Mischverfassung', p. 264; ibid., *Machtteilung*, pp. 113–40.

25 'Qui in Veneta ciuitate, cuius repub. Mixta esse dixi ex region, populari & optimatiu statu, referunt optimatium statum: ac media queda sunt quibus extremae partes, status scilicet popularis, magnu consilium, ac princes qui Regis personam gerit, inuice uinciuntur. Sic inquit Plato in Timeo extrema elementa, terram ac igne medijs elementis uinciri: sic in diapason cosonantia extremae uoces medijs diatessaron ac diapente uouibus inuicem metuntur'. Contarini, *De magistratibus*, p. 96. Cf. Plato, 'Timaios', I 7 31b–32c.

26 Cf. Bodin, *Les six livres de la République*, p. 260 f. (II 1). Cf. hereto Riklin, 'Die venezianische Mischverfassung', p. 274.

27 Bodin, *Les six livres de la République*, p. 253 (II 1). Cf. Aristoteles, *Politics*, II 1266a 1–5.

28 Bodin, *Les six livres de la République*, p. 951 (VI 4).

29 Ibid. p. 973 (VI 5).

30 'Et tout ainsi que deux simples en extremité de froideur & de chaleur sont autant de poisons, et neantmoins composés & temperés l'vn avec l'autre, font vne medecine fort salutaire: aussi ces deux proportions de gouuernement Arithmetique et Geometrique'. Ibid., p. 1021 (VI 6).

31 Contarini, *The commonwealth*. Cf. for the translation and its importance: Peltonen, *Classical Humanism*, pp. 102–18 and the restrained estimation of the significance to the history of reception at Pocock, *The Machiavellian Moment*, pp. 320–30. Cf. also Skinner, *The Foundations of Modern Political Thought*, vol. 1, pp. 141 et seq.

32 Cf. Pocock, *The Machiavellian Moment*.

33 Cf. Fortescue, *The Governance of England*, chap. I. Cf. See also Vile, *Constitutionalism*, pp. 37 et seq.

34 Cf. especially Nippel, *Mischverfassungstheorie*; Peltonen, *Classical Humanism*.

35 Ponet, A Shorte Treatise (without pagination).

36 Aristotle, *Politiqves*. Cf. Peltonen, *Classical Humanism*, p. 112.

37 Cf. Peltonen, *Classical Humanism*, pp. 123 et seq.

38 Cf. Goldie, 'Absolutismus', p. 309; Mendle, *Dangerous Positions*; Nippel, *Mischverfassungstheorie*, pp. 258–65; Vile, *Constitutionalism*, p. 39.

39 Nippel, *Mischverfassungstheorie*, pp. 167 et seq.

40 Hunton, *A Treatise of Monarchy*. Cf. Nippel, *Mischverfassungstheorie*, p. 276.

41 Hunton, *A Treatise of Monarchy*, Chap. III, Sect. I. Cf. Nippel, *Mischverfassungstheorie*, p. 277.

42 Filmer, *The Anarchy of a Limited or Mixed Monarchy*.

43 Filmer, *Observations upon Aristotle's Politiques*, p. 8.

44 Milton, *Eikonoklastes*, pp. 31 et seq.

45 Ibid., p. 42.

46 So Goldie, 'Absolutismus', p. 313.

47 Sidney, *Discourses Concerning Government*, p. 448 (III 22).

48 Cf. Goldie, 'Absolutismus', pp. 334 et seq.

49 Bolingbroke, *A Dissertation upon Parties*, p. 159 f. (Letter XII).

50 Hume, 'Of the liberty of the press', pp. 10 et seq.

51 Althusius, *Politik*, pp. 197 et seq. (XIX § 10).

52 Ibid, p. 197 (XIX § 9).

53 Cf. also Dreitzel, *Absolutismus und ständische Verfassung in Deutschland*, p. 26.

54 Althusius, *Politik*, p. 421 (XXXIX § 2).

55 Cf. Schmittlein, *L'aspect politique du differend Bossuet-Fénelon*; Engrand, 'Les préoccupations politiques de Fénelon'.

56 Cf. for the history of reception: Cherel, *Fénelon au XVIIIe siècle*; Hillenaar (ed.), *Nouvel état présent des travaux sur Fénelon*.

57 'Savez-vous [ ... ] ce que c'est que l'anarchie; ce que c'est que la puissance arbitraire, et ce que c'est que la royauté réglée par les lois, milieu entre les deux extrémités?' Fénelon, *Examen de conscience sur les devoirs de la royauté*, p. 977. Cf. hereto: Gallouédec-Genuys, *La conception du Prince*; Hobert, 'Fénelon als Denker'; Hübinger, 'Fénelon als politischer Denker'; Mohr, *Fénelon und der Staat*.

58 Cf. Le Brun, 'Notice'; Faille, 'Autour de l'examen'.

59 Cf. Molino, 'L'"Essai philosophique sur le gouvernement civil" – Ramsay ou Fénelon?'.

60 Ramsay, 'Essai sur le Gouvernement civil', p. 3. Cf. concerning the person: Baldi, *Verisimile, non vero*; Henderson, *Chevalier Ramsay*; Schiffmann, *Andreas Michael Ramsay*.

61 Cf. ibid., p. 1.

62 'Entre ces deux extrêmitez un Peuple d'ailleurs si sage ne pût trouver le milieu'. Ibid., p. 112.

63 'La Royauté est comme le point d'appui d'un levier, qui en s'approchant de l'un ou de l'autre de ces deux extrêmitez les tient dans l'équilibre'. Ibid., p. 154.

64 Ibid., p. 181.

65 Cf. pp. 182 et seq.

66 Cf. Desgraves, *Montesquieu*, p. 132.

67 Cf. Montesquieu, 'Lettres Persanes (1721)', p. 252 (Lettre LXXX), 313 (Lettre CXXII), 327 (Lettre CXXXI).

68 Cf. Montesquieu, *Considérations sur les causes de la grandeur des Romains* (1734), p. 119 (chap. IX); ibid., 'Mes Pensées', pp. 1151–53 (No. 631–33).

69 Cf. Shakleton, *Montesquieu*, p. 238.

70 Cf. Desgraves, *Montesquieu*, pp. 228 et seq.

71 Cf. Seyssel, *La Grand' Monarchie de France*, p. 13. 'Comme ceste moderation et refrenation de la puissance absolue des roys, est à leur grand honneur et proffit'. Cf. hereto Kuhfuss, *Mäßigung und Politik*, pp. 133, 170 et seq., 185. Concerning the historical background: Fenske, *Der moderne Verfassungsstaat*, pp. 110–12.

72 'Je le dis, et il me semble que je n'ai fait cet ouvrage que pour le prouver: l'esprit de modération doit être celui du législateur; le bien politique, comme le bien morale, se trouve toujours entre deux limites' (Montesquieu, 'De L'esprit des lois', vol. XXIX, chap. 1, p. 865). Cf. also Kuhfuss, *Mäßigung und Politik*; Riklin, 'Montesquieus freiheitliches Staatsmodell'.

73 Vol. XIV, chap. 2, p. 476 (La 'sensibilité pour les plaisirs [ ... ] sera plus grande dans les pays tempérés; dans les pays chauds, elle sera extrême').

74 Vol. XVII, chap. 2, p. 523 ('Il ne faut donc pas être étonné que la lâcheté des peuples des climats chauds les ait presque toujours rendus esclaves, et que le courage des peuples des climats froids les ait maintenus libres').

75 Cf. vol. XVII, chap. 4, p. 529.

76 Cf. vol. XVII, chap. 5, p. 528.

77 Cf. vol. XVII, chap. VI.

78 Vol. III, chap. 10, p. 259 ('une obéissance extrême').

79 Cf. vol. IV, chap. 3, p. 265.

80 Vol. XIII, chap. 13, p. 467.

81 'Elles doivent être extrêmement esclaves'. Vol. VII, chap. IX, p. 341.

82 Vol. XVI, chap. 9, p. 515.

83 Vol. V, chap. 11, p. 290.

84 Vol. VIII, chap. 2, pp. 349, 351.

85 Vol. VIII, chap. 3, p. 352.
86 Vol. VIII, chap. 6, p. 354.
87 Vol. V, chap. 7, p. 281.
88 Vol. VIII, chap. 2, p. 351.
89 Vol. VIII, chap. 5, p. 353.
90 Vol. XIX, chap. 27, p. 583.
91 Thus, the résumé of a detailed study especially in the England chapter at: Riklin, *Machtteilung*, pp. 276 et seq. Cf. also ibid., 'Montesquieus freiheitliches Staatsmodell'; Brühlmeier, 'Verfassungstheorie und Grundrechtsdenken bei Montesquieu'; Chaimowicz, *Freiheit und Gleichgewicht*, pp. 62–72.
92 Cf. Riklin, *Machtteilung*, p. 269.
93 Diderot, *Œuvres Complètes*, p. 81.
94 Voltaire, 'Extrême', p. 53.
95 Cf. Wilhelm, *Der deutsche Frühliberalismus*, p. 125.
96 So Dreitzel, *Absolutismus und ständische Verfassung in Deutschland*, p. 104.
97 Cf. Justi, *Vergleichungen*, pp. 52 et seq., 493–549.
98 Justi, *Natur und Wesen*, p. 217.
99 Ibid., p. 330.
100 Cf. Lutz, 'The Relative Influence of European Writers on Late Eighteenth-Century American Political Thought', pp. 194 et seq.
101 Cf. Publius (Madison), Federalist No. 14, p. 115: 'If Europe has the merit of discovering this great mechanical power in government, by the simple agency of which the will of the largest political body may be concentred, and its force directed to any object which the public good requires, America can claim the merit of making the discovery the basis of unmixed and extensive republics'. Cf. concerning the interpretation: Bose, *Republik und Mischverfassung*, pp. 89 et seq.
102 Cf. Gebhardt, *Die Krise des Amerikanismus*, p. 26.
103 Cf. also Chinard, 'Polybius and the American Constitution'.
104 Cf. Nolte, 'Aristotelische Tradition'; Riklin, 'John Adams und die gewaltenteilige Mischverfassung'; Thompson, *John Adams and the Spirit of Liberty*, especially pp. 174–249; Walsh, *The Political Science of John Adams*.
105 Adams, 'A Defense of the Constitution', p. 111.
106 Cf. Nolte, 'Aristotelische Tradition', pp. 231 et seq.
107 Adams, 'Three Letters', p. 428. Cf. also Thompson, *John Adams and the Spirit of Liberty*, pp. 188 et seq.
108 Mercier, *Tableau de Paris*, Chap. 348. An example for the later literary popularity of this bon mot can be seen in the social novel by Jeanne Mussard, *Les extrêmes se touchent*, 1872, although nothing contributes to the substance of the formula.
109 Bien, 'Revolution, Bürgerbegriff und Freiheit'.
110 Löhneyß, 'Aulico Politica', pp. 410 et seq. (Chap. 8). Another important impressive example concerning the history of terms of the extremes from the English-speaking world is Ford, *The Golden Meane*. Cf. also Singer, *Die Fürstenspiegel in Deutschland im Zeitalter des Humanismus und der Reformation*.
111 Luther, 'An den christlichen Adel', p. 154.
112 Cf. also Dieter, *Der junge Luther und Aristoteles*.
113 Cf. Scheible, *Melanchthon. Eine Biographie*, p. 91. Cf. also ibid., Art. 'Melanchthon', pp. 371–410.
114 Melanchthon, *Loci communes 1521*, p. 61 (2, 35).
115 Melanchthon, 'Enarrationes', p. 311 (secundum librum, caput II: 'De mediocritate').
116 Cf. Scheible, 'Melanchthon neben Luther', pp. 164 et seq.
117 Cf. Melanchthon, 'Commentarii'.
118 Cf. ibid., 'Widmungsvorrede'. Cf. Scheible, *Melanchthon. Eine Biographie*, p. 93.
119 Cf. Melanchthon, 'De officio principum', p. 394 (margin no. 245). Cf. hereto detailed Estes, 'Melanchthon's Confrontation'.

120 Gardiner, *A Declaration*. The *Oxford English Dictionary* (vol. 3, Oxford, 1961, p. 476) marks the Gardiner quote as first proof of the old-fashioned, but not common, 'extremist' synonym word. Cf. with person and the historical background: Armstrong, 'Gardiner, Stephen'; Muller, *Stephen Gardiner and the Tudor Reaction*; Smith, *Tudor Prelates and Politics, 1536–58*; Skinner, *The Foundations of Modern Political Thought*, vol. 2: The Age of Reformation, p. 84.

121 Cf. MacCulloch, *Die zweite Phase der englischen Reformation*, p. 33.

122 Gonzales de Leon, Controversiae, p. 249.

123 Thirty and two Extremes of these times.

124 This topos can be seen several times. Cf. e.g., Smyth [Lord Bishop of Exeter], The Tendency to Extremes; The Via Media; Garbett, 'Protestant Truth'. But there can also be seen attempts to find a course between the extremes: Beaulieu, *Take heed of both Extremes*; T.A. [Thomas Aiton, Minister of the Gospel at Alyth], The Original Constitution of the Christian Church.

125 This passage is seen as the first lexical reference to the term 'Extremismus': *Deutsches Wörterbuch*, p. 2535.

126 Cf. Camerarius, *Politicorum et oeconomicorum Aristotelis interpretationes et explicationes accuratae*, pp. 89, 161, 178.

127 Cf. Schuber, Art. 'Camerarius, Ludwig'. Cf. concerning the father, Stählin, Art. 'Camerarius, Joachim'.

128 'Camerarius to Behaim', Groningen, 9/19 May 1648, p. 231.

129 'Camerarius to Behaim', Groningen, 18/28 April 1646, p. 209.

130 Cf. concerning the phobia of Camerarius about Jesuits: Ernstberger, 'Einleitung', p. 16.

131 Cf. Machiavelli, *Geschichte von Florenz*, pp. 420–22 (Vol. VII). Cf. also with the following the basic article: Faul, 'Verfemung, Duldung und Anerkennung des Parteiwesens in der Geschichte des politischen Denkens', pp. 60–80.

132 Machiavelli, *Discorsi*, p. 19 (I 4).

133 Ibid., *Discorsi*. In: ibid., *Opere, a cura di Corrado Vivanti*, pp. 193–525, here 209 (I 4). Cf. also Aristotle, *Politik*, V 1302b.

134 Münkler, *Machiavelli*, p. 379.

135 Machiavelli, 'Denkschrift über die Reform des Staates von Florenz', p. 351; ibid., 'Discursus Florentinarum rerum post mortem iunioris Laurentii Medices', p. 738 (marginno. 14). Cf. hereto also Münkler, *Machiavelli*, pp. 379 et seq.

136 Montesquieu, *Considérations*, pp. 679 et seq.

137 Cf. hereto detailed: Kluxen, 'Die Herkunft der Lehre von der Gewaltentrennung'; Shakleton, 'Montesquieu, Bolingbroke and the Separation of Powers'.

138 Cf. Jäger, Art. 'Opposition', p. 476; ibid., *Politische Partei und parlamentarische Opposition*, pp. 75–155.

139 Cited according to Jäger, Art. Opposition, p. 478.

140 Edmund Burke, Speech on Fox's East India Bill (December 1, 1783), in ibid., *Select Works*, ed. by E.J. Payne, vol. 4, Indianapolis, 1990, p. 165.

141 Cf. Rousseau, *Der Gesellschaftsvertrag oder Die Grundsätze des Staatsrechts*, p. 59 (II, 3).

142 Chamberlayne, *L'Estat présent de l'Angleterre*, p. 59. The first part of this book was published in 1669; the second part, from which the quotes have been taken, was added to the third edition from 1672. Cf. the quotation at S.L., Art. 'Chamberlayne, Edward', pp. 8 et seq. References to the book by Chamberlayne can be found in Mackenzie, *Les relations de l'Angleterre et de la France d'après le vocabulaire*, p. 82; Mönch, Der politische Wortschatz der französischen Restauration in Parlament und Presse, pp. 54 et seq.

143 Marcel Gauchet suspects this as a new creation of an old differentiation: ibid., 'La droite et la gauche', p. 396.

144 Cf. the reference at Gauchet: ibid., pp. 398 et seq. Cf. hereto also Retat, 'Partis et factions en 1789', pp. 82 et seq.; Brasart, *Paroles de la Révolution*, pp. 102–4.

145 Cf. Buchez/Roux-Lavergne, *Histoire parlementaire*. Cited according to Rémond, *Les droites en France*, p. 389.
146 Cf. Defrasne, *La gauche en France de 1789 à nos jours*; Petitfils, *La droite en France de 1789 à nos jours*.
147 Cf. the reference at Frey, *Les transformations du vocabulaire français*, p. 46; Gauchet, La droite et la gauche, pp. 399 and 461, note 14; Brunot, Histoire de la langue française, pp. 769 et seq.
148 Cited according to Gauchet, 'La droite et la gauche', p. 461, note 14.
149 Cf. Frey, *Les transformations du vocabulaire français*, p. 34.
150 Cf. ibid., p. 35. Cf. to this well-documented use of the term also: Bianchi, 'Fanatique(s)/Fanatisme (1789–94)'.
151 Cf. Frey, *Les transformations du vocabulaire français*, pp. 30, 34.
152 Ibid., pp. 105 et seq.
153 'Il me paraît infecté de ce coupable modérantisme qui [ … ] voudrait assassiner la liberté'. Cited according to ibid., p. 154.
154 Burke, 'Reflections on the Revolution in France', p. 136.
155 Ibid., p. 137.
156 Humboldt, 'Ideen über Staatsverfassung', p. 84.
157 Wieland, 'Unparteiische Betrachtungen', p. 488.
158 Wieland, 'Die Französische Republik', p. 524.
159 Ibid., p. 534.
160 Ibid., p. 535 (emphasis in the original).
161 Halem, *Blicke auf einen Theil Deutschlands*, p. 303.
162 'Forster to Heyne', 12 July 1791, p. 653.
163 'Forster to Therese Forster', Paris, 19/20 December 1793, p. 764.
164 'Washington to the Marquis de Lafayette', 10 June 1792, p. 54.
165 Cf. concerning the incidents: Furet, 'La République jacobine'.
166 Staël-Holstein, 'De l'influence des passions', p. 143 (Chap. VII: De l'esprit de parti): 'Ce sont des esprits crédules, soit qu'ils se passionnent pour ou contre les vieilles erreurs; et leur violence, sans arrêt, leur donne le besoin de se placer à l'extrême de toutes les idées, pour y mettre à l'aise leur jugement et leur caractère. [ … ] On a dit souvent, dans le cours de la révolution de France, que les aristocrates et les jacobins tenaient le même langage, étaient aussi absolu dans leurs opinions, et, selon la diversité des situations, adoptaient un système de conduite également intolérant. Cette remarque doit être considérée comme une simple conséquence du même principe. Les passions rendent les hommes semblables entre eux, comme la fièvre jette dans le même état des tempéraments divers'.
167 Constant, *Des réactions politiques*, pp. 89, 95. Cf. concerning the historical background: Barudio, *Madame de Staël und Benjamin Constant*; Gauchet, 'Constant, Staël et la Révolution française'; Todorov, *Benjamin Constant*.
168 Constant, 'De la souveraineté du peuple', pp. 14 et seq.
169 Cf. Adams, 'Review of the Propositions for Amending the Constitution', pp. 546 et seq.
170 Cf. Schalk, *Exempla*, p. 73; Spaemann, '"Fanatisch" und "Fanatismus"'.

### 4 Extreme ideologies in the political laboratory of the nineteenth century

1 Mönch, Der politische Wortschatz der französischen Restauration in Parlament und Presse, p. 54.
2 Ibid., p.57.
3 Cf., Boiste, *Dictionnaire universel de la langue française*, pp. 244 et seq., 302, 340; Duclerc/Paguerre, *Dictionnaire Politique*, p. 394.
4 Cf., e.g. Wilbert, 'Qu'est-ce que le côté droit?'
5 Cf. e.g. Dupont, 'Lettre d'avis'. Cf. the following newspapers: *L'extrême droite. Journal du droit et des principes vrais*, Dir. Adrien Peladan, Nîmes, 1875–77

(weekly); *L'Avenir de Bézier*. Organe de la démocratie extrême gauche, paraissant trois fois par semaine, Bézier, 1881/1882; *L'Extrême-gauche* (Alliance radicale-socialiste), paraissant le dimanche, Dir. Emile Brousse, Saint-Mandé (Seine) 1883; *L'Extrême-gauche*, Vincennes 1883/1884; *La Démocratie du Midi*. Journal radical extrême-gauche, paraissant tous les dimanches, Bézier 1886; *Le Courrier de Bézier et de l'arrondissement*. Journal politique, littéraire et commercial, later: Organe de la démocratie radicale extrême-gauche et socialiste révisionniste, later: Organe radical socialiste. Hebdomadaire, later: bihebdomadaire, Bézier 1891–93; *L'Extrême-gauche*, Lyon 1904; *Germinal*. Journal républicain d'extrême-gauche, Carpentras 1912/1913 (authors e.g. Edouard Daladier and Edouard Herriot); *Le Cri du peuple du Sud-Est*. Hebdomadaire, later: Hebdomadaire d'extrême-gauche, Lyon 1920–21.

6 Cf., Thiers, *Discours parlementaires* – with numerous examples.

7 Cf., Laponce, *Left and Right*, p. 52. See also Backes, 'Rechts-Links-Unterscheidung'; Decker, 'Jenseits von rechts und links?'; Eatwell, 'Rise of "Left–Right" Terminology'; Hoff, *Rechts und Links*; Rossi-Landi, *Le chassé croisé*; Slama, *Les chasseurs d'absolu*.

8 Cf., Laponce, *Left and Right*, p. 53.

9 As Laponce, *Left and Right*, seems to assume (p. 54).

10 Eisenmann, *Die Parteyen der teutschen Reichsversammlung*, pp. 8, 13, 19, 24, 38.

11 As in Kramer, *Fraktionsbindungen in den deutschen Volksvertretungen*, pp. 50 et seq. (emphases in the original).

12 Verhandlungen der badischen Zweiten Kammer, 1822, vol. 8, pp. 145 et seq. Cited according to Kramer, *Fraktionsbindungen in den deutschen Volksvertretungen*, p. 42.

13 Welcker, *Die Universal- und die juristisch-politische Encyclopädie*, p. XXVI.

14 Besoigne Jérôme (anonymous), *Juste Milieu. Qu'il faut tenir dans les disputes de religion*, o.O., 25 August 1735 ('le vice de l'Extrême, qui consisteroit à outrer les choses, et à donner dans un excès pour en éviter un autre').

15 Cf., Spuller, *Royer-Collard*, p. 135.

16 Cf. also Starzinger, *Middlingness*, pp. 20–35.

17 Cf., Rosanvallon, *Le Moment Guizot*.

18 Guizot, *Mémoires pour servir à l'histoire de mon temps*, vol.1, pp. 95 et seq.

19 Ibid., p. 157.

20 Guizot, *Du Gouvernement de la France depuis la Restauration*, p. 232. For the contemporary use of the language, see also Des Ultra en 1818, et de la note secrète, par le Chev. De N., Paris 1818.

21 Starzinger, *Middlingness*, p. 4.

22 Cited according to ibid., p. 9.

23 Cf., Brougham, 'High-Tory Principles', p. 150. As to person, see Stewart, *Henry Brougham*.

24 Brougham, 'Balances and Checks', p. 7. cf., Starzinger, *Middlingness*, p. 32. In later years, Brougham presented a comprehensive work about the history and the functioning of the British mixed constitution: Brougham, *The British Constitution*.

25 *Le Moniteur Universel*, No. 31, 31 January 1831: 'Nous chercherons à nous tenir dans un juste milieu également éloigné des excès du pouvoir populaire et des abus du pouvoir royal'.

26 Anon. (Regis-Jean-Francois Vaysse de Villiers), Le juste milieu en toutes choses, et surtout en politique, Paris, 1832, p. 3. In this vein, see also Dosquet, *Le Juste-Milieu dévoilé, ou la France en 1832*.

27 'On devait prévoir que cette monarchie, transaction définitive entre tous les systèmes et tous les partis, blesserait les extrêmes en tout genre, les disposerait à se coaliser ou fournir en commun leur part de sophismes et de déclamations'. Thiers, *La Monarchie de 1830*, p. I.

28 'Le juste milieu, ce qui n'est ni juste ni milieu'. Marie Joseph de la Fayette an Karl von Rotteck, Lagrange. The German spokesmen of Vormärz liberalism also expressed criticism regarding the reign of Louis-Philippe, even though they claimed the term 'middle' for themselves. See only Rotteck, 'Vorwort zur ersten Auflage'.

29 'Blicke auf die politischen halbperiodischen Schriften der Franzosen'. In: *Augsburger Allgemeine Zeitung*, Supplement No. 149, 28 November 1818, p. 594.

30 Görres, 'Teutschland und die Revolution (1819)', p. 101. Görres also later defended the constitutional monarchy as the middle road between despotism and anarchy. cf. ibid., 'Weltlage', p. 16. See also: Dieter J. Weiss, Joseph von Görres (1776–1848). In: Heidenreich (ed.), *Politische Theorien*, pp. 139–54.

31 Cf. Heuvel, *German Life in the Age of Revolution*, pp. 241–51.

32 Murhard, art. 'Absolutismus', p. 156 (emphasis in the original). As to biography, see: Weidemann, 'Friedrich Murhard'; Schäfer, 'Friedrich Murhard'.

33 Cf. Fouquet, 'Ancillon', pp. 265 et seq.

34 Cf. Ancillon, *Zur Vermittlung der Extreme in den Meinungen*. A French translation was published in the year Ancillon died: Ancillon, *Du Juste Milieu ou du Rapprochement des Extrêmes dans les Opinions*.

35 Pölitz, 'Friedrich Ancillon als politischer Schriftsteller', p. 313.

36 Ibid., *Die Staatswissenschaften im Lichte unserer Zeit*, p. VIII. Cf. with Pölitz' Staatslehre: Connerton, Karl Heinrich Ludwig Pölitz and the Politics of the Juste Milieu in Germany, p. 58; Stolleis, *Geschichte des öffentlichen Rechts in Deutschland*, pp. 165 et seq. For a critique of Pölitz' system, see: Wolgast, Art. 'Reform, reformation', pp. 350 et seq.

37 Cf. foremost: Boldt, *Deutsche Verfassungsgeschichte*; Fehrenbach, *Verfassungsstaat und Nationsbildung*; Grimm, *Deutsche Verfassungsgeschichte*.

38 Cf. hereto e.g. Haake, *Johann Peter Friedrich Ancillon und Kronprinz Friedrich Wilhelm IV von Preußen*.

39 Welcker, Art. 'Ancillon', p. 520 (emphasis in the original). See also the critique by Friedrich von Gagern: ibid., 'Die rechte Mitte'. As to the person of Welcker, see foremost: Mueller-Dietz, *Das Leben des Rechtslehrers und Politikers Karl Theodor Welcker*; ibid., 'Karl Theodor Welcker'; ibid., 'Der Freiburger Einfluss: Rotteck und Welcker'; Wild, *Karl Theodor Welcker*.

40 Münch, *Historische Rückblicke, politische Zeitstimmen und patriotische Ermahnungen*, p. 14.

41 Jordan, *Selbstverteidigung*, p. 13. See in this vein already: ibid., *Versuche über allgemeinen Staatsrecht*, pp. 6–12. As to biography, see: Kleinknecht, *Sylvester Jordan*.

42 Cf. Bleek, 'Friedrich Christoph Dahlmann (1785–1860)'; Kraus, 'Die deutsche Rezeption und Darstellung'; Wilhelm, *Die englische Verfassung und der vormärzliche deutsche Liberalismus*.

43 Cf. Backes, *Liberalismus und Demokratie*, pp. 123–29. See also: Schöttle, *Politische Theorien*.

44 Cf. with 'radicalism': Wende, *Radikalismus im Vormärz*. For the importance of the Staatslexikon, see foremost: Brandt, 'Das Rotteck-Welckersche "Staats-Lexikon". Einleitung zum Neudruck'; Zehntner, *Das Staatslexikon von Rotteck und Welcker*.

45 Rotteck, 'Vorwort zur ersten Auflage (1834)', pp. XXI et seq. (emphasis in the original). For a similar position, see Schwarz, *Gedanken über die richtige Mitte in der innern Politik*. For Rotteck's understanding of the constitution, see: Brandt, 'Karl von Rotteck (1775–1840)'; Ehmke, *Karl von Rotteck, der 'politische Professor'*; Jobst, 'Die Staatslehre Karl von Rottecks'.

46 Rotteck, Art. 'Abgeordnete', p. 104 (emphasis in the original). See also ibid., Art. 'Census', p. 154.

47 Schulz, *Deutsches Noth- und Hilfsbüchlein für vorsichtig liberale Esser und Trinker,* pp. VIII et seq.
48 Ibid., p. 3.
49 Cf., Backes, *Liberalismus und Demokratie,* pp. 91 et seq. As to biography, see in detail: Grab, *Dr. Wilhelm Schulz aus Darmstadt.*
50 Schulz, Art. 'Revolution', p. 555.
51 Oppenheim, 'Zur Kritik der Demokratie in Deutschland'. As to biography: Hentschel, 'Nationalpolitische und sozialpolitische Bestrebungen in der Reichsgründungszeit'; Klenner, 'Heinrich Bernhard Oppenheim als Rechtsphilosoph'.
52 Ruge, 'Kritik und Partei. Der Vorwurf gegen die neueste Geistesentwicklung', pp. 1175 et seq., 1177–80, 1181 et seq., here 1179. Cf. also Walter, *Demokratisches Denken zwischen Hegel und Marx,* pp. 236–38.
53 Ruge, 'Kritik und Partei. Der Vorwurf gegen die neueste Geistesentwicklung', p. 1180.
54 Hegel, *Phänomenologie des Geistes.* Cf. for the contemporary analysis of Hegel's theses: Günther, *Die Juste-Milieus in der deutschen Philosophie gegenwärtiger Zeit.*
55 For Krug's biography, see foremost: Holz, Art. 'Krug, Wilhelm Traugott'; Prantl, Art. 'Krug, Wilhelm Traugott', pp. 220–22; Riedel, Art. 'Krug, Wilhelm Traugott'. One of Krug's students published an acknowledgement in appreciation of his achievements after the death of his teacher, which contains a great deal of material: Vogel, *D. Wilhelm Traugott Krug.* Krug himself described his 'Lebensreise' for the first time in 1825: *Urceus, Meine Lebensreise.* An updated autobiography appeared in the year of his death: *Krug's Lebensreise in sechs Stationen,* and, in addition, Volkmar Reinhardt's letters to the publisher, Leipzig, 1842. A further important biographical source is found in Krug's extensive correspondence with the Dresden theologian, classical scholar and author August Boettiger, which is kept at the Saechsische Staats- und Landesbibliothek Dresden (Mscr. Dresd. H. 37, 4°, vol. 112, 113).
56 For Krug's theological and church–political position, see in detail: Graf, *Theonomie,* pp. 52–76.
57 Cf. Heyer, 'Professor Wilhelm Traugott Krug in Leipzig', pp. 67–75; Löschburg, 'Wilhelm Traugott Krug und der nationale Befreiungskampf des griechischen Volkes', pp. 208–22.
58 Cf. hereto foremost. Kemper, *Gesunder Menschenverstand.*
59 Cf. hereto foremost: Fiedler, *Die staatswissenschaftlichen Anschauungen und die politisch–publizistische Tätigkeit des Nachkantianers Wilhelm Traugott Krug.*
60 Cf. Zwahr, 'Von der zweiten Universitätsreform bis zur Reichsgründung', pp. 141 et seq.; ibid., *Revolutionen in Sachsen,* pp. 94–100.
61 Cf. Reinhardt, Die sächsischen Unruhen der Jahre 1830–31 und Sachsens Übergang zum Verfassungsstaat, pp. 37–43; Schlechte, Die Vorgeschichte der sächsischen Verfassung vom 4 September 1831, pp. 61 et seq.; Hammer, *Volksbewegung und Obrigkeiten,* pp. 123–43.
62 Cf. with the History of the Saxon Federal State Parliament: Matzerath, 'Landstände und Landtage in Sachsen 1438 bis 1831'; ibid., *Aspekte sächsischer Landtagsgeschichte.*
63 Cf. Franke, *Zensur und Preßaufsicht in Leipzig 1830–48,* p. 84.
64 Cf. Krug, *Aretologie oder philosophische Tugendlehre,* p. 84.
65 Haller, *Restauration der Staats-Wissenschaft.*
66 Cf. for Haller's political theory, among others: Brandt, *Landständische Repräsentation im deutschen Vormärz,* pp. 59–64; Martin, 'Weltanschauliche Motive im altkonservativen Denken'; Reinhard, 'Der Streit um K.L. von Hallers "Restauration der Staatswissenschaft"'; Weilenmann, Untersuchungen zur Staatstheorie Carl Ludwig von Hallers.
67 Cf. Müller-Schmid, 'Adam Müller (1779–1829)'.

68 Krug, 'Die Staatswissenschaft im Restaurazionsprozesse der Herren v. Haller, Adam Müller und Konsorten betrachtet (1817)', p. 327. cf. For Krug's quarrel with Haller and Müller, see also: Fiedler, *Die staatswissenschaftlichen Anschauungen und die politisch–publizistische Tätigkeit des Nachkantianers Wilhelm Traugott Krug*, pp. 32–37.

69 Krug, 'Geschichtliche Darstellung des Liberalismus alter und neuer Zeit', p. 325.

70 Ibid., p. 376.

71 Ibid., p. 377.

72 Ibid., p. 377.

73 Ibid., p. 398.

74 Ibid., 'Der falsche Liberalismus unsrer Zeit', p. 334.

75 Cf. ibid., p. 335.

76 Ibid., p. 338.

77 Ibid., p. 367.

78 Ibid., p. 377.

79 Ibid., p. 379. Cf. for the republicanism of part of the 'Hambachians': Hüls, *Johann Georg August Wirth (1798–1848)*.

80 Krug, Art. 'Ultraismus', p. 260.

81 Ibid., 'Der Kampf zwischen Konservativen und Destruktiven und das europäische Ober-Studien-Direktorium', p. 202.

82 Ibid.

83 Ibid., p. 204.

84 Ibid., p. 203.

85 Cf. ibid., 'Dikäopolitik oder neue Restaurazion der Staatswissenschaft mittels Rechtsgesetzen (1824)', pp. 455–94; see already ibid., 'Das Repräsentativsystem'.

86 Krug, 'Dikäopolitik oder neue Restaurazion der Staatswissenschaft mittels Rechtsgesetzen (1824)', pp. 393 et seq.

87 Cf. for the classification: Brandt, *Landständische Repräsentation im deutschen Vormärz*, pp. 223–26.

88 Krug, 'Das Repräsentativsystem', p. 297.

89 Cf. ibid., pp. 307–17. See hereto also: Böckstiegel, *Volksrepräsentation in Sachsen*, pp. 60–69.

90 Cf. Krug, *Ueber Opposizions-Parteien in und außer Deutschland und ihr Verhältniß zu den Regierungen*. See hereto also: Jäger, Art. 'Opposition', pp. 492 et seq.

91 Cf. Backes, *Liberalismus und Demokratie*, pp. 375–409.

92 This work is seen as 'the most important philosophical handbook of the nineteenth century': Wolters, Art. 'Krug, Friedrich, Wilhem Traugott', p. 503.

93 Krug, *Allgemeines Handwörterbuch der philosophischen Wissenschaften nebst ihrer Literatur und Geschichte*, p. 394.

94 Cf. only Bernhardi, 'Unsere Verfassung im Sinn der extremen und im Sinn der gemäßigten Parteien (1858)'; Droysen, 'Die Extreme'; Ernst II. Herzog von Sachsen-Coburg-Gotha, 'Denkschrift über die Gründung des "Vereins" (1853)'; Radowitz, 'Der Kampf der Extreme'; Werro, *Les partis extrêmes dans le Canton de Fribourg*; Der extreme Liberalismus. Seine Irrtümer und sein dem Werk der Einigung Deutschlands verderblicher Einfluss. Nach den Erlebnissen der letztverflossenen fünfzig Jahre kritisch beleuchtet von einem Siebenziger, Wiesbaden, 1881.

95 Rohmer, *Lehre von den politischen Parteien*, pp. 104 et seq.

96 Ibid., p. 305.

97 Ibid., pp. 307 et seq.

98 Ibid., pp. 309 et seq.

99 Ibid., p. 313.

100 Sybel, *Die politischen Parteien der Rheinprovinz in ihrem Verhältniß zur preußischen Verfassung geschildert*, pp. 4, 45.

101 Ibid., p. 44.

102 Ibid.
103 Bluntschli, Art. 'Friedrich und Theodor Rohmer', p. 648.
104 Bluntschli, Art. 'Parteien, politische', p. 726.
105 Cf. Besier/Lindemann, *Im Namen der Freiheit*, pp. 94–107; Gara, 'Who was an abolitionist?'; Mayer, *All on Fire*; Perry, *Radical Abolitionism*; Thomas, *The Liberator*.
106 Demos, 'The Antislavery Movement and the Problem of Violent "Means"', p, 502.
107 Garrison, 'To the public'.
108 Calculator, 'Gradual emancipation' (emphasis in the original).
109 'A Brief Criticism', in *The Liberator*, 3 (1833) 7, pp. 26 et seq. (emphasis in the original).
110 'To the Senate and House of Representatives', in *The Liberator*, 4 (1834) 7, p. 25.
111 'Anti-Slavery Fanatics', in *The Liberator*, 4 (1834) 25, p. 97.
112 Owing to the independence of his judgement, the observations by Friedrich von Raumer, who travelled the USA at the beginning of the 1840s, are extremely informative for the evaluation of this question: Raumer, *America and the American People*, Chap. XII: 'The Races of Mankind and Slavery'.
113 'The Ultra-Abolitionists', in *The Liberator*, 13 (1843) 19, p. 73. The quotation comes from Cooke, *An essay on the gospel's relations to civil law*, p. 12.
114 'From the Haverhill Gazette', in *The Liberator*, 12 (1842) 7, p. 24.
115 'From the Mercantile Journal', in *The Liberator*, 11 (1841) 21, p. 84. That the abolitionists did not reject 'moderation' in every form is shown by Zinn, 'Abolitionists, Freedom-Riders, and the Tactics of Agitation'. See also the contributions in Kraut (ed.), *Crusaders and Compromisers*.
116 Webster, 'The Constitution and the Union', p. 358. Webster's remark is listed as a first proof in: *A Dictionary of American English*, vol. 2, p. 915. Cf. as to the person: Poore, *The Political Register and Congressional Directory*, p. 688; Smith, *Defender of the Union*.
117 Olmsted, *A Journey in the Seaboard Slave States*, p. 177.
118 Cf. Williams, *Lincoln and the Radicals*; Dumond, *Antislavery Origins of the Civil War in the United States*.
119 Cf. for biography: Poore, *The Political Register and Congressional Directory*, p. 348.
120 Cox, *Eight Years in Congress*, p. 21.
121 Ibid., p. 20.
122 Ibid., p. 188.
123 Ibid., p. 189 (speech of 6 January 1861).
124 Cf. for this designation: Coleman, 'The Use of the Term "Copperhead" During the Civil War', pp. 263 et seq.
125 'The Extremists at Work', in *New York Times*, 22 January 1867, p. 4 ('Silvery tongues and Jesuitical pens').
126 *The American*, 13 (1887) 341 (19 February), p. 276. Cf. for the historical background: Clark, 'Prohibition and Temperance'.
127 Cf. for example 'The left', in *The Times* (London), 28 October 1873; 'Prolongation of Marshal Macmahon's Powers', in *The Times* (London), 5 November 1873, p. 5.
128 In a letter, the president of the American 'Fenian Brotherhood' of 1865 spoke in a non-political context about 'these days of extravagance and extremism'; Roberts, 'The Fenians in America', p. 2.
129 'Indian Fanatics', in *The Times* (London), 14 October 1871, p. 12.
130 Cf. Klimkeit, *Der politische Hinduismus*, pp. 226–42.
131 Government of Bombay, *Source Material for a History of the Freedom Movement in India*, p. 205.
132 Cf. Majumdar, *History of the Freedom Movement in India*, pp. 427 et seq. For an intellectual background, see: Varma, *Modern Indian Political Thought*, pp. 202–80; Inamdar, 'The Political Ideas of Lokmanya Tilak'.

133 'The Unrest in Bengal', in *The Times* (London), 15 October 1906, p. 8; 'India. The National Congress', in *The Times* (London), 16 December 1907, p. 5; 'Disorderly Scenes at the National Congress', in *The Times* (London), 27 December 1907, p. 7; 'The Split at Surat', in *The Times* (London), 30 December 1907, p. 3 ('meeting the extremists'); 'The Indian National Congress', in *The Times* (London), 27 January 1908, p. 4; 'The National Congress', in *The Times* (London), 10 December 1908, p. 5. Cf. about these struggles: Ripathi, *The Extremist Challenge*; Rothermund, *Die politische Willensbildung in Indien 1900–960*, pp. 47–70.

134 Documentation about the Tilak trial contains numerous press articles from the years 1906 to 1908 and gives a good insight into the contemporary use of the language: 'Full and Authentic report of the Tilak Trial'. For further evidence, see: *The Oxford Dictionary*, vol. III, p. 476.

## 5 Extremism at the beginning of the 'age of extremes'

1 Paul Valery to A.A. Coste (1915). See also *Trésor de la Langue Française*, vol. 8, p. 536.
2 Cf. 'Le gouvernement provisoire veut calmer les extrémistes', in *Le Matin*, 27 March 1917, p. 3; 'L'entretien du général Kornilow avec les extrémistes', in *Le Matin*, 28 March 1917, p. 3; 'Campagne des extrémistes contre M. Milioukow', in *Le Matin*, 5 May 1917, p. 3; 'Un mouvement des extrémistes à Cronstadt', in *Le Matin*, 4 June 1917, p. 2; 'Une victoire sur les extrémistes', in *Le Matin*, 4 October 1917, p. 1; 'La révolution maximaliste', in *Le Matin*, 10 November 1917, p. 3; 'Les extrémistes attaquent le Kremlin', in *Le Matin*, 20 November 1917, p. 1; 'L'agitation extrémiste et le gouvernement', in *Le Figaro*, 6 May 1917, p. 2 ; 'Les manifestations extrémistes à Petrograd', in *L'Humanité*, 3 July 1917, p. 3; 'Les extrémistes et l'opinion', in *L'Humanité*, 7 July 1917, p. 3; 'Le gouvernement contre les extrémistes', in *L'Humanité*, 8 July 1917, p. 1; 'La note de M. Milioukoff et les extrémistes', in *L'Action Française*, 5 May 1917, p. 2.
3 The word 'maximalism' probably goes back to the Erfurt Parteitag of German social democracy (1891). There, a tendency demanded to carry on the political fight on the basis of a maximal programme, whereas another pleaded for a reformistic minimal programme. In Russia, one spoke of 'maximalism' in the social revolutionary party as of the revolution of 1905. Bolshevism and maximalism constituted two leanings, although they frequently blended in the time that followed. Therefore, the word 'maximalisme' was not used uniformly. After the October Revolution, the extreme left formations who were independent of the Bolshevists were given this designation. Cf. e.g. Reed, *Zehn Tage*, p. 21. For the history of the word, see Bongiovanni, 'Massimalismo'; Gayman, 'Maximalisme'.
4 See already 'Russia Prospects of the New Ministry', in: *Daily Chronicle*, 20 March 1917, p. 2. ('substantial concessions to the extremists'); Harold Williams, 'Likelihood of Revolutionary Regime', in *Daily Chronicle*, 26 March 1917, p. 3 ('the Council of Workmen's and Soldiers' Deputies [ ... ] was largely at the mercy of the Extremists'). The term 'extremist' for the radical revolutionaries in Russia is also often found in the language of diplomacy of the time. Cf. e.g. Buchanan, *My Mission to Russia and Other Diplomatic Memories*, pp. 129, 137, 219; Lloyd George, *War Memoirs*, p. 1120.
5 Cf. 'Salomon Grumbach', in *Internationales Biographisches Archiv* No. 36, 25 August 1952.
6 Cf. with Grimm's role, among others, Jost, *Die Altkommunisten*, p. 47.
7 *L'Humanité*, 11 May 1916, p. 1. Two additional spellings are also used: 'extrèmiste' and 'extrémiste'. This shows the newness and insecurity of the use of the language. See also Grumbach, *L'erreur de Zimmerwald-Kienthal*; ibid., *Brest-Litowsk*. Both works use the term 'maximalist' and not 'extremist'.

8 *L'Humanité*, 21 March 1917, p. 2.
9 Buchanan, *My Mission to Russia and Other Diplomatic Memories*, p. 137.
10 *L'Humanité*, 21 March 1917, p. 3.
11 Cf. 'Qui êtes-vous?', p. 13.
12 Anet, *La Révolution russe*, vol. 1, p. 111 (25 March) (emphasis in the original). This book contains a collection of articles that appeared on a daily basis in the *Petit Parisien*. See also *L'Action Française*, 26 March 1917, p. 1.
13 This does not necessarily contradict the claim that the words 'extremism' and 'extremist' had only become known in the Russian language 'since the 1930s'. So Cernych, *Istoriko-etimologicsekij*, p. 444.
14 Lenin, 'Die Machenschaften der republikanischen Chauvinisten', p. 376. Lenin cites Claude Anet's formulation 'de l'ancien redacteur d'un journal extrémiste'. In the Russian version, this reads: 'бывшим редактором экстремистской [ ... ] газеты'. Lenin, *Werke* (Polnoe sobranie sočinenij), vol. 31 (March–April 1917), p. 81.
15 Lenin, 'Briefe aus der Ferne', p. 329.
16 Lenin, 'Drei Krisen', p. 169. In the Russian version, Lenin did not use the word 'ėkstremistkoj' but 'krainost' for the menshivists and Bolshevists, who with their radical/uncompromising attitude worked right into the hands of the counter-revolution: 'своими крайностями контрреволюции'. Lenin, *Werke* (Polnoe sobranie sočinenij), vol. 32 (May–July 1917), p. 430.
17 Paléologue, *La Russie des tsars pendant la grande guerre*, p. 305.
18 See e.g. the unfavourable evaluation in: Kerenski, *La Révolution russe 1917*, p. 337.
19 Ibid., p. 306.
20 See Peschanski (ed.), *Marcel Cachin*, p. 85 (Monday, 16 April 1917).
21 Williams, *The Spirit of the Russian Revolution*, p. 11. See also the evaluation by the German historian Gustav Mayer: Lademacher (ed.), *Die Zimmerwalder Bewegung*, pp. 518–20.
22 Peschanski (ed.), *Marcel Cachin*, p. 98 (Friday, 20 April 1917).
23 Ibid., p. 105 (Saturday, 21 April 1917). During his trip from Paris to Saint Petersburg, Cachin often used the attribute 'extremist' for the Zimmerwaldian left and Lenin's followers. See e.g. ibid., p. 48 (Monday, 2 April 1917), p. 54 (Wednesday, 4 April 1917), p. 73 (Friday, 13 April 1917), p. 87 (Tuesday, 17 April 1917).
24 Ibid., p. 137 (Wednesday, 2 May 1917).
25 Cf. Stillig, *Die Russische Februarrevolution 1917 und die sozialistische Friedenspolitik*, pp. 69–73.
26 Paléologue, *La Russie des tsars pendant la grande guerre*, p. 307.
27 Ibid., p. 308.
28 So the evaluation of a 'Jusqu' au boutiste'; Maxe, *De Zimmerwald au bolchévisme ou le triomphe du marxisme pangermaniste*, p. 72.
29 Guilbeaux, 'La Révolution russe et la paix'.
30 Guilbeaux, *La fin des Soviets*, p. 11. Guilbeaux now strongly took the USSR to task, which had brought misery and slavery to the Russian people and covered the world with war (p. 171).
31 S. Drudzo, 'Lénine', in *Journal du peuple*, 14 May 1917, p. 1. There is no biography available for Lozowski. As different as the spelling sometimes is, so are parts of the biographical data. Cf. for the inconsistencies, the doctoral thesis by Gomolinski, Salomon Abramovitch Dridzo dit Alexandre Lozovsky (1878–1952); Tosstorff, *Profitern*, pp. 717–25. See beyond that the following literature: Art. 'Lozovsky', pp. 318 et seq., Kießling, *Partner im 'Narrenparadies'*, pp. 196 et seq., 204 et seq.; Redlich, *War, Holocaust and Stalinism*, pp. 5, 8, 146; Rapoport, *Hammer, Sichel, Davidstern*, 149 et seq.
32 *L'Union des Métaux*, no. 67/May 1917. See quotations and commentaries in Merrheim, *Amsterdam ou Moscou?*, p. 6. The formula 'Revolution jusqu'au bout' was derived from the then popular expression of 'jusqu'au boutisme', meaning the

unconditional supporters of the war. See in this context: Guilbeauz, ' ... et demain?'.

33  Rolland, *Journal des années de guerre 1914–19*, p. 1190. See also the entry on p. 1179.
34  Cf. explanation by Cachin and Frossard at the meeting of Congress on 22 July, in *The Communist Internationale*, 2 (1920) 13, pp. 266 et seq.
35  Frossard, 'Sur la Révolution Russe'.
36  Kalinine, 'La Révolution russe et ses perspectives'. In spite of the different short form of the first name, this seems to be the editor of *Pravda* at the time, the later head of state of the Soviet Union, Michail Kalinin (1875–1946). Cf. *Internationales Biographisches Archiv* 03/1965, 11 January 1965.
37  Stillig, *Die Russische Februarrevolution 1917 und die sozialistische Friedenspolitik*, p. 27.
38  Anet, *La Révolution russe*, vol. 1, p. 241 (23 May). See also: Thomas, 'Journal de Russie'. and the introduction by Sinanoglou, ibid., pp. 86–92.
39  Vandervelde, *Trois aspects de la Révolution russe*, p. XII.
40  Anet, *La Révolution russe*, vol. 2, p. 216 (6 Nov.).
41  Cf. Ferro, *La Révolution russe de 1917*, p. 547; Pipes, *Die Russische Revolution*, vol. 2, pp. 222 et seq.
42  Anet, *La Révolution russe*, vol. 2, pp. 277–78 (18 Nov.).
43  Buchanan, *My Mission to Russia and Other Diplomatic Memories*, p. 218.
44  See e.g. the following articles: 'The council of workers and soldiers', in *Vorwärts*, 25 March 1917, p. 1; 'Meeting in the Tauric Palace', in *Vorwärts*, 22 March 1917, p. 1 (both refer to information from the *Daily Chronicle* correspondent 'Harald William'; correct name: Harold Williams); 'The provisional government issues numerous appeals to call the "extremists" to order', in *Leipziger Volkszeitung*, 27 March 1917, p. 2 (based on an article from the Paris newspaper *Le Temps*); 'The announcement by the maximalists', in *Frankfurter Zeitung*, Morgenblatt 7 July 1917, p. 2 (names the source: *Telegraaf*, Den Hague); 'The battle in Petersburg against Lenin', in *Germania*, addition 29 July 1917 (the author cites a long passage from *La Stampa*, Torino); 'The uncertainty in Petersburg', in *Germania*, 11 September 1917, p. 1 (source: *Le Temps*, Paris); 'How is Kornilov doing?', in *Vorwärts*, 18 September 1917 (source: information from a Dutch news agency); 'The extremists in the majority', in *Germania*, 16 November 1917, p. 1 (the article refers to a report by the *Daily News* correspondent Arthur Ransome); 'The counter-revolutionary movement in Russia', in *Grenzboten*, 76 (1917) 35, pp. 257–68, here 258 (source: Russian newspapers). Apparently, the German–Swiss press avoided the neologism even more consistently. An article in the *Neue Zürcher Zeitung* about the events in Russia frequently referred to the reports of the Milan press and constantly translated the word 'estremisti' as 'extremes'. Cf. e.g.: 'The conditions in Russia', in *Neue Zürcher Zeitung*, 1 Abendblatt, 13 April 1917, p. 1; 'The conditions in Russia', in *Neue Zürcher Zeitung*, 2 Morgenblatt, 19 April 1917, p. 1.
45  Cf. 'Denkschrift des Grafen Brockdorff-Rantzau für das Auswärtige Amt vom 2 April 1917', p. 48. See hereto also: Scheidemann, *Ulrich Graf Brockdorff-Rantzau (1869–1928)*, pp. 294–333.
46  Cf. with this German political line the summary by: Kielmansegg, *Deutschland und der Erste Weltkrieg*, pp. 490–513. See also: Zechlin, 'Friedensbestrebungen und Revolutionierungsversuche'.
47  Cf. the telegram from the German Embassy in Stockholm to the Berlin Ministry of 20 March 1917.
48  Cf. Zeman (ed.), *Germany and the Revolution in Russia 1915–18*, pp. VII–XI; Scharlau/Zeman, *Freibeuter der Revolution*; Hahlweg (ed.), *Lenins Rückkehr nach Russland 1917*. See the summary about the state of the research in: Pipes, *Die Russische Revolution*, vol. 2, pp. 96–98.

49 Cf. Sigel, *Die Lensch–Cunow–Haenisch-Gruppe*; Ribhegge, *August Winnig*, pp. 85–114.
50 Cf. Reinhardt, Art. 'Flake, Otto'.
51 Flake, 'Lenin'.
52 Ibid., p. 359.
53 Ibid., p. 360.
54 Augé, *Larousse Mensuel Illustré*, vol. 3, p. 378. The first lexicographic entry is found in: Augé, *Larousse Mensuel Illustré*, vol. 4, p. 414: 'extrêmisme n. m. Tendance à adopter les idées extrêmistes ou à prendre les décisions extrêmes: L'extrêmisme en politique, en sciences, en philosophie'. – 'extrêmiste adj. et n. Qui propose une doctrine en la poussant jusqu'à des limites extrêmes: Des pragmatistes Extrêmistes. Favorables aux idées ou aux opinions extrêmes: les tendances Extrêmistes en politique'.
55 Merrheim, 'Ce qui paralyse et tue les révolutions'.
56 Ibid., p. 2.
57 Cf. the polemics between Ludovic-Oscar Frossard and Merrheim: Confédération Générale du Travail. 21ème congrès national corporatif, pp. 348–93. See hereto: Papayanis, *Alphonse Merrheim*, pp. 136–40.
58 Merrheim, 'Préface', p. 21.
59 Cf. Merrheim, 'Ceux que l'on accuse d'outrager la Révolution russe'; ditto, 'Outrager la vérité'. Also at the following CGT meeting, Merrheim held on to his positions: Confédération Générale du Travail. 22ème congrès national corporatif, pp. 220–41. However, here he no longer reached back to the extremism formula.
60 Cf. Bonnefous, *Notice sur la vie et les travaux de Maxime Leroy (1873–1957)*; *In memoriam Maxime Leroy*; Racine, Art. 'Leroy, Maxime Auguste'; Schnur, 'Über Maxime Leroy'.
61 Cf. Leroy, *Les techniques nouvelles du syndicalisme*, p. 92.
62 Ibid., p. 94.
63 Ibid., p. 95.
64 Ibid., p. 96.
65 Ibid., p. 97.
66 Lenin, 'Der "linke Radikalismus", die Kinderkrankheit im Kommunismus'.
67 Leroy, 'Préface', pp. XIX–XX.
68 Ibid., p. 106.
69 Ibid., p. 163.
70 'The program of the extremists', in *Corriere della Sera*, 1 April 1917, p. 1.
71 See e.g.: 'Il movimento dei partiti in Russia e le tendenze per il futuro regime. La mossa dei socialisti tedeschi. Ammonimenti agli estremisti', in *Corriere della Sera*, 10 April 1917, p. 2; 'Un grande convegno di soldati. Reazione contro gli estremisti', in *Corriere della Sera*, 15 April 1917, p. 1; 'Monito di Brussilow agli estremisti', in *Corriere della Sera*, 18 April 1917, p. 2; 'Dov'è Lenin?', in *Corriere della Sera*, 22 July 1917, p. 1 (Lenin as 'capo estremista').
72 'Junior, I partiti politici in Russia mentre si sviluppa la rivoluzione', in *Avanti*, 12 April 1917, p. 1; 'rabbioso tono dei vari "Temps", "Times" and "Corriere della Sera" dalla loro ostinazione nel denigrare l'opera degli "estremisti", "demagoghi" o "anarchici". [ ... ] Attraverso i vari dispaci dei giornali italiani, francesi ed inglesi si poteva capire che il Governo ed i circoli dirigenti dei liberali e conservatori facevano tutto il possibile per trovare nelle altre classi sociali e nell'esercito un appoggio contro le tendenze "estremiste" del Consiglio operaio'. Cf. also F. Ciccotti, 'Le "alcune difficoltà" russe', in *Avanti*, 17 April 1917, p. 1.
73 'Nella Russia', in *Il Popolo d'Italia*, 15 April 1917, p. 1; Cf. also 'I graduatori del progresso', in *Il Popolo d'Italia*, 15 April 1917, p. 1; 'Il germanofilo Lenin', in *Il Popolo d'Italia*, 1 May 1917, p. 1; 'L'Internazionale di Lenine', in *Il Popolo d'Italia*, 22 July 1917, p. 1.

74 Mussolini, 'Da Stürmer a Lenine': 'infame opera di tradimento compiuta dagli estremisti ai servizi della Germania'. Cf. also: ibid., 'Duplice colpo! Il Tramonto di Zimmerwald', p. 29; ibid., 'Viva Kerensky!', p. 78.

75 Ibid., 'Impudenza e mistificazione', p. 109: 'lo stato d'animo predominante fra i tesserati'.

76 Ibid., 'Avanti, il Mikado!', p. 41.

77 Ibid., p. 42; 'l'avvento al potere degli estremisti russi può significare la pace separata'.

78 'Il Comitato Centrale dei Fasci di Combattimento, I Fasci Italiani di Combattimento al Proletariato Italiano', in *Il Popolo d'Italia*, 27 April 1920, p. 6 (Mussolini, *Opera Omnia*, vol. XIV, Florence, 1954, p. 426) 'Lavoratori! [ ... ] Lo sciopero generale di Torino, voluto dai mistificatori dell'estremismo socialista e finito dopo ventotto giorni nella più grande disfatta del proletariato, dev'essere un monito per voi'. Cf. also *Il Popolo d'Italia*, 14 August 1921, p. 8 (*Opera Omnia*, vol. XVII, Florence, 1955, pp. 98 et seq.).

79 So Bourdeau, 'Préface', p. 11.

80 The speech by Lloyd George is printed in: Francesco Nitti, *L'Europa senza pace*, Florence, 1921, pp. 93–97, quote here from pp. 96 et seq.

81 Cf. Gentile, *Storia del Partito Fascista*, p. 63; Petracchi, *La Russia rivoluzionaria nella politica italiana*.

82 Cf. Payne, *A History of Fascism 1914–45*, p. 89.

83 See the definition for 'estremista' in: Panzini, *Dizionario Moderno*, p. 217.

84 Cf. Craig, *Geschichte Europas 1815–1980*, p. 435.

85 Cf. Petersen, 'La nascita del concetto di "Stato totalitario" in Italia'; ibid., 'Die Entstehung des Totalitarismusbegriffs in Italien'; Goetz, 'Über den Ursprung des Totalitarismusbegriffs'; ibid., 'Totalitarismus. Ein historischer Begriff'; Brudny, 'Le totalitarisme: histoire du terme et statut du concept'. See for the conceptual history foremost: Bruneteau, *Les totalitarismes*; Gleason, *Totalitarianism*; Huttner, *Totalitarismus und säkulare Religionen*; Möll, *Gesellschaft und totalitäre Ordnung*; Traverso (ed.), *Le totalitarisme*.

86 Cf. Amendola, 'Il governo di domani (22 July 1922)', p. 4. See also: ibid., 'Il mezzogiorno e la crisi politica italiana (1 Oct. 1922)', p. 177, where he speaks of the necessity of 'sfuggire ai pericolosi estremi'.

87 See hereto: Schäfer, 'Luigi Sturzo als Totalitarismustheoretiker'.

88 Cf. Durand, 'Italien', pp. 474–83.

89 Sturzo, 'Il nostro "centrismo"', p. 243.

90 Ibid., p. 244 (emphasized in the text): 'I socialisti dicono: il male viene dall'ordinamento borghese della società; bisogna abbatterlo, dopo verrà il novus ordo: essi sono estremisti, perché arrivano ad una concezione assoluta. I fascisti dicono: la nazione potrà prosperare solo quando sarà "fascistizzata" negli ordinamenti, nel pensiero, nella vita sociale; essi tendono ad un assoluto e quindi sono anch'essi "estremisti". Chiamiamoli per pura comodità gli uni estremisti di sinistra, gli altri estremisti di destra, e ciò in riferimento alla società borghese; ma la tendenza "monopolista", "assolutista", "estremista" è nella natura del loro movimento'.

91 Ibid.

92 In his later writings, Sturzo often used the expression 'estremismo' for fascism as well as Bolshevism. Cf. e.g. Sturzo, *Pensiero antifascista*, p. 90. He was not consistent in using it. Sometimes, he reserved the term for the violent wing of fascism. Cf. ibid., *L'Italie et le fascisme*, pp. 90, 121, 186, 218.

93 Cf. Molony, *The Emergence of Political Catholicism in Italy*.

94 Cf. Belardinelli, 'Die politische Philosophie des christlichen Personalismus'. The important biography derives from: De Rosa, *Luigi Sturzo*. See also: Moos, 'Don Luigi Sturzo – Christian Democrat'; Caponigri, 'Don Luigi Sturzo'; 'Luigi Sturzo nella storia d'Italia'.

95 Cf. Timasheff, *The Sociology of Luigi Sturzo*; Campanini, *Il pensiero politico di Luigi Sturzo*.

96 So Sturzo wrote the first book of this title about the 'totalitarian state': Sturzo, *El estado totalitario*. For Sturzo's role in the dispersal of this term, see among others, Huttner, *Totalitarismus und säkulare Religionen*, pp. 36–39.

97 Cf. e.g. 'Georg Plechanov' (Russian source), in *Frankfurter Zeitung*, second morning paper, 17 April 1917, p. 3; 'Die Kundgebung der Maximalisten' (Dutch source), in *Frankfurter Zeitung*, second morning paper, 7 July 1917, p. 2; 'Die Schlacht in Petersburg gegen Lenin' (Italian source), in *Germania*, additional paper, 29 July 1917; 'Die Unsicherheit in Petersburg' (French source), in *Germania*, 11 September 1917, p. 1; 'Wie steht es um Kornilow?' (Dutch source), in *Vorwärts*, 18 September 1917; 'Ein englisches Urteil über die neue Regierung' (English source, in *Frankfurter Zeitung*, first morning paper, 11 October 1917, p. 2; 'Die Extremisten in der Mehrheit' (English source), in *Germania*, 11 November 1917, p. 2.

98 Cf. Lichtenberger, *Deutschland und Frankreich in ihren gegenwärtigen Beziehungen*, e.g. pp. 36, 39, 42, 51, 71 et seq. The French original: Lichtenberger, *L'Allemagne d'aujourd'hui*.

99 Cf. e.g. Landau-Aldanov, *Lenin und der Bolschewismus*, p. 17 (preface of the first French edition of 1919).

100 Cf. Quendt, 'Sozialisten und Kommunisten in Frankreich'. For a (later) English source, see Churchill, *Nach dem Kriege*, pp. 69, 73.

101 'The elections in Italy', in *Frankfurter Zeitung*, 18 May 1921 (evening paper), p. 1. See hereto also: Funk, 'Das faschistische Italien im Urteil der "Frankfurter Zeitung" (1920–32)', p. 263.

102 'But Lenin's revolutionary totalitarianism already seeks to form the specifically ideological glue between the republics and those other "people's states" which the Petersburg government would like to see arising in all of Europe and Asia'. Paquet, 'Die Wendung des imperialistischen Russland', p. 861. See hereto also ibid., *Im kommunistischen Russland*, p. 111.

103 See e.g. Bernstein, *Wesen und Aussichten des bürgerlichen Radikalismus*; Rohrbach, 'Die radikale Linke und die Revolution in Russland'; 'Die Revolution in Rußland', in *Historisch-politische Blätter für das katholische Deutschland*, 159 (1917) 81, pp. 575–98; Nieder, *Der Radikalismus am Ruder*; Meusel, 'Der Radikalismus'; Plessner, *Grenzen der Gemeinschaft*. See also the collection of election posters in: Buchstab/Kaff/Kleinmann (eds), *Keine Stimme dem Radikalismus*. The title of the Lenin paper '"Der linke Radikalismus", die Kinderkrankheit im Kommunismus' (German edition, Berlin/Hamburg, 1920) is called 'L'estremismo, malattia infantile del comunismo', Milano, 1920. This very clearly shows the difference in the use of the language.

104 Cf. Wende, *Radikalismus im Vormärz*; Backes, *Liberalismus und Demokratie*, pp. 55–60. See also for France: Avril, 'Radicalisme'; Kayser, *Les grandes batailles du radicalisme des origines aux portes du pouvoir 1820–1901*.

105 Keller, Art. 'Radikalismus'.

106 Verhandlungen des Reichstags, first election period, vol. 361, 392. Meeting of 22 November 1923, p. 12180.

107 J.E., 'Fascisten und Kommunisten', in *Vossische Zeitung*, morning edition, 17 October 1922, pp. 1 et seq.

108 Verhandlungen des Reichstags, first election period, vol. 361, 391. Meeting of 20 November 1923, p. 12174.

109 Ibid., p. 12173.

110 The Reichstag and Federal State Parliament speeches documented in the following volume give a good impression of the language of the parliamentarian examinations of communism and national socialism: Schönhoven/Vogel (eds), *Frühe Warnungen vor dem Nationalsozialismus*.

111  Severing, 'Der Kampf gegen den Radikalismus'. See also for the historical background as well as the terminology: ibid., *Mein Lebensweg*, vol. II.
112  Georg, 'Unfruchtbarkeit des Radikalismus'.
113  Schramm, *Radikale Politik*, p. 41. See for biography: Mohler, *Die Konservative Revolution in Deutschland 1918–32*, pp. 448 et seq.
114  Ibid., pp. 45 et seq.
115  Ibid., p. 46.
116  Ibid., p. 82.
117  Ibid., p. 83.
118  Cf. Schulz, *Von Brüning zu Hitler*, pp. 349–51; Martiny, 'Die Entstehung und politische Bedeutung'.
119  Rathmann, 'Positiver Radikalismus', p. 2.
120  Ibid., p. 1.
121  Ibid., p. 7.
122  Ibid., p. 2.
123  Ibid., p. 6.
124  Ibid.
125  Cf. from the national socialist viewpoint: Weiß, 'Die Gefahr des Radikalismus'.
126  Cf. Kershaw, *Hitler 1889–1936: Hubris*, pp. 277–330. Hitler's 'world view' is analysed in context in: Syring, *Hitler*; Zitelmann, *Hitler*. Agreements and differences as to how the protagonists envisaged the world are worked out precisely by: Kroll, *Utopie als Ideologie*. The complete spectrum of ideas of the anti-liberal right-wing is missing in: Breuer, *Ordnungen der Ungleichheit*. Beyond that as readable as ever: Sontheimer, *Antidemokratisches Denken in der Weimarer Republik*.
127  Hitler, *Mein Kampf*, p. 371 (book I, chap. 12: 'The adolescence of the German national socialist workers' party'). See hereto the commentary by Zehnpfenning, *Hitlers Mein Kampf*.
128  Ibid., pp. 580 et seq.
129  Ibid., p. 581.
130  Ibid., p. 217.
131  Hitler, *Mein Kampf*, p. 581.
132  Ibid., p. 583.
133  Ibid., p. 585.
134  Ibid., p. 591.
135  Ibid., p. 592.
136  Hitler, speech at the NSDAP meeting in Plauen i.V. (11 June 1925). In: Ibid., pp. 90 et seq.
137  Hitler, The social mission of the nation. Speech at the NSDAP meeting in Stuttgart (16 December 1925). In: Ibid., p. 259.
138  Hitler, speech at the NSDAP meeting in Altenburg (11 April 1926). In: Ibid., p. 371.
139  Hitler, Freedom and Bread. Speech at the NSDAP meeting in Doerflas (26 June 1927), pp. 394 et seq.
140  Ibid., p. 402.
141  Hitler, A fight for Germany's freedom. Speech at the NSDAP meeting in Kulmbach (5 February 1928), pp. 667 et seq.
142  Hitler, Speech at the NSDAP meeting in Braunschweig (4 November 1925), p. 209.
143  Ibid., p. 210.
144  Hitler, 'Politik der Woche', in *Illustrierter Beobachter*, 31 May 1930, p. 214.
145  Hitler, 'Ein neues Kampfjahr bricht an', in *Illustrierter Beobachter*, 3 January 1931, p. 170.
146  Hitler, Speech at the NSDAP meeting in Kaiserslautern (16 April 1931), p. 170.
147  Hitler, 'Warum musste ein 8 November kommen?', p. 645.
148  Ibid., p. 653.

## 6 Extreme terms in the political language of German ideocracies

1 Cf. Leo, *Studien und Skizzen zu einer Naturlehre des Staates*. See for the coinage of terms: Dierse, 'Ideologie', p. 143. For the importance of Leo and his state doctrine: Krägelin, *Heinrich Leo*; Maltzahn, *Heinrich Leo*; Stolleis, *Geschichte des öffentlichen Rechts in Deutschland*, p. 149.
2 Bluntschli, 'Ideokratie und Theokratie', p. 289.
3 Cf. Gurian, 'Totalitarianism as Political Religion', p. 123. For Gurian's concept of totalitarianism, see: Hürten, *Waldemar Gurian*.
4 Cf. Bernholz, 'Ideology, Sects, State and Totalitarianism: A General Theory'; ditto, 'Ideocracy and totalitarianism'; Piekalkiewicz/Penn, *Politics of Ideocracy*.
5 For the scientific research discussion, see foremost: Heydemann/Oberreuter (eds), *Diktaturen in Deutschland*; Linz, *Totalitäre und autoritäre Regime*; Pohlmann, *Deutschland im Zeitalter des Totalitarismus*; Schmiechen-Ackermann, *Diktaturen im Vergleich*.
6 *Meyers Lexikon*, vol. 3, column 1210.
7 Cf. Chapter 6, part 4 in this volume.
8 Goebbels, 'Das Volk will es!' ('This is what the people want!'), p. 1.
9 Ibid., 'Speech at the meeting of the German student association against the un-German spirit" (Berlin Opera Square, 10 May 1933), p. 108.
10 Ibid., 'Speech at the mass rally of the NSDAP region Hamburg (Hamburg, on the square in front of the Eulenburg in the former zoo', 16 July 1933), p. 119 (emphasized in the original).
11 Cf. with this conflict: Diehl-Thiele, *Partei und Staat im Dritten Reich*.
12 Goebbels, 'Tagebücher', part I, vol. 3/II, p. 126 (27 October 1934).
13 Ibid., p. 288 (12 December 1936). The rather rare term 'extremism' Goebbels had already used in the 'Kampfzeit'. In July 1924, he had read the Bebel memoirs and was impressed by his rise from lowly origins to becoming the 'feared socialist leader'. In its beginnings, Bebel's socialism was sound, as it fought the 'then almighty liberalism'. 'It also had been fatherland-minded', but then it became 'contaminated by the Jewry'. Bolshevism, however, remained 'sound in its core. What we see today is crèche-hunting, incapability, immaturity and cowardice. These fantastic extremist leaders of German communism are being destroyed by the German middle-class'. Goebbels, 'Tagebücher', part I, vol. 1/I, p. 162 (7 July 1924).
14 Goebbels, 'Tagebücher', part I, vol. 4, p. 267 (16 August 1937).
15 Ibid.
16 Goebbels, 'Tagebücher', part I, vol. 6, p. 174 (5 November 1938).
17 Goebbels, 'Tagebücher', part I, vol. 8, p. 409 (7 November 1940).
18 Goebbels, 'Wesen, Methoden und Ziele der Propaganda' (Special meeting of the region and district propaganda leaders on the occasion of the seventh Reich's party conference of the NSDAP, Nürnberg, Apollo Theatre, 16 September 1935), p. 247 (emphasized in the original).
19 Ibid., p. 247 (emphasized in the original).
20 Ibid., p. 249 (emphasized in the original).
21 Ibid., p. 254 (emphasized in the original).
22 Ibid., p. 234 (emphasized in the original).
23 Goebbels, 'Der Bolschewismus'. Speech at the party congress in Nürnberg, 1936, p. 10.
24 Goebbels, 'Tagebücher', part I, vol. 5, pp. 269 et seq. (23 April 1938).
25 Goebbels, 'Tagebücher', part I, vol. 6, p. 182 (11 November 1938).
26 Ibid., p. 185 (13 November 1938).
27 Goebbels, 'Tagebücher', part II, vol. 1, p. 384 (9 September 1941).
28 Ibid., p. 392 (10 September 1941).

29  Goebbels, Speech at the giant rally of the Upper Danube region of the NSDAP on the occasion of the fourth anniversary of the 'Anschluss' (Linz, South Railway Station Hall, 15 March 1942), pp. 100 et seq.
30  Goebbels, 'Tagebücher', part II, vol. 2, p. 241 (6 November 1941).
31  Goebbels, 'Tagebücher', part II, vol. 1, p. 254 (18 August 1941).
32  Ibid., p. 218 (12 August 1941).
33  Cf. ibid., p. 254 (18 August 1941).
34  Goebbels, 'Tagebücher', part II, vol. 3, p. 432 (7 March 1942).
35  Ibid., p. 561 (27 March 1942).
36  Ibid., p. 320 (15 February 1942).
37  Ibid., p. 506 (20 March 1942), see also ibid., p. 496 (19 March 1942).
38  Beetz, 'Totalitäre Rhetorik und Konstruktivismus', p. 185. For the importance of the superlatives and elatives in Goebbels' propaganda language, see also: Beisswenger, *Totalitäre Sprache und textuelle Konstruktion*, pp. 38–40.
39  Goebbels, Speech at the rally to honour the tenth anniversary of the seizure of power (Berlin, Sportpalast, 30 January 1943), p. 161 (emphasized in the original).
40  Ibid., pp. 160 et seq. (emphasized in the original).
41  Goebbels, Speech at the rally of the Berlin region of the NSDAP (Berlin, Sportpalast, 18 February 1943), p. 205.
42  Cf. Moltmann, 'Goebbels' Rede zum totalen Krieg am 18 Februar 1943', p. 29.
43  Goebbels, Speech at the Rally of the Berlin region of the NSDAP (Berlin, Sportpalast, 18 February 1943), p. 183.
44  Ibid., p. 187.
45  Ibid., p. 182 (emphasized in the original).
46  Ibid., p. 183 (emphasized in the original).
47  Cf. Fetscher, *Joseph Goebbels im Berliner Sportpalast 1943*, p. 101, footnote 10.
48  Goebbels, Speech at the rally of the Berlin region of the NSDAP (Berlin, Sportpalast, 18 February 1943), p. 177.
49  Kershaw, *Hitler 1936–45: Nemesis*, p. 734.
50  Ley, 'Fanatiker des Glaubens!', pp. 1 et seq.
51  Goebbels, Rede auf der Kundgebung der NSDAP anläßlich der Verleihung von Ritterkreuzen des Kriegsverdienstkreuzes (Berlin, Sportpalast, 5 June 1943), p. 235 (emphasized in the original).
52  Cited according to Domarus, *Hitler. Reden und Proklamationen 1932–45*, vol. II/2, pp. 2204 et seq.
53  Goebbels, 'Tagebücher', part II, vol. 15, p. 686 (8 April 1945).
54  Klemperer, 'Notizbuch eines Philologen', p. 66. See hereto also Schmitz-Berning, *Vokabular des Nationalsozialismus*, pp. 224–29.
55  Marx, 'Kritik des Hegelschen Staatsrechts (1843)', p. 293.
56  Cf. Lokatis, 'Falsche Fragen an das Orakel?'.
57  Schirdewan, 'Die westdeutschen Wahlen zum Bundestag', p. 874.
58  Ulbricht, *Die gegenwärtige Lage und die neuen Aufgaben der Sozialistischen Einheitspartei Deutschlands*. Lecture and final commentary at the 2nd Party Conference of the SED, Berlin, 9–12 July 1952, p. 18.
59  *Ausschuss für deutsche Einheit, Wer zog die Drähte? Der Juni-Putsch 1953 und seine Hintergründe*, p. 55.
60  Verner, 'Zu den Bundestagswahlen in Westdeutschland', p. 1005. See also 'Der Zusammenbruch des faschistischen Abenteuers', in *Neues Deutschland*, 19 June 1953, p. 1.
61  Polak, 'Der Prozeß gegen die KPD', p. 707.
62  Neumann, 'Das Verbot der KPD', p. 811.
63  Ibid., p. 810.
64  Neumann, 'Die Funktion der bürgerlichen Parteien in Westdeutschland', p. 272.
65  Ibid., p. 273.

66 Ibid., p. 272.
67 'Die Verbrechen der Harich-Gruppe', in *Neues Deutschland*, 9 March 1957, p. 4.
68 Schmidt/Schröder, 'Der Angriff der Ultras auf die Reste der bürgerlichen Demokratie in Westdeutschland', pp. 132 et seq.
69 Ulbricht, 'Rede auf einer Wahlversammlung der Nationalen Front des demokratischen Deutschland in Ost-Berlin (25 August 1961)', p. 233.
70 Brandt, 'Erklärung des Regierenden Bürgermeisters von Berlin vor dem Abgeordnetenhaus von Berlin (13 August 1961)', p. 13.
71 *Dokumente zur Deutschlandpolitik*, IVth series, vol. 7/1, p. 177.
72 Ibid., p. 138.
73 Ibid., p. 139. See also Schnitter, 'Die Bonner Ultras und die Atomstreitmacht der NATO'.
74 'Der Faschismus und die Arbeiterklasse. Bericht des Genossen Dimitroff auf dem VII. Weltkongress der Kommunistischen Internationale' (17 August 1935). In: Pirker (ed.), *Komintern und Faschismus*, p. 187.
75 Cf. Stasch, 'Eine Theorie des Neofaschismus'.
76 Neubert, 'Offener Nationalismus in Westdeutschland', p. 1175.
77 Schröder, 'Der westdeutsche Neonazismus in NPD und CDU/CSU', p. 209.
78 Heyden, 'Weltanschauliche Grundlagen des Sozialdemokratismus', p. 150. See also: Richter/Wrona, 'Ideologie des Sozialdemokratismus in der Gegenwart'; Academy of the Sciences of the CSSR (ed.), *Ideologie des Sozialdemokratismus in der Gegenwart*.
79 Hoeft, 'Parteitag der reaktionärsten und aggressivsten Kräfte des westdeutschen Monopolkapitals', p. 79.
80 Herrmann, 'Zur Formierung des Rechtsblocks in der BRD', p. 1088.
81 Ulbricht, 'Bemerkungen zu den Beziehungen zwischen der DDR und der BRD'.
82 Ullrich, 'Ist der Neofaschismus in Deutschland eine reale Gefahr?', p. 1314.
83 See only Weißbecker/Wimmer, 'Wesen und Erscheinungsformen des Faschismus', p. 488.
84 See Birch/Hillmann, 'Die Krise im Herrschaftssystem des USA-Imperialismus' with the part 'Der Rechtsextremismus und seine Bindungen zur herrschenden Klasse', pp. 1178 et seq.; Herrmann, 'Zur Formierung des Rechtsblocks in der BRD', pp. 1197–1100.
85 Art. 'Radikalismus', in *Meyers Neues Lexikon*, vol. 6, p. 789.
86 Lenin, 'Der "linke Radikalismus", die Kinderkrankheit im Kommunismus (1920)'.
87 'Der "linke Radikalismus", die Kinderkrankheit im Kommunismus'. In: *Wörterbuch des Wissenschaftlichen Kommunismus*, Berlin (East), 1982, p. 235. See also 'Radikalismus', in *Kleines, politisches Wörterbuch*, Berlin (East), pp. 783 et seq.
88 Cf. only Albrecht, *Marxismus*.
89 Cf. e.g. Gerns/Steigerwald/Weiß, *Opportunismus heute*, pp. 32 et seq.; Harder, *Klassenkampf und 'linke' Kunsttheorien*.
90 Cf. Adamo, *Antileninismus in der BRD*; Steigerwald, *Marxistische Klassenanalyse oder spätbürgerliche Mythen*; Wingert, *Die marxistisch–leninistische Lehre*.
91 Nörenberg, *Planwirtschaft im Zerrspiegel des Linksradikalismus*, p. 9.
92 Cf. collective of authors under the leadership of Norbert Madloch, *Links-Radikalismus*, p. 17.
93 'Linksradikalismus', in *Wörterbuch des Wissenschaftlichen Kommunismus*, p. 237.
94 Ibid.
95 Collective of authors under the leadership of Norbert Madloch, *Links-Radikalismus*, p. 18.
96 Cf. for the biography: Baumgartner, 'Schleifstein, Josef'.
97 Schleifstein, 'Gedanken zur Bewegung der studentischen Jugend in Westdeutschland', p. 913.

98  Weichold, *Zwischen Götterdämmerung und Wiederauferstehung*, p. 232.
99  'Zur Rolle der Studentenbewegung in Westdeutschland', in *Einheit*, 25 (1970), pp. 115 et seq., here 115. See also Hesselbarth, 'Aufbruch der Studenten in der kapitalistischen Welt', pp. 1354–66.
100  Heyden, 'Das antikommunistische Wesen des heutigen Trotzkismus', p. 211.
101  X Parteitag der SED, 11–16 April 1981 in Berlin. Bericht des ZK der Sozialistischen Einheitspartei Deutschlands an den X Parteitag der SED, p. 92.
102  Cf. only Pabst, Sozialpsychologische Problem der Herausbildung des Linksradikalismus; Schadow, Marxistisch–leninistische Politökonomische Auseinandersetzung; Weichold, Probleme des Linksradikalismus in unserer Epoche.
103  Weißbecker, 'Die historisch–politische Funktion des Neonazismus und der Nationaldemokratischen Partei in Westdeutschland', p. 849.
104  Elm, 'Traditionen und Tendenzen des Konservatismus in der BRD', pp. 861–78.
105  Knobelsdorf, 'Zu einigen Entwicklungstendenzen des modernen Rechtsextremismus', p. 106.
106  Winkler, *Neo-Faschismus in der BRD*, p. 5.
107  Weißbecker, 'Der Faschismus in der Gegenwart', p. 267.
108  Cf. Moreau, 'Der westdeutsche Kommunismus in der Krise'.
109  Hoeft, 'Strauß und Barzel', p. 633.
110  Cf. Hirsch, *Kommen die Nazis wieder?*, p.174.
111  Cf. e.g. PDI (ed.), Die Union und der Neonazismus. Verharmlosung als Methode, PDI special edition no. 13; PDI-Blick nach rechts, special edition, no. 5, August 1982; Köhler, *Union konkret*, PDI-Blick nach rechts, special edition no. 10, Munich, February 1983; Kühnl, 'Der Einfluss rechtsradikalen Gedankenguts auf die Arbeitnehmer', PDI-Blick nach rechts, special edition, no. 7, Munich, September 1982.
112  Knabe, *Die unterwanderte Republik. Stasi im Westen*, p. 112.
113  On a more modest level, they continued with the political work of the DKP and its comrades in belief within the PDS. Cf. only Moreau/Lang, *Linksextremismus*.
114  Cf. 'Der Streit der Ideologien und die gemeinsame Sicherheit', in *Einheit*, 42 (1987), pp. 771–80.
115  This also included the violently fought against totalitarianism concept. Cf. Jesse, Die 'Die "Totalitarismus-Doktrin" aus DDR-Sicht', pp. 458–83.
116  Cf. Madloch, 'Vorwort'.
117  Like the KPD/ML. Cf. Wunschik, *Die maoistische KPD/ML*.
118  Cf. Peters, *Tödlicher Irrtum*, pp. 537–91.

## 7 Extremism as an element of the official/semi-official language of the Federal Republic of Germany

1  Cf. Eschenburg, *Jahre der Besatzung 1945–49*.
2  Cf. Backes/Jesse, 'Antiextremistischer Konsens. Prinzipien und Praxis', pp. 142–45.
3  Cf. Klocksin, *Kommunisten im Parlament*; Backes/Jesse, 'Antiextremistischer Konsens. Prinzipien und Praxis', pp. 142–45.
4  Kommentar zur Fassung des Allgemeinen Redaktionsausschusses, 16 December 1948, Drucksache 374. Cited according to Scherb, *Präventiver Demokratieschutz als Problem der Verfassungsgebung nach 1945*, p. 193.
5  Protokoll der 6th Sitzung des Kombinierten Ausschusses, 24 September 1948, p. 174.
6  24th Sitzung des Ausschusses für Organisation des Bundes, 1 December 1948, p. 851.
7  Walter Strauß (CDU) deemed this fear exaggerated: 'if that happens, the complete German constitution (Grundgesetz) is a waste'. 10th Sitzung des Ausschusses für Verfassungsgerichtshof, 11 January 1949, p. 1546.
8  Letter from the military governors of 14 April 1949 to the parliamentary council about the regulation of the permission the Federal Government had in the realm

of the police, p. 669. Cf. hereto Badura, 'Die Legitimation des Verfassungsschutzes', p. 28.

9 According to the state secretary in the federal interior ministry, Ritter von Lex: *Deutscher Bundestag*, 1st voting period, 65th meeting of 1 June 1950, p. 2387.

10 Ibid., p. 2390.

11 Ibid., p. 2391.

12 Ibid., p. 2392.

13 Protokoll des Ausschusses zum Schutz der Verfassung, 3rd Meeting of 22 November 1949, p. 5. Cited according to Schiffers, *Verfassungsschutz und parlamentarische Kontrolle in der Bundesrepublik Deutschland 1949–57*, p. 15.

14 Decree by the federal minister of the interior of 19 September 1950: Political activities by the members of public service against the democratic basic order, cited after being printed by Erhard Denninger (ed.), *Freiheitliche demokratische Grundordnung*, Materials for the understanding of the state and for the constitutional reality in the Federal Republic, vol. II, Frankfurt a.M., 1977, pp. 509 et seq., here p. 509.

15 Bundesgesetzblatt, no. 42/1950, p. 682.

16 Cf. Schiffers, *Verfassungsschutz und parlamentarische Kontrolle in der Bundesrepublik Deutschland 1949–57*, pp. 179 et seq.

17 BVerfGE 1/1952, pp. 12 et seq. See also: Sattler, *Die rechtliche Bedeutung der Entscheidung für die streitbare Demokratie*.

18 Ibid., p. 23.

19 BVerfGE 14/1956, p. 139.

20 Ibid., p. 137.

21 Ibid., p. 139.

22 Cf. only the headwords in: Hall (ed.), *The Oxford Companion to the Supreme Court of the United States*.

23 Cf. Ragan, 'Justice Oliver Wendell Homes'.

24 Cf. with the former legal interpretation of this doctrine: Jahrreiss, 'Demokratie. Selbstbewusstsein – Selbstgefährdung – Selbstschutz'; Scheuner, 'Der Verfassungsschutz im Bonner Grundgesetz'. To this concept, see also: Backes/Jesse, *Politischer Extremismus in demokratischen Verfassungsstaaten*, pp. 461–88.

25 Cited according to Jaschke, *Streitbare Demokratie und innere Sicherheit. Grundlagen, Praxis und Kritik*, p. 124. For the history of its creation, see: Imle, *Zwischen Vorbehalt und Erfordernis*.

26 The anti-Semitic and Nazi incidents from 25 December 1959 until 28 January 1960. White Paper of the Government of the Federal Republic of Germany.

27 'Bericht nach den Erkenntnissen der Verfassungsschutzbehörden. Rechtsradikalismus in der Bundesrepublik. Ein Erfahrungsbericht'.

28 'Erfahrungen aus der Beobachtung und Abwehr rechtsradikaler und antisemitische Tendenzen im Jahre 1962', p. 3.

29 Cf. 'Erfahrungen aus der Beobachtung und Abwehr rechtsradikaler und antisemitischer Tendenzen im Jahre 1963'.

30 'Erfahrungen aus der Beobachtung und Abwehr rechtsradikaler und antisemitischer Tendenzen im Jahre 1964', p. 3.

31 Ibid., p. 9.

32 Ibid., p. 8.

33 Ibid., p. 9.

34 Ibid., p. 11.

35 Ibid., p. 13.

36 Ibid., p. 15.

37 Ibid., p. 19.

38 Ibid., p. 23.

39 'Erfahrungen aus der Beobachtung und Abwehr rechtsradikaler und antisemitischen Tendenzen im Jahre 1965', p. 3.

40 'Erfahrungen aus der Beobachtung und Abwehr rechtsradikaler und antisemitischer Tendenzen im Jahre 1966', p. 3.
41 Ibid., p. 4.
42 'Die kommunistische Tätigkeit in der Bundesrepublik im Jahre 1964'.
43 Cf. 'Die kommunistische Tätigkeit in der Bundesrepublik im Jahre 1965'; 'Die kommunistische Tätigkeit in der Bundesrepublik im Jahre 1966'.
44 'Erfahrungen aus der Beobachtung und Abwehr rechtsradikaler und antisemitischer Tendenzen im Jahre 1967', p. 4.
45 'Linksradikalismus in der Bundesrepublik im Jahre 1967'.
46 Bundesministerium des Innern (ed.), *Verfassungsschutzberichte*, pp. 5, 7, 39, 44, 51, 98.
47 Cf. Borgs-Maciejewski (ed.), *Radikale im öffentlichen Dienst*, p. 9.
48 Cf. regarding the terminology, e.g.: Braunthal, *Politische Loyalität und Öffentlicher Dienst*; Frisch, *Extremistenbeschluss*; Jesse, *Streitbare Demokratie*; Koschnik, *Der Abschied vom Extremistenbeschluss*; Schönbohm (ed.), *Verfassungsfeinde als Beamte?*. According to administrative legal terminology, it was without a doubt a 'resolution' as no new law had been created.
49 Hessischer Landtag, 7th election period, 35th meeting of 9 March 1972, p. 1913.
50 This is exemplified in the documentation by Borgs-Maciejewski (ed.), *Radikale im öffentlichen Dienst*.
51 *Verfassungsschutzbericht* (VSB) 1974, p. 4. Cf. hereto also Jesse, 'Verfassungsschutzberichte des Bundes und der Länder im Vergleich'.
52 Deutscher Bundestag, 7th election period, 132nd Meeting of 15 November 1974, p. 8960.
53 Maihofer, 'Politische Kriminalität', p. 367.
54 In this form already in the VSB 1971, p. 86, where it was otherwise still called 'right' and 'left' efforts.
55 As e.g. in the report of the year 1978: VSB 1978, pp. 112–25.
56 Cf. VSB 2005.
57 Bundesamt für Verfassungsschutz (ed.), *Bundesamt für Verfassungsschutz*, p. 25.
58 Staatsministerium des Innern/Landesamt für Verfassungsschutz Sachsen (ed.), *Verfassungsschutzbericht 1993*, p. 15.
59 VSB 2005, p. 17.
60 Cf. Ministerstvo vnitra CR Odbor bezpecnostni politiky (ed.), *Informace o problematico extremismu na uzemi ceske republiky v roce 2004*.
61 Cf. Bundesministerium für Inneres/Bundesamt für Verfassungsschutz und Terrorismusbekämpfung (ed.), *Verfassungsschutzbericht 2005*; Bundesamt für Polizei (ed.), *Bericht innere Sicherheit der Schweiz 2004*, p. 17.
62 Cf. Allgemene Inlichtingen- en Veiligheidsdienst (ed.), *Jaarverslag 2004*, p. 6.
63 Cf. the presentation of the report for 2004: www.cncdh.fr/ (6 July 2009).
64 Government of the United Kingdom/Home Office (ed.), *Preventing Extremism Together. Places of Worship*, p. 2.
65 Cf. the definition in the following report: US Department of Justice/FBI (ed.), *Terorism 2000/2001*, p. IV.
66 Ibid., p. 26.
67 Cf. Michael, *Confronting Right-Wing Extremism and Terrorism in the USA*, pp. 167–69.
68 See www.adl.org/main_Extremism/default.htm (13 December 2005).
69 Cf. only Bird, 'Racist Speech or Free Speech?'; Brugger, 'Verbot oder Schutz von Hassrede?'; Walker, *Hate Speech*; Zimmer, *Hate Speech im Völkerrecht*.

**8 Lines of development of the extremism concept in the twentieth century**

1 Borkenau, *The Totalitarian Enemy*, p. 11. Cf. for Borkenau's intellectual development: Lange-Enzmann, *Franz Borkenau als politischer Denker*. For the historic

background: Gleason, *Totalitarianism*, pp. 90, 229; Jones, *The Lost Debate*, pp. 118–24; ditto, 'The Path from Weimar Communism to the Cold War'; Möll, *Gesellschaft und totalitäre Ordnung*, pp. 77 et seq.

2 Borkenau, *The totalitarian Enemy*, p. 13.
3 Cf. ibid., pp. 22, 241.
4 Ibid., p. 250.
5 Ibid., p. 151: 'There exists a very close connection between the extreme forms of the mob rule and the extreme forms of autocratic tyranny'.
6 Ibid., p. 231.
7 Rühle, 'Brauner und Roter Faschismus', p. 20. See as to Rühle's political development: Schmeitzner, 'Roter und brauner Faschismus?'.
8 Rühle, 'Brauner und Roter Faschismus', p. 41.
9 Ibid., p. 42.
10 Cf. concerning the appreciation of life and work: Ooyen, 'Ein moderner Klassiker der Verfassungstheorie'.
11 Loewenstein, 'Militant Democracy and Fundamental Rights'.
12 Loewenstein, 'Legislative Control of Political Extremism in European Democracies'; ditto, *Contrôle legislative de l'extrémisme politique dans les démocraties européennes*.
13 Loewenstein (anonym), 'Der Staatsschutz in den europäischen Demokratien'. In: NZZ, no. 659 13 April 1937, p. 1 and no. 662 14 April 1937, p. 2, quote no. 659.
14 Ibid., no. 659.
15 Loewenstein, 'Der Kommunismus und die amerikanische Verfassung', p. 9.
16 Comité Consultativo de Emergencia para la Defensa Política (ed.), *Legislación para la defensa política en las Repúblicas Americanas*, vol. II, p. 103.
17 Ibid., vol. I, p. 45.
18 Cf. ibid, vol. II, pp. 105 et seq.
19 Cf. ibid, vol. I, p. 582.
20 Ibid., vol. II, p. 465.
21 Loewenstein, 'Der Kommunismus und die amerikanische Verfassung', p. 9.
22 *Offener Horizont*, pp. 229–54.
23 Arendt, *The Origins of Totalitarianism*. For Arendt's totalitarianism concept, see foremost: Canovan, 'The Leader and the Masses'; Whitfield, *Into the Dark*.
24 Ibid., p. 471.
25 Ibid., p. 477.
26 Brinton, *Die Revolution und ihre Gesetz*, p. 43.
27 Ibid., p. 142.
28 Ibid., pp. 178 et seq.
29 Ibid., p. 179.
30 Ibid., p. 208.
31 Ibid., p. 212.
32 Ibid., p. 220.
33 Ibid., p. 254.
34 Ibid., p. 265.
35 Ibid., pp. 269 et seq.
36 Ibid., p. 291.
37 Ibid., p. 256.
38 Ibid., p. 364.
39 Löwenthal, 'Totalitäre und demokratische Revolution'. Cited according to the reprint in: Seidel/Jenkner (eds), *Totalitarismusforschung*, p. 367. The contribution had appeared in an altered form in the magazine *Commentary*: Löwenthal, 'Totalitarianism Reconsidered'. For the historical classification, see: Backes, 'Vom Marxismus zum Antitotalitarismus'.
40 Ibid., p. 378.

41  Ibid., p. 361. However, he saw the totalitarian dynamics as having come to an end in the first half of the 1960s. See ibid., p. 379 (supplement 1966).
42  For the research development, see e.g. the contributions in the following volumes: Seidel/Jenkner (ed.), *Totalitarismusforschung*; Jesse (ed.), *Totalitarismus im 20. Jahrhundert*.
43  Cf. as pioneering: Linz, *Totalitäre und autoritäre Regime*.
44  Hofstätter, *Einführung in die Sozialpsychologie*, pp. 193 et seq.
45  Ibid., p. 195.
46  Cf. Hofstätter, *Gruppendynamik*, pp. 71–91.
47  Allport/Hartman, 'The Measurement and Motivation of Atypical Opinion in a Certain Group', p. 740.
48  Ibid., p. 749.
49  The differentiation between 'tender-minded' and 'tough-minded' goes back to: James, *Pragmatism*, p. 12.
50  Cf. already Eysenck, 'General social attitudes'.
51  Cf. Eysenck, *The Psychology of Politics*, p. 111.
52  Adorno, *Studien zum autoritären Charakter*, p. 150. The volume contains Adorno's contributions from the following study: Ditto/Frenkel-Brunswik/Levinson/Sanford, *The Authoritarian Personality*.
53  Ibid., p. 277.
54  Shils, 'Authoritarianism: "Right" and "Left"', p. 28.
55  Carlson, *Under Cover*, p. 520. See in a similar vein: Sayers/Kahn, *Sabotage!*.
56  Cf. only Lerner, *It is Later than you Think*. See also ditto, 'Das Grundmuster der Diktatur'. See in detail as to this discussion: Boventer, *Grenzen politischer Freiheit im demokratischen Staat*, pp. 59–66.
57  Freyhold, *Autoritarismus und politische Apathie*, p. 19.
58  Cf. Shils, 'Authoritarianism: "Right" and "Left"', pp. 48 et seq.
59  For the appreciation of person and work, see: Moynihan, 'Introduction'.
60  Shils, *The Torment of Secrecy*, p. 15.
61  Ibid., p. 132.
62  Ibid., p. 91.
63  Ibid., p. 95.
64  Ibid., p. 225.
65  Ibid., p. 228.
66  Ibid., p. 226.
67  Ibid., p. 227.
68  Lipset/Raab, Politics of Unreason, p. 5.
69  Ibid., p. 6.
70  Ibid., p. 7.
71  Cf. already Lipset, 'Socialism – Left and Right – East and West', p. 173. See also ditto, 'Social Stratification and "Right-Wing Extremism"'; Lipset, 'Democracy and Working-Class Authoritarianism'.
72  Cf. Lipset, 'Der "Faschismus": die Linke, die Rechte und die Mitte' (1959). This contribution caused lively discussion and was reprinted in several languages. See e.g.: ditto, '"Faschismus", rechts, links und in der Mitte'; (Original English version: ditto, *Political Man*); ditto, 'Der "Faschismus", die Linke, die Rechte und die Mitte' (1967).
73  Cf. summarizing Falter, *Hitlers Wähler*.
74  Scheuch, 'Theorie des Rechtsradikalismus in westlichen Industriegesellschaften', p. 22.
75  Ibid.
76  Ibid., p. 23.
77  Cf. also for the terminology and the scientific yield: Arzheimer/Falter, 'Die Pathologie des Normalen'.

78 Cf. only 'Projekt Rechtsradikalismus: Analysen zur Wählerschaft der NPD', in *Jahrbuch der Universität zu Köln*, 3 (1968), pp. 371–73.
79 Cf. Scheuch, 'Die NPD als rechtsextreme Partei'.
80 Scheuch, 'Zum Wiedererstehen der Erlösungsbewegungen', p. 130.
81 Scheuch, 'Politischer Extremismus in der Bundesrepublik', p. 462.
82 Cf. Herz, Soziale Bedingungen für Rechtsextremismus, pp. 43 et seq.
83 Cf. Lipset/Raab, *The Politics of Unreason*. p. 428.
84 Scheuch, 'Politischer Extremismus in der Bundesrepublik', p. 462.
85 Cf. Klingemann/Pappi, *Politischer Radikalismus*, pp. 73–75.
86 Cf. *Politischer Protest in der Sozialwissenschaftlichen Literatur*. Eine Arbeit in der Infratest Wirtschaftsforschung GmbH; *politischer Protest in der Bundesrepublik Deutschland. Beiträge zur sozialempirischen Untersuchung des Extremismus*. Eine Arbeit der Infratest Wirtschaftsforschung GmbH.
87 Kaase, 'Linksextremismus', p. 219.
88 Cf. hereto Chapter 7, part 3.
89 Funke, 'Extremismus und offene Gesellschaft', p. 21.
90 Ibid., p. 18.
91 Ibid., p. 19.
92 Flechtheim, 'Extremismus und Radikalismus', pp. 59 et seq. Cf. also ditto, 'Radikalismus contra Extremismus'.
93 Ibid., p. 60.
94 Ibid., p. 61.
95 Cf. Mudde, 'Politischer Extremismus und Radikalismus in Westeuropa'.
96 Cf. e.g. Besier/Betz, *Postmodern Politics in Germany*, pp. 126–32 ('From Right-Wing Radicalism to Right-Wing Extremism?'); Funke, *Rechtsextremismus in Deutschland*, p. 13; Lepszy/Veen, *'Republikaner' und DVU in kommunalen und Landesparlamenten sowie im Europaparlament*, pp. 3 et seq; Minkenberg, *Die neue radikale Rechte im Vergleich*, p. 34; Pekonen, *The New Radical Right in Finland*; Stöss, *Rechtsextremismus im vereinten Deutschland*, p. 12.
97 Jaschke, *Rechtsextremismus und Fremdenfeindlichkeit*, p. 27.
98 Cf. Otto/Merten, 'Rechtsradikale Gewalt im vereinigten Deutschland', p. 19.
99 Jaschke, *Rechtsextremismus und Fremdenfeindlichkeit*, p. 27.
100 Cf. Backes, *Politischer Extremismus in demokratischen Verfassungsstaaten*, p. 68.
101 Cf. ibid., pp. 103 et seq.
102 Cf. Backes/Jesse, *Politischer Extremismus in der Bundesrepublik Deutschland*, 1989. Last edition: Backes/ Jesse, *Politischer Extremismus in der Bundesrepublik*, Neuausgabe, 1996.
103 Backes/Jesse (eds), *Jahrbuch Extremismus & Demokratie*. Detailed information is offered on the *Jahrbuch* webpage: www.tu-chemnitz.de/phil/politik/pspi/jahrbuch/ (accessed 6 July 2009).
104 'Authoritarianism' in this sense is therefore not to be mistaken for 'authoritarian system', a term used in comparative dictatorship research. Cf. Linz, *Totalitäre und autoritäre Regime*.
105 Cf. for critique, Roghmann, *Dogmatismus und Autoritarismus*, pp. 83 et seq.; Keiler/Stadler (eds), *Erkenntnis oder Dogmatismus?* For the development of research, see: Lederer, *Jugend und Autorität*.
106 Cf. Rokeach, *The Open and Closed Mind*; ditto, *Political and Religious Dogmatism*.
107 One of the few exceptions was the – back then violently feuded over – Allensbacher Studie by Noelle-Neumann/Ring, *Das Extremismus-Potential*.
108 Cf. Lederer/Kindervater, 'Internationale Vergleiche'.
109 Cf. McFarland/Ageyev/Abalakina-Paap, 'Authoritarianism in the Former Soviet Union'; McFarland, 'Communism as Religion'.
110 Cf. Greenberg/Jonas, 'Psychological Motives and Political Orientation'.

111  Cf. Altemeyer, *The Authoritarian Specter*, p. 10.
112  Cf. for the history of words: Art. 'fundamentalism', in *The Oxford English Dictionary*, vol. VI, second edition, Oxford, 1989, p. 267; for the history of terms: Barr, 'Fundamentalismus'.
113  Meyer, *Fundamentalismus*.
114  Cf. Jäggi/Krieger, *Fundamentalismus*.
115  Salamun, 'Fundamentalismus', p. 36.
116  Cf. Popper, *Das Elend des Historizismus*; ditto, *Die offene Gesellschaft und ihre Feinde*; Albert, 'Das Gewissheitsbedürfnis und die Suche nach Wahrheit'; Salamun, 'Der holistische Grundzug'. See hereto also: Fritze, Kritik des totalitären Denkens'; Backes, 'Totalitäres Denken'.
117  Salamun, 'Fundamentalismus', pp. 37–43.
118  Cf. Jaschke, *Fundamentalismus in Deutschland*.
119  Marty/Appleby, *Herausforderung Fundamentalismus*, p. 10.
120  Bornhausen, 'Faszismus und Fundamentalismus in den Vereinigten Staaten'. See the remark in: Laqueur, *Faschismus*, p. 225.
121  Cf. Laqueur, *Faschismus*, pp. 251–59.
122  Breuer, *Ästhetischer Fundamentalismus*.
123  Grebing, *Linksradikalismus gleich Rechtsradikalismus*, pp. 8 et seq. For a critique, see also: Pfahl-Traughber, 'Politischer Extremismus'.
124  Cf. hereto in detail Chapter 6 in this volume. In addition: *Wörterbuch des Wissenschaftlichen Kommunismus*, pp. 237 et seq.
125  Cf. e.g. Tronti, *Extremismus und Reformismus*. The following writings also agree with this understanding of the term: Bravo, *Critica dell' estremismo*; ditto, *L'estremismo in Italia*. In France, one mostly spoke of 'gauchisme' in this context and in Portugal of 'esquerdismo'. Cf. only Biard, *Dictionnaire de l'extrême gauche de 1945 à nos jours*; Ruas, Art. 'Extremismo'.
126  Stöss, 'Einleitung', p. 304. Similar argumentation in: Butterwegge, *Rechtsextremismus, Rassismus und Gewalt*, pp. 64–78.
127  Neugebauer/Stöss, *Die PDS*, p. 13.
128  Wippermann, 'Verfassungsschutz und Extremismusforschung', p. 269. See also ditto, 'Doch ein Begriff muss bei dem Worte sein'.
129  Cf. Bobbio, *Rechts und Links.* p. 76.
130  Ibid., p. 78.
131  Ibid., p. 79.
132  Ibid., p. 83.
133  Ibid., p. 84.
134  Ibid.
135  Ibid.
136  Ibid.
137  Saposs, 'The Rôle of the Middle Class in Social Development', p. 395.
138  Geiger, 'Panik im Mittelstand', pp. 637–54. A reprint of the contribution is found in the: Hamburger Institut für Sozialforschung (ed.), *Reader*.
139  Cf. Winkler, 'Extremismus der Mitte?', p. 186.
140  Cf. Falter, *Hitlers Wähler*; ditto, 'Radikalisierung des Mittelstandes oder Mobilisierung der Unpolitischen?'.
141  Kraushaar, 'Extremismus der Mitte', p. 26.
142  Kopp, 'Die Begegnung der dritten Art.', p. 2. In this sense, see also: Schüßlburner, 'Liberalextremismus'.
143  Riehl, 'Der Kampf geht weiter'.
144  Schwab, 'Wer unterwandert die deutschen Burschenschaften'.
145  According to the Saxon Parliament Representative: Apfel, 'Volksgemeinschaft statt "kontrollierter" Zuwanderung!'.
146  Cf. REP Press Report, 27 April 2002.

**9 Political extremism: final results, classification of terms and outlook**

1 Cf. with the terminus Schottmann, *Politische Schlagwörter*, who, however, did not include 'radicalism' or 'extremism' in the dictionary of catch phrases.
2 Dolf Sternberger even remarks: 'Any understanding of the constitutional state, all of "constitutionalism" as the Anglo-Saxons call it, also that of the late Middle Ages and the Modern Age, has sprung from the Aristotelian root'. Ditto, *Drei Wurzeln der Politik*, p. 105.
3 In contrast to the history of the terms of the extremes, the history of 'tyrannis' and 'despoteia' is well researched. Compare only Mandt, Art. 'Tyrannis, Despotie'; ditto, 'Das klassische Verständnis: Tyrannis und Despotie'; Turchetti, *Tyrannie et tyrannicide de l'Antiquité à nos jours*.
4 Cf. Adler, *Naming and Addressing*, pp. 93–166.
5 Cf. with this term: Hermanns, 'Brisante Wörter'.
6 Cf. Link, *Versuch über den Normalismus*.
7 Cf. Koselleck, *Vergangene Zukunft*, pp. 211–59. See also Richter, 'Aristoteles und der klassische griechische Begriff der Despotie', p. 24.
8 Cf. Canu, *Der Schutz der Demokratie in Deutschland und Frankreich*, p. 32.
9 Arcille, Militants! in *Le Titre Enchaîné*, no. 3, 21 January 1919, p. 1. In this context, see also the neutral use of the term in: Tchernoff, *L'extrême-gauche socialiste-révolutionnaire en 1870/71*, p. 4 ('républicains extrémistes', 'fractions extrémistes').
10 However, not always. See only: Kraushaar, 'Extremismus der Mitte'.
11 Nozick, 'The Characteristic Features of Extremism', pp. 296–99.
12 Cf. Backes, *Politischer Extremismus in demokratischen Verfassungsstaaten*, p. 103.
13 Mudde, 'Radikale Parteien in Europa', p. 13.
14 Cf. Lucardie, 'Demokratischer Extremismus'.
15 Cf. Sartori, Parties and Party Systems, pp. 132 et seq. See hereto also the critique by: Kailitz, *Politischer Extremismus in der Bundesrepublik Deutschland*, p. 16.
16 Cf. in this vein, Agassi, 'The Logic of Consensus and of Extremes'.
17 Breton/Galeotti/Salmon/Wintrobe, 'Introduction', p. xiii.
18 Marx, 'Kritik des Hegelschen Staatsrechts (1843)', p. 293.
19 Cf. Bravo, *Critica dell'estremismo*; Grispigni, *Elogio dell'estremismo*.
20 Reitz, 'Editorial', p. 461.
21 Wippermann, 'Extreme Radikale'.
22 Initiative gegen jeden Extremismusbegriff (INEX), *Das Ende des Extremismus*.
23 Cf. with the controversy reaching back to Ernst Fraenkel's concept of neopluralism, especially: Detjen, 'Pluralismus und klassische politische Philosophie'; Sutor, 'Traditionelles Gemeinwohl und liberale politische Theorie'.
24 Cf. Loewenstein, *Verfassungslehre*, pp. 26–29.
25 Cf. Dahl, *Polyarchy*, p. 5. Hereto, see also: Merkel, *Systemtransformation*, pp. 31–34.
26 See hereto the differentiation by: Finer, *The History of Government*, vol. III, pp. 1567 et seq.
27 Cf. Popper, *Das Elend des Historizismus*.
28 Lübbe, 'Heilsmythen nach der Aufklärung', p. 286, speaks of 'ideology – political coexistence – incapable needs for recognition'.
29 See hereto Reis, *Ambiguitätstoleranz*.
30 Cf. also Salamun, 'Demokratische Kultur und antidemokratisches Denken', p.154.
31 Cf. Bleicken, *Die athenische Demokratie*, pp. 289 et seq.
32 Cf. e.g. Kägi, 'Rechtsstaat und Demokratie'; Kielmansegg, 'Die "Quadratur des Zirkels"'; Laufer, 'Die Widersprüche im freiheitlichen demokratischen System'.
33 Cf. Riklin, *Machtteilung*; Sternberger, 'Die neue Politie'.
34 Cf. Friedrich, *Der Verfassungsstaat der Neuzeit*.

35 Regarding this typology cf. also: Backes, *Liberalismus und Demokratie*, pp. 49 et seq.
36 Both elements are central, even though the ideological concepts of the NS leadership were far more heterogeneous and considerably less formulated than the structure of ideas in Marxism–Leninism. See foremost: Ackermann, *Heinrich Himmler als Ideologe*; Bärsch, *Die politische Religion des Nationalsozialismus*; Höver, *Joseph Goebbels*; Kroll, *Utopie als Ideologie*; Syring, *Hitler*; Zehnpfennig, *Hitlers Mein Kampf*; Zitelmann, *Hitler*.
37 Cf. Bobbio, *Rechts und Links*, p. 76.
38 The term does not grasp the forms of a 'fundamentalism of escapism' grasped by Martin Riesebrodt. Cf. ditto, *Fundamentalismus als patriarchalische Protestbewegung*, pp. 201–14.
39 In regard to this question cf. also: Backes/Jesse, 'Islamismus', pp. 201–14.
40 For the way of thinking of extremist 'perpetrators with a good conscience', see most of all: Fritze, *Täter mit gutem Gewissen*; ditto, 'Kommunistische und nationalsozialistische Weltanschauung', pp. 151 et seq.
41 Goebbels, 'Was wollen wir im Reichstag' (30 April 1928), p. 71.
42 This is Haller, *Restauration der Staats-Wissenschaft*.
43 See Huntington, *The Third Wave*.
44 Cf. Chehabi/Linz (eds), *Sultanistic Regimes*.
45 Cf. e.g. Bendel/Croissant/Rüb (eds), *Zwischen Demokratie und Diktatur*; Carothers, 'The End of the Transition Paradigm'.
46 Cf. Hardt/Negri, *Empire*; Holloway, *Change the World without Taking Power*. Cf. hereto Moreau/Steinborn, 'Die Bewegung der Altermondialisten'.
47 Cf. Chomsky, 'Powers and Prospects'. Cf. also: Ward, *Anarchism*.
48 Cf. Benoist, *Demokratie*, p. 32; ditto, *Communisme et nazisme*, pp. 133–40.
49 Cf. Al Qathafi, *The Green Book*; Qutb, *Milestones* (Ma'alim fi al-tariq).
50 Cf. Kepel, *Das Schwarzbuch des Dschihad*. In addition, critically: Tibi, 'Vom klassischen Djihad zum terroristischen Djihadismus'.
51 Cf. Besier/Lübbe (eds), *Politische Religion und Religionspolitik*; Weinberg/Pedahzur (eds), *Religious Fundamentalism and Political Extremism*.
52 This is how the particular problem is expressed in: Kielmansegg, *Das Experiment der Freiheit*.

# Bibliography

## 1 Sources

### Printed press

*L'Action française*, Paris, 1917–19.
*Der Angriff*, Berlin, 1933–45.
*L'Atelier*, Paris, 1919 et seq.
*L'Atelier*. Hebdomadaire Syndicaliste, Paris, 1920.
*Augsburger Allgemeine Zeitung*, Augsburg, 1818–32.
*L'Avanti*, Milano, 1917–24.
*L'Avenir de Bézier*. Organe de la démocratie radicale extrême gauche, paraissant trois fois par semaine, Bézier, 1881/1882.
*Corriere della Sera*, Milano, 1917–24.
*Le Courrier de Bézier et de l'arrondissement*. Journal politique, littéraire et commercial, then: Organe de la démocratie radicale extrême-gauche et socialiste révisionniste, then: Organe radical socialiste. Hebdomadaire, then: bihebdomadaire, Bézier 1891–93.
*Le Cri du peuple du Sud-Est*. Hebdomadaire, then. Hebdomadaire d'extrême-gauche, Lyon 1920–21.
*Daily Chronicle*, London, 1917–19.
*La Démocratie du Midi*. Journal radical extrême-gauche, 1886.
*Deutschlands Erneuerung*, München, 1932/33.
*Dresdner Neueste Nachrichten*, Dresden, 1917–19.
*L'extrême droite*. Journal du droit et des principes vrais, Dir. Adrien Peladan, Nîmes, 1875–77 (weekly).
*L'Extrême-gauche* (Alliance radicale-socialiste), paraissant le dimanche, Dir. Emile Brousse, Saint-Mandé (Seine) 1883.
*L'Extrême-gauche*, Lyon 1904.
*L'Extrême-gauche*, Vincennes 1883/1884.
*Le Figaro*, Paris, 1917–19.
*Frankfurter Zeitung*, Frankfurt a.M., 1917–33.
*Germania*, Berlin, 1917 et seq.
*Germinal*. Journal républicain d'extrême-gauche, Carpentras, 1912 et seq.
*L'Humanité*, Paris, 1915–19.
*Le Journal du Peuple*, Paris, 1917.
*Leipziger Volkszeitung*, 1917–19.

*Le Matin*, Paris, 1917–19.
*Neues Deutschland*, Berlin (East), 1946–89.
*Neue Zürcher Zeitung*, 1917–19.
*The New York Times*, New York, 1860–88, 1917–19.
*Il Popolo d'Italia*, Roma, 1917–23.
*Il Popolo Nuovo*, Roma, 1923.
*Das Schwarze Korps*, Berlin, 1935–45.
*La Stampa*, Torino, 1917–19.
*Telegraaf*, Den Haag, 1917–19.
*Le Temps*, Paris, 1917–23.
*The Times*, London, 1865, 1906–8, 1917–23.
*Le Titre Censuré*. Journal hebdomadaire et doctrinaire, Paris, 1919.
*La Vie Ouvrière*, Paris, 1920.
*Völkischer Beobachter*, München, 1933–45.
*Vorwärts*, Berlin, 1917–19.
*Vossische Zeitung*, Berlin, 1917–32.

### Books, essays, articles

Adamo, Hans: *Antileninismus in der BRD. Tendenzen, Inhalt und Methoden der Lenin-fälschung in der Bundesrepublik unter besonderer Berücksichtigung des internationalen Leninjahres 1970*, Frankfurt a.M.: Verlag Marxistische Blätter, 1970.
Adams, John: 'A Defense of the Constitution of Government of the United States of America, against the attack of M. Turgot, in his letter to Dr. Price, dated the twenty-second day of March, 1778'. In: ditto, *Works*, pp. 3–496.
——'Review of the Propositions for Amending the Constitution submitted by Mr. Hillhouse to the Senate of the United States in 1808'. In: ditto, *Works*, vol. VI, Boston: Little, Brown, 1851, pp. 523–50.
——'Three Letters to Roger Sherman, on the Constitution of the United States'. In: ditto, *Works*, S. 427–36.
——*Works*, with a Life of the Author, notes and illustrations, by his grandson Charles Francis Adams, vol. V, Boston: Little, Brown, 1851.
Adorno, Theodor W./Frenkel-Brunswik, Else/Levinson, Daniel J./Sanford, R. Nevitt: *The Authoritarian Personality. Studies in Prejudice*, ed. by Max Horkheimer and Samuel H. Flowerman, New York: Harper, 1950.
——*Studien zum autoritären Charakter* (1950), Frankfurt a.M.: Suhrkamp, 1982.
Aeschylus: 'Eumenides'. In: *Aeschylus* in two volumes, with an English translation by Herbert Weir Smyth, Cambridge/London: Harvard University Press/William Heinemann, 1983, pp. 267–371.
Agassi, Joseph: 'The Logic of Consensus and of Extremes'. In: Fred D'Agostino/I.C. Jarvine (eds): *Freedom and Rationality. Essays in Honor of John Watkins. From his Colleagues and Friends*, Dordrecht: Kluwer, 1989, pp. 3–21.
Aiton, Thomas [T.A., Minister of the Gospel of Alyth]: The Original Constitution of the Christian Church: Wherein the Extremes on either Hand are Stated and Examined. To which is added an Appendix containing The Rise of the Jure Divino Prelatists; and an Answer to their Arguments, by Episcopal Divines, Edinburgh: Printed for John Paton; and sold at his shop, 1730.
Alberti Magni ratisbonensis episcopi, ordinis praedicatorum, Opera Omnia, ex editione lugdunensi religiose castigate, et pro auctoritatibus ad fidem vulgatae versionis

accuratiorumque patrologiae textuum revocata, auctaque B. Alberti vita ac bibliographia operum a PP. Quétif et Echard Exaratis, etiam revisa et locupletata, cura ac labore Augusti Borgnet, sacerdotis dioecesis Remensis, annuente faventeque Pont. Max. Leone XIII, volumen septimum Ethicorum Lib. X, Paris: L. Viv'es, 1891.

Alberti Magni ratisbonensis episcopi, ordinis praedicatorum, Opera Omnia, ex editione lugdunensi religiose castigate, et pro auctoritatibus ad fidem vulgatae versionis accuratiorumque patrologiae textuum revocata, auctaque B. Alberti vita ac bibliographia operum a PP. Quétif et Echard Exaratis, etiam revisa et locupletata, cura ac labore Augusti Borgnet, sacerdotis dioecesis Remensis, annuente faventeque Pont. Max. Leone XIII, volumen octavum Politicorum Lib. VIII, Paris: L. Viv'es, 1891.

Albrecht, Richard: *Marxismus – bürgerliche Ideologie – Linksradikalismus. Zur Ideologie und Sozialgeschichte des westeuropäischen Linksradikalismus*, Berlin (Ost): Akademie, 1975.

Allgemene Inlichtingen- en Veiligheidsdienst (ed.): *Jaarverslag 2004*, Den Haag, 2005.

Allport, Floyd H./Hartman, D.A.: 'The Measurement and Motivation of Atypical Opinion in a Certain Group'. In: APSR, 19 (1925), pp. 735–60.

Al Qathafi, Muammar: *The Green Book*, www.geocities.com/Athens/8744/readgb.htm (accessed 6 July 2009).

Althusius, Johannes: *Politik*, übersetzt von Heinrich Janssen, in Auswahl herausgegeben, überarbeitet und eingeleitet von Dieter Wyduckel, Berlin: Duncker und Humblot, 2003.

Amendola, Giovanni: 'Il governo di domani (22 July 1922)'. In: ditto, *La democrazia italiana contro il fascismo*, Milano: Riccardi, 1960, p. 4.

——'Il mezzogiorno e la crisi politica italiana (1 Oct. 1922)'. In: ditto, *Una battaglia liberale. Discorsi politici (1919–23)*, Torino: Gobetti, 1924, pp. 157–77.

Ancillon, Friedrich: *Zur Vermittlung der Extreme in den Meinungen*, Berlin: Duncker und Humblot, 1828.

——*Du Juste Milieu ou du Rapprochement des Extrêmes dans les Opinions*, traduit de l'allemand de Frédéric Ancillon, par Mme. la Baronne de S., 2 vols, Bruxelles: Hauman, Cattoir et Cie, 1837.

Anet, Claude: *La Révolution russe*, vol. 1: A Petrograd et aux armées (mars–mai 1917), vol. 2: Grandeur et décadence d'Alexandre Feodorovitch Kerenski, l'affaire Kornilof – le grand jour et le coup d'État maximaliste (juin–novembre 1917), Paris: Phébus, 1919.

*The Anti-Semitic and Nazi Incidents from 25 December 1959 until 28 January 1960*. White Paper of the Government of the Federal Republic of Germany, Bonn: Government Publication, 1960.

Apfel, Holger: 'Volksgemeinschaft statt "kontrollierter" Zuwanderung! Leitlinien für eine nationaldemokratische Politik'. In: *Deutsche Stimme*, no. 8/2005, p. 4.

Arendt, Hannah: *Elemente und Ursprünge totaler Herrschaft*. I. Antisemitismus, II. Imperialismus, III. Totale Herrschaft, new edition, Munich: Piper, 1986.

——'Ideologie und Terror: eine neue Staatsform (1953)'. In: ditto: *Elemente*, pp. 703–30.

——*The Origins of Totalitarianism*, new edition with added prefaces, San Diego/New York/London: Harcourt, 1985.

——*Vita activa oder Vom tätigen Leben*, Munich: Piper, 1992 (1967).

Aristotle: *Erste Analytik/Zweite Analytik*, Herausgegeben, übersetzt, mit Einleitungen und Anmerkungen versehen von Hans Günter Zekl, Hamburg: Meiner, 1998.

——*Metaphysik*, übersetzt und eingeleitet von Thomas Alexander Szlezák, Berlin: Akademie, 2003.

——*Nicomachean Ethics*, translated and edited by Roger Crisp, Cambridge: Cambridge University Press, 2000.

——*Nikomachische Ethik*, Übersetzung und Nachwort von Franz Dirlmeier, Anmerkungen von Ernst A. Schmidt, Stuttgart: Reclam, 1983.

——*Opera omnia*. Graece et Latine cum indice nominum et rerum absolutissimo, edidit Cats Bussemaker, Hildesheim: Olms, 1998, vols I and II.

——*The Politics*, translated and with an introduction, notes and glossary by Carnes Lord, Chicago/London: University Press, 1984.

——*Politik*, übersetzt und hrsg. von Olof Gigon, 6th edition, Munich: DTV, 1986.

——*Politiqves, or Discourse of Government*, translated by I.D., London, 1598.

——*Prior and Posterior Analytics*, edited and translated by John Warrington, London/ New York: Dent, 1964.

——*Topik*, herausgegeben, übersetzt, mit Einleitung und Anmerkungen versehen von Hans Günter Zekl, Darmstadt/Hamburg: Meiner, 1997.

Art. 'Radikalismus'. In: *Meyers Neues Lexikon in acht Bänden*, vol. 6, Leipzig: Bibliographisches Institut, 1963, pp. 789 et seq.

Augé, Claude: *Larousse Mensuel Illustré*, vol. 4: 1917 à 1919, Paris: Larousse, 1919.

Augé, Paul: *Larousse du Xxe siècle en six volumes*, vol. 3, Paris: Larousse, 1930.

*Ausschuss für deutsche Einheit, Wer zog die Drähte? Der Juni-Putsch 1953 und seine Hintergründe*, Berlin (Ost): Kongreß-Verlag, 1954.

Beaulieu, Luke de: *Take heed of both Extremes: or, Plain and useful Cautions against Popery, and Presbytery: By way of Dialogue*. In two parts, London: Printed for Henry Brome, 1675.

'Bericht nach Erkenntnissen der Verfassungsschutzbehörden. Rechtsradikalismus in der Bundesrepublik. Ein Erfahrungsbericht'. In: APuZ, B 20/1962, pp. 241–52.

Bernhardi, Theodor von: 'Unsere Verfassung im Sinn der extremen und im Sinn der gemäßigten Parteien (1858)'. In: ditto, *Vermischte Schriften*, vol. 2, Berlin: Reimer, 1879, pp. 182–210.

Besoigne, Jérôme (anonymous): *Juste Milieu. Qu'il faut tenir dans les disputes de religion*, o.O., 25 August 1735.

Birch, Heinz/Hillmann, Günter: 'Die Krise im Herrschaftssystem des USA-Imperialismus'. In: *Einheit*, 24 (1968), pp. 1174–83.

Bluntschli, Johann Caspar: 'Friedrich und Theodor Rohmer'. In: ditto/Brater (eds), *Staats-Wörterbuch*, vol. 8, pp. 643–51.

——'Parteien, politische'. In: ditto/Brater (eds), *Staats-Wörterbuch*, vol. 7, pp. 717–47.

——Brater, Karl (eds), *Deutsches Staats-Wörterbuch*, 11 vols, Stuttgart: Expedition des Staats-Wörterbuchs, 1857–70.

——'Ideokratie und Theokratie'. In: ditto/Karl Brater (eds): *Deutsches Staats-Wörterbuch*, vol. 5, Stuttgart: Expedition des Staats-Wörterbuchs, 1860, pp. 279–90.

——Seiler, Sebastian: *Die Kommunisten in der Schweiz nach den bei Weitling vorgefundenen Papieren*. Wörtlicher Abdruck des Kommissionalberichts an die Hohe Regierung des Standes Zürich (1843), Nachdruck Glashütten im Taunus: Auvermann, 1973.

Bobbio, Norbert: *Rechts und Links. Gründe und Bedeutungen einer politischen Unterscheidung*, Berlin: Wagenbach, 1994.

Bodin, Jean: *Les six livres de la République*, avec l'apologie de René Herpin, deuxième réimpression de l'édition de Paris 1583, Aalen: Scienta, 1977.

Boiste, P.C.F.: *Dictionnaire universel de la langue française, avec le latin et les étymologies*, 8th edition, Paris: Lecointe et Pougin, 1834.

Bolingbroke, Saint-John, Henry Viscount: *A Dissertation upon Parties*, London: Printed for R. Francklin, 1739.

Borkenau, Franz: *The Totalitarian Enemy*, London: Faber and Faber, 1940.

Bornhausen, Karl Eduard: 'Faszismus und Fundamentalismus in den Vereinigten Staaten'. In: *Die Christliche Welt*, 38 (1923) 14/15, col. 235–43.

Bourdeau, Jean: 'Préface'. In: Jean Alazard, *Communisme et 'fascio' en Italie*, Paris: Bossard 1922, p. 11.

Brandt, Willy: 'Erklärung des Regierenden Bürgermeisters von Berlin vor dem Abgeordnetenhaus von Berlin (13 August 1961)'. In: *Dokumente zur Deutschlandpolitik*, IV. Reihe, vol. 7/1, hg. vom Bundesministerium für innerdeutsche Beziehungen, Frankfurt a.M., 1976, pp. 13–18.

Bravo, Gian Mario: *Critica dell'estremismo*, Milano: Saggiatore, 1977.

——*L'estremismo in Italia*, Roma: Ed. Ruinti, 1982.

Brinton, Crane: *Die Revolution und ihre Gesetze*, Frankfurt a.M., 1959 (*The Anatomy of Revolution*, New York: W.W. Norton & Co., 1938).

Brougham, Henry Lord: *The British Constitution. Its History, Structure, and Working*, London: Richard Griffin & Co., 1860.

——'High-Tory Principles'. In: ditto, *Contributions to the Edinburgh Review*, vol. II, London, 1856, pp. 506–40.

——'Of Balances and Checks'. In: ditto, *Political Philosophy*, part II, London, 1844, pp. 5–16.

Brucioli, Antonio: *Dialogi*, a cura di Aldo Landi, Neapel, 1982.

Bruni, Leonardo: *Politicorum Libri Commentarii*, Paris: Henr. Stephanus, 1506.

Buchanan, George: *My Mission to Russia and Other Diplomatic Memories*, vol. 2, London: Cassel, 1923.

Buchstab, Günter/Kaff, Brigitte/Kleinmann, Hans-Otto (eds), *Keine Stimme dem Radikalismus. Christliche, liberale und konservative Parteien in den Wahlen 1930–33*, Berlin: Colloquium, 1984.

Bundesamt für Polizei, EJPD (ed.): *Bericht innere Sicherheit der Schweiz 2004*, Bern, 2005.

Bundesamt für Verfassungsschutz (ed.): *Bundesamt für Verfassungsschutz. Aufgaben – Befugnisse – Grenzen*, Köln: Bundesamt für Verfassungsschutz, 1999.

Bundesgesetzblatt, no. 42/1950.

Bundesministerium des Inneren (ed.): *Verfassungsschutzberichte (VSB)*, Bonn: BMI, 1969–96, Berlin: BMI, 1997–2006.

Bundesministerium für Inneres/Bundesamt für Verfassungsschutz und Terrorismusbekämpfung (ed.): *Verfassungsschutzbericht 2005*, Wien: Bundesministerium für Inneres, 2005.

Bundesverfassungsgericht, *Entscheidungen*, Karlsruhe, 1952 et seq.

Burke, Edmund: Speech on Fox's East India Bill (1783). In: ditto, *Works*, vol. II, with an introduction by F.W. Raffety, London: Oxford University Press, 1907.

——'Reflections on the Revolution in France and on the Proceedings in Certain Societies in London relative to that event': In a letter intended to have been sent to a gentleman in Paris 1790. In: ditto, *Works*, vol. IV, with an introduction by F.W. Raffety, London, 1907.

Calculator, 'Gradual emancipation'. In: *The Liberator*, 3 (1833) 23, p. 89.

Camerarius, Joachim: *Politicorum et oeconomicorum Aristotelis interpretationes et explicationes accuratae, nunc primum a filijs in lucem ediae*, Frankfurt a.M.: Apud A. Wechelum, 1581.

Camerarius, Ludwig: 'Brief an Lukas Friedrich Behaim vom 9/19 Mai 1648'. In: Ludwig Camerarius und Lukas Friedrich Behaim. *Ein politischer Briefwechsel über den Verfall des Reiches 1636–48, Herausgegeben von Anton Ernstberger,* München: Beck, 1961, pp. 230–32.

——'Brief an Lukas Friedrich Behaim vom 18/28 April 1646'. In: ibid., p. 209.

Carlson, John Roy: *Under Cover. My Four Years in the Nazi Underworld of America. The Amazing Revelation of How Axis Agents and Our Enemies Within Now Plotting to Destroy the United States,* New York: Dutton, 1943.

Chamberlayne, Edward: *L'Estat présent de l'Angleterre.* Avec plusieurs reflexions sur son ancien estat, troisième édition, seconde partie, Amsterdam: Blaeu, 1672.

Changeux, Pierre-Jacques: *Traité des Extrêmes ou Eléments de la Science de la Réalité,* vol. 1, Amsterdam: Darkstee & Merkus, 1767.

Churchill, Winston S.: *Nach dem Kriege,* Zürich: Amalthea, 1930.

Cicero, Marcus Tullius: *De officiis/Vom pflichtgemäßen Handeln,* Lateinisch/Deutsch, übersetzt, kommentiert und herausgegeben von Heinz Gunermann, Stuttgart: Reclam, 1976.

——*De Re Publica/Vom Gemeinwesen,* Lateinisch/Deutsch, übersetzt und herausgegeben von Karl Büchner, Stuttgart: Reclam, 2004

Ciconia, E.A. (ed.): *De republica veneta fragmenta,* Venedig: ex typographia Picottiana, 1830.

Comité Consultativo de Emergencia para la Defensa Política (ed.): *Legislación para la defensa política en las Repúblicas Americanas,* 2 vols, Montevideo: Milton Reyes, 1947.

Confédération Générale du Travail, 21ème congrès national corporatif. Tenu à Orléans du 27 septembre au 2 octobre 1920. Compte rendu des travaux, Villeneuve-Saint-Georges: BIT, 1920.

——22ème congrès national corporatif. Tenu à Lille du 25 au 30 juillet 1921. Compte rendu des travaux, Villeneuve-Saint-Georges: BIT, 1921.

Constant, Benjamin: *Des Réactions politiques,* An V (1797).

——'De la souveraineté du peuple'. In: ditto, *Œuvres politiques,* avec introduction, notes et index par Charles Louandre, Paris: Charpentier, 1874, pp. 2–16.

Contarini, Gasparo: *De magistratibus & re publica Venetorum libri quinque,* Basel, 1544.

——*The commonwealth and government of Venice,* translated by Lewes Lewkenor, London: Iohn Windet for Edmund Mattes, 1599.

Cooke, Parsons: *An essay on the gospel's relations to civil law,* second edition, Boston, 1843.

Dante Alighieri: *Monarchia.* Studienausgabe Lateinisch/Deutsch, Einleitung, Übersetzung und Kommentar von Ruedi Imbach und Christoph Flüeler, Stuttgart: Reclam, 1998.

'Denkschrift des Grafen Brockdorff-Rantzau für das Auswärtige Amt vom 2 April 1917', abgedruckt bei Werner Hahlweg (ed.), *Lenins Rückkehr nach Rußland 1917. Die deutschen Akten,* Leiden: Brill, 1957, pp. 47–49.

'Der "linke Radikalismus", die Kinderkrankheit im Kommunismus'. In: *Wörterbuch des Wissenschaftlichen Kommunismus,* Berlin (Ost): Dietz, 1982, p. 235.

Des Ultra en 1818, et de la note secrète, par le Chev. De N., Paris, 1818.

Deutscher Bundestag, *Stenographische Berichte,* Bonn, 1949 et seq., Berlin, 1999 et seq.

*A Dictionary of American English,* vol. 2. On Historical Principles Compiled at the University of Chicago, London: Oxford University Press, 1960.

Diderot: *Œuvres Complètes*, tome VIII: Encyclopédie IV, édition critique et annotée, présentée par John Lough et Jacques Proust, Paris: Hermann, 1976.

Dionysius of Halikarnassus: *The Roman Antiquities*, with an English translation by Earnest Cary, on the basis of the version of Edward Spelman, vol. IV, revised edition, London/Cambridge: Harvard University Press, 1962.

Domarus, Max: *Hitler. Reden und Proklamationen 1932–45*, vol. II: Untergang. II. semi vol. 1941–45, Wiesbaden: Löwit, 1973.

Dosquet, Emile: *Le Juste-Milieu dévoilé, ou la France en 1832*, Metz, 1832.

Droysen, Johann Gustav: 'Die Extreme (1848)'. In: ditto: *Politische Schriften*. Im Auftrage der preußischen Akademie der Wissenschaften herausgegeben von Felix Gilbert, München: Oldenbourg, 1933, pp. 149–52.

Duclerc, E./Paguerre: *Dictionnaire Politique*. Encyclopédie du Langage et de la Science Politiques, rédigé par une réunion de députés, de publicistes et de journalistes, avec une introduction par Louis Antoine Garnier-Pagès, Paris: Pagnerre, 1842.

Dupont (de l'Eure): 'Lettre d'avis Le Comité Electoral de l'extrême gauche', 1846 (BN, Impr. Lb 51–4091).

Egidio Colonna (Aegidius Romanus): *De Regimine Principum Libri III*, recogniti et una com vita auctoris in lucem editi per F. Hieronymum Samaritanium, Neudruck der Ausgabe Rom 1607, Aalen: Scienta, 1967.

Eisenmann, Gottfried: *Die Parteyen der teutschen Reichsversammlung, ihre Programme, Statuten und Mitgliederverzeichnisse*, Erlangen: Enke, 1848.

Elm, Ludwig: 'Traditionen und Tendenzen des Konservatismus in der BRD'. In: ZfG, 24 (1976), pp. 861–78.

Engelbert von Admont: *De regimine principum*, libri seu tract. VII. Primum post quadringentos et amplius annos in lucem evulgati, cum in exempto monasterio mellicensi ord. S. Bened. Praeside A.R.D.P. Carolomanno Hueber, ejusdem monasterii professo et theologo nobilis ac eruditus dominus Jo. Georgius Theophil. Huffnagl, franco Albimoeniensis ex universa philosophia publice responderet cum facultate superiorum, Ratisbonae o.O. (1725).

Engels, Friedrich: 'Die Entwicklung des Sozialismus von der Utopie zur Wissenschaft (1880)'. In: Karl Marx/ditto: *Werke* (MEW), vol. 19, Berlin (Ost). Dietz, 1962, pp. 189–228.

'Erfahrungen aus der Beobachtung und Abwehr rechtsradikaler und antisemitischer Tendenzen im Jahre 1962'. In: APuZ, B 14/1963, pp. 3–22.

'Erfahrungen aus der Beobachtung und Abwehr rechtsradikaler und antisemitischer Tendenzen im Jahre 1963'. In: APuZ, B 26/1964, pp. 3–21.

'Erfahrungen aus der Beobachtung und Abwehr rechtsradikaler und antisemitischer Tendenzen im Jahre 1964'. In: APuZ, B 11/1965, pp. 3–23.

'Erfahrungen aus der Beobachtung und Abwehr rechtsradikaler und antisemitischer Tendenzen im Jahre 1965'. In: APuZ, B 11/1966, pp. 3–28.

'Erfahrungen aus der Beobachtung und Abwehr rechtsradikaler und antisemitischer Tendenzen im Jahre 1966'. In: APuZ, B 24/1967, pp. 3–37.

'Erfahrungen aus der Beobachtung und Abwehr rechtsradikaler und antisemitischer Tendenzen im Jahre 1967'. In: APuZ, B 15/1968, pp. 3–39.

'Erklärung Cachins und Frossards auf der Kongress-Sitzung vom 22 Juli'. In: *Die Kommunistische Internationale*, 2 (1920) 13, pp. 266 et seq.

'Erlass des Bundesministeriums des Innern vom 19 September 1950, Politische Betätigung der Angehörigen des Öffentlichen Dienstes gegen die demokratische Grundordnung'. In: Erhard Denninger (ed.): *Freiheitliche Demokratische Grundordnung*.

Materialien zum Staatsverständnis und zur Verfassungswirklichkeit in der Bundesrepublik, vol. II, Frankfurt a.M.: Suhrkamp, 1977, pp. 509 et seq.

Ernst II. Herzog von Sachsen-Coburg-Gotha: 'Denkschrift über die Gründung des "Vereins" (1853)'. In: ditto, *Aus meinem Leben und aus meiner Zeit*, 5th edition, Berlin: Hertz, 1888, pp. 306–15.

Ernstberger, Anton (ed.): *Ludwig Camerarius und Lukas Friedrich Behaim. Ein politischer Briefwechsel über den Verfall des Reiches 1636–48*, München: Beck, 1961.

Eysenck, Hans Jürgen: 'General social attitudes'. In: *Journal of Social Psychology*, 19 (1944), pp. 207–27.

——*The Psychology of Politics*, London: Routledge & Kegan Paul, 1954.

Fénelon, François de Salignac de la Mothe: *Examen de conscience sur les devoirs de la royauté, Œuvres*, édition présentée, établie et annotée par Jacques Le Brun, vol. 2, Paris: Gallimard, 1997, pp. 971–1009.

Filmer, Robert: *The Anarchy of a Limited or Mixed Monarchy. Or, a succinct examination of the Fundamentals of Monarchy, both in this and other Kingdoms, as well as about the Right of Power in Kings, as of the Original of Naturall Liberty of the People. A Question never yet disputed, though most necessary in these Times*, o.O., 1648.

——*Observations upon Aristotle's Politiques, touching Forms of Government. Together with directions for obedience to Governours in dangerous and doubtfull times*, London: R. Royston, 1652.

Flake, Otto: 'Lenin'. In: *Die Glocke*, 3 (1917) 35 (1 December), pp. 358–60.

Flechtheim, Ossip K.: 'Extremismus und Radikalismus. Eine Kontraststudie'. In: Funke (ed.): *Extremismus*, pp. 47–61.

——'Radikalismus contra Extremismus'. In: *Neues Hochland*, 66 (1974), pp. 485–93.

Ford, John (anonym): *The Golden Meane*, lately written, as occasion served, to a great Lord [Leffery Chorlton]. Discoursing the Noblenesse of perfect Virtue in extreames, London, 1613 (British Library C.124.b.27.12).

Forster, Georg: 'Brief an Heyne, 12 July 1791'. In: Günther (ed.): *Die Französische Revolution*, pp. 652–55.

——'Brief an Therese Forster, Paris, 19/20 December 1793'. In: Günther (ed.): *Die Französische Revolution*, pp. 764–66.

Fortescue, John: *The Governance of England. The Difference between Absolute and Limited Monarchy*, edited by Charles Plummer, Oxford: Clarendon Press, 1885.

Freyhold, Michaela von: *Autoritarismus und politische Apathie. Analyse einer Skala zur Ermittlung autoritätsgebundener Verhaltensweisen*, Frankfurt a.M.: Europäische Verlagsanstalt, 1971.

Frossard, Louis-Oscar: 'Sur la Révolution Russe'. In: *Le Populaire*. Journal-Revue hebdomadaire de propagande Socialiste & Internationaliste, No. 48 of 14–20 May 1917, pp. 3 et seq.

'Full and Authentic Report of the Tilak Trial'. Being the Only Authorised Verbatim Account, with introduction, character sketch of Bal Gangadhar Tilak and Press Opinion, Bombay, September 1908.

Funke, Manfred (ed.): *Extremismus im demokratischen Rechtsstaat. Ausgewählte Texte und Materialien zur aktuellen Diskussion*, Bonn: Bundeszentrale für politische Bildung, 1978.

——'Extremismus und offene Gesellschaft – Anmerkungen zur Gefährdung und Selbstgefährdung des demokratischen Rechtsstaats'. In: Funke (ed.): *Extremismus*, pp. 15–46.

——*Rechtsextremismus in Deutschland. Historische Entwicklungen und aktuelle Bedrohung*, Sankt Augustin: Knoth, 1994.

Gagern, Friedrich von: 'Die rechte Mitte (1837/38)'. In: Heinrich von Gagner, *Das Leben des Generals Friedrich von Gagnern*, vol. 3, Leipzig/Heidelberg 1856, pp. 259–65

Garbett, Edward: 'Protestant Truth; its position between the two Extremes of Infidelity and Popery', being a sermon, preached in the episcopal chapel, Gray's Inn Lane, on Sunday evening, November 17, London: Thames Ditton printed, 1850.

Gardiner, Stephen: *A Declaration of such true articles as G. Joye hath gone about to confute as false*, London: J. Herforde, 1546, fol. Xx.

Garrison, William Lloyd: 'To the public'. In: *The Liberator*, 1 (1831) 1, p. 1.

Geiger, Theodor: 'Panik im Mittelstand'. In: *Die Arbeit*, (1930) 10, pp. 637–54.

Georg, Manfred: 'Unfruchtbarkeit des Radikalismus. Thomas Mann gegen politisches und kulturelles Obskurantentum'. In: *Neue Leipziger Zeitung*, 15 June 1930.

Gerns, Willi/Steigerwald, Robert/Weiß, Günter: *Opportunismus Heute*, Frankfurt a.M.: Marxistische Blätter, 1974.

Giannotti, Donato: *Die Republik Florenz* (1534), herausgegeben und eingeleitet von Alois Riklin, übersetzt und kommentiert von Daniel Höchli, München: Fink, 1997.

Goebbels, Joseph: 'Ansprache auf der Großkundgebung des Gaues Oberdonau der NSDAP zum 4 Jahrestag des "Anschlusses" (Linz, Südbahnhofhalle, 15 March 1942)'. In: Heiber (ed.), *Goebbels-Reden*, vol. 2, pp. 83–111.

——'Ansprache auf der Kundgebung der Deutschen Studentenschaft "wider den undeutschen Geist" (Berlin Opernplatz, 10 May 1933)'. In: Heiber (ed.), *Goebbels-Reden*, vol. 1, pp. 108–12.

——'Ansprache auf der Massenkundgebung des Gaues Hamburg der NSDAP (Hamburg, Platz vor der Eulenburg im ehemaligen Zoo, 16 July 1933)'. In: Heiber (ed.), *Goebbels-Reden*, vol. 1, pp. 113–23.

——'Das Volk will es!'. In: *Der Angriff*, 7 March 1933, p. 1.

——'Der Bolschewismus'. Rede auf dem Parteikongress in Nürnberg 1936, München: Franz Eher Nachf., 1936.

——'Rede auf der Kundgebung der NSDAP anlässlich der Verleihung von Ritterk reuzen des Kriegsverdienstkreuzes (Berlin, Sportpalast, 5 June 1943)'. In: Heiber (ed.), *Goebbels-Reden*, vol. 2, pp. 218–39.

——'Rede auf der Kundgebung des Gaues Berlin der NSDAP (Berlin, Sportpalast, 18 February 1943)'. In: Heiber (ed.), *Goebbels-Reden*, vol. 2, pp. 172–208.

——'Rede auf der Kundgebung zum 10 Jahrestag der Machtübernahme (Berlin, Sportpalast, 30 January 1943)'. In: Heiber (ed.), *Goebbels-Reden*, vol. 2, pp. 158–71.

——'Tagebücher', im Auftrag des Instituts für Zeitgeschichte herausgegeben von Elke Fröhlich, Teil I & II, München 1994–2005.

——'Was wollen wir im Reichstag (30 April 1928)'. In: ditto: *Der Angriff. Aufsätze aus der Kampfzeit*, 2nd edition, München: Franz Eher Nachf., 1935, pp. 71–73.

——'Wesen, Methoden und Ziele der Propaganda (Sondertagung der Gau- und Kreispropagandaleiter anlässlich des 7 Reichsparteitags der NSDAP, Nürnberg, Apollo-Theater, 16 September 1935)'. In: Heiber (ed.), *Goebbels-Reden*, vol. 1, pp. 230–64.

Gonzales de Leon, F. Joanne: Controversiae inter defensores libertatis et praeicatores gratiae, de auxiliis divinae gratiae, tam excitantis quam adjuvantis, tam operantis quam cooperantis, tam sufficientis quam efficacies, et de extremis Haereticorum erroribus circa eandem, Roma, 1635.

Görres, Joseph: 'Teutschland und die Revolution (1819)'. In: ditto, *Gesammelte* Schriften, Herausgegeben von der Görres-Gesellschaft, vol. 13: Politische Schriften (1817–22), Köln, 1929.

——'Weltlage (1838)'. In: ditto, *Gesammelte Schriften*, vol. 16/1, pp. 1–40.

Government of Bombay, *Source Material for a History of the Freedom Movement in India* (Collected from Bombay Governmen Records), vol. II: 1885–1920, Bombay, 1958.

Government of the United Kingdom/Home Office (ed.): *Preventing Extremism Together. Places of Worship*, London, 6 October 2005.

Grebing, Helga: *Linksradikalismus gleich Rechtsradikalismus. Eine falsche Gleichung*, Stuttgart: Kohlhammer, 1971.

Grimm, Jacob/ Grimm, Wilhelm: *Deutsches Wörterbuch*, Neubearbeitung, Herausgegeben von der Berlin-Brandenburgischen Akademie der Wissenschaften und der Akademie der Wissenschaften zu Göttingen, vol. 8, Stuttgart: Hirzel, 1999.

Grispigni, Marco: *Elogio dell'estremismo*. Storiografia e movimenti, Roma: manifestolibri, 2000.

Grumbach, Salomon: *L'erreur de Zimmerwald-Kienthal*, Paris: L'Humanité, 1917.

——*Brest-Litowsk*, Lausanne: Payot, 1918:

Grün, Karl: *Die soziale Bewegung in Frankreich und Belgien. Briefe und Studien* (1845), Nachdruck Hildesheim: Gerstenberg, 1974.

Günther, Anton: *Die Juste-Milieus in der deutschen Philosophie gegenwärtiger Zeit*, Wien: Beck, 1838.

Günther, Horst (ed.): *Die Französische Revolution. Berichte und Deutungen deutscher Schriftsteller und Historiker*, Frankfurt a.M.: Deutscher Klassiker-Verlag, 1985.

Guilbeaux, Henri: *La fin des Soviets*, Paris: Soc. française d'éd. littéraires et techn., 1937.

——'La Révolution russe et la paix'. In: *Demain*, 2 (1917) 13 (May), p. 3.

——' … et demain?' In: *Demain*, 1 (1916) 1 (January), pp. 1–3.

Guizot, François: *Mémoires pour servir à l'histoire de mon temps*, vol. 1, Paris: Levy, 1858.

——*Du Gouvernement de la France depuis la Restauration, et du ministère actuel*, 4th edition Paris: Ladvocat, 1821.

Halem, Gerhard Anton von: *Blicke auf einen Theil Deutschlands, der Schweiz und Frankreichs bey einer Reise vom Jahre 1790*, nach der Ausgabe von 1791 mit den Korrekturen und Ergänzungen aus Halems Handexemplar neu herausgegeben, erläutert und mit einem Nachwort versehen von Wolfgang Griep und Cord Sieberns, Bremen: Ed. Temmen, 1990.

Haller, Carl Ludwig von: *Restauration der Staats-Wissenschaft*, 6 vols, 2nd edition, Winterthur: Steiner, 1820–25.

——*Restaurazion der Staatswissenschaft oder Theorie des natürlich-geselligen Zustands, der Schimäre des künstlich-bürgerlichen entgegengesezt.* 1 vol.: Darstellung, Geschichte und Kritik der bisherigen falschen Systeme. Allgemeine Grundsätze der entgegengesezten Ordnung Gottes und der Natur, Winterthur: Steiner, 1816.

Hamburger Institut für Sozialforschung (ed.): *Reader: Die Kontroverse über den Zusammenbruch der Mittelschichtparteien und den Aufstieg der NSDAP am Ende der Weimarer Republik*, Hamburg 1994.

Harder, Jürgen: *Klassenkampf und 'linke' Kunsttheorien. Zum Antikommunismus kunsttheoretischer Konzeptionen des Linksradikalismus in der BRD (1965–75)*, Berlin (Ost): Dietz, 1978.

Hardt, Michael/Negri, Antonio: *Empire*, Cambridge/London: Harvard University Press, 2001.

Hegel, Georg Wilhelm Friedrich: *Phänomenologie des Geistes*, mit einem Nachwort von Georg Lukács, Text-Auswahl und Kommentar zur Rezeptionsgeschichte von Gerhard Göhler, Frankfurt a.M.: Ullstein, 1970, pp. 286 et seq. (BB. Der Geist, 454–56).

Heiber, Helmut (ed.): *Goebbels-Reden*, vol. 1: 1932–39, München, 1971.

——*Goebbels-Reden*, vol. 2: 1939–45, Düsseldorf, 1972.

Herodot: *Historien*, übersetzt von Walter Marg, München: DTV, 1991.

Herodotus of Halicarnassus, *Histories*, translated and introduced by Harry Carter, London: Oxford University Press, 1962.

Herrmann, Klaus Dieter: 'Zur Formierung des Rechtsblocks in der BRD'. In: *Einheit*, 26 (1970), pp. 1088–1100.

Herz, Thomas A.: Soziale Bedingungen für Rechtsextremismus in der Bundesrepublik Deutschland und in den Vereinigten Staaten, Dissertation, Köln, 1973.

Hesselbarth, Hellmut: 'Aufbruch der Studenten in der kapitalistischen Welt'. In: *Einheit*, 24 (1969), pp. 1354–66.

Heyden, Günter: 'Das antikommunistische Wesen des heutigen Trotzkismus'. In: *Einheit*, 27 (1972), pp. 211–20.

——'Weltanschauliche Grundlagen des Sozialdemokratismus'. In: *Einheit*, 27 (1971), pp. 150–60.

Himmler, Heinrich: 'Rede des Reichsführers-SS bei der SS-Gruppenführertagung in Posen am 4 Oktober 1943 (Dokument 1919-PS)'. In: *Der Prozess gegen die Hauptkriegsverbrecher vor dem internationalen Militärgerichtshof, Nürnberg*, 14 November 1945–1 Oktober 1946, Urkunden und anderes Beweismaterial, vol. 29, Nürnberg: Delphin, 1948, pp. 110–73.

Hippokrates: 'Die Regelung der Lebensweise'. In: ditto, *Schriften*. Die Anfänge der abendländischen Medizin, übersetzt und mit Einführungen, einem Essay 'Zum Verständnis der Schriften' und einer Bibliographie hg. von Hans Diller, Reinbek: Rowohlt, 1962.

Hirsch, Kurt: *Kommen die Nazis wieder? Gefahren für die Bundesrepublik*, München: Desch, 1967.

Hitler, Adolf: 'Die soziale Sendung der Nation'. Rede auf NSDAP-Versammlung in Stuttgart (16 December 1925). In: Hitler, *Reden*, vol. I, pp. 239–62.

——'Ein Kampf um Deutschlands Freiheit'. Rede auf NSDAP-Versammlung in Kulmbach (5 February 1928). In: Hitler, *Reden*, vol. II, Teil 1, pp. 662–68.

——'Ein neues Kampfjahr bricht an' (*Illustrierter Beobachter*, 3 January 1931). In: Hitler, *Reden*, vol. IV, Teil 1, pp. 170–72.

——'Freiheit und Brot'. Rede auf NSDAP-Versammlung in Dörflas (26 Juni 1927). In: Hitler, *Reden*, vol. II, Teil 1, pp. 386–403.

——*Mein Kampf*. Zwei Bände in einem Band, München, o.J. (Original: vol. 1: 1925, vol. 2: 1927).

——'Politik der Woche' (*Illustrierter Beobachter*, 31 May 1930). In: Hitler, *Reden*, vol. III, Teil 3, München, 1995, pp. 211–14.

——'Rede auf NSDAP-Versammlung in Altenburg' (11 April 1926). In: Hitler, *Reden*, vol. I, pp. 370–74.

——'Rede auf NSDAP-Versammlung in Braunschweig' (4 November 1925). In: Hitler, *Reden*, vol. I, pp. 208–10.

——'Rede auf NSDAP-Versammlung in Kaiserslautern' (16 April 1931). In: Hitler, *Reden*, vol. IV, Teil 1, pp. 305–14.

——'Rede auf NSDAP-Versammlung in Plauen i.V.' (11 June 1925). In: Hitler, *Reden*, vol. I, pp. 90 et seq.

——*Reden*, vol. I, hg. und kommentiert von Clemens Vollnhals, München: Saur, 1992.

——*Reden*, vol. II, hg. und kommentiert von Bärbel Duzik, München: Saur, 1992.

——*Reden*, vol. III, hg. und kommentiert von Christian Hartmann, München: Saur, 1995.

——*Reden*, vol. IV, hg. und kommentiert von Constantin Goschler, München: Saur, 1994.

——'Warum musste ein 8. November kommen?' In: *Deutschlands Erneuerung*, XI (1933), pp. 642–54.

Hoeft, Klaus-Dieter: 'Parteitag der reaktionärsten und aggressivsten Kräfte des westdeutschen Monopolkapitals'. In: *Einheit*, 25 (1969), pp. 79–90.

——'Strauß und Barzel'. In: *Einheit*, 28 (1973), pp. 633–36.

Holloway, John: *Change the World without Taking Power. The Meaning of Revolution Today*, London: Pluto, 2002.

Horaz, Q.H. Flaccus: *Oden und Epoden*, hg. und übersetzt von Gerhard Fink, Düsseldorf: Artemis und Winkler, 2002.

——*Satiren – Briefe. Sermones – Epistulae*, übersetzt von Gerd Herrmann. Herausgegeben von Gerhard Fink, Düsseldorf: Artemis und Winkler, 2000.

Humboldt, Wilhelm von: 'Ideen über Staatsverfassung, durch die neue französische Constitution veranlasst' (August 1791). In: ditto, *Werke*, ed. by Albert Leitzmann, vol. 1: 1785–95, Berlin: Behr, 1903, pp. 77–85.

Hume, David: 'Of the liberty of the press'. In: ditto: *Essays. Moral, Political, and Literary*, ed. and with a Foreword, Notes, and Glossary by Eugene F. Miller, revised edition, Indianapolis: Liberty Fund, 1987, pp. 9–13.

Hunton, Philip: *A Treatise of Monarchy*, containing two parts: I. Concerning Monarchy in General. II. Concerning This Particular Monarchy, London: Printed for and sold by Richard Baldwin, 1643.

*Ideologie des Sozialdemokratismus in der Gegenwart*. Herausgegeben von der Akademie der Wissenschaften der USSR, Berlin (Ost): Staatsverlag der DDR, 1971.

Initiative gegen jeden Extremismusbegriff (INEX), *Das Ende des Extremismus*, 16 October 2008, http://inex.blogsport.de (accessed 11 March 2009).

Isidori Hispalensis Episcopi Etymologiarum sive Originum, ed. by W.M. Lindsay, Oxford, 1957.

Isokrates: 'Rede an Nikokles'. In: ditto, *Sämtliche Werke*, vol. 1, übersetzt von Christine Ley-Hutton, eingeleitet und erläutert von Kai Brodersen, Stuttgart: Hiersemann, 1993.

Jäggi, Christian J./Krieger, David J.: *Fundamentalismus. Ein Phänomen der Gegenwart*, Zürich: Orell Füssli, 1991.

Jahrreiss, Hermann: 'Demokratie. Selbstbewusstsein – Selbstgefährdung – Selbstschutz (Zur deutschen Verfassungsproblematik seit 1945)'. In: *Festschrift Richard Thoma zum 75th Geburtstag*, Tübingen: Mohr (Siebeck), 1950, pp. 71–91.

James, William: *Pragmatism. A New Name for Some Old Ways of Thinking*. Popular Lectures on Philosophy, New York: Longmans, 1909.

Jordan, Sylvester: *Selbstvertheidigung Dr Sylvester Jordan's in der wider ihn geführten Criminaluntersuchung, Theilnahme an Hochvrath betreffend*. Nebst der Appellationsschrift seines Vertheidigers, Ober-Gerichts-Anwalt C.F. Schantz zu Marburg, und einer Denkschrift, die Rechtfertigung der Beschwerden und zugleich einen Beitrag zur Lehre vom Indicienbeweise enthaltend, Mannheim: Bassermann, 1844.

——*Versuche über allgemeinen Staatsrecht*, in systematischer Ordnung und mit Bezugnahme auf Politik, Marburg, 1828.

Justi, Johann Heinrich Gottlob von: *Vergleichungen der Europäischen mit den Asiatischen und andern vermeintlich Barbarischen Regierungen*, in drey Büchern verfasset, Berlin: Scriptor, 1762.

——*Natur und Wesen der Staaten als die Quelle aller Regierungswissenschaften und Gesezze*, mit Anmerkungen hg. von Heinrich Godfried Scheidemantel, Mitau: Steidel, 1771.

Kaase, Max: 'Linksextremismus'. In: Dieter Nohlen (ed.): *Piper's Wörterbuch zur Politik*, vol. 2: Westliche Industriegesellschaften. Wirtschaft – Gesellschaft – Politik. Herausgegeben von Manfred G. Schmidt, München: Piper, 1983, pp. 218–21.

Kalinine, W.: 'La Révolution russe et ses perspectives'. In: *Demain*, 2 (1917) 15 (July), pp. 156–65.

Kant, Immanuel: *Metaphysik der Sitten* (1797), mit einer Einleitung herausgegeben von Hans Ebeling, Stuttgart: Reclam, 1990.

Keller, Franz: Art. 'Radikalismus'. In: Hermann Sacher (ed.), *Staatslexikon*, 5 von Grund aus neubearb. Auflage, Freiburg im Brsg., 1931: Herder, vol. 4, col. 507 et seq.

Kepel, Gilles: *Das Schwarzbuch des Dschihad. Aufstieg und Niedergang des Islamismus*, München/Zürich: Piper, 2002.

Kerenski, Alexandre: *La Révolution russe 1917*, Paris: Payot, 1928.

Klemperer, Victor: LTI. *Notizbuch eines Philologen*, Berlin: Aufbau, 1949.

Klingemann, Hans D./Pappi, Franz U.: *Politischer Radikalismus*. Theoretische und methodische Probleme der Radikalismusforschung, dargestellt am Beispiel einer Studie anlässlich der Landtagswahl 1970 in Hessen, München: Oldenbourg, 1972.

Knobelsdorf, Wlodzimierz: 'Zu einigen Entwicklungstendenzen des modernen Rechtsextremismus'. In: Ludwig Elm (ed.), *Konservatismus in der BRD*, Hg. im Auftrag des Wissenschaftlichen Rates für Grundfragen des ideologischen Kampfes zwischen Sozialismus und Imperialismus, Arbeitsgruppe Konservatismus, Berlin (Ost): Dietz, 1982, pp. 104–8.

Köhler, Otto: *Union konkret: Sicherheitsbeauftragter Friedrich Zimmermann*, PDI-Blick nach rechts, Sonderausgabe No. 10, München, February 1983.

'Die Kommunistische Tätigkeit in der Bundesrepublik im Jahre 1964'. In: APuZ, B 33/1965, pp. 3–36.

'Die Kommunistische Tätigkeit in der Bundesrepublik im Jahre 1965'. In: APuZ, B 20/1966, pp. 3–30.

'Die Kommunistische Tätigkeit in der Bundesrepublik im Jahre 1966'. In: APuZ, B 28/1967, pp. 3–32.

Kopp, Hans-Ulrich: 'Die Begegnung der dritten Art. Liberal-Extremismus'. In: Junge *Freiheit*, Jan./Feb. 1992.

Krug, Wilhelm Traugott: *Allgemeines Handwörterbuch der philosophischen Wissenschaften nebst ihrer Literatur und Geschichte*. Nach dem heutigen Standpuncte der Wissenschaft bearbeitet und herausgegeben, zweite verbesserte und vermehrte Auflage, vol. 5 als Supplement. Erste Abteilung, Leipzig: F.A. Brockhaus, 1838.

——*Aretologie oder philosophische Tugendlehre*, Königsberg: Unzer, 1818.

——Art. 'Ultraismus'. In: ditto, *Allgemeines Handwörterbuch der philosophischen Wissenschaften nebst ihrer Literatur und Geschichte*, vol. 4: St bis Z, Leipzig: F.A. Brockhaus, 1829, pp. 259 et seq.

——'Dikäopolitik oder neue Restaurazion der Staatswissenschaft mittels Rechtsgesetzen (1824)'. In: ditto, *Gesammelte Werke*, vol. 6, pp. 282–565.

——'Der falsche Liberalismus unsrer Zeit. Ein Beitrag zur Geschichte des Liberalismus und eine Mahnung für künftige Volksvertreter (1832)'. In: ditto, *Gesammelte Schriften*, vol. 5, pp. 331–84.

——*Gesammelte Schriften*, 12 vols, Braunschweig: Friedrich Vieweg, 1830–41.

——'Geschichtliche Darstellung des Liberalismus alter und neuer Zeit. Ein historisch-politischer Versuch (1823)'. In: ditto, *Gesammelte Schriften*, vol. 4, pp. 323–404

——'Der Kampf zwischen Konservativen und Destruktiven und das europäische Ober-Studien-Direktorium. Auch ein Versuch, das Politisch-Böse unsrer Zeit auszurotten (1835)'. In: ditto, *Gesammelte Schriften*, vol. 6, pp. 193–230.

——'Korrespondenz Krugs mit dem Dresdner Theologen, Altphilologen und Schriftsteller Karl August Böttiger, Sächsische Landes- und Universitätsbibliothek Dresden' (Mscr. Dresd. H. 37, 4°, vol. 112, 113).

——'Das Repräsentativsystem. Oder Ursprung und Geist der stellvertretenden Verfassungen, mit besonderer Hinsicht auf Deutschland und Sachsen (1816)'. In: ditto, *Gesammelte Schriften*, vol. 3, pp. 277–319.

——'Die Staatswissenschaft im Restaurazionsprozesse der Herren v. Haller, Adam Müller und Konsorten betrachtet (1817)'. In: ditto, *Gesammelte Schriften*, vol. 1, pp. 321–92.

——*Ueber Opposizions-Parteien in und außer Deutschland und ihr Verhältniß zu den Regierungen. Nebst einem Nachwort über eine merkwürdige politische Prophezeiung*, Leipzig: Kollmann, 1835.

——*Urceus, Meine Lebensreise. In sechs Stazionen*, Leipzig, 1825.

——*Allgemeines Handwörterbuch*, vol. 5 als Supplement. Erste Abtheilung, Leipzig, 1838.

——*Krug's Lebensreise in sechs Stationen, von ihm selbst beschrieben, nebst Franz Volkmar Reinhardt's Briefen an den Verfasser*, Leipzig: Baumgärtner, 1842.

Kühnl, Reinhard: 'Der Einfluss rechtsradikalen Gedankenguts auf die Arbeitnehmer, PDI-Blick nach rechts', Sonderausgabe No. 7, München, September 1982.

Lafayette, Marie Joseph de: 'Brief an Karl von Rotteck, Lagrange, 24 October 1833'. Abdruck bei Claudia Igelmund, Frankreich und das Staatslexikon von Rotteck und Welcker. Eine Studie zum Frankreichbild des süddeutschen Frühliberalismus, Frankfurt a.M.: Lang, 1987, appendix.

Landau-Aldanow, M.A.: *Lenin und der Bolschewismus*, aus dem Französischen von Viktor Bergmann, Berlin: Ullstein, 1920.

Lenin, Wladimir Iljitsch: 'Briefe aus der Ferne. Brief 2: Die neue Regierung und das Proletariat'. In: Lenin, *Werke*, vol. 23, pp. 323–57.

——'Drei Krisen'. In: Lenin., *Werke*, vol. 25, pp. 166–67.

——'Der "linke Radikalismus", die Kinderkrankheit im Kommunismus (1920)'. In: Lenin, *Werke*, vol. 31, pp. 5–106.

——'Die Machenschaften der republikanischen Chauvinisten'. In: Lenin, *Werke*, vol. 23, pp. 374–77.

——*Werke* (Polnoe sobranie socinenij), vol. 31 (März–April 1917), Moskau: Progress, 1969, pp. 79–82.

——*Werke* (Polnoe sobranie socinenij), Hg. vom Institut für Marxismus–Leninismus des ZK der KPdSU, 40 vols, Berlin (Ost): Universum-Bücherei, 1955–65.

——'Wie soll man den Wettbewerb organisieren? (7–10 January 1918)'. In: ditto: *Werke*, vol. 26, pp. 402–14.

Leo, Heinrich: *Studien und Skizzen zu einer Naturlehre des Staates*, Halle: Anton, 1833.

Lerner, Max: 'Das Grundmuster der Diktatur (Original: The Patterns of Dictatorship, 1935)'. In: Seidel/Jenkner (eds): *Totalitarismusforschung*, pp. 30–48.

——*It is Later than you Think. The Need for a Militant Democracy* (1943), New Brunswick, NJ: Transaction Publishers, 1989.

Leroy, Maxime: *Les techniques nouvelles du syndicalisme*, Paris: Garnier, 1921.

——'Préface'. In: H.-G. Wells, *La Russie telle que je viens de la voir*, Paris: Ed. du progrès civique, 1921, pp. I–XXXII.

Ley, Robert: 'Fanatiker des Glaubens!' In: *Der Angriff*, 23 February 1943, pp. 1 et seq.

Lichtenberger, Henri: *Deutschland und Frankreich in ihren gegenwärtigen Beziehungen*, in deutscher Bearbeitung von Rudolf Berger, Leipzig: Ernst Oldenbourg, 1924.

——*L'Allemagne d'aujourd'hui. Dans ses relations avec la France*, Paris: G. Crès, 1922.

'Linksradikalismus in der Bundesrepublik im Jahre 1967'. In: APuZ, B 30/1968, pp. 3–32.

Lipset, Seymour M.: 'Democracy and Working-Class Authoritarianism'. In: *American Sociological Review*, 24 (1959), pp. 482–501.

——'Der "Faschismus", die Linke, die Rechte und die Mitte'. In: Ernst Nolte (ed.), *Theorien über den Faschismus*, 6th edition, Königstein/Ts.: Athenäum, 1984 (1967), pp 449–91.

——'Der "Faschismus", die Linke, die Rechte und die Mitte'. In: KZfSS, 11 (1959), pp. 401–44.

——'"Faschismus" – rechts, links und in der Mitte'. In: ditto, *Soziologie der Demokratie*, Neuwied: Luchterhand, 1962, pp. 131–89.

——*Political Man. The Social Basis of Politics*, New York: Doubleday, 1960.

——Raab, Earl: *The Politics of Unreason. Right-Wing Extremism in America, 1790–1977*, 2nd edition, Chicago: University of Chicago Press, 1978 (1970).

——'Socialism – Left and Right – East and West'. In: *Confluence*, 7 (1958), pp. 173–92.

——'Social Stratification and "Right-Wing Extremism"'. In: *British Journal of Sociology*, 10 (1959), pp. 346–82.

Loewenstein, Karl: *Contrôle legislative de l'extrémisme politique dans les démocraties européennes*, Paris 1939.

——'Der Kommunismus und die amerikanische Verfassung'. In: JZ, 7 (1952), pp. 2–10.

——'Legislative Control of Political Extremism in European Democracies'. In: *Columbia Law Review*, 38 (1938), pp. 591–622, 725–74.

——'Militant Democracy and Fundamental Rights'. In: APSR, 31 (1937), pp. 417–32, 638–58.

——(anonym) 'Der Staatsschutz in den europäischen Demokratien'. In: NZZ, No. 659, 13 April 1937, p. 1.

——(anonym) 'Der Staatsschutz in den europäischen Demokratien'. In: NZZ, No. 662, 14 April 1937, p. 2.

——*Verfassungslehre*, 2nd edition, Tübingen: Mohr, 1969.

Löhneyß, Georg Engelhard von: 'Aulico Politica, oder Hof-, Staats- und Regierungskunst (Remlingen 1622/24)'. In: Hans-Otto Mühleisen/Theo Stammen/Michael Philipp (eds), *Fürstenspiegel der frühen Neuzeit*, Frankfurt a.M.: Insel, 1997, pp. 394–419.

Löwenthal, Richard: 'Totalitäre und demokratische Revolution'. In: *Der Monat*, 13 (1960/61) 146, pp. 29–40.

——'Totalitäre und demokratische Revolution'. In: Seidel/Jenkner (eds), *Totalitarismusforschung*, pp. 359–81.

——'Totalitarianism Reconsidered'. In: *Commentary*, 29 (1960), pp. 504–12.

Lloyd George, David: 'Rede'. In: Nitti, Francesco: *L'Europa senza pace*, Firenze: R. Bemporad, 1921, pp. 93–97.

——*War Memoirs*, vol. 2, London: Nicholson & Watson, 1936.

Ludendorff, Erich: *Der totale Krieg*, Munich: Ludendorff, 1935.

Luther, Martin: 'An den christlichen Adel deutscher Nation von des christlichen Standes Besserung'. In: ditto, *Studienausgabe*, in Zusammenarbeit mit Helmar Junghans, Joachim Rogge und Günther Wartenberg, Herausgegeben von Hans-Ulrich Delius, vol. 2, Berlin (Ost): Evangelische Verlagsanstalt, 1982, pp. 89–167.

Machiavelli, Niccolò: 'Denkschrift über die Reform des Staates von Florenz'. In: ditto, *Politische Schriften*, Herausgegeben von Herfried Münkler, Frankfurt a.M.: Fischer-Taschenbuch-Verlag, 1991, pp. 347–57.

——*Discorsi. Gedanken über Politik und Staatsführung*, deutsche Gesamtausgabe, übersetzt, eingeleitet und erläutert von Rudolf Zorn, zweite verbesserte Auflage, Stuttgart: Kröner, 1977.

——'Discorsi'. In: ditto, *Opere*, vol. 1, pp. 193–525.

——'Discursus Florentinarum rerum post mortem iunioris Laurentii Medices'. In: ditto, *Opere*, vol. 1, pp. 733–47.

——*Geschichte von Florenz*, mit einem Nachwort von Kurt Kluxen, 3rd edition, Zürich: Manesse, 1993.

——*Opere*, a cura di Corrado Vivanti, Torino, 1997.

Madloch, Norbert: 'Vorwort'. In: Akademie für Gesellschaftswissenschaften beim ZK der SED/Autorenkollektiv unter der Leitung von Norbert Madloch (eds), *Links-Radikalismus*, Berlin (Ost): Dietz 1989, pp. 5–8.

Marx, Karl: 'Kritik des Hegelschen Staatsrechts (1843)'. In: MEW 1, p. 293.

Maxe, Jean: *De Zimmerwald au bolchévisme ou le triomphe du marxisme pangermaniste. Essai sur les menées internationalistes pendant la guerre 1914–20*, Paris: Bossard, 1920.

Melanchthon, Philipp: 'Commentarii in aliquot politicos libros Aristotelis (1530)'. In: Karl Gottlieb Bretschneider/Heinrich Ernst Bindseil (eds), *Corpus Reformatorum*, Halle: Schwetschke, 1850, vol. 16, pp. 416–51.

——'De officio principum, quod mandatum Dei praecipiat eis tollere abusus Ecclesiasticos (1539)'. In: ditto, *Werke*, vol. 1: Reformatorische Schriften, Herausgegeben von Robert Stupperich, Gütersloh: Bertelsmann, 1951, pp. 387–410.

——'Enarrationes aliquot librorum ethicorum Aristotelis (1529)'. In: ditto, *Werke*, vol. 1, pp. 276–415.

——*Loci communes 1521*. Lateinisch–Deutsch, übersetzt und mit kommentierten Anmerkungen versehen von Horst Georg Pöhlmann, Herausgegeben vom Lutherischen Kirchenamt der Vereinigten Evangelisch-Lutherischen Kirche Deutschlands, zweite durchgesehene und korrigierte Auflage, Gütersloh: Gütersloher Verlagshaus, 1997.

——'Widmungsvorrede vom 5 August 1537'. In: ditto, *Briefwechsel. Kritische und kommentierte Gesamtausgabe*, im Auftrag der Heidelberger Akademie der Wissenschaften Herausgegeben von Heinz Scheible, vol. 7: Texte 1536–37, bearbeitet von Christine Mundhenk, unter Mitwirkung von Heidi Hein und Judith Steiniger, Stuttgart–Bad Cannstatt: Frommann-Holzboog, 2006.

Mercier, Louis Sébastien: *Tableau de Paris*, vol. 4, Amsterdam, 1788.

Merrheim, Alphonse: *Amsterdam ou Moscou?*, Paris, 1921.

——'Ce qui paralyse et tue les révolutions'. In: *L'information ouvrière et sociale*, No. 224, 13 Juni 1920, pp. 1 et seq.

——'Ceux que l'on accuse d'outrager la Révolution russe'. In: *L'Atelier*, 11 September 1920, p. 3.

——'Outrager la vérité ou "outrager" la Révolution russe?' In: *L'Atelier*, 18 September 1920, p. 3.

——'Préface'. In: Max Hoschiller, *Le mirage du soviétisme*, Paris: Payot, 1921, pp. 7–24.

*Meyer's Lexikon*, vol. 3, 8th edition, Leipzig, 1937.

*Meyer's Neues Lexikon* in acht Bänden, vol. 6, Leipzig: Bibliographisches Institut, 1963.

Meyer, Thomas: *Fundamentalismus. Aufstand gegen die Moderne*, Reinbek: Rowohlt, 1989.

Milton, John: *Eikonoklastes in Answer to a Book Intitl'd Eikon Basilike. The Portrature of his Sacred Majesty in his Solitudes and Sufferings*, London: Printed by Matthew Simmons, 1649.

Minerstvo vnitra ĈR Odbor bezpeĉnostní politiky (ed.): *Informace o problematice extremismu na území ĉeské republiky v roce 2004*, Prague, 2005.

Minkenberg, Michael: *Die neue radikale Rechte im Vergleich. USA, Frankreich, Deutschland*, Opladen/Wiesbaden: Westdeutscher Verlag, 1998.

Montaigne, Michel de: *Essais*, Nachdruck der von Peter Coste ins Deutsche übertragenen Ausgabe von 1753/54 mit einer editorischen Notiz und Inhaltsübersicht, Redaktion Winfried Stephan, vol. 3, Zürich: Diogenes, 1992.

——'Von der Mäßigung seines eignen Willens (1580)'. In: ditto, *Essais*, vol. 3, pp. 212–57.

Montesquieu, Charles de: *Considérations sur les causes de la grandeur des Romains et de leur décadence*, avec commentaries et notes de Frédéric-le-Grand, edition collationnée sur le texte de 1734, avec une introduction par J. Charvet, réimpression de l'édition de Paris 1876, Genf: Slatkine Reprints, 1971.

——'Considérations sur les causes de la granndeur des Romains et de leur décadence (1734)'. In: ditto, *Œuvres complètes*, vol. 2, pp. 69–209.

——'De l'esprit des lois ou du rapport que les lois doivent avoir avec la constitution de chaque gouvernement, les moeurs, le climat, la religion, le commerce, etc. (1748)'. In: ditto, *Œuvres complètes*, vol. 2, pp. 227–995.

——'Lettres Persanes (1721)'. In: ditto, *Œuvres complètes*, vol. 1, pp. 129–373.

——'Mes Pensées'. In: ditto, *Œuvres complètes*, vol. 1, pp. 973–1574.

——*Œuvres complètes*, texte présenté et annoté par Roger Caillois, 'Bibliothèque de la Pléiade', 2 vols, Paris: Gallimard, 1996.

Münch, Ernst: *Historische Rückblicke, politische Zeitstimmen und patriotische Ermahnungen. An die Teutschen*, 1st Heft, Braunschweig, 1831.

Murhard, Friedrich: Art. 'Absolutismus' (1835). In: Carl von Rotteck/Carl Welcker (eds), *Das Staats-Lexikon. Encyklopädie der sämmtlichen Staatswissenschaften für alle Stände*. In Verbindung mit vielen der angesehensten Publicisten Deutschlands hg. von Carl von Rotteck und Carl Welcker, neue durchaus verbesserte und vermehrte Auflage, mit einer Einleitung zum Neudruck von Hartwig Brandt und einem Verzeichnis der Mitarbeiter von Helga Albrecht, Frankfurt a.M.: Keip, 1990, vol. 1, pp. 146–57.

Mussard, Jeanne: *Les extrêmes se touchent*, Cluny, 1872.

Mussolini, Benito: 'Avanti, il Mikado!' In: *Il Popolo d'Italia*, 11 November 1917, p. 4 (Opera Omnia, vol. X, pp. 41–43).

——'Da Stürmer a Lenine'. In: *Il Popolo d'Italia*, 25 July 1917, pp. 1 und 4. Abdruck in: Benito Mussolini, *Opera Omnia*, a cura di Edoardo e Duilio Susmel, vol. IX, Firenze: La Fenice, 1952, pp. 74–76.

——'Duplice colpo! Il Tramonto di Zimmerwald'. In: *Il Popolo d'Italia*, 9 July 1917, p. 4 (*Opera Omnia*, vol. IX, pp. 29–35).

——'Impudenza e mistificazione'. In: *Il Popolo d'Italia*, 13 August 1917, p. 4 (*Opera Omnia*, vol. IX, pp. 109–12).

——*Opera Omnia*, a cura di Edoardo e Duilio Susmel, 44 vols, Firenze: La Fenice, 1952–80.

——'Viva Kerensky!' In: *Il Popolo d'Italia*, 26 July 1917, p. 4 (*Opera Omnia*, vol. IX, pp. 77 et seq.).

Neubert, Wolfram: 'Offener Nationalismus in Westdeutschland'. In: *Einheit*, 22 (1966), pp. 1174–86.

Neumann, Oskar: 'Das Verbot der KPD – ein gefährlicher Angriff auf Frieden, Demokratie und Wiedervereinigung Deutschlands'. In: *Einheit*, 11 (1956), pp. 809–14.

——'Die Funktion der bürgerlichen Parteien in Westdeutschland'. In: *Einheit*, 11 (1956), pp. 271–78.

Nieder, Ludwig: *Der Radikalismus am Ruder. Tatsachen und Gedanken*, Mönchen-Gladbach: Volksverein, 1919.

Nieke, W.: 'Extremismus'. In: Ritter (ed.), *Historisches Wörterbuch*, vol. 2, col. 883 et seq.

Noelle-Neumann, Elisabeth/Ring, Erp: *Das Extremismus-Potential unter jungen Leuten in der Bundesrepublik Deutschland 1984*, Bonn: Bundesminister des Innern, 1984.

Nörenberg, Günther: *Planwirtschaft im Zerrspiegel des Linksradikalismus*, Berlin (Ost): Die Wirtschaft, 1984.

Nozick, Robert: 'The Characteristic Features of Extremism'. In: ditto: *Socratic Puzzles*, Cambridge, MA: Harvard University Press, 1997, 296–99.

*Offener Horizont, Festschrift für Karl Jaspers*, München: Piper, 1953.

Olmsted, Frederick Law: *A Journey in the Seaboard Slave States. With Remarks on their Economy*, New York, 1856.

Oppenheim, Heinrich Bernhard: 'Zur Kritik der Demokratie in Deutschland'. In: *Deutsche Monatsschrift für Politik, Wissenschaft, Kunst und Leben*, 1 (1850), pp. 7 et seq.

Oresme, Nicole: *Le livre de éthique d'Aristote*, ed. by Albert D. Menut, New York: G.E. Stechert, 1940.

——'Le livre de politiques d'Aristote'. In: *Transactions of the American Philosophical Society*, vol. 60, Teil 6, Herausgegeben von Albert Douglas Menut, Philadelphia: American Philosophical Society, 1970.

Otto, Hans Uwe/Merten, Roland: 'Rechtsradikale Gewalt im vereinigten Deutschland: Jugend im Kontext von Gewalt, Rassismus und Rechtsextremismus'. In: ditto (eds): *Rechtsradikale Gewalt im vereinigten Deutschland. Jugend im gesellschaftlichen Umbruch*, Opladen: Leske und Buderich, 1993, pp. 13–33.

*The Oxford English Dictionary*, vol. III, Oxford: Clarendon Press, 1961.

Pabst, Manfred: Sozialpsychologische Problem der Herausbildung des Linksradikalismus der 60er Jahre in den entwickelten kapitalistischen Ländern, besonders in der BRD und in Westberlin, Diss. A, Philosophische Fakultät, Martin-Luther-Universität Halle-Wittenberg, Halle, 1984.

Paléologue, Maurice: *La Russie des tsars pendant la grande guerre. 19 août 1916–17 mai 1917*, Paris: Plon, 1922.

Panzini, Alfredo: *Dizionario Moderno. Supplemento ai Dizionari Italiani*, 4° edizione rinnovata e aumentata Milano: U. Hoepli, 1923.

Paquet, Alfons: 'Die Wendung des russischen Imperialismus'. In: *Die Glocke*, 3 (1918) 49 (9 March), pp. 852–61.

——*Im kommunistischen Russland. Briefe aus Moskau*, Jena: Diedrichs, 1919.

*Der Parlamentarische Rat 1948–49. Akten und Protokolle*, Vol. 13: Ausschuss für Organisation des Bundes/Ausschuss für Verfassungsgerichtshof und Rechtspflege, bearbeitet von Edgar Büttner und Michael Wettengel, semi vol. I & II, München, 2002.

Pascal, Blaise: *Pensées publiées dans leur texte authentique*, avec une introduction, des notes et des remarques par Ernest Havet, 5th éd. revue et corrigée, vol. 1, Paris: Delagrave, 1897.

PDI-Blick nach rechts, Sonderausgabe No. 5, August 1982: 'Streit und Intrigen in der Strauß-Partei'.

PDI (ed.), Die Union und der Neonazismus. Verharmlosung als Methode, PDI-Sonderheft No. 13, München: PDI, 1980.

Pekonen, Kyösti: *The New Radical Right in Finland*, Kopijyvä, 1999.

Pirker, Theo (ed.): *Komintern und Faschismus. Dokumente zur Geschichte und Theorie des Faschismus*, Stuttgart: Deutsche Verlagsanstalt, 1965.

Plato: *Werke* in acht Bänden, Griechisch und Deutsch, herausgegeben von Gunther Eigler, Sonderausgabe, Darmstadt: Wissenschaftliche Buchgesellschaft, 1990.

——*Laws*, translated by Benjamin Jowett, Mineola/New York: Dover; David & Charles, 2006.

——'Nomoi'. In: ditto, *Werke*, vol. 8/1 and 2.

——'Politeia'. In: Platon, *Werke*, vol. 4.

——'Politikos'. In: ditto, *Werke*, vol. 6.

——*The Republic*, ed. by G.R.F. Ferrari, translated by Tom Griffith, Cambridge: Cambridge University Press, 2000.

——'Timaios'. In: ditto, *Werke*, vol. 7.

Plessner, Helmut: *Grenzen der Gemeinschaft. Eine Kritik des sozialen Radikalismus*, 9th edition, Bonn: F. Cohen, 1924.

Plutarch: *Lives*, with an English translation by Bernardotte Perrin, vol. II, Cambridge/London: W. Heinemann, 1985.

——*Vitae Parallelae* = Plutarchi Chaeronensis quae supersunt, omnia: graece et latine, vol. 1, principibus ex editionibus castigavit, virorumque doctorum suisque annotationibus instruxit Johann Jacob Reiske, Leipzig, 1774.

Polak, Karl: 'Der Prozeß gegen die KPD – ein Bestandteil der Kriegspolitik der Adenauer-Regierung'. In: *Einheit*, 8 (1953), pp. 702–13.

*Politischer Protest in der Bundesrepublik Deutschland. Beiträge zur sozialempirischen Untersuchung des Extremismus.* Eine Arbeit der Infratest Wirtschaftsforschung GmbH, Stuttgart: Kohlhammer, 1980.

*Politischer Protest in der sozialwissenschaftlichen Literatur.* Eine Arbeit der Infratest Wirtschaftsforschung GmbH, Stuttgart: Kohlhammer, 1978.

Pölitz, Karl Heinrich Ludwig: *Die Staatswissenschaften im Lichte unserer Zeit*, vol. 1, Leipzig: Hinrichs, 1823.

——'Friedrich Ancillon als politischer Schriftsteller'. In: *Jahrbücher für Geschichte und Staatskunst*, 10 (1837), pp. 289–313.

Polybios: *Geschichte*. Gesamtausgabe in zwei Bänden, eingeleitet und übertragen von Hans Drexler, Zürich/Stuttgart: Artemis, 1961.

Ponet, John: A Shorte Treatise of politike pouuer, and of the true obedience which subiectes owe to kynges and other ciuile Gouvernours, with an Exhortacion to all true naturall Englishe men, compyled by D.I.P.B.R. VV., o.O., 1556 (unpaginiert).

Poore, Perley: *The Political Register and Congressional Directory.* A Statistical Record of the Federal Officials, Legislative, Executive, and Judicial, of the United States of America, 1776–1878, Boston, MA: Houghton, Osgood and Co., 1878.

Popper, Karl R.: *Das Elend des Historizismus*, fünfte verbesserte Auflage, Tübingen: Mohr, 1979 (1965).

——*The Open Society and Its Enemies*, vol. I: The spell of Plato, reprint, London/New York: Routledge, 1993.

Protokoll der 6th Sitzung des Kombinierten Ausschusses vom 24 September 1948. In: *Der Parlamentarische Rat 1948–49*, semi vol. I.

Ptolemy of Lucca: *On the Government of Rulers/De Regimine Principum*, with portions attributed to Thomas Aquinas, translated by James M. Blythe, Philadelphia, 1997.

Publius (Madison), Federalist No. 14. In: Alexander Hamilton/James Madison/John Jay, *Die Federalist Papers*, übersetzt, eingeleitet und mit Anmerkungen versehen von Barbara Zehnpfennig, Darmstadt: WBG, 1993, pp. 114–19.

Quendt, Eugen: 'Sozialisten und Kommunisten in Frankreich'. In: *Deutsche Politik*, 6 (1921) 26, pp. 614–17.

*Qui êtes-vous? Annuaire des contemporains, notices biographiques*, Paris: Ruffy, 1924.

Qutb, Sayyid: *Milestones*, http://web.youngmuslims.ca/online_library/books/milestones/hold/index_2.htm (accessed 6 July 2009).

Radowitz, Joseph Maria von: 'Der Kampf der Extreme'. In: ditto, *Ausgewählte Schriften*, hg. von Wilhelm Corvinus, vol. 2, Regensburg: Habbel, o.J. (1916), pp. 432 et seq.

Ramsay, Andreas Michael: Essai sur le Gouvernement civil, où l'on traite de la Nécessité, de l'Origine, des Droits, des Bornes, & des differentes formes de la Souveraineté; selon les Principes De feu M. François de Salignac de la Mothe-Fénelon, Archevêque Duc de Cambray, troisième édition, revûë, corrigée, & augmentée, London: Compagnie, 1722.

Rathmann, August: 'Positiver Radikalismus'. In: *Neue Blätter für den Sozialismus*, 2 (1931) 1, pp. 1–7.

Raumer, Frederick von: *America and the American People* (1846), reprint, translated by William W. Turner, New York, 1970.

Reed, John: *Zehn Tage, die die Welt erschütterten* (1919), Berlin (Ost): Dietz, 1984.

Richter, Friedrich/Wrona, Vera: 'Ideologie des Sozialdemokratismus in der Gegenwart'. In: *Einheit*, 28 (1972), pp. 221–27.

Riehl, Jürgen: 'Der Kampf geht weiter. Überlegungen zur Strategie, Weltanschauung und Sprache'. In: *Recht und Wahrheit*, 10 (1994) 7/8, p. 12.

Ritter, Joachim (ed.): *Historisches Wörterbuch der Philosophie*, neubearb. Ausgabe des 'Wörterbuchs der Philosophischen Begriffe' von Rudolf Eisler, vol. 2, Stuttgart, 1972.

Roberts, W.R.: 'The Fenians in America'. In: *The Daily Telegraph* (London), 29 December 1865, p. 2.

Rohmer, Friedrich: *Lehre von den politischen Parteien*, Erster Teil: Die Vier Parteien, durch Theodor Rohmer, Zürich: Beyel, 1844.

Rohrbach, Paul: 'Die radikale Linke und die Revolution in Russland'. In: *Deutsche Politik*, 2 (1917) 17, pp. 521–28.

Rokeach, Milton: *The Open and Closed Mind*, New York: Basic Books, 1960.

——*Political and Religious Dogmatism: An Alternative to the Authoritarian Personality*, Psychological Monographs: General and Applied, vol. 70, no. 18, Washington, DC, 1956.

Rolland, Romain: *Journal des années de guerre 1914–19*. Notes et documents pour servir à l'histoire morale de l'Europe de ce temps, texte établi par Marie Romain Rolland, Paris: Albin Michel, 1952.

Rotteck, Karl von: 'Vorwort zur ersten Auflage (1834)'. In: ditto/Welcker (eds), *Staats-Lexikon*, vol. 1, pp. III–XXIII.

——Art. 'Abgeordnete' (1835). In: ditto/Welcker (eds), *Staatslexikon*, vol. 1, pp. 102–11.

——Art. 'Census' (1836). In: ditto/Welcker (eds), *Staatslexikon*, vol. 3, pp. 145–60.

——Welcker, Karl Theodor (eds): *Das Staats-Lexikon*. Encyclopädie der sämtlichen Staatswissenschaften für alle Stände, zweite Auflage, mit einer Einleitung zum Neudruck von Hartwig Brandt, Frankfurt a.M.: Keip, 1990.

Rousseau, Jean-Jacques: *Der Gesellschaftsvertrag oder Die Grundsätze des Staatsrechts*, mit einer Einleitung von Paul Ritterbusch, Leipzig, undated.

Ruas, Henrique Barrilaro: Art. 'Extremismo'. In: *Polis. Enciclopédia VERBO da Sociedado e do Estado. Antropologia – Direito – Economia – Ciência Política*, vol. 2, Lissabon, 1984, Sp. 1346–50.

Ruge, Arnold: 'Kritik und Partei. Der Vorwurf gegen die neueste Geistesentwicklung'. In: *Deutsche Jahrbücher für Wissenschaft und Kunst*, 5 (1842) 294 (10 December), 295 (12 December), 296 (13 December), pp. 1175 et seq., 1177–80, 1181 et seq.

Rühle, Otto: 'Schriften. Brauner und Roter Faschismus (1939)'. In: ditto: *Schriften. Perspektiven einer Revolution in hochindustrialisierten Ländern*. Herausgegeben von Gottfried Mergner, Reinbek: Rowohlt, 1971, pp. 7–71.

Saposs, David J.: 'The Rôle of the Middle Class in Social Development. Fascism, Populism, Communism, Socialism'. In: *Economic Essays in Honour of Wesley Clair Mitchell*, presented to him by his former students on the occasion of his sixtieth birthday, New York: Columbia University Press, 1935, pp. 393–424.

Sartori, Giovanni: *Parties and Party Systems: A Framework for Analysis*, 2nd edition, New York: Cambridge University Press, 1993.

Sayers, Michael/Kahn, Albert E.: *Sabotage! The Secret War Against America*, New York: Harper & Brothers, 1942.

Schadow, Dietmar: Marxistisch–leninistische Politökonomische Auseinandersetzung mit den Angriffen des gegenwärtigen Linksradikalismus auf den realen Sozialismus, Diss. A, Gesellschaftswissenschaftliche Fakultät, Humboldt-Universität Berlin, Berlin, 1982.

Scheuch, Erwin K., unter Mitarbeit von Hans D. Klingemann: 'Theorie des Rechtsradikalismus in westlichen Industriegesellschaften'. In: *Hamburger Jahrbuch für Wirtschafts- und Gesellschaftspolitik*, 12 (1967), pp. 11–29.

——'Die NPD als rechtsextreme Partei'. In: *Hamburger Jahrbuch für Wirtschafts- und Gesellschaftspolitik*, 15 (1970), pp. 320–33.

——'Politischer Extremismus in der Bundesrepublik'. In: Richard Löwenthal/Hans-Peter Schwarz (eds): *Die zweite Republik. 25 Jahre Bundesrepublik Deutschland – eine Bilanz*, 2nd edition, Stuttgart: Seewald, 1974, pp. 433–69.

——'Zum Wiedererstehen der Erlösungsbewegungen'. In: Kurt Sontheimer/Gerhard A. Ritter/Brita Schmitz-Hübsch/Paul Kevenhörster/Erwin K. Scheuch: *Der Überdruss an der Demokratie. Neue Linke und alte Rechte – Unterschiede und Gemeinsamkeiten*, Köln: Markus, 1970, pp. 129–206.

Schirdewan, Karl: 'Die westdeutschen Wahlen zum Bundestag'. In: *Einheit*, 4 (1949), pp. 873–82.

Schleifstein, Josef: 'Gedanken zur Bewegung der studentischen Jugend in Westdeutschland'. In: *Einheit*, 24 (1968), pp. 912–14.

Schmidt, Max/Schröder, Otto: 'Der Angriff der Ultras auf die Reste der bürgerlichen Demokratie in Westdeutschland'. In: *Einheit*, 18 (1962), pp. 130–42.

Schnitter, Helmut: 'Die Bonner Ultras und die Atomstreitmacht der NATO'. In: *Einheit*, 21 (1965), pp. 66–74.

Schramm, Wilhelm von: *Radikale Politik. Die Welt diesseits und jenseits des Bolschewismus*, München: Duncker & Humblot, 1932.

Schreiben der Militärgouverneure vom 14 April 1949 an den Parlamentarischen Rat über die Regelung der der Bundesregierung auf dem Gebiet der Polizei zustehenden Befugnisse, abgedruckt bei Hermann von Mangoldt, *Das Bonner Grundgesetz*, Berlin: Vahlen, 1953, Anhang Nr. 1.

Schröder, Otto: 'Der westdeutsche Neonazismus in NPD und CDU/CSU'. In: *Einheit*, 23 (1967), pp. 208–26.

Schulz, Wilhelm: Art. 'Communismus'. In: Rotteck/Welcker (eds): *Staats-Lexikon*, vol. XI, pp. 290–339.

——Art. 'Revolution' (1842). In: Staatslexikon, vol. XI, pp. 550–62.

——*Deutsches Noth- und Hilfsbüchlein für vorsichtig liberale Esser und Trinker*. Mit drei unsichtbaren Bildern von berühmten Meistern, und einem unpassenden, aber keineswegs überflüssigen Anhange. Zur lustigen Fastnachtszeit des Jahres 1844, Zürich/Winterthur: Literar, 1844.

Schüßlburner, Josef: 'Liberalextremismus'. In: *Staatsbriefe* 9/10 (1996), pp. 5–18.

Schwab, Jürgen: 'Wer unterwandert die deutschen Burschenschaften – nationale Intellektuelle oder der Verfassungsschutz?' In: *Deutsche Stimme*, No. 7/2001, pp. 16 et seq.

Schwarz, Christian Wilhelm: *Gedanken über die richtige Mitte in der innern Politik, den Bürgern der Stadt Ulm mitgetheilt und gewidmet von ihrem designierten Abgeordneten zur nächsten Ständeversammlung*, Ulm: Wohler, 1832.

Severing, Karl: 'Der Kampf gegen den Radikalismus. Die Wirtschaftsnot und die extremen Parteien'. In: *Neue Freie Presse* (Wien), 29 March 1931.

——*Mein Lebensweg*, vol. II: Im Auf und Ab der Republik, Köln: Greven, 1950.

Seyssel, Claude de: *La Grand' Monarchie de France*, Paris: Galiot Du Pré, 1557.

Shils, Edward A.: 'Authoritarianism: "Right" and "Left"'. In: Richard Christie/Marie Jahoda (eds): *Studies in the Scope and Method of 'The Authoritarian Personality'*. Continuities in Social Research, Glencoe, IL: Free Press, 1954, pp. 24–49.

——*The Torment of Secrecy. The Background and Consequences of American Security Policies*, Melbourne: Heinemann, 1956.

Sidney, Algernon: *Discourses Concerning Government*, edited by Thomas G. West, Indianapolis: Liberty Classics, 1990.

Sinanoglou, Ioannis: 'Einführung'. In: *Les Cahiers du monde russe et soviétique*, 14 (1973) 1–2, pp. 86–92.

Smyth, T.S. [Lord Bishop of Exeter]: The Tendency to Extremes in Religious Opinions, shewn and constrasted with the moderation of the Church of England. A Sermon, preached at the Visitation, held at Bodmin, 24 July 1828.

Solon: 'Die große Staatselegie'. In: ditto, *Dichtungen*. Sämtliche Fragmente, im Versmaß des Urtextes ins Deutsche übertragen von Eberhard Preime, 3rd edition, München: Heimeran, 1945, pp. 17–19.

——'Elegiac poetry'. In: Douglas E. Gerber (ed.), *Greek Elegiac Poetry. From the Seventh to the Fifth Centuries BC*, Cambridge/London: Harvard University Press, 1999, pp. 106–65.

Sophokles: 'Oidipus auf Kolonos'. In: ditto, *Tragödien*, übersetzt von Wilhelm Willige, überarbeitet von Karl Bayer, mit einer Einführung und Erläuterungen von Bernhard Zimmermann, München: DTV, 1990, pp. 319–76.

——'Oedipus at Colonos'. In: *The Death-Song of Thamyris and other Poems*, done into English verse by E.H. Pember, London: Printed at the Chiswick Press, 1899, pp. 103–200.

Staatsministerium des Innern/Landesamt für Verfassungsschutz Sachsen (eds): *Verfassungsschutzbericht 1993. Ereignisse, Gruppierungen, Hintergründe*, Dresden, 1994.

Staël-Holstein, Madame de: 'De l'influence des passions sur le bonheur des individus et des nations (1796)'. In: *Œuvres complètes*, Genève: Slatkine Reprints, 1967, vol. I.

Stasch, Albert: 'Eine Theorie des Neofaschismus'. In: *Einheit*, 2 (1947), pp. 629–43.

Stöss, Richard: 'Einleitung: Struktur und Entwicklung des Parteiensystems der Bundesrepublik – Eine Theorie'. In: ditto (ed.): *Parteien-Handbuch. Die Parteien der Bundesrepublik Deutschland 1945–80*, vol. 1: AUD bis EFP, Opladen: Westdeutscher Verlag, 1983, pp. 17–309.

——*Rechtsextremismus im vereinten Deutschland*, Bonn: FES, 1999.

Sturzo, Luigi: 'Il nostro "centrismo"'. In: *Il Popolo Nuovo* (Roma), 26 August 1923. Wiederabdruck in: ditto, *Il Partito Popolare Italiano*, vol. 2: Popolarismo e Fascismo, Torino, 1924, pp. 241–48.

——*Pensiero antifascista*, Torino: Gobetti, 1925.

——*L'Italie et le fascisme*, Paris: F. Alcan, 1927.

——*El estado totalitario*, Madrid 1935.

Sybel, Heinrich von: *Die politischen Parteien der Rheinprovinz in ihrem Verhältniß zur preußischen Verfassung geschildert*, Düsseldorf: Buddeus, 1847.

Tchernoff, Jouda: *L'extrême-gauche socialiste-révolutionnaire en 1870/71*, Paris: Bureaux de l'Action Nationale, 1918 (Collection de l'Action Nationale).

Telegramm der deutschen Botschaft in Stockholm an das Berliner Ministerium vom 20 März 1917, abgedruckt bei André Scherer/Jacques Grunewald (eds), *L'Allemagne et les problèmes de la paix pendant la première guerre mondiale*. Documents extraits des archives de l'Office allemand des Affaires étrangères, Paris: Presses Univ. de France, 1966, p. 42.

Theophrast: *Charaktere, übersetzt und herausgegeben von Dietrich Klose*, mit einem Nachwort von Peter Steinmetz, Stuttgart: Reclam, 1970.

Theophrastus: *Characters*. Edited with an introduction, translation and commentary by James Diggle, Cambridge: Cambridge University Press, 2004.

Thiers, Adolphe: *Discours parlementaires*, publiés par M. Calmon, première partie (1830–36), vols II & III, Paris: Calmann Lévy, 1879.

——*La Monarchie de 1830*, Paris: A. Mesnier, 1831.

Thirty and two Extremes of these times discovered and reduced to sixteene Golden Meanes, tending to the reducing of strayers, the stablishing of Waverers, and the uniting of Judgements and Hearts together in the Truth, London, 1647 (British Library 669. f. 11. [66]).

Thomas, Albert: 'Journal de Russie'. In: *Les Cahiers du monde russe et soviétique*, 14 (1973) 1–2, pp. 93–204.

Thomas von Aquin: *Opera omnia*, ut sunt in indice thomistico additis 61 scriptis ex aliis medii aevi auctoribus, curante Roberto Busa S.I., vol. 4: Commentaria in Aristotelem et alios, Stuttgart-Bad Cannstatt: Frommann-Holzboog, 1980.

——*De regimine principum ad regem Cypri et De regimine Judaeorum ad ducissam Brabantiae*, politica opuscula duo, ad finem optimarum editionum diligenter recusa, Joseph Mathis curante, Torino/Roma: Marietti, 1948.

——*Summe der Theologie*, zusammengefasst, eingeleitet und erläutert von Joseph Bernhart, vol. 2: Die sittliche Weltordnung, 3rd edition, Stuttgart: Kröner, 1985.

——*Über die Herrschaft der Fürsten*, Übersetzung von Friedrich Schreyvogel, Nachwort von Ulrich Matz, Stuttgart: Reclam, 1999.

Thukydides: *Geschichte des Peloponnesischen Krieges*, griechisch–deutsch, übersetzt und mit einer Einführung und Erläuterung versehen von Georg Peter Landmann, München: Artemis & Winkler, 1993, pt. 2.

*Trésor de la Langue Française. Dictionnaire de la Langue du XIXe et du XXe siècle* (1789–1960), vol. 8, Paris: CNRS, 1980.

Tronti, Mario: *Extremismus und Reformismus*, Berlin: Merve, 1971.

Ulbricht, Walter: 'Bemerkungen zu den Beziehungen zwischen der DDR und der BRD'. In: ND vom 16 Juni 1970.

——*Die gegenwärtige Lage und die neuen Aufgaben der Sozialistischen Einheitspartei Deutschlands*. Referat und Schlusswort auf der II Parteikonferenz der SED, Berlin, 9 bis 12 Juli 1952, Berlin (Ost): Dietz, 1952.

——'Rede auf einer Wahlversammlung der Nationalen Front des demokratischen Deutschland in Ost-Berlin (25 August 1961)'. In: *Dokumente zur Deutschlandpolitik*, IV Reihe, vol. 7/1, pp. 231–41.

Ullrich, Siegfried: 'Ist der Neofaschismus in der BRD eine reale Gefahr?' In: *Einheit*, 35 (1980), pp. 1314–18.

US Department of Justice/FBI (eds): *Terrorism 2000/2001*, Washington DC, 2004.

Valéry, Paul: *Lettres à quelques-uns*, Paris: Gallimard, 1952.

Vandervelde, Émile: *Trois aspects de la Révolution russe, 7 mai–25 juin 1917*, Paris: Berger-Levrault, 1918.

Verhandlungen der badischen Zweiten Kammer, 1822, vol. 8, pp. 145 et seq. Zitiert nach Kramer, Fraktionsbindungen, p. 42.

Verhandlungen des Reichstags, 1st Wahlperiode, vol. 361, 391. Sitzung vom 20 November 1923 und 392. Sitzung vom 22 November 1923.

Verner, Paul: 'Zu den Bundestagswahlen in Westdeutschland'. In: *Einheit*, 8 (1953), pp. 1003–11.

The Via Media. An Ecclesiastical Chart, showing that the Church of England holds the middle place of Truth between the two extremes of Sectarian Error and Popish Heresy, Haselbury, June 1843.

Vogel, Emil Ferdinand: *D. Wilhelm Traugott Krug in drey vertraulichen Briefen an einen Freund im Auslande*, Neustadt an der Orla: Wagner, 1844.

Voltaire: 'Extrême'. In: Diderot: *Œuvres complètes*, nouvelle édition, Dictionnaire philosophique III, Paris 1879, reprint Nendeln/Lichtenstein: Kraus, 1967, vol. 19, pp. 52–54.

Washington, George: 'Brief an den Marquis de Lafayette, 10 Juni 1792'. In: ditto, *Writings*, edited by John C. Fitzpatrick, from the original manuscript sources 1754–99, vol. 32, Washington DC: US Government Printing Office, 1939.

Webster, Daniel: 'The Constitution and the Union'. Speech of 7 March 1850. In: ditto, *Works*, vol. 5, Boston, MA: Little & Brown, 1851, pp. 324–67.

Weichold, Jochen: Probleme des Linksradikalismus in unserer Epoche. Eine vergleichende Studie zu den Ursachen des Linksradikalismus in den entwickelten kapitalistischen Ländern in den drei Etappen der allgemeinen Krise des Kapitalismus, Diss. B, Akademie für Gesellschaftswissenschaften beim ZK der SED, Institut für Imperialismusforschung, Berlin (Ost), 1985.

Weiß, Heinrich L.: 'Die Gefahr des Radikalismus'. In: *Deutschlands Erneuerung*, 7 (1932), pp. 413–16.

Weißbecker, Manfred: 'Die historisch–politische Funktion des Neonazismus und der Nationaldemokratischen Partei in Westdeutschland'. In: ZfG, 16 (1968), pp. 837–54.

——'Der Faschismus in der Gegenwart: Grundlagen – Erscheinungsformen – Aktivitäten – Organisationen'. In: Klaus Drobisch et al., *Faschismus in Deutschland – Faschismus der Gegenwart*, Köln: Pahl-Rugenstein, 1980, pp. 249–79.

——Wimmer, Walter: 'Wesen und Erscheinungsformen des Faschismus'. In: *Einheit*, 38 (1983), pp. 485–91.

Welcker, Karl Theodor: *Die Universal- und die juristisch-politische Encyclopädie und Methodologie zum Gebrauche bei Vorlesungen und für das Selbststudium. Das innere und äußere System*, vol. 1, Stuttgart: Metzler, 1829.

——Art. 'Ancillon' (1845). In: Rotteck/Welcker (eds): *Staatslexikon*, vol. 1, pp. 519–28.

Werro, R.: *Les partis extrêmes dans le Canton de Fribourg*, 1848.

Wieland, Christoph Martin: 'Die Französische Republik (September 1792)'. In: Günther (ed.), *Die Französische Revolution*, pp. 517–36.

——'Unparteiische Betrachtungen über die dermalige Staats-Revolution in Frankreich (1790)'. In: Günther (ed.), *Die Französische Revolution*, pp. 485–517.

Wilbert, Alc. [ibiade], avocat: 'Qu'est-ce que le côté droit? ou Itinéraire du Ministère Polignac', tracé par les membres de l'extrême droite depuis le 14 octobre 1815 jusqu'au 31 juillet 1829, Paris, 1829.

Williams, Harold: *The Spirit of the Russian Revolution*, London: Avenue Press, 1919.

Winkler, Arno: *Neo-Faschismus in der BRD. Erscheinungen, Hintergründe, Gefahren*, Berlin (Ost): Dietz, 1980.

Wippermann, Wolfgang: '"Doch ein Begriff muss bei dem Worte sein". Über "Extremismus", "Faschismus", "Totalitarismus" und "Neofaschismus"'. In: Siegfried Jäger/Alfred Schobert (eds): *Weiter auf unsicherem Grund. Faschismus – Rechtsextremismus – Rassismus. Kontinuitäten und Brüche*, Duisburg: DISS, 2000, pp. 21–47.

——'Verfassungsschutz und Extremismusforschung: Falsche Perspektiven'. In: Jens Mecklenburg (ed.): *Braune Gefahr. DVU, NPD, REP – Geschichte und Zukunft*, Berlin: Elefanten Press, 1999, pp. 268–80.

*Wörterbuch des Wissenschaftlichen Kommunismus*, Berlin (Ost): Dietz, 1982.

X Parteitag der SED. 11 bis 16 April 1981 in Berlin. Bericht des Zentralkomitees der Sozialistischen Einheitspartei Deutschlands an den X Parteitag der SED. Berichterstatter: Genosse Erich Honecker, Berlin (Ost): Dietz, 1981.

Zedler, Johann Heinrich: *Großes vollständiges Universal-Lexicon aller Wissenschaften und Künste*, vol. 9, Halle: Zedler, 1735.

## 2 Literature

Aalders, G.J.D.: *Die Theorie der gemischten Verfassung im Altertum*, Amsterdam: Hakkert, 1968.

Ackermann, Josef: *Heinrich Himmler als Ideologe*, Göttingen: Musterschmidt, 1970.

Adler, Max K.: *Naming and Addressing. A Sociolinguistic Study*, Hamburg: Buske Helmut, 1978.

Albert, Hans: 'Das Gewissheitsbedürfnis und die Suche nach Wahrheit. Ideologisches Denken zwischen Fundamentalismus und Pragmatismus'. In: Friedrich Schneider/ Rudolf Strasser/Klar Vodrazka (eds): *Pragmatismus versus Fundamentalismus*, Wien: Orac, 1993, pp. 11–30.

Albertini, Rudolf von: *Das florentinische Staatsbewusstsein im Übergang von der Republik zum Prinzipat*, Bern: Francke, 1955.

Altemeyer, Bob: *The Authoritarian Specter*, Cambridge, MA: Harvard University Press, 1996.

Annas, Julia: 'Platon'. In: Fetscher/Münkler, *Piper's Handbuch*, vol. 1, pp. 369–95.

Armstrong, Colin D.C.: 'Gardiner, Stephen'. In: *Oxford Dictionary of National Biography*, Oxford: Oxford University Press, 2004, pp. 435–59.

Art. 'Lozovsky'. In: Jean Maitron (ed.), *Dictionnaire Biographique du Mouvement Ouvrier Français*, troisième partie: 1871–1914, vol. 13, Paris: Editions Ouvriéres, 1975.

Arzheimer, Kai/Falter, Jürgen W.: 'Die Pathologie des Normalen. Eine Anwendung des Scheuch-Klingemann-Modells zur Erklärung rechtsextremen Denkens und Verhaltens'. In: Fuchs/Roller/Wessels (eds), *Bürger und Demokratie*, pp. 85–107.

Avril, Pierre: 'Radicalisme'. In: Olivier Duhamel/Yves Mény (eds), *Dictionnaire Constitutionnel*, Paris: Presses Univ. de France, 1992, pp. 856 et seq.

Baal, Gérard: *Histoire du radicalisme*, Paris: Éd. La Découverte, 1994.

Backes, Uwe: 'Extrême, Extrémité, Extrémisme. Une esquisse de l'histoire de ces mots dans la langue politique française'. In: *Mots*, 55 (1998), pp. 142–52.

——*Liberalismus und Demokratie – Antinomie und Synthese. Zum Wechselverhältnis zweier politischer Strömungen im Vormärz*, Düsseldorf: Droste, 2000.

——*Politischer Extremismus in demokratischen Verfassungsstaaten. Elemente einer normativen Rahmentheorie*, Opladen: Westdeutscher Verlag, 1989.

——(ed.): *Rechtsextreme Ideologien in Geschichte und Gegenwart*, Köln: Böhlau, 2003.

——'Die Rechts-Links-Unterscheidung. Betrachtungen zu ihrer Geschichte, Logik, Leistungsfähigkeit und Problematik'. In: Backes/Jesse (eds), *Vergleichende Extremismusforschung*, pp. 99–120.

——'"Totalitäres Denken" – Konzeptgeschichte, Merkmale und herrschaftspraktische Wirkungen'. In: *Religion – Staat – Gesellschaft*, 4 (2003) 1, pp. 41–56.

——'Vom Marxismus zum Antitotalitarismus. Ernst Fraenkel und Richard Löwenthal'. In: Schmeitzner (ed.): *Totalitarismuskritik von links*, pp. 327–54.

——Courtois, Stéphane (eds): 'Ein Gespenst geht um in Europa'. In: *Das Erbe kommunistischer Ideologien*, Köln: Böhlau, 2002.

——Jesse, Eckhard: 'Antiextremistischer Konsens. Prinzipien und Praxis'. In: ditto (eds), *Vergleichende Extremismusforschung*, pp. 185–200.

——Jesse, Eckhard: 'Islamismus – Djihadismus – Totalitarismus – Extremismus. Herausforderungen des demokratischen Verfassungsstaates'. In: ditto (eds), *Vergleichende Extremismusforschung*, pp. 201–14.

——Jesse, Eckhard (eds): *Jahrbuch Extremismus & Demokratie*, vol. 1–6, Bonn: Bouvier, 1989–94, vol. 7–17, Baden-Baden: Nomos, 1995 et seq.

——Jesse, Eckhard: *Politischer Extremismus in der Bundesrepublik Deutschland*, vol. 1: Literatur, vol. 2: Analyse, vol. 3: Dokumentation, Köln: Verlag Wissenschaft und Politik, 1989.

——Jesse, Eckhard: *Politischer Extremismus in der Bundesrepublik Deutschland*, Neuausgabe, Bonn: Bundeszentrale für Politische Bildung, 1996.

——Jesse, Eckhard (eds): *Vergleichende Extremismusforschung*, Baden-Baden: Nomos, 2005.

Badura, Peter: 'Die Legitimation des Verfassungsschutzes'. In: Bundesamt für Verfassungsschutz (ed.), *Verfassungsschutz*, pp. 27–51.

Baldi, Marialuisa: *Verisimile, non vero. Filosofia e politica in Andrew Michael Ramsay*, Milano: Angeli, 2002.

Baron, Hans: *The Crisis of the Early Italian Renaissance. Civic Humanism and Republican Liberty in an Age of Classicism and Tyranny*, Princeton, NJ: Princeton University Press, 1966.

Barr, James: 'Fundamentalismus'. In: *Evangelisches Kirchenlexikon. Internationale theologische Enzyklopädie*, vol. 1, 3rd edition, Göttingen: Vandenhoeck & Ruprecht, 1986, pp. 1404–6.

Bärsch, Klaus-Eckehard: *Die politische Religion des Nationalsozialismus. Die religiöse Dimension der NS-Ideologie in den Schriften von Dietrich Eckart, Joseph Goebbels, Alfred Rosenberg und Adolf Hitler*, München: Fink, 1998.

Barudio, Günter: *Madame de Staël und Benjamin Constant. Spiele mit dem Feuer*, Berlin: Rowohlt, 1996.

Bauer, Yehuda: 'Der dritte Totalitarismus'. In: *Die Zeit*, 31 July 2003.

Baum, Wilhelm (ed.): 'Engelbert von Admont und die Aristotelesrezeption in Padua'. In: ditto, *Engelbert von Admont. Vom Ursprung und Ende des Reiches und andere Schriften*, Graz: Leykam, 1998, pp. 222–40.

Baumgartner, Gabriel: 'Schleifstein, Josef'. In: ditto/Dieter Hebig (eds): *Biographisches Handbuch der SBZ/DDR 1945–90*, vol. 2, München, 1997, p. 779.

Beetz, Manfred: 'Totalitäre Rhetorik und Konstruktivismus. Zu Goebbels' Proklamation des totalen Krieges im Berliner Sportpalast am 18 Februar 1943'. In: Albert F. Herbig (ed.), *Konzepte rhetorischer Kommunikation*, St. Ingbert: Röhrig, 1995, pp. 171–208.

Beißwenger, Michael: *Totalitäre Sprache und textuelle Konstruktion von Welt am Beispiel ausgewählter Aufsätze von Joseph Goebbels über 'die Juden'*, Stuttgart: Ibidem, 2000.

Belardinelli, Sergio: 'Die politische Philosophie des christlichen Personalismus'. In: Karl Graf Ballestrem/Henning Ottmann (eds), *Politische Philosophie des 20 Jahrhunderts*, München: Oldenbourg, 1990, pp. 243–62.

Bendel, Petra/Croissant, Aurel/Rüb, Friedbert W. (eds): *Zwischen Demokratie und Diktatur. Zur Konzeption und Empire demokratischer Grauzonen*, Opladen: Leske & Buderich, 2002.

Benoist, Alain de: *Communisme et nazisme. 25 réflexions sur le totalitarisme au XXe siècle (1917–89)*, Paris: Le Labyrinthe, 1998.

——*Demokratie: Das Problem*, Tübingen: Hohenrain, 1986.

Benz, Wolfgang: *Der Holocaust*, 5th edition, München: Beck, 2001.

Bergsdorf, Wolfgang: *Politik und Sprache*, München: Olzog, 1978.

Berlin-Brandenburgische Akademie der Wissenschaften (ed.): *Polybios-Lexikon*, bearbeitet von Arno Mauersberger, zweite verbesserte Auflage von Christian-Friedrich Collatz, Melsene Gützlaf und Hadwig Helms, vol. 1, Lieferung 1, Berlin, 2000, vol. 2, Lieferung 2, Berlin: Akademie, 2003.

Bernholz, Peter: 'Ideology, Sects, State and Totalitarianism: A General Theory'. In: Hans Maier/Michael Schäfer (eds), *Totalitarismus und politische Religion. Konzepte des Diktaturvergleichs*, vol. 2, Paderborn: Ferdinand, 1997, pp. 271–98.

——'Ideocracy and totalitarianism: A formal analysis incorporating ideology'. In: *Public Choice*, 108 (2001), pp. 33–75.

Bernstein, Eduard: *Wesen und Aussichten des bürgerlichen Radikalismus*, München: Duncker und Humblot, 1915.

Besier, Gerhard/Lindemann, Gerhard: *Im Namen der Freiheit. Die amerikanische Mission*, Göttingen: Vandenhoeck & Ruprecht, 2006.

——Lübbe, Hermann (eds): *Politische Religion und Religionspolitik. Zwischen Totalitarismus und Bürgerfreiheit*, Göttingen: Vandenhoeck und Ruprecht, 2005.

——Betz, Hans-Georg: *Postmodern Politics in Germany. The Politics of Resentment*, New York: St. Martin's Press, 1991.

Bianchi, Serge: 'Fanatique(s)/Fanatisme (1789–94)'. In: Annie Geffroy/Jacques Guil-haumon/Sylvia Moreno (eds), *Dictionnaire des usages socio–politiques (1770–1815)*, fasc. 1: Désignants socio-politiques, Paris: Klincksieck, 1985, pp. 71–78.

Biard, Roland: *Dictionnaire de l'extrême gauche de 1945 à nos jours*, Paris: Belfond, 1978.

Bielefeldt, Heiner: 'Von der päpstlichen Universalherrschaft zur autonomen Bürgerre-publik. Aegidius Romanus, Johannes Quidort von Paris, Dante Alighieri und Marsilius von Padua im Vergleich'. In: *Zeitschrift der Savigny-Stiftung für Rechtsgeschichte*. Kanonistische Abteilung, 73 (1987), pp. 70–130.

Bien, Günther: *Die Grundlegung der politischen Philosophie bei Aristoteles*, dritte unveränderte Auflage, Freiburg im Brsg.: Alber, 1985.

——'Revolution, Bürgerbegriff und Freiheit. Über die neuzeitliche Transformation der alteuropäischen Verfassungstheorie in politische Geschichtsphilosophie'. In: *Philo-sophisches Jahrbuch*, 79 (1972), pp. 1–18.

Bird, Karen L.: 'Racist Speech or Free Speech? A Comparison of the Law in France and the United States'. In: *Comparative Politics*, 32 (2000), pp. 399–418.

Bleek, Wilhelm: 'Friedrich Christoph Dahlmann (1785–1860)'. In: Heidenreich (ed.), *Politische Theorien*, pp. 329–41.

Bleicken, Jochen: *Die athenische Demokratie*, 2nd edition, Paderborn: Schöningh, 1994.

——'Zur Entstehung der Verfassungstypologie im 5. Jahrhundert v. Chr. (Monarchie, Aristokratie, Demokratie)'. In: *Historia*, 28 (1979), pp. 149–72.

Bluche, Frédéric: *Le bonpartisme. Aux origines de la droite autoritaire (1800–850)*, Paris: PUF, 1980.

Blythe, James M.: *Ideal Government and the Mixed Constitution in the Middle Ages*, Princeton, NJ: Princeton University Press, 1992.

Bobbio, Norberto: *Rechts und Links. Gründe und Bedeutung einer politischen Unterschei-dung*, Berlin: Klaus Wagenbach, 1994.

——Matteucci, Nicola/Pasquino, Gianfranco (eds): *Dizionario di Politica*, seconda edi-zione interamente riveduta e ampliata, Torino, 1983.

Böckstiegel, Elke: *Volksrepräsentation in Sachsen. Zur Entwicklung der Repräsentation des sächsischen Volkes von 1789 bis 1850*, München: VVF, 1998.

Boldt, Hans: *Deutsche Verfassungsgeschichte*, vol. 2: Von 1806 bis zur Gegenwart, München: DTV, 1990.

Bongiovanni, Bruno: 'Massimalismo'. In: Bobbio/Matteucci/Pasquino (eds), *Dizionario di Politica*, pp. 641 et seq.

Bonnefous, Édouard: *Notice sur la vie et les travaux de Maxime Leroy (1873–1957)*, lue dans la séance du 2 mars 1959, Paris: impr. Firmin-Didot et Cie, 1959.

Borgs-Maciejewski, Hermann (ed.): *Radikale im öffentlichen Dienst. Dokumente, Debatten, Urteile*, Bonn-Bad Godesberg: Godesberger Taschenbuch-Verl., 1973.

Borst, Arno: 'Religiöse und geistige Bewegungen im Hochmittelalter'. In: *Propyläen Weltgeschichte*, Herausgegeben von Golo Mann und August Nitschke, vol. 5, Berlin/Frankfurt a.M.: Propyläen, 1991, pp. 489–561.

Bose, Harald von: *Republik und Mischverfassung – zur Staatsformenlehre der Federalist Papers*, Frankfurt a.M.: Lang, 1989.

Boventer, Gregor: *Grenzen politischer Freiheit im demokratischen Staat. Das Konzept der streitbaren Demokratie in einem internationalen Vergleich*, Berlin: Duncker und Humblot, 1985.

Bracher, Karl-Dietrich: *Die totalitäre Erfahrung*, München: Piper, 1987.

——*Zeit der Ideologien. Eine Geschichte des politischen Denkens im 20 Jahrhundert*, Stuttgart: DVA, 1982.

Brandt, Hartwig: 'Karl von Rotteck (1775–1840)'. In: Heidenreich (ed.), *Politische Theorien*, pp. 369–82.

——*Landständische Repräsentation im deutschen Vormärz. Politisches Denken im Einflussfeld des monarchischen Prinzips*, Neuwied: Luchterhand, 1968.

——'Das Rotteck-Welckersche "Staats-Lexikon". Einleitung zum Neudruck'. In: Rotteck/Welcker (eds), *Das Staats-Lexikon*, vol. 1, pp. 5–27.

Brasart, Patrick: *Paroles de la Revolution. Les Assemblees parlementaires 1789–94*, Paris: Minerve, 1988.

Braunthal, Gerard: *Politische Loyalität und Öffentlicher Dienst. Der 'Radikalenerlass' von 1972 und seine Folgen*, Marburg: Schüren, 1992.

Breton, Albert/Galeotti, Gianluigi/Salmon, Pierre/Wintrobe, Ronald: 'Introduction'. In: ditto (eds), *Political Extremism and Rationality*, Cambridge: Cambridge University Press, 2002, pp. xi–xxi.

Breuer, Stefan: *Ästhetischer Fundamentalismus. Stefan George und der deutsche Antimodernismus*, Darmstadt: WBG, 1995.

——*Ordnungen der Ungleichheit. Die deutsche Rechte im Widerstreit ihrer Ideen 1871–1945*, Darmstadt: WBG, 2001.

Brudny, Michelle-Irène: 'Le totalitarisme: histoire du terme et statut du concept'. In: *Communisme*, 47/48 (1996), pp. 13–32.

Brugger, Winfried: 'Verbot oder Schutz von Hassrede? Rechtsvergleichende Beobachtungen zum deutschen und amerikanischen Recht'. In: AöR, 128 (2003), pp. 372–411.

Brühlmeier, Daniel: 'Verfassungstheorie und Grundrechtsdenken bei Montesquieu'. In: *Archiv für Rechts- und Sozialphilosophie*, 67 (1981), pp. 233–41.

Bruneteau, Bernard: *Les totalitarismes*, Paris: Colin, 1999.

Brunner, Otto/Conze, Werner/Koselleck, Reinhart (eds): *Geschichtliche Grundbegriffe. Historisches Wörterbuch zur politisch–sozialen Sprache in Deutschland*, 8 vols, Stuttgart 1972–97.

Brunot, Fernand: *Histoire de la langue française des origines à nos jours*, vol. IX: La Révolution et l'Empire, pt. 2: Les événements, les institutions et la langue, Paris: Colin, 1967.

Buchez, Philippe/Roux-Lavergne, Pierre: *Histoire parlementaire de la Révolution francaise. Journal des assemblées nationales depuis 1789 jusqu'en 1815*, Paris: Paulin, 1834.

Bundesamt für Verfassungsschutz (ed.): *Bundesamt für Verfassungsschutz. 50 Jahre im Dienst der inneren Sicherheit*, Köln: Heymanns, 2000.

——*Verfassungsschutz in der Demokratie. Beiträge aus Wissenschaft und Praxis*, Köln: Heymanns, 1999.

Buonarroti, Philippo: *Babeuf und die Verschwörung für die Gleichheit (1828), mit dem durch sie veranlassten Prozess und den Belegstücken*, übersetzt und eingeleitet von Anna und Wilhelm Blos, Stuttgart, 1909, Nachdruck, 2nd Edition, Berlin: Dietz, 1975.

Butterwegge, Christoph: *Rechtsextremismus, Rassismus und Gewalt. Erklärungsmodelle in der Diskussion*, Darmstadt: Primus, 1996.

Butterworth, Charles E.: 'Die politischen Lehren von Avicenna und Averroës'. In: Fetscher/ Münkler (eds), *Piper's Handbuch*, vol. 2, München: Piper, 1993, pp. 141–73.

Button, John: *The Radicalism Handbook. A Complete Guide to the Radical Movement in the Twentieth Century*, London: Cassell, 1995.

Cabet, Etienne: *Voyage en Icarie*, Paris: Au Bureau du Populaire, 1848.

Campanini, Giorgio: *Il pensiero politico di Luigi Sturzo*, Caltanissetta: Salvatore Sciascia Editore, 2001.

Canovan, Margaret: 'The Leader and the Masses. Hannah Arendt on Totalitarianism and Dictatorship'. In: Peter Baehr/Melvin Richter (eds), *Dictatorship in History and Theory. Bonapartism, Caesarism, and Totalitarianism*, Cambridge, MA: Cambridge University Press, 2004, pp. 241–60.

Canu, Isabelle: *Der Schutz der Demokratie in Deutschland und Frankreich. Ein Vergleich des Umgangs mit politischem Extremismus vor dem Hintergrund der europäischen Integration*, Opladen: Leske und Buderich, 1997.

Caponigri, A. Robert: 'Don Luigi Sturzo'. In: *The Review of Politics*, 14 (1952), pp. 147–65.

Carothers, Thomas: 'The End of the Transition Paradigm'. In: *Journal of Democracy*, 13 (2002), pp. 5–21.

Černych, P. Ja.: *Istoriko-ètimologičeskij slovar' sovremennogo russkogo jazyka*, vol. 2, Moskwa: Russkij Jazyk, 1994.

Chaimowicz, Thomas: *Freiheit und Gleichgewicht im Denken Montesquieus und Burkes. Ein analytischer Beitrag zur Geschichte der Lehre vom Staat im 18. Jahrhundert*, Wien: Springer, 1985.

Chehabi, H.E./Linz, Juan J. (eds): *Sultanistic Regimes*, Baltimore, MD: Johns Hopkins University Press, 1998.

Chenu, M.-D.: *Das Werk des Hl. Thomas von Aquin*, Heidelberg: Kerle, 1960.

Cherel, Albert: *Fénelon au XVIIIe siècle en France (1715–1820). Son prestige – son influence*, Paris: Hachette, 1917.

Chinard, Gilbert: 'Polybius and the American Constitution'. In: *Journal of the History of Ideas*, 1 (1940), pp. 38–58.

Chomsky, Noam: 'Powers and Prospects. Reflections on Human Nature and the Social Order'. In: Matthew Festenstein/Michael Kenny (eds): *Political Ideologies. A Reader and Guide*, Oxford: Oxford University Press, 2005, pp. 375–79.

Clark, Norman H.: 'Prohibition and Temperance'. In: Jack P. Greene (ed.), *Encyclopedia of American Political History. Studies of the Principal Movements and Ideas*, vol. 3, New York: Scribner, 1984, pp. 1005–17.

Colas, Dominique: *Civil Society and Fanaticism. Conjoined Histories*, Stanford, CA: Stanford University Press, 1997.

——'Säubernde und gesäuberte Einheitspartei: Lenin und der Leninismus'. In: Backes/Courtois (eds): *Ein Gespenst geht um in Europa*, pp. 147–86.

Coleman, Charles H.: 'The Use of the Term "Copperhead" During the Civil War'. In: *The Mississippi Valley Historical Review*, 25 (1938), pp. 263 et seq.

Connerton, Daniel Patrick: Karl Heinrich Ludwig Pölitz and the Politics of the Juste Milieu in Germany, 1794–1838, PhD thesis, University of North Carolina, Chapel Hill, NC, 1973.

Courtois, Stéphane et al.: *Das Schwarzbuch des Kommunismus. Unterdrückung, Verbrechen und Terror*, München: Piper, 1998.

Cox, Samuel S.: *Eight Years in Congress, from 1857 to 1865. Memoir and Speeches*, New York: Appleton, 1965.

Craig, Gordon A.: *Geschichte Europas 1815–1980. Vom Wiener Kongress bis zur Gegenwart*, München: Beck, 1983.

Dahl, Robert A.: *Polyarchy. Participation and Opposition*, New Haven, CN: Yale University Press, 1971.

Decker, Frank: 'Jenseits von rechts und links? Zum Bedeutungswandel der politischen Richtungsbegriffe'. In: Backes/Jesse (eds), *Jahrbuch Extremismus & Demokratie*, Baden-Baden: Nomos, vol. 10, pp. 33–48.

Defrasne, Jean: *La gauche en France de 1789 à nos jours*, 3rd Edition, Paris: Presses Univ. de France, 1983 (1972).

Demos, John: 'The Antislavery Movement and the Problem of Violent "Means"'. In: *The New England Quarterly*, 37 (1964), pp. 501–26.

Dempf, Alois: *Sacrum Imperium. Geschichts- und Staatsphilosophie des Mittelalters und der politischen Renaissance*, München/Berlin: Oldenbourg, 1929.

Desgraves, Louis: *Montesquieu*, Frankfurt a.M.: Frankfurter Societäts-Dr., 1992.

Detjen, Joachim: 'Pluralismus und klassische politische Philosophie'. In: *Jahrbuch für Politik*, 1 (1991), pp. 151–89.

Devegnaucourt, Gilles/Guignet, Philippe (eds): *Fénelon. Evêque et pasteur en son temps 1695–1715*, Paris, 1996.

Diehl-Thiele, Peter: *Partei und Staat im Dritten Reich. Untersuchung zum Verhältnis von NSDAP und allgemeiner innerer Staatsverwaltung*, München: Beck, 1969.

Dierse, Ulrich: 'Ideologie'. In: Brunner/Conze/Koselleck (eds), *Geschichtliche Grundbegriffe*, Stuttgart: Klett, vol. 3, pp. 131–69.

Dieter, Horst: 'Zum Begriff der Moderatio bei Cicero'. In: *Eirene* 6 (1967), pp. 69–91.

Dieter, Theodor: *Der junge Luther und Aristoteles. Eine historisch-systematische Untersuchung zum Verhältnis von Theologie und Philosophie*, Berlin: de Gruyter, 2001.

Dreitzel, Horst: *Absolutismus und ständische Verfassung in Deutschland. Ein Beitrag zu Kontinuität und Diskontinuität der politischen Theorie in der frühen Neuzeit*, Mainz: von Zabern, 1992.

Duberman, Martin (ed.), *The Antislavery Vanguard. New Essays on the Abolitionists*, Princeton, NJ: Princeton University Press, 1965.

Duhamel, Olivier/Mény, Yves (eds), *Dictionnaire Constitutionnel*, Paris: Presses Univ. de France, 1992.

Dumond, Dwight Lowell: *Antislavery Origins of the Civil War in the United States*, reprint Westport, CN: Greenwood Press, 1980 (1959).

Durand, Jean-Dominique: 'Italien'. In: Jean-Marie Mayeur et al. (eds), *Die Geschichte des Christentums. Religion – Politik – Kultur*, vol. 12: Erster und Zweiter Weltkrieg. Demokratien und Totalitäre Systeme (1914–58), Freiburg im Brsg.: Herder, 1992, pp. 440–98

Düring, Ingemar: *Von Aristoteles bis Leibniz. Einige Hauptlinien in der Geschichte des Aristotelismus*, Darmstadt: Wissenschaftliche Buchgesellschaft, 1968.

Eatwell, Roger: 'The Rise of "Left–Right" Terminology: The Confusions of Social Science'. In: ditto/O'Sullivan (eds), *Nature of the Right*, pp. 32–46.

——'Zur Natur des "generischen Faschismus"'. In: Backes (ed.): *Rechtsextreme Ideologien*, Köln, Wien: Böhlau, pp. 93–122.

——O'Sullivan, Noel (eds): *The Nature of the Right. American and European Politics and Political Thought since 1789*, Boston, MA: Twayne Publishers Inc., 1989.

Ehmke, Horst: *Karl von Rotteck, der 'politische Professor'*, Karlsruhe: C.F. Müller, 1964.

Eliasberg, George: *Der Ruhrkrieg von 1920*, Bonn-Bad Godesberg: Neue Gesellschaft, 1974.

Engrand, Charles: 'Les préoccupations politiques de Fénelon'. In: Devegnaucourt/Guignet (eds), *Fénelon*, pp. 233–42.

Ernstberger, Anton: *Ludwig Camerarius und Lukas Friedrich Behaim. Ein politischer Briefwechsel über den Verfall des Reiches 1636–48*, München: Beck, 1961.

——'Einleitung'. In: ditto (ed.): *Ludwig Camerarius*, pp. 1–19.

Eschenburg, Theodor: *Jahre der Besatzung 1945–49*, mit einem einleitenden Essay von Eberhard Jäckel, Stuttgart: DVA, 1983.

Estes, James M.: 'Melanchthon's Confrontation with the "Erasmian" Via media in Politics: The De officio principum of 1539'. In: Loehr (ed.), *Dona Melanchthoniana*, Stuttgart-Bad Cannstatt: Frommann-Holzboog, pp. 83–101.

*Europäischer Philhellenismus. Die europäische philhellenische Presse bis zur Hälfte des 19. Jahrhunderts*, Frankfurt a.M.: Lang, 1994.

Everts, Carmen: *Politischer Extremismus. Theorie und Analyse am Beispiel der Parteien REP und PDS*, Berlin: Weissensee, 2000.

Faille, R.: 'Autour de l'examen de conscience pour un roi de Fénelon'. In: *Revue française d'histoire du livre*, 1974, pp. 7–77.

Falter, Jürgen W.: *Hitlers Wähler*, München: Beck, 1991.

——'Radikalisierung des Mittelstandes oder Mobilisierung der Unpolitischen? Die Theorien von Seymour Martin Lipset und Reinhard Bendix über die Wählerschaft der NSDAP im Lichte neuerer Forschungsergebnisse'. In: Steinbach, Peter (ed.): *Probleme politischer Partizipation im Modernisierungsprozeß*, Stuttgart: Klett-Cotta, 1982, pp. 438–69.

Faul, Erwin: 'Verfemung, Duldung und Anerkennung des Parteiwesens in der Geschichte des politischen Denkens'. In: PVS, 5 (1964), pp. 60–80.

Fehrenbach, Elisabeth: *Verfassungsstaat und Nationsbildung 1815–71*, München: R. Oldenbourg, 1992.

Fenske, Hans: *Der moderne Verfassungsstaat. Eine vergleichende Verfassungsgeschichte von der Entstehung bis zum 20. Jahrhundert*, Paderborn: Schöningh, 2001.

Ferro, Marc: *La Révolution russe de 1917*, Paris: Mursia, 1967.

*Festschrift Herbert Batliner*, Vaduz: Rita Batliner, 1988.

Fetscher, Iring: *Joseph Goebbels im Berliner Sportpalast 1943 'Wollt ihr den totalen Krieg?'*, Hamburg: EVA, 1998.

——Münkler, Herfried (eds): *Piper's Handbuch der politischen Ideen*, vol. 1: Frühe Hochkulturen und europäische Antike; vol. 2: Mittelalter: Von den Anfängen des Islams bis zur Reformation; vol. 3: Neuzeit: Von den Konfessionskriegen bis zur Aufklärung; vol. 4: Nuzeit: Von der Französischen Revolution bis zum europäischen Nationalismus; vol. 5: Neuzeit: Vom Zeitalter des Imperialismus bis zu den neuen sozialen Bewegungen, München: Piper, 1985–93.

Fiedler, Alfred: *Die staatswissenschaftlichen Anschauungen und die politisch–publizistische Tätigkeit des Nachkantianers Wilhelm Traugott Krug*, Dresden: Risse, 1933.

Finer, Samuel E.: *The History of Government. From the Earliest Times*, vol. III: Empires, Monarchies, and the Modern State, Oxford: Oxford University Press, 1999.

Flasch, Kurt: *Das philosophische Denken im Mittelalter. Von Augustin zu Machiavelli*, Stuttgart: Reclam, 1986.

——*Das philosophische Denken im Mittelalter. Von Augustin zu Machiavelli*, zweite revidierte und erweiterte Auflage, Stuttgart: Reclam, 2001.

Flashar, Hellmut: 'Aristoteles'. In: *Überweg*, Antike 3, Basel: Schwabe, 1983, pp. 175–437.

——(ed.): *Die Philosophie der Antike*, vol. 4: Die hellenistische Philosophie, Basel: Schwabe, 1994.

Flüeler, Christoph: *Rezeption und Interpretation der Aristotelischen Politica im späten Mittelalter*, pt. 1, Amsterdam/Philadelphia: Grüner, 1992.

Fouquet, Richard: 'Ancillon'. In: NDB, Herausgegeben von der historischen Kommission bei der Bayerischen Akademie der Wissenschaften, vol. 1, Berlin: Duncker und Humblot, 1953, pp. 265 et seq.

Franke, Richard Walter: *Zensur und Preßaufsicht in Leipzig 1830–48*, mit einem Überblick über die gleichzeitige sächsische Preßgesetzgebung, Leipzig: Börsenverl. der deutschen Buchhändler, 1930.

Frey, Max: *Les transformations du vocabulaire français à l'époque de la Révolution (1789–1800)*, Paris: Presses Universitaires de France, 1925.

Friedrich, Carl J. (ed.): 'Totalitarianism' Proceedings of a Conference held at the American Academy of Arts and Sciences, Cambridge, MA: Harvard University Press, 1953.

——*Der Verfassungsstaat der Neuzeit*, Berlin: Springer, 1953.

Frisch, Peter: *Extremistenbeschluss*. Zur Frage der Beschäftigung von Extremisten im öffentlichen Dienst mit grundsätzlichen Erläuterungen, Argumentationskatalog, Darstellung extremistischer Gruppen und einer Sammlung einschlägiger Vorschriften, Urteile und Stellungnahmen, 4th Edition, Leverkusen: Heggen, 1977.

Fritz, Kurt von: *Platon in Sizilien und das Problem der Philosophenherrschaft*, Berlin: de Gruyter, 1968.

——*The Theory of the Mixed Constitution in Antiquity. A Critical Analysis of Polybius' Political Ideas*, New York: Columbia University Press, 1954.

Fritze, Lothar: 'Kommunistische und nationalsozialistische Weltanschauung – Strukturelle Parallelen und inhaltliche Unterschiede'. In: *Totalitarismus und Demokratie*, 2 (2005), pp. 101–52.

——'Kritik des totalitären Denkens. Hans Alberts methodischer Kritizismus und Totalitarismusforschung'. In: *Aufklärung und Kritik*, Sonderheft 5/2001, pp. 67–87.

——*Täter mit gutem Gewissen. Über menschliches Versagen im diktatorischen Sozialismus*, Köln: Böhlau, 1998.

Fuchs, Dieter/Roller, Edeltraud/Wessels, Bernhard (eds): *Bürger und Demokratie in Ost und West*. Studien zur politischen Kultur und zum politischen Prozess. Festschrift für Hans-Dieter Klingemann, Wiesbaden: Westdeutscher Verlag, 2002.

Fukuyama, Francis: *The End of History and the Last Man*, New York: Free Press, 2006.

Funk, Michael: 'Das faschistische Italien im Urteil der "Frankfurter Zeitung" (1920–32)'. In: *Quellen und Forschungen aus italienischen Archiven und Bibliotheken*, 69 (1989), pp. 255–311.

Funke, Manfred: Art. 'Extremismus'. In: Wolfgang W. Mickel (ed.): *Handlexikon zur Politikwissenschaft*, München: Ehrenwirth, 1983, pp. 132–36.

Furet, François: 'La République jacobine'. In: ditto, *La Révolution*, vol. 1, Paris: Gallimard, 1988, pp. 181–257.

——Nolte, Ernst: *'Feindliche Nähe'. Kommunismus und Faschismus im 20. Jahrhundert. Ein Briefwechsel*, München: Herbig, 1998.

——Mona Ozouf (eds): *The French Revolution and the Creation of Modern Political Culture*, vol. 3: The Transformation of Political Culture 1789–1848, Oxford: Pergamon, 1989.

Gallouédec-Genuys, Françoise: *La conception du Prince dans L'œuvre de Fénelon*, Paris: Presses Universitaires de France, 1963.

Gara, Larry: 'Who was an abolitionist?' In: Duberman (ed.), *Antislavery*, Princeton NJ: Princeton University Press, 1965, pp. 32–51.

Gasman, Daniel: *The Scientific Origins of National Socialism*, New Brunswick, NJ: Transaction Publishers, 2004 (1971).

Gauchet, Marcel: 'La droite et la gauche'. In: Nora (ed.), *Les lieux de mémoire*, Paris: Gallimard, vol. III, pp. 395–467.

——'Constant, Staël et la Révolution française'. In: Furet/Ozouf (eds), *The French Revolution*, Belknap Press, pp. 159–72.

Gautier-Dalché, Jean: 'Oresme et son temps'. In: Souffrin/Segonds (eds), *Nicolas Oresme*, Paris: Les Belles Lettres, 1988. pp. 7–80.

Gawlick, Günter/Görler, Woldemar: 'Cicero'. In: Flashar, *Philosophie*, Basel: Schwabe, 1983, vol. 4, pp. 993–1168.

Gayman, Jean-Marc: 'Maximalisme'. In: George Labica/Gérard Bensussan (eds), *Dictionnaire critique du marxisme*, 2e édition refondue et augmentée, Paris: Presses Universitaires de France, 1985 (1982), pp. 732 et seq.

Gebhardt, Jürgen: *Die Krise des Amerikanismus. Revolutionäre Ordnung und gesell-schaftliches Selbstverständnis in der amerikanischen Republik*, Stuttgart: Klett, 1976.

Gentile, Emilio: *Storia del Partito Fascista, 1919–22*, Bari: Laterza, 1989.

Gigon, Olof: 'Cicero und Aristoteles'. In: *Hermes* 87 (1959), pp. 143–62.

Gleason, Abbott: *Totalitarianism. The Inner History of the Cold War*, New York: Oxford University Press, 1995.

Goertz, Hansjosef: 'Staat und Widerstandsrecht bei Thomas von Aquin'. In: *Freiburger Zeitschrift für Philosophie und Theologie*, 17 (1970), pp. 308–43.

Goetz, Helmut: 'Über den Ursprung des Totalitarismusbegriffs'. In: NZZ, 27/28 May 1976, Fernausgabe No. 73.

——'Totalitarismus. Ein historischer Begriff'. In: *Schweizerische Zeitschrift für Geschichte*, 32 (1982), pp. 163–74.

Goldie, Mark: 'Absolutismus, Parlamentarismus und Revolution in England'. In: Fetscher/Münkler (eds), *Piper's Handbuch*, München: Piper, 1985–93, vol. 3, pp. 275–352.

Gomolinski, Olivia: Salomon Abramovitch Dridzo dit Alexandre Lozovsky (1878–1952): Parcours d'un dirigeant juif bolchevik. Matériaux pour une approche bio-graphique, mémoire pour le Diplôme d'études approfondies, sous la direction de Monsieur Jean-Louis Robert et de Madame Annette Wieviorka, Université de Paris I – Panthéon-Sorbonne, U.F.R. d'Histoire, Centre de recherches d'histoire des mouvements sociaux et du syndicalisme, Paris, July 1999.

Grab, Walter: *Dr. Wilhelm Schulz aus Darmstadt. Weggefährte von Georg Büchner und Inspirator von Karl Marx*, Frankfurt/M.: Büchergilde Gutenberg, 1987.

Grabmann, Martin: *Die Geschichte der scholastischen Methode*, vol. 1: Die scholastische Methode von ihren ersten Anfängen in der Väterliteratur bis zum Beginn des 12. Jahr-hunderts, vol. 2: Die scholastische Methode im 12. und beginnenden 13. Jahrhundert, Darmstadt: Wissenschaftliche Buchgesellschaft, 1956.

——*Die mittelalterlichen Kommentare zur Politik des Aristoteles*, Sitzungsberichte der Bayerischen Akademie der Wissenschaften, Philosophisch-historische Abteilung, vol. II, no. 10, München 1941.

——*Thomas von Aquin. Persönlichkeit und Gedankenwelt. Eine Einführung*, München: J. Kösel, 1949.

Graeber, Edwin: *Die Lehre von der Mischverfassung bei Polybios*, Bonn: Bouvier, 1968.

Graf, Friedrich Wilhelm: *Theonomie. Fallstudien zum Integrationsanspruch neuzeitlicher Theologie*, Gütersloh: Gütersloher Verlagshaus G. Mohn, 1987.

Gralher, Martin: 'Mitte – Mischung – Mäßigung. Strukturen, Figuren, Bilder und Metaphern in der Politik und im politischen Denken'. In: Haungs, Peter (ed.), *Res*

*Publica. Studien zum Verfassungswesen.* Dolf Sternberger zum 70. Geburtstag, München: W. Fink, 1977, pp. 82–114.

Greenberg, Jeff/Jonas, Eva: 'Psychological Motives and Political Orientation – The Left, the Right, and the Rigid: Comment on Jost et al'. In: *Psychological Bulletin*, 129 (2003), pp. 376–82.

Greenstein, Fred I./Polsby, Nelson W. (eds): *Handbook of Political Science*, vol. 3: Macropolitical Theory, Reading, MA: Addison-Wesley Publishing Co., 1975.

Griffin, Roger: *The Nature of Fascism*, London: Pinter, 1991.

Grignaschi, Mario: 'Nicolas Oresme et son commentaire à la "Politique" d'Aristote'. In: *Album Helen Maud Cam. Studies presented to the International Commission for the History of Representative and Parliamentary Institutions*, vol. XXIII, Louvain: Publications Universitaires de Louvain, 1960, pp. 95–125.

Grimm, Dieter: *Deutsche Verfassungsgeschichte 1776–1866*, Frankfurt a.M.: Suhrkamp, 1988.

Günther, Horst (ed.): *Die Französische Revolution. Berichte und Deutungen deutscher Schriftsteller und Historiker*, Frankfurt a.M.: Suhrkamp, 1985.

Gurian, Waldemar: 'Totalitarianism as Political Religion'. In: Friedrich (ed.), *Totalitarianism*, New York: Grosset & Dunlap, 1964, pp. 119–29.

Haake, Paul: *Johann Peter Friedrich Ancillon und Kronprinz Friedrich Wilhelm IV von Preußen*, München: Oldenbourg, 1920.

Hahlweg, Werner (ed.): *Lenins Rückkehr nach Russland 1917. Die deutschen Akten*, Leiden: E.J. Brill, 1957.

Hall, Kermit L. (ed.): *The Oxford Companion to the Supreme Court of the United States*, New York: Oxford University Press, 1992.

Hammer, Karl/Hartmann, Peter Claus (eds): *Le bonapartisme. Phénomène historique et mythe politique.* Actes du 13e colloque historique franco-allemand de l'Institut Historique Allemand de Paris à Augsbourg du 26 jusqu'au 30 septembre 1975, München: Artemis, 1977.

Hammer, Michael: *Volksbewegung und Obrigkeiten. Revolution in Sachsen 1830/31*, Weimar/Köln/Wien: Böhlau, 1997.

Harder, Jürgen: *Klassenkampf und 'linke' Kunsttheorien. Zum Antikommunismus kunsttheoretischer Konzeptionen des Linksradikalismus in der BRD (1965–75)*, Berlin (Ost): Dietz, 1978.

Hartmann, Nicolai: 'Die Wertdimensionen der Nikomachischen Ethik (1944)'. In: ditto, *Kleinere Schriften*, Berlin: de Gruyter, 1957, pp. 191–214.

Heidenreich, Bernd (ed.): *Politische Theorien des 19. Jahrhunderts. Konservatismus – Liberalismus – Sozialismus*, zweite völlig neu bearbeitete Auflage, Berlin: Akad.-Verlag, 2002.

Henderson, G.D.: *Chevalier Ramsay*, London: Nelson, 1952.

Hentschel, Volker: 'Nationalpolitische und sozialpolitische Bestrebungen in der Reichsgründungszeit. Das Beispiel Heinrich Bernhard Oppenheim'. In: *Jahrbuch des Instituts für Deutsche Geschichte der Universität Tel Aviv*, 5 (1976), pp. 299–345.

Hermann, Wilhelm: *Der Begriff der Mäßigung in der patristischen und scholastischen Ethik von Klemens von Alexandrien bis Albert d. Gr.*, Aachen, 1913.

Hermanns, Fritz: 'Brisante Wörter. Zur lexikographischen Bedeutung parteisprachlicher Wörter und Wendungen in Wörterbüchern der deutschen Gegenwartssprache'. In: Herbert Ernst Wiegand (ed.): *Studien zur neuhochdeutschen Lexikographie II*, Hildesheim: Georg Olms, 1982, pp. 87–108.

Heuvel, Jon Vanden: *German Life in the Age of Revolution. Joseph Görres, 1776–1848*, Washington DC: Catholic University of America Press, 2001.

Heydemann, Günther/Oberreuter, Heinrich (eds): *Diktaturen in Deutschland – Vergleichs-aspekte. Strukturen, Institutionen und Verhaltensweisen*, Bonn: Bundeszentrale für politische Bildung, 2003.

Heyer, Friedrich: 'Professor Wilhelm Traugott Krug in Leipzig und Leibarzt Hufeland in Berlin: Ihr philhellenischen Aufrufe und ihre Stourdza-Beziehungen. Arnold Ruge, der Sympathisant in Festungshaft'. In: *Europäischer Philhellenismus*, Frankfurt a.M.: Lang, 1994, pp. 67–75.

Hillenaar, Henk (ed.): *Nouvel état présent des travaux sur Fénelon*, Amsterdam: Rodopi, 2000.

Hirschfeld, Gerhard/Krumeich, Gerd/Renz, Irina/Pohlmann, Markus (eds): *Enzyklopädie Erster Weltkrieg*, Paderborn: Schöningh, 2004.

Hobert, Winfried: *Fénelon als Denker der politischen und sozialen Reform*, Diss. phil., Braunschweig, 1975.

Hobsbawm, Eric: *Age of Extremes. The Short Twentieth Century 1914–91*, London: Michael Joseph, 1994.

Höchli, Daniel: *Der Florentiner Republikanismus. Verfassungswirklichkeit und Verfassungsdenken zur Zeit der Renaisssance*, Bamberg: Haupt, 2004.

——'Zur Übersetzung'. In: Giannotti, *Die Republik Florenz*, pp. 117–24.

Hoff, Klaus: *Rechts und Links – zwei Schlagworte auf dem Prüfstand*, Krefeld: Sinus, 1992.

Höffe, Otfried: 'Ausblick: Aristoteles oder Kant – wider eine plane Alternative'. In: ditto, *Aristoteles. Die Nikomachische Ethik*, Berlin: Akademie Verlag, 1995, pp. 277–304.

Hofstätter, Peter: *Einführung in die Sozialpsychologie*, Stuttgart: Kröner, 1954.

——*Gruppendynamik. Die Kritik der Massenpsychologie*, Hamburg: Rowohlt, 1957.

Holz, Friedbert: Art. 'Krug, Wilhelm Traugott'. In: NDB, Herausgegeben von der Historischen Kommission bei der Bayerischen Akademie der Wissenschaften, vol. 13, Berlin: Duncker und Humblot, 1982, pp. 114 et seq.

Honnefelder, Ludger: 'Die philosophiegeschichtliche Bedeutung Alberts des Großen'. In: ditto et al. (eds), *Albertus Magnus und die Anfänge der Aristoteles-Rezeption im lateinischen Mittelalter. Von Richardus Rufus bis zu Franciscus de Mayronis*, Münster: Aschendorff, 2005, pp. 249–79.

Höver, Ulrich: *Joseph Goebbels. Ein nationaler Sozialist*, Bonn: Bouvier, 1992.

Hübinger, Paul Egon: 'Fénelon als politischer Denker'. In: *Historisches Jahrbuch*, 57 (1937), pp. 61–85.

Hüls, Elisabeth: *Johann Georg August Wirth (1798–1848). Ein politisches Leben im Vormärz*, Düsseldorf: Droste, 2004.

Huntington, Samuel P.: *The Third Wave. Democratization in the Late Twentieth Century*, 2nd edition, London: University of Oklahoma Press, 1993.

Hürten, Heinz: *Waldemar Gurian. Ein Zeuge der Krise unserer Welt in der ersten Hälfte des 20. Jahrhunderts*, Mainz: Matthias Grünewald, 1972.

Hüttinger, Daniela: 'Platon'. In: Maier/Denzer (eds), *Klassiker*, pp. 15–32.

Huttner, Markus: *Totalitarismus und säkulare Religionen. Zur Frühgeschichte totali-tarismuskritischer Begriffs- und Theoriebildung in Großbritannien*, Bonn: Bouvier, 1999.

Imbach, Ruedi: 'Kommentar', In: Dante Aligheri, *Monarchia*, pp. 330–34.

Imle, Walter: *Zwischen Vorbehalt und Erfordernis. Eine historische Studie zur Entstehung des nachrichtendienstlichen Verfassungsschutzes nach 1945*, München: Tuduv-Verlagsge-sellschaft, 1984.

Inamdar, N.R.: 'The Political Ideas of Lokmanya Tilak'. In: Pantham/Deutsch (eds), *Political Thought in Modern India*, New Delhi: Sage Publications, 1986, pp. 110–21.

*In memoriam Maxime Leroy, 1873–1957*, Paris, 1958.

Jaeger, Werner: *Paideia. Die Formung des griechischen Menschen*, 2. ungekürzter photomechanischer Nachdruck in einem Band, Berlin: de Gruyter, 1989 (1933, 1944, 1947).

Jäger, Wolfgang: Art. 'Opposition'. In: Brunner/Conze/Koselleck (eds), *Geschichtliche Grundbegriffe*, vol. 4, Stuttgart: Klett, 1978, pp. 469–517.

——*Politische Partei und parlamentarische Opposition. Eine Studie zum politischen Denken Lord Bolingbrokes und David Humes*, Berlin: Duncker und Humblot, 1971.

Jaschke, Hans-Gerd: *Fundamentalismus in Deutschland. Gottesstreiter und politische Extremisten bedrohen die Gesellschaft*, Hamburg: Hoffmann & Campe, 1998.

——*Rechtsextremismus und Fremdenfeindlichkeit. Begriffe, Positionen, Praxisfelder*, 2nd Edition, Wiesbaden: Westdeutscher Verlag, 2001.

——*Streitbare Demokratie und innere Sicherheit. Grundlagen, Praxis und Kritik*, Opladen: Westdeutscher Verlag, 1991.

Jesse, Eckhard: 'Antiextremistischer Konsens. Von der Weimarer Republik bis zur Gegenwart'. In: Karl G. Kick/Stephan Weingart/Ulrich Bartosch (eds), *Wandel durch Beständigkeit. Studien zur deutschen und internationalen Politik*. Jens Hacker zum 65. Geburtstag, Berlin: Duncker und Humblot, 1998, pp. 151–69.

——*Streitbare Demokratie. Theorie, Praxis und Herausforderungen in der Bundesrepublik Deutschland*, Berlin: Colloquium, 1980.

——'Die "Totalitarismus-Doktrin" aus DDR-Sicht'. In: Jesse (ed.), *Totalitarismus*, Bonn: Bundeszentrale für politische Bildung, 1996, pp. 458–83.

——(ed.): *Totalitarismus im 20. Jahrhundert. Eine Bilanz der internationalen Forschung*, 2nd edition, Baden-Baden: Nomos, 1999.

——'Verfassungsschutzberichte des Bundes und der Länder im Vergleich. Zwischen Kontinuität und Wandel'. In: Backes/ditto: *Vergleichende Extremismusforschung*, pp. 379–96.

Jobst, Hans: 'Die Staatslehre Karl von Rottecks'. In: *Zeitschrift für die Geschichte des Oberrheins*, 103 (1955), pp. 468–98.

Jones, William: 'The Path from Weimar Communism to the Cold War. Franz Borkenau and the "totalitarian enemy"'. In: Söllner/Wieland/Walkenhaus (eds), *Totalitarismus*, Berlin: Akademie Verlag, 1997, pp. 35–52.

Jones, William David: *The Lost Debate. German Socialist Intellectuals and Totalitarianism*, Urbana: University of Illinois Press, 1999.

Jost, Hans Ulrich: *Die Altkommunisten. Linksradikalismus und Sozialismus in der Schweiz 1919 bis 1921*, Frauenfeld: Huber, 1977.

Kägi, Werner: 'Rechtsstaat und Demokratie. Antinomie und Synthese'. In: Matz (ed.): *Grundprobleme*, pp. 107–46.

Kailitz, Steffen: *Die politische Deutungskultur im Spiegel des 'Historikerstreits'*, Wiesbaden: Westdeutscher Verlag, 2001.

——*Politischer Extremismus in der Bundesrepublik Deutschland. Eine Einführung*, Wiesbaden: Westdeutscher Verlag, 2004.

Kalchreuter, Hermann: Die Mesotes bei und vor Aristoteles, Diss. phil., Tübingen, 1911.

Kaltenbrunner, Gerd-Klaus (ed.): *Konservatismus in Europa*, Freiburg im Brsg.: Rombach, 1972.

Kayser, Jacques: *Les grandes batailles du radicalisme des origines aux portes du pouvoir 1820–1901*, Paris: M. Rivière, 1962.

Keiler, Peter/Stadler, Michael (eds): *Erkenntnis oder Dogmatismus? Kritik des 'Dogmatismus'-Konzepts*, Köln: Pahl-Rugenstein, 1978.

Kemper, Adolf: *Gesunder Menschenverstand und transzendentaler Synthetismus. W.T. Krug – Philosoph zwischen Aufklärung und Idealismus*, Münster: Lit, 1988.

Kershaw, Ian: *Hitler 1889–1936: Hubris*, London: Allen Lane, 2000.

——*Hitler 1936–45: Nemesis*, London: Allen Lane, 2000.

——*The 'Hitler Myth'. Image and Reality in the Third Reich*, revised edition, Oxford: Oxford University Press, 2001.

Kielmansegg, Peter Graf: *Deutschland und der Erste Weltkrieg*, 2nd Edition, Stuttgart: Klett, 1980.

——*Das Experiment der Freiheit. Zur gegenwärtigen Lage des demokratischen Verfassungsstaates*, Stuttgart: Klett, 1988.

——'Die "Quadratur des Zirkels". Überlegungen zum Charakter der repräsentativen Demokratie'. In: Matz (ed.): *Aktuelle Herausforderungen*, pp. 9–41.

Kießling, Wolfgang: *Partner im 'Narrenparadies'. Der Freundeskreis um Noel Field und Paul Merker*, Berlin: Dietz, 1994.

Kleinknecht, Günter: *Sylvester Jordan (1792–1861). Ein deutscher Liberaler im Vormärz*, Marburg: Presseamt der Stadt Marburg, 1983.

Klenner, Hermann: 'Heinrich Bernhard Oppenheim als Rechtsphilosoph'. In: *Zeitschrift für Religions- und Geistesgeschichte*, 48 (1996), pp. 303–13.

Klimkeit, Hans-Joachim: *Der politische Hinduismus. Indische Denker zwischen religiöser Reform und politischem Erwachen*, Wiesbaden: Harrassowitz, 1981.

Klingeis, Rupert: 'Das aristotelische Tugendprinzip der richtigen Mitte in der Scholastik'. In: *Divus Thomas*, VII (1920), pp. 33–49, 142–72, 269–88, VIII (1921), pp. 1–14, 83–112.

Klocksin, Jens Ulrich: *Kommunisten im Parlament. Die KPD in Regierungen und Parlamenten der westdeutschen Besatzungszonen und der Bundesrepublik Deutschland (1945–56)*, 2nd Edition, Bonn: Verlag im Hof, 1994.

Kluxen, Kurt: 'Die Herkunft der Lehre von der Gewaltentrennung'. In: Heinz Rausch (ed.): *Zur heutigen Problematik der Gewaltentrennung*, Darmstadt: Wissenschaftliche Buchgesellschaft, 1969, pp. 130–52.

Knabe, Hubertus: *Die unterwanderte Republik. Stasi im Westen*, Berlin: Propyläen, 1999.

Knops, Jan Pieter Hubert: *Etudes sur la traduction française de la Morale à Nicomache d'Aristote par Nicole Oresme*, La Haye: Excelsior, 1952.

Koch-Baumgarten, Sigrid: *Aufstand der Avantgarde. Die Märzaktion der KPD 1921*, Frankfurt a.M.: Campus, 1986.

Kohoutek, Marie Luise von: Die Differenzierung des anthropinon agathon. Eine Studie zur Werttafel der Nikomachischen Ethik, Diss. phil. masch., Marburg, 1924.

Koschnik, Hans: *Der Abschied vom Extremistenbeschluss*, Bonn: Verlag Neue Gesellschaft, 1979.

Koselleck, Reinhart: 'Einleitung'. In: Brunner/Conze/Koseleck (eds): *Geschichtliche Grundbegriffe*, vol. I, 4th Edition, Stuttgart: Klett, 1992, pp. XIII–XXVI.

——*Vergangene Zukunft*, Frankfurt a.M.: Suhrkamp, 1979.

Krägelin, Paul: *Heinrich Leo*, Leipzig: Voigtländer, 1908.

Krämer, Hans Joachim: *Arete bei Platon und Aristoteles. Zum Wesen und zur Geschichte der platonischen Ontologie*, Heidelberg: Winter, 1959.

Kramer, Helmut: *Fraktionsbindungen in den deutschen Volksvertretungen 1819–49*, Berlin: Duncker und Humblot, 1968.

Kraus, Hans-Christof: 'Die deutsche Rezeption und Darstellung der englischen Verfassung im neunzehnten Jahrhundert'. In: Rudolf Muhs/Johannes Paulmann/Willibald

Steinmetz (eds), *Aneignung und Abwehr. Interkultureller Transfer zwischen Deutschland und Großbritannien im 19. Jahrhundert*, Bodenheim: Philo, 1998, pp. 89–126.

Kraushaar, Wolfgang: 'Extremismus der Mitte. Zur Geschichte einer soziologischen und sozialhistorischen Interpretationsfigur'. In: Hans-Martin Lohmann (ed.): *Extremismus der Mitte. Vom rechten Verständnis deutscher Nation*, Frankfurt a.M.: Fischer Taschenbuch Verlag, 1994, pp. 23–50.

——'Extremismus der Mitte. Zur Logik einer Paradoxie'. In: Leonhard Fuest/Jörg Löffler (eds): *Diskurse des Extremen. Über Extremismus und Radikalität in Theorie, Literatur und Medien*, Würzburg: Königshausen & Neumann, 2005, pp. 13–22.

Kraut, Alan M. (ed.): *Crusaders and Compromisers. Essays on the Relationship of the Antislavery Struggle to the Antebellum Party System*, Westport, CN: Greenwood Press, 1983.

Krockow, Christian Graf von: 'Edmund Burke'. In: Fetscher/Münkler (eds), *Piper's Handbuch*, vol. 4, pp. 71–79.

Kroll, Frank-Lothar: *Utopie als Ideologie. Geschichtsdenken und politisches Handeln im Dritten Reich*, 2nd Edition, Paderborn: Schöningh, 1999.

Kucher, Felix: 'Der Bildungsgang und das philosophische Umfeld Engelberts von Admont'. In: Wilhelm Baum (ed.), *Engelbert von Admont. Vom Ursprung und Ende des Reiches und anderen Schriften*, Graz: Leykam, 1998, pp. 222–40.

Kuhfuss, Walter: *Mäßigung und Politik. Studien zur politischen Sprache und Theorie Montesquieus*, München: W. Fink, 1975.

Lademacher, Horst (ed.): *Die Zimmerwalder Bewegung. Protokolle und Korrespondenzen*, vol. 1: Protokolle, La Hague: Mouton, 1967.

Lambertini, Roberto: 'A proposito della "costruzione" dell'oeconomica in Egidio Romano'. In: *Medioevo. Rivista di storia della filosofia medievale*, 14 (1988), pp. 315–70.

Landi, Aldo: 'Nota critica'. In: Brucioli, *Dialogi*, pp. 551–88.

Lange-Enzmann, Birgit: *Franz Borkenau als politischer Denker*, Berlin: Duncker & Humblot, 1996.

Laponce, Jean A.: *Left and Right. The Topography of Political Perceptions*, Toronto: University Press, 1981.

Laqueur, Walter: *Faschismus. Gestern – Heute – Morgen*, Berlin: Propyläen, 1997.

Laue, Heinrich von: *Maß und Mitte. Eine problemgeschichtliche Untersuchung zur frühen griechischen Philosophie und Ethik*, maschinenschriftliche Abhandlung, Universitätsbibliothek Münster, 1960.

Laufer, Heinz: 'Die Widersprüche im freiheitlichen demokratischen System oder Die Demokratie als eine coincidentia oppositorum'. In: Leonart Reinisch (ed.): *Freiheit & Gleichheit oder Die Quadratur des Kreises*, München: Bayrische Landeszentrale für politische Bildungspolitik, 1974, pp. 15–26.

Le Brun, Jacques: 'Notice'. In: Fénelon, *Œuvres*, vol. 2, pp. 1664 et seq.

Lederer, Gerda: *Jugend und Autorität. Über den Einstellungswandel zum Autoritarismus in der Bundesrepublik Deutschland und in den USA*, Opladen: Westdeutscher Verlag, 1983.

——Kindervater, Angela: 'Internationale Vergleiche'. In: Gerda Lederer/Peter Schmidt (eds): *Autoritarismus und Gesellschaft. Trendanalysen und vergleichende Jugenduntersuchungen 1945–93*, Opladen: Leske und Budrich, 1995, pp. 167–88.

Lefèvre, Eckard: *Horaz. Dichter im augusteischen Rom*, München: C.H. Beck, 1993.

Leggewie, Claus/Meier, Horst: *Republikschutz. Maßstäbe für die Verteidigung der Demokratie*, Reinbek: Rowohlt, 1995.

Lehmann, Hartmut/Richter, Melvin (eds*): The Meaning of Historical Terms and Concepts. New Studies on Begriffsgeschichte*, Washington, DC: German Historical Institute, 1996.

Lepszy, Norbert/Veen, Hans-Joachim: *'Republikaner' und DVU in kommunalen und Landesparlamenten sowie im Europaparlament*, Interne Studien und Berichte, no. 63, II. Fassung. Herausgegeben von der Konrad-Adenauer-Stiftung, Sankt Augustin: Konrad-Adenauer-Stiftung, 1994.

Levinson, Ronald B.: *In Defense of Plato*, Cambridge, MA: Harvard University Press, 1953.

Ley, Klaus: 'Dante Alighieri'. In: Maier/Denzer (eds), *Klassiker*, pp. 95–106.

Link, Jürgen: *Versuch über den Normalismus. Wie Normalität produziert wird*, 3rd Edition, Göttingen: Vandenhöck und Ruprecht, 2006.

Linz, Juan J.: *Totalitäre und autoritäre Regime*, Herausgegeben von Raimund Krämer, Berlin: Berliner Debatte Wissenschaftsverlag, 2000.

——'Totalitarian and Authoritarian Regimes'. In: Greenstein/Polsby (eds): *Political Science*, vol. 3, pp. 3–411.

Loehr, Johanna (ed.): *Dona Melanchthoniana*. Festgabe für Heinz Scheible zum 70. Geburtstag, Stuttgart-Bad Cannstatt: Frommann-Holzboog, 2001.

Löschburg, Winfried: 'Wilhelm Traugott Krug und der nationale Befreiungskampf des griechischen Volkes'. In: Ernst Engelberg (ed.), *Karl-Marx-Universität Leipzig 1409– 1959*. Beiträge zur Universitätsgeschichte, vol. 1, Leipzig: Verlag Enzyklopädie, 1959, pp. 208–22.

Lokatis, Siegfried: 'Falsche Fragen an das Orakel? Die Einheit der SED'. In: Simone Barck/Martina Langermann/Siegfried Lokatis (eds), *Zwischen 'Mosaik' und 'Einheit'. Zeitschriften in der DDR*, Berlin: Ch. Links, 1999, pp. 592–601.

Löwenstein, Karl: *Verfassungslehre*, 2nd Edition, Tübingen: J.C.B. Mohr, 1969.

Lübbe, Hermann: 'Heilsmythen nach der Aufklärung. Geschichtsphilosophie als Selbstermächtigungsideologie'. In: Jacob Taubes (ed.), *Religionstheorie und Politische Theologie*, vol. 3: Theokratie, Munich: Schöningh/Fink, 1987, pp. 279–92.

Lucardie, Paul: Demokratischer Extremismus: ein Widerspruch in sich? Paper presented at the Annual Meeting of the DVPW-Group 'Extremismusforschung', 2006, https://www.dvpw.de/fileadmin/docs/2006Extrem.pdf.

Luigi Sturzo nella storia d'Italia: Atti del Convegno internazionale di studi promosso dall'Assemblea Regionale Siciliana (Palermo-Caltagirone, 26–28 novembre 1971), vol. 2: Comunicazioni, Roma, 1973.

Lutz, Donald S.: 'The Relative Influence of European Writers on Late Eighteenth-Century American Political Thought'. In: APSR, 78 (1984), pp. 189–97.

Maccoby, Simon: *English Radicalism 1832–52*, London: Allen & Unwin, 1935.

MacCulloch, Diarmaid: *Die zweite Phase der englischen Reformation (1547–1603) und die Geburt der anglikanischen Via Media*, Münster: Aschendorff, 1998.

McFarland, Sam G.: 'Communism as Religion'. In: *International Journal for the Psychology of Religion*, 8 (1998), pp. 33–48.

——Ageyev, Vladimir S./Abalakina-Paap, Marina A.: 'Authoritarianism in the Former Soviet Union'. In: *Journal of Personality and Social Psychology*, 63 (1992), pp. 1004–10.

Mackenzie, Fraser: *Les relations de l'Angleterre et de la France d'après le vocabulaire*, vol. 1: Les infiltrations de la langue et de l'esprit anglais. Anglicismes français, Paris: Droz, 1939.

Maier, Hans: 'Zur Lehrgeschichte der politischen Wissenschaft'. In: ditto, *Politische Wissenschaft. Aufsätze zur Lehrtradition und Bildungspraxis*, München: Piper, 1969, pp. 15–52.

——*Totalitarismus und politische Religionen. Konzepte des Diktaturvergleichs*, Paderborn: Schöningh, 1996.

——(ed.): *Totalitarismus und politische Religionen. Konzepte des Diktaturvergleichs*, vol. 3: Deutungsgeschichte und Theorie, Paderborn: Schöningh, 2003.

——Schäfer, Michael (eds): *Totalitarismus und politische Religionen. Konzepte des Diktaturvergleichs*, vol. 2, Paderborn: Schöningh, 1997.

——et al. (eds): *Politik, Philosophie, Praxis*. Festschrift für Wilhelm Hennis zum 65. Geburtstag, Stuttgart: Klett-Cotta, 1988.

——Denzer, Horst (eds): *Klassiker des politischen Denkens*, vol. 1: Von Plato bis Hobbes, Neuausgabe, München: C.H. Beck, 2001.

Maihofer, Werner: 'Politische Kriminalität'. In: *Meyers Enzyklopädisches Lexikon*, vol. 14, Mannheim: Bibliographisches Institut, 1975, pp. 365–69.

Majumdar, R.C.: *History of the Freedom Movement in India*, vol. I, Kalkutta: Firma K.L. Mukhopadhyay, 1962.

Maltzahn, Christoph Freiherr von: *Heinrich Leo (1799–1878). Ein politisches Gelehrtenleben zwischen romantischem Konservatismus und Realpolitik*, Göttingen: Vandenhoeck und Ruprecht, 1979.

Mandt, Hella: Art. 'Tyrannis, Despotie'. In: Brunner/Conze/Koselleck (eds): *Geschichtliche Grundbegriffe*, vol. 6, pp. 651–706.

——'Das klassische Verständnis: Tyrannis und Despotie'. In: Maier (ed.), *Totalitarismus*, vol. 3, pp. 29–106.

Martin, Alfred von: 'Weltanschauliche Motive im altkonservativen Denken'. In: Kaltenbrunner (ed.), *Konservatismus*, S. 139–80.

Martiny, Martin: 'Die Entstehung und politische Bedeutung der "Neuen Blätter für den Sozialismus" und ihres Freundeskreises'. In: VfZ, 25 (1977), pp. 373–419.

Marty, Martin E./Appleby, R. Scott: *Herausforderung Fundamentalismus. Radikale Christen, Moslems und Juden im Kampf gegen die Moderne*, Frankfurt a.M.: Campus, 1996.

Matz, Ulrich: *Aktuelle Herausforderungen der repräsentativen Demokratie*, Köln: Heymann, 1985.

——(ed.): *Grundprobleme der Demokratie*, Darmstadt. Wissenschaftliche Buchgesellschaft, 1973.

——'Nachwort'. In: Thomas von Aquin, *Über die Herrschaft der Fürsten*, pp. 73–89.

Matzerath, Josef: 'Landstände und Landtage in Sachsen 1438 bis 1831. Zur Entstehung, Gewichtung und Tagungsweise der sächsischen Ständeversammlung in vorkonstitutioneller Zeit'. In: Karlheinz Blaschke, *700 Jahre politische Mitbestimmung in Sachsen*, Dresden: Sächsischer Landtag, 1994, pp. 17–30.

——*Aspekte sächsischer Landtagsgeschichte. Umbrüche und Kontinuitäten 1815 bis 1868*, Dresden: Sächsischer Landtag, 2000.

Mayer, Henry: *All on Fire. William Lloyd Garrison and the Abolition of Slavery*, New York: St. Martin's Press, 1998.

Meißner, Franz-Joseph: 'Maistre Nicolas Oresme et la lexicographie française'. In: *Cahiers de Lexicologie*, 40 (1982), pp. 51–66.

Mendle, Michael: *Dangerous Positions. Mixed Government, the Estates of the Realm, and the Making of the Answer to the six propositions*, Alabama: University of Alabama Press, 1985.

Merkel, Wolfgang: *Systemtransformation*, Opladen: Leske und Budrich, 1999.

Meusel, Alfred: 'Der Radikalismus'. In: *Kölner Vierteljahreshefte für Soziologie*, 4/5 (1924/26), pp. 44–48.

Michael, George: *Confronting Right-Wing Extremism and Terrorism in the USA*, New York: Routledge, 2003.

Miethke, Jürgen: 'Der Weltanspruch des Papstes im späten Mittelalter. Die Politische Theorie der Traktate De Potestate Papae'. In: Fetscher/Münkler (eds), *Pipers Handbuch*, vol. 2, pp. 351–445.

Mittelstraß, Jürgen: 'Oresme'. In: ditto (ed.): *Enzyklopädie Philosophie und Wissenschaftstheorie*, vol. 2, Mannheim: Bibliographisches Institut Wissenschaftsverlag, 1984, pp. 1089–91.

Mohler, Armin: *Die Konservative Revolution in Deutschland 1918–32*. Ein Handbuch 3, um einen Ergänzungsband erweiterte Auflage, Darmstadt: Wissenschaftliche Buchgesellschaft, 1989.

Mohr, Eva: Fénelon und der Staat, Diss. phil., Frankfurt a.M., 1971.

Molino, Jean: 'L'"Essai philosophique sur le gouvernement civil" – Ramsay ou Fénelon?' In: *La regence*, Paris: Colin, 1970, pp. 276–93.

Möll, Marc-Pierre: *Gesellschaft und totalitäre Ordnung. Eine theoriegeschichtliche Auseinandersetzung mit dem Totalitarismus*, Baden-Baden: Nomos, 1998.

Molony, John N.: *The Emergence of Political Catholicism in Italy. Partito Popolare 1919–26*, London: C. Helm, 1977.

Moltmann, Günter: 'Goebbels' Rede zum totalen Krieg am 18. Februar 1943'. In: VfZ, 12 (1964), pp. 13–43.

Mommsen, Wolfgang J.: *Die Urkatastrophe Deutschlands. Der Erste Weltkrieg 1914–18*, Stuttgart: Klett-Cotta, 2002.

Mönch, Bernhard: Der politische Wortschatz der französischen Restauration in Parlament und Presse, Diss. phil. masch., Bonn 1960.

Moos, Malcolm: 'Don Luigi Sturzo – Christian Democrat'. In: APSR, 39 (1945), pp. 269–92.

Moraux, Paul: *Der Aristotelismus bei den Griechen. Von Andronikos bis Alexander von Aphrodisias*, vol. 1: Die Renaissance des Aristotelismus im 1. Jh. v. Chr., Berlin/New York: de Gruyter, 1973.

Moreau, Patrick/Lang, Jürgen P.: *Linksextremismus. Eine unterschätzte Gefahr*, Bonn: Bouvier, 1996.

——Steinborn, Eva: 'Die Bewegung der Altermondialisten – Eine Gefahr für die Demokratie?' In: Backes/Jesse (eds): *Jahrbuch Extremismus & Demokratie*, vol. 2, pp. 170–206.

——'Der westdeutsche Kommunismus in der Krise'. In: Uwe Backes/Eckhard Jesse (eds), *Jahrbuch Extremismus & Demokratie*, vol. 2, pp. 170–206.

Moynihan, Daniel P.: 'Introduction'. In: Shils: *Torment of Secrecy*, Carbondale, IL: Southern Illinois University Press, pp. VII–XXIII.

Mudde, Cas: 'Politischer Extremismus und Radikalismus in Westeuropa – Typologie und Bestandsaufnahme'. In: Backes/Jesse (eds): *Gefährdungen der Freiheit*, Göttingen: Vandenhoeck & Ruprecht, pp. 87–104.

——'Radikale Parteien in Europa'. In: APuZG, B 47/2008, pp. 12–19.

Muller, James Arthur: *Stephen Gardiner and the Tudor Reaction*, London: SPCK, 1926.

Müller-Dietz, Heinz: *Das Leben des Rechtslehrers und Politikers Karl Theodor Welcker*, Freiburg im Brsg.: Verlag Eberhard Albert.

——'Karl Theodor Welcker – Politiker, Strafrechtslehrer und Vollzugsreformer'. In: *Zeitschrift für Strafvollzug*, 16 (1967), pp. 13–23.

——'Der Freiburger Einfluss: Rotteck und Welcker'. In: Elmar Wadle (ed.), *Philipp Jakob Siebenpfeiffer und seine Zeit im Blickfeld der Rechtsgeschichte*, Sigmaringen: Jan Thorbecke, 1991.

Müller-Schmid, Peter Paul: 'Adam Müller (1779–1829)'. In: Heidenreich (ed.), *Politische Theorien*, Berlin: Akademie-Verlag, 2002, pp. 109–38.

Münkler, Herfried: *Machiavelli. Die Begründung des politischen Denkens der Neuzeit aus der Krise der Republik Florenz*, Frankfurt a.M.: Europäische Verlagsanstalt, 1982.

Müri, Walter: 'Der Maßgedanke bei griechischen Ärzten'. In: *Gymnasium*, 57 (1950), pp. 183–201.

Neugebauer, Gero/Stöss, Richard: *Die PDS. Geschichte, Organisation, Wähler, Konkurrenten*, Opladen: Leske und Budrich, 1996.

Nippel, Wilfried: *Mischverfassungstheorie und Verfassungsrealität in Antike und früher Neuzeit*, Stuttgart: Klett-Cotta, 1980.

——'Cicero'. In: Maier/ Denzer (eds), *Klassiker*, pp. 53–64.

Nipperdey, Thomas/Doering-Manteuffel, Anselm/Thamer, Hans-Ulrich (eds): *Weltbürgerkrieg der Ideologien. Antworten an Ernst Nolte*, Berlin: Propyläen-Verlag, 1993.

Nolte, Ernst: *Der europäische Bürgerkrieg, 1917–45. Nationalsozialismus und Bolschewismus*, Frankfurt a.M.: Propyläen-Verlag, 1987.

——*Der Faschismus in seiner Epoche. Die Action française – Der italienische Faschismus – Der Nationalsozialismus*, 5th Edition, München: Piper, 1979 (1963).

——'Vergangenheit, die nicht vergehen will'. In: *'Historikerstreit'. Die Dokumentation der Kontroverse um die Einzigartigkeit der nationalsozialistischen Judenvernichtung*, München: Piper, 1987, pp. 39–47.

Nolte, Paul: 'Aristotelische Tradition und amerikanische Revolution. John Adams und das Ende der klassischen Politik'. In: *Der Staat*, 14 (1988), pp. 209–32.

Nora, Pierre (ed.): *Les lieux de mémoire*, vol. III, Les France, 1. Conflits et partages, Paris: Gallimard, 1993.

Ooyen, Robert Chr. van: 'Ein moderner Klassiker der Verfassungstheorie: Karl Loewenstein'. In: ZfP, 51 (2004), pp. 68–86.

Panagopoulos, Epaminondas Peter: *Essays on the History and Meaning of Checks and Balances*, Lanham: University Press of America, 1985.

Pantham, Thomas/Deutsch, Kenneth L. (eds): *Political Thought in Modern India*, New Delhi: Sage, 1986.

Papayanıs, Nicholas: *Alphonse Merrhem, The Emergence of Reformism in Revolutionary Syndicalism 1871–1925*, Dordrecht: Martinus Nijhoff Publ., 1985.

Payne, Stanley: *A History of Fascism 1914–45*, 2nd edition, London: University of Wisconsin Press, 1997.

Peltonen, Markku: *Classical Humanism and Republicanism in English Political Thought, 1570–1640*, Cambridge: Cambridge University Press, 1995.

Perry, Lewis: *Radical Abolitionism. Anarchy and the Government of God in Antislavery Thought*, reprint, Knoxville, TN: University of Tennessee Press, 1995 (1973).

Peschanski, Denis (ed.): *Marcel Cachin. Carnets 1906–47*, vol. 2: 1917–20, édition établie et annotée par Gilles Candar, Brigitte Studer et Nicolas Werth, Paris: CNRS, 1993.

Peters, Butz: *Tödlicher Irrtum. Die Geschichte der RAF*, Berlin: Argon-Verlag, 2004.

Petersen, Jens: 'La nascita del concetto di "Stato totalitario" in Italia'. In: *Annali dell'Istituto storico italo-germanico in Trento* (Bologna), 1 (1975), pp. 143–67.

——'Die Entstehung des Totalitarismusbegriffs in Italien'. In: Eckhard Jesse (ed.), *Totalitarismus im 20. Jahrhundert. Eine Bilanz der internationalen Forschung*, 2nd Edition, Baden-Baden: Nomos, 1999, pp. 95–117.

Petitfils, Jean-Christian: *La droite en France de 1789 à nos jours*, 3rd Edition, Paris: Presses Universitaires de France, 1983 (1973).

Petracchi, Giorgio: *La Russia rivoluzionaria nella politica italiana. Le relazioni italo-sovietiche, 1917–25*, Bari: Laterza, 1982.

Pfahl-Traughber, Armin: 'Politischer Extremismus – was ist das überhaupt? Zur Definition von und Kritik an einem Begriff'. In: Bundesamt für Verfassungsschutz (ed.): *Bundesamt für Verfassungsschutz. 50 Jahre im Dienst der inneren Sicherheit*, Köln: Heymann, 2000, pp. 185–211.

Piekalkiewicz, Jaroslaw/Penn, Alfred Wayne: *Politics of Ideocracy*, New York: State University of New York Press, 1995.

Pipes, Richard: *Die Russische Revolution*, vol. 2: Die Macht der Bolschewiki, Berlin: Rowohlt, 1992.

Piron, Sylvain: *Nicolas Oresme: violence, langage et raison politique*, European University Institute Working Paper HEC No. 97/1, Florence: European University Institute, Department of History and Civilization, 1997.

Pocock, John G.A.: *The Machiavellian Moment. Florentine Political Thought and the Atlantic Republican Tradition*, second edition with a new afterword by the author, Princeton, NJ: Princeton University Press, 2003 (1975).

Pohlmann, Friedrich: *Deutschland im Zeitalter des Totalitarismus. Politische Identitäten in Deutschland zwischen 1918 und 1989*, München: Olzog, 2001.

Popper, Karl R.: *Das Elend des Historizismus*, fünfte verbesserte Auflage, Tübingen: J.C.B. Mohr, 1979 (1965).

——*Die offene Gesellschaft und ihre Feinde*, vol. I: Der Zauber Platons, siebte Auflage mit weitgehenden Verbesserungen und neuen Anhängen, Tübingen: Mohr, 1992 (Original: 1944).

Prantl, Art. 'Krug, Wilhelm Traugott'. In: ADB, Herausgegeben durch die Historische Kommission bei der Königlichen Akademie der Wissenschaften, vol. 17, Leipzig, 1883, pp. 220–22.

Puschner, Uwe/Schmitz, Walter/Ulbricht, Justus H. (eds): *Handbuch der 'Völkischen Bewegung' 1871–1918*, München: Saur, 1996.

——*Die völkische Bewegung im wilhelminischen Kaiserreich. Sprache – Rasse – Religion*, Darmstadt: Wissenschaftliche Buchgesellschaft, 2001.

Quillet, Jeannine: 'Nicole Oresme Traducteur d'Aristote'. In: Souffrin, Pierre/Segonds, Alain Philippe (eds): *Nicolas Oresme. Tradition et innovation chez un intellectuel du XIVe siècle*, Paris: Belles Lettres, 1988, pp. 81–91.

——(ed.): *Autour de Nicole Oresme*. Actes du Colloque Oresme organisé à l'Université de Paris XII, Paris: Librairie philosophique Vrin, 1990.

Racine, Nicole: Art. 'Leroy, Maxime Auguste'. In: Maitron/Pennetier (eds), *Dictionnaire biographique*, vol. 34, pp. 309 et seq.

Raeder, Hans: *Platons philosophische Entwicklung*, Leipzig: Teubner, 1905.

Ragan, Fred: 'Justice Oliver Wendell Homed, Jr., Zechariah Chafee, Jr., and the Clear and Present Danger Test for free Speech: The First Year, 1919'. In: *Journal of History*, 58 (1971), pp. 24–45.

Rapoport, Louis: *Hammer, Sichel, Davidstern. Judenverfolgung in der Sowjetunion*, Berlin: Links, 1992.

Rathmann, Lothar (ed.): *Alma Mater Lipsiensis. Geschichte der Karl-Marx-Universität Leipzig*, Leipzig: Edition Leipzig, 1984.

Redlich, Shimon: *War, Holocaust and Stalinism. A Documented Study of the Jewish Anti-Fascist Committee in the USSR*, Australia: Harwood Academic Publ., 1995.

Reichardt, Sven: *Faschistische Kampfbünde. Gewalt und Gemeinschaft im italienischen Squadrismus und in der deutschen SA*, Köln: Böhlau, 2002.

Reimann, Aribert: 'Der Erste Weltkrieg – Urkatastrophe oder Katalysator?' In: APuZ, B 29–30/2004, pp. 30–38.

Reinhard, Ewald: 'Der Streit um K.L. von Hallers "Restauration der Staatswissenschaft"'. In: *Zeitschrift für die gesamte Staatswissenschaft*, 111 (1955), pp. 115–30.

Reinhardt, Olaf: Art. 'Flake, Otto'. In: Wolfgang Benz/Hermann Graml (eds), *Biographisches Lexikon zur Weimarer Republik*, München: Beck, 1988, p. 88.

Reinhardt, Paul: Die sächsischen Unruhen der Jahre 1830–31 und Sachsens Übergang zum Verfassungsstaat, Diss. phil., Halle, 1915.

Reis, Jack: *Ambiguitätstoleranz. Beiträge zur Entwicklung der Persönlichkeitskonstruktion*, Heidelberg: Asanger, 1997.

Reitz, Tilman: 'Editorial'. In: *Das Argument*, 237/2000, pp. 461–62.

Rémond, René: *Les droites en France*, Neuausgabe, Paris: Aubier-Montaigne, 1982 (1954).

Retat, Pierre: 'Partis et factions en 1789: émergence des désignants politiques'. In: *Mots*, 16 (1988), pp. 69–89.

Ribhegge, Wilhelm: *August Winnig. Eine historische Persönlichkeitsanalyse*, Bonn-Bad Godesberg: Neue Gesellschaft, 1973.

Richter, Melvin: 'Appreciating a Contemporary Classic: The Geschichtliche Grundbegriffe and Future Scholarship'. In: Lehmann/ditto (eds): *Meaning of Historical Terms*, pp. 7–19.

——'Aristoteles und der klassische griechische Begriff der Despotie'. In: Maier et al. (eds): *Politik, Philosophie, Praxis*, pp. 21–37.

——*The History of Political and Social Concepts. A Critical Introduction*, Oxford: Oxford University Press, 1995.

Riedel, Manfred: 'Aristoteles-Tradition am Ausgang des 18. Jahrhunderts. Zur ersten deutschen Übersetzung der "Politik" durch Johann Georg Schlosser'. In: *Alteuropa und die moderne Gesellschaft*. Festschrift für Otto Brunner, Herausgegeben vom Historischen Seminar der Universität Hamburg, Göttingen: Vandenhoeck und Ruprecht, 1963, pp. 278–315.

Riedel, Wolfgang: Art. 'Krug, Wilhelm Traugott'. In: Walther Illy: *Literaturlexikon. Autoren und Werke deutscher Sprache*, vol. 7, München: Bertelsmann Lexikon Verlag, 1990, pp. 47 et seq.

Riesebrodt, Martin: *Fundamentalismus als patriarchalische Protestbewegung*, Tübingen: Mohr, 1990.

Riklin, Alois: 'Aristoteles und die Mischverfassung'. In: *Festschrift Herbert Batliner*, pp. 341–51.

——'Donato Giannotti – ein verkannter Staatsdenker der Florentiner Renaissance'. In: *Giannotti, Die Republik Florenz*, pp. 17–75.

——'John Adams und die gewaltenteilige Mischverfassung'. In: ZfP, 38 (1991), pp. 274–93.

——*Machtteilung. Geschichte der Mischverfassung*, Darmstadt: Wissenschaftliche Buchgesellschaft, 2006.

——'Montesquieus freiheitliches Staatsmodell. Die Identität von Machtteilung und Mischverfassung'. In: PVS, 30 (1989), pp. 420–42.

——'Die venezianische Mischverfassung im Lichte von Gasparo Contarini (1483–1542)'. In: ZfP, 37 (1990), S. 264–91.

Ripathi, Amales: *The Extremist Challenge. India between 1890 and 1910*, Bombay: Orient Longmans, 1967.

Roghmann, Klaus: *Dogmatismus und Autoritarismus. Kritik der theoretischen Ansätze und Ergebnisse dreier westdeutscher Untersuchungen*, Meisenheim am Glan: Hain, 1966.

Romilly, Jean de: 'Le classement des constitutions d'Hérodote à Aristote'. In: *Revue des études grecques*, 72 (1959), pp. 80–99.

Rosa, Gabriele De: *Luigi Sturzo*, Torino: UTET, 1977.

Rosanvallon, Pierre: *Le Moment Guizot*, Paris: Gallimard, 1985.

Rossi-Landi, Guy: *Le chassé croisé. La droite et la gauche en France de 1789 à nos jours*. Essai, Paris: J.C. Lattès, 1978.

Rothermund, Dietmar: *Die politische Willensbildung in Indien 1900–960*, Wiesbaden: Harrassowitz, 1965.

Rüstow, Alexander: *Ortsbestimmung der Gegenwart. Eine universalgeschichtliche Kulturkritik*, vol. 3: Herrschaft oder Freiheit?, Erlenbach-Zürich: Rentsch, 1957.

Ryffel, Heinrich: ΜΕΤΑΒΟΛΗ ΠΟΛΙΤΕΙΩΝ. *Der Wandel der Staatsverfassungen*, Bern: Haupt, 1949.

Salamun, Kurt: 'Demokratische Kultur und antidemokratisches Denken. Vorbemerkungen zur demokratischen Kultur'. In: ditto (ed.): *Geistige Tendenzen der Zeit. Perspektiven der Weltanschauungstheorie und Kulturphilosophie*, Frankfurt a.M.: Lang, 1996, pp. 151–65.

——'"Fundamentalismus" – Versuch einer Begriffserklärung und Begriffsbestimmung'. In: ditto (ed.): *Fundamentalismus 'interdisziplinär'*, Wien: LIT, 2005, pp. 21–45.

——'Der holistische Grundzug in Herbert Marcuses neomarxistischer Gesellschaftstheorie und Ideologiekritik'. In: ditto (ed.): *Aufklärungsperspektiven. Weltanschauungsanalyse und Ideologiekritik*, Tübingen: J.C.B. Mohr, 1989, pp. 69–80.

Sattler, Andreas: *Die rechtliche Bedeutung der Entscheidung für die streitbare Demokratie*. Untersucht unter besonderer Berücksichtigung der Rechtsprechung des Bundesverfassungsgerichts, Baden-Baden: Nomos, 1982.

Schäfer, Herbert: 'Friedrich Murhard (1778–1853). Geschichte einer politischen Verfolgung'. In: Stadtsparkasse Kassel (ed.), *Friedrich und Karl Murhard – gelehrte Schriftsteller und Stifter in Kassel*, Kassel: Buch- und Kunstverlag Weber & Weidemeyer, o.J. (1988), pp. 14–35.

Schäfer, Michael: 'Luigi Sturzo als Totalitarismustheoretiker'. In: Maier (ed.), *Totalitarismus*, pp. 37–47.

Schalk, Fritz: *Exempla romanischer Wortgeschichte*, Frankfurt a.M.: Klostermann, 1966.

Scharlau, W. B. /Zeman, Z. A. B.: *Freibeuter der Revolution – Parvus-Helphand. Eine politische Biographie*, Köln: Verlag Wissenschaft und Politik, 1964.

Scheible, Heinz: Art. 'Melanchthon'. In: *Theologische Realenzyklopädie, Herausgegeben von Gerhard Müller*, vol. 12, Berlin: de Gruyter, 1992, pp. 371–410.

——'Melanchthon neben Luther'. In: ditto, *Melanchthon und die Reformation. Forschungsbeiträge*, Herausgegeben von Gerhard May und Rolf Decot, Mainz: P. von Zabern, 1996, pp. 153–70.

——*Melanchthon. Eine Biographie*, München: Beck, 1997.

Scheidemann, Christiane: *Ulrich Graf Brockdorff-Rantzau (1869–1928). Eine politische Biographie*, Frankfurt a.M.: Lang, 1998.

Scherb, Armin: *Präventiver Demokratieschutz als Problem der Verfassungsgebung nach 1945*, Frankfurt a.M.: Lang, 1987.

Scheuner, Ulrich: 'Der Verfassungsschutz im Bonner Grundgesetz'. In: *Um Recht und Gerechtigkeit. Festgabe für Erich Kaufmann zu seinem 70. Geburtstag*, Stuttgart: Kohlhammer, 1950, pp. 313–30.

Schiffers, Reinhard: *Verfassungsschutz und parlamentarische Kontrolle in der Bundesrepublik Deutschland 1949–57*. Mit einer Dokumentation zum 'Fall John' im Bundestagsausschuss zum Schutz der Verfassung, Düsseldorf: Droste Verlag, 1997.

——*Zwischen Bürgerfreiheit und Staatsschutz. Wiederherstellung und Neufassung des politischen Strafrechts in der Bundesrepublik Deutschland 1949–51*, Düsseldorf: Droste Verlag, 1989.

Schiffmann, Gustav Adolf: *Andreas Michael Ramsay. Eine Studie zur Geschichte der Freimaurerei*, Leipzig: Zechel, 1878.

Schilling, Harald: *Das Ethos der Mesotes. Eine Studie zur Nikomachischen Ethik des Aristoteles*, Tübingen: Mohr, 1930.

Schilling, Otto: *Die Staats- und Soziallehre des hl. Thomas von Aquin*, Paderborn: Schöningh,1923.

Schlechte, Alexander: Die Vorgeschichte der sächsischen Verfassung vom 4. September 1831, Diss. iur., Borna-Leipzig, 1927.

Schmeitzner, Mike: 'Brauner und roter Faschismus? Otto Rühles rätekommunistische Totalitarismustheorie'. In: ditto. (ed.): *Totalitarismuskritik von links. Deutsche Diskurse im 20. Jahrhundert*, Göttingen: Vandenhoeck und Ruprecht, 2007, pp. 205–27.

Schmidinger, Heinrich: *Romana Regia Potestas. Staats- und Reichsdenken bei Engelbert von Admont und Enea Silvio Piccolomini*, Basel: Helbing und Lichtenhahn, 1978.

Schmiechen-Ackermann, Detlef: *Diktaturen im Vergleich*, Darmstadt: Wissenschaftliche Buchgesellschaft, 2002.

Schmitt, Charles B.: *Aristotle and the Renaissance*, Cambridge, MA: Harvard University Press, 1983.

Schmittlein, Raymond: *L'aspect politique du differend Bossuet-Fénelon*, Mainz, 1956.

Schmitz-Berning, Cornelia: *Vokabular des Nationalsozialismus*, Berlin: de Gruyter, 1998.

Schnur, Roman: 'Über Maxime Leroy'. In: ARSP, 41 (1954/55), pp. 510–27.

Schönbohm, Wulf (ed.): *Verfassungsfeinde als Beamte? Die Kontroverse um die streitbare Demokratie*, München: Olzog, 1979.

Schönhoven, Klaus/Vogel, Hans-Jochen (eds): *Frühe Warnungen vor dem Nationalsozialismus. Ein historisches Lesebuch*, Bonn: Dietz, 1998.

Schöttle, Rainer: *Politische Theorien des süddeutschen Liberalismus im Vormärz. Studien zu Rotteck, Welcker, Pfizer, Murhard*, Baden-Baden: Nomos, 1994.

Schottmann, Christian: *Politische Schlagwörter in Deutschland zwischen 1929 und 1934*, Stuttgart: Heinz, 1997.

Schuber, Friedrich Hermann: Art. 'Camerarius, Ludwig'. In: NDB, Herausgegeben von der Kommission bei der Bayerischen Akademie der Wissenschaften, vol. 3, Berlin: Duncker und Humblot, 1957, pp. 105–7.

Schulz, Gerhard: *Von Brüning zu Hitler. Der Wandel des politischen Systems in Deutschland 1930–33*, Berlin: de Gruyter, 1992.

Schumann, Dirk: *Politische Gewalt in der Weimarer Republik 1918–33. Kampf um die Straße und Furcht vor dem Bürgerkrieg*, Essen: Klartext Verlag, 2001.

Schwartz, Michael: *Sozialistische Eugenik. Eugenische Sozialtechnologien in Debatten und Politik der deutschen Sozialdemokratie, 1890–1933*, Bonn: Dietz, 1995.

Schwarz, Hans-Peter: *Das Gesicht des Jahrhunderts. Monster, Retter und Mediokritäten*, Berlin: Siedler, 1998.

Schwenn: Art. 'Kybele'. In: *Paulys Real-Encyclopädie der Classischen Altertumswissenschaft*, vol. 11, Stuttgart: Metzler, 1922, col. 2250–98.

Seidel, Bruno/Jenkner, Siegfried (eds): *Wege der Totalitarismusforschung*, Darmstadt: Wissenschaftliche Buchgesellschaft, 1968.

Shahar, Shulamith: 'Nicolas Oresme, un penseur politique indépendant de l'entourage du roi Charles V'. In: *L'Information historique*, 32 (1970), pp. 203–9.

Shakleton, Robert: *Montesquieu. A Critical Biography*, Oxford: Oxford University Press, 1961.

——'Montesquieu, Bolingbroke and the Separation of Powers'. In: *French Studies*, 3 (1949), pp. 25–38.

Shils, Edward A.: *The Torment of Secrecy. The Background and Consequences of American Security Policies*, Neuausgabe, Chicago: Ivan R. Dee, 1996 (1956).

Sigel, Robert: *Die Lensch–Cunow–Haenisch-Gruppe. Eine Studie zum rechten Flügel der SPD im Ersten Weltkrieg*, Berlin: Duncker und Humblot, 1976.

Singer, Bruno: *Die Fürstenspiegel in Deutschland im Zeitalter des Humanismus und der Reformation*, München: Fink, 1981.

Skinner, Quentin: *The Foundations of Modern Political Thought*, vol. 1: The Renaissance; vol. 2: The Age of Reformation, Cambridge, MA: Cambridge University Press, 1978.

S.L., Art. 'Chamberlayne, Edward'. In: *The Dictionary of National Biography*, founded in 1882 by George Smith, edited by Sir Leslie Stephen and Sir Sidney Lee, from the Earliest Times to 1900, vol. IV, Oxford: Oxford University Press, 1917, pp. 8 et seq.

Slama, Alain-Gérard: *Les chasseurs d'absolu. Genèse de la gauche et de la droite*, Paris: Bernard Grasset, 1980.

Smith, Craig R.: *Defender of the Union. The Oratory of Daniel Webster*, New York.: Greenwood Press, 1989.

Smith, Lacey Baldwin: *Tudor Prelates and Politics, 1536–58*, Princeton, NJ: Princeton University Press, 1953.

Sontheimer, Kurt: *Antidemokratisches Denken in der Weimarer Republik. Die politischen Ideen des deutschen Nationalismus zwischen 1918 und 1933*, 2nd Edition, München: DTV, 1983 (1962).

Souffrin, Pierre/Segonds, Alain Philippe (eds): *Nicolas Oresme. Tradition et innovation chez un intellectuel du XIVe siècle*, Paris: Belles Lettres, 1988.

Spaemann, Robert: '"Fanatisch" und "Fanatismus"'. In: *Archiv für Begriffsgeschichte*, 15 (1971), pp. 256–74.

Spahn, Peter: 'Oikos und Polis. Beobachtungen zum Prozess der Polisbildung bei Hesiod, Solon und Aischylos'. In: *HZ*, 231 (1980), pp. 529–64.

Spuller, Eugène: *Royer-Collard*, Paris: Hachette, 1895.

Stählin, Friedrich: Art. 'Camerarius, Joachim'. In: NDB, Herausgegeben von der Kommission bei der Bayerischen Akademie der Wissenschaften, vol. 3, Berlin: Duncker und Humblot, 1957, pp. 104 et seq.

Stark, Rudolf: *Aristotelesstudien. Philologische Untersuchungen zur Entwicklung der aristotelischen Ethik*, München: Beck, 1954.

Starzinger, Vincent E.: *Middlingness. 'Juste Milieu' Political Theory in France and England, 1815–48*, Charlottesville, VA: University Press of Virginia, 1965.

Steigerwald, Robert: *Marxistische Klassenanalyse oder spätbürgerliche Mythen*. Lenin-Verfälschung in der BRD – "Links"-revisionistische Sozialismus-Kritik – Bürgerliche Ideologie in linker Verkleidung – Antikommunismus, seine Grundmythen und Grundmechanismen, Berlin (Ost): Akademie-Verlag, 1972.

Sternberger, Dolf: *Drei Wurzeln der Politik*, Taschenbuchausgabe, Frankfurt a.M.: Suhrkamp, 1984 (1978).

——'Die neue Politie. Vorschläge zu einer Revision der Lehre vom Verfassungsstaat'. In: JöR, 33 (1984), pp. 1–40.

Sternhell, Zeev: *La droite révolutionnaire. Les origines française du fascisme 1885–1914*, Paris: Seuil, 1978.

——*Maurice Barrès et le nationalisme français*, Paris: Ed. Complexe, 1985 (1972).

Stewart, Robert: *Henry Brougham 1778–1868. His Public Career*, London: Bodley Head, 1985.

Stillig, Jürgen: *Die Russische Februarrevolution 1917 und die sozialistische Friedenspolitik*, Köln: Böhlau, 1977.

Stolleis, Michael: *Geschichte des öffentlichen Rechts in Deutschland*, vol. 2: Staatslehre und Verwaltungswissenschaft 1800–1914, München: Beck, 1992.

Sutor, Bernhard: 'Traditionelles Gemeinwohl und liberale politische Theorie'. In: Karl Graf Ballestrem/Henning Ottmann (eds): *Theorie und Praxis*. Festschrift für Nikolaus Lobkowicz zum 65. Geburtstag, Berlin: Duncker und Humblot, 1996, pp. 155–77.

Syring, Enrico: *Hitler. Seine politische Utopie*, Berlin: Propyläen, 1994.

Taeger, Fritz: *Die Archaeologie des Polybios*, Stuttgart: Kohlhammer, 1922.

Talmon, Jacob L.: *The Origins of Totalitarian Democracy*, London: Mercury Books, 1961.

——*Political Messianism. The romantic phase*, London: Secker & Warburg, 1960.

Taylor, Robert: 'Les néologismes chez Nicole Oresme, traducteur du XIXe siècle'. In: Georges Straka (ed.), *Actes du Xe congrès international de linguistique et philologie romanes*, vol. 2, Paris: Klicksieck, 1965, pp. 727–36.

Thomas, John L.: *The Liberator. William Lloyd Garrison*, Boston, MA: Little Brown, 1963.

Thompson, C. Bradley: *John Adams and the Spirit of Liberty*, Lawrence, KS: University Press of Kansas, 1998.

Tibi, Bassam: *Der neue Totalitarismus. 'Heiliger Krieg' und westliche Sicherheit*, Darmstadt: Primus-Verlag, 2004.

——'Vom klassischen Djihad zum terroristischen Djihadismus – Der irreguläre Krieg der Islamisten und die neue Weltordnung'. In: Backes/Jesse (eds): *Jahrbuch Extremismus & Demokratie*, vol. 14, pp. 27–44.

Tierney, Brian: 'Aristotle, Aquinas, and the Ideal Constitution'. In: Proceedings of the Fourth Mid-Atlantic States Conference on Patristic, Medieval, and Renaissance Studies at Villanova University, 28 September 1979, pp. 1–11.

Timasheff, Nicolas S.: *The Sociology of Luigi Sturzo*, Baltimore, MD: Helicon Press, 1962.

Todorov, Tzvetan: *Benjamin Constant. La passion démocratique*, Paris: Hachette, 1997.

Tosstorff, Reiner: *Profitern. Die Rote Gewerkschaftsinternationale 1920–77*, Paderborn: Schöningh, 2004.

Trampedach, Kai: *Platon, die Akademie und die zeitgenössische Politik*, Stuttgart: Steiner

Traverso, Enzo (ed.): *Le totalitarisme. Le Xxe siècle en débat*, Paris: Seuil, 2001.

Turchetti, Mario: *Tyrannie et tyrannicide de l'Antiquité à nos jours*, Paris: Presse Universitaires de France, 2001.

Ubl, Karl: 'Einleitung'. In: ditto (ed.), *Schriften*, pp. 1–91.

——*Engelbert von Admont. Ein Gelehrter im Spannungsfeld von Aristotelismus und christlicher Überlieferung*, München: Oldenbourg, 2000.

——(ed.): *Die Schriften des Alexander von Roes und des Engelbert von Admont*, pt. 2: Engelbert von Admont, Speculum virtutum (Monumenta Germaniae Historica. Staatsschriften des späteren Mittelalters. vol. I, pt. 2), Hannover: Hahnsche Buchhandlung, 2004.

——'Zur Entstehung der Fürstenspiegel Engelberts von Admont'. In: *Deutsches Archiv für Erforschung des Mittelalters*, 55 (1999), pp. 499–548.

Ullmann, Walter: *Medieval Foundations of Renaissance Humanism*, Ithaca, NY: Cornell University Press, 1977.

Urmson, J.O.: 'Aristotle's Doctrine of the Mean'. In: Amélie Oksenberg Rorty (ed.): *Essays on Aristotle's Ethics*, Berkeley, CA: University of California Press, 1980, pp. 157–70.

V.A.L., Art. 'Extrême'. In: *Encyclopédie ou Dictionnaire raisonné des sciences, des arts et des métiers*, nouvelle impression de l'édition de 1751–80, Stuttgart-Bad Cannstatt: Frommann-Holzboog, 1967, Supplement, vol. 2 (1776), pp. 928–32.

Varma, Vishwanath Prasad: *Modern Indian Political Thought*, 8th edition, Agra: Lakshmi Narain Agarwal, 1985 (1961).

Vile, Maurice J.C.: *Constitutionalism and the Separation of Powers*, Oxford: Clarendon Press, 1967.

Walker, Samuel: *Hate Speech. The History of an American Controversy*, Lincoln, NE: University of Nebraska Press, 1994.

Walsh, Correa Moylan: *The Political Science of John Adams. A Study in the Theory of Mixed Government and the Bicameral System*, reprint, Freeport, ME: Books for Libraries Press, 1969 (1915).

Walter, Stefan: *Demokratisches Denken zwischen Hegel und Marx. Die politische Philosophie Arnold Ruges. Eine Studie zur Geschichte der Demokratie in Deutschland*, Düsseldorf: Droste, 1995.

Ward, Colin: *Anarchism. A Very Short Introduction*, Oxford: Oxford University Press, 2004.

Weber, Thomas: 'Extreme'. In: Wolfgang Fritz Haug (ed.): *Historisch-kritisches Wörterbuch des Marxismus*, vol. 3, Hamburg: Argument-Verlag, 1997, col. 1198–1208.

Wehrli, Fritz: 'Ethik und Medizin. Zur Vorgeschichte der aristotelischen Mesonlehre'. In: *Museum Helveticum*, 8 (1951), pp. 36–62.

——Wöhrle, Georg/Zhmud, Leonid: 'Der Peripatos bis zum Beginn der römischen Kaiserzeit'. In: Helmut Flashar (ed.): *Die Philosophie der Antike*, vol. 3: Ältere Akademie – Aristoteles – Peripatos, zweite durchgesehene und erweiterte Auflage, Basel: Schwabe, 2004, pp. 493–639.

Weichold, Jochen: *Zwischen Götterdämmerung und Wiederauferstehung. Linksradikalismus im Wandel*, Berlin (Ost): Verlag Neues Leben, 1989.

Weidemann, Wilhelm: 'Friedrich Murhard (1778–1853) und der Altliberalismus'. In: *Zeitschrift für Hessische Geschichte und Landeskunde*, 55 (1926), pp. 229–76.

Weikart, Richard: *Socialist Darwinism. Evolution in German Socialist Thought from Marx to Bernstein*, San Francisco: International Scholars Publications, 1998.

Weilenmann, Heinz: Untersuchungen zur Staatstheorie Carl Ludwig von Hallers. Versuch einer geistesgeschichtlichen Einordnung, Diss. phil., Bern, 1955.

Weinberg, Leonard/Pedazhur, Ami (eds): *Religious Fundamentalism and Political Extremism*, London: Cass, 2004.

Weiß, Dieter J.: 'Joseph von Görres (1776–1848)'. In: Heidenreich (ed.), *Politische Theorien*, pp. 139–54.

Wende, Peter: *Radikalismus im Vormärz. Untersuchungen zur politischen Theorie der frühen deutschen Demokratie*, Wiesbaden: Steiner, 1975.

——'Radikalismus'. In: Brunner/Conze/Koselleck (eds), *Grundbegriffe*, vol. 5, pp. 113–33.

Werth, Nicolas: 'Ein Staat gegen sein Volk. Gewalt, Unterdrückung und Terror in der Sowjetunion'. In: Courtois, Stéphane et al, *Das Schwarzbuch des Kommunismus. Unterdrückung, Verbrechen und Terror*, München: Piper, 1998, pp. 51–295.

Whitfield, Stephen J.: *Into the Dark. Hannah Arendt and Totalitarianism*, Philadelphia: Temple University Press, 1980.

Wild, Karl: *Karl Theodor Welcker. Ein Vorkämpfer des älteren Liberalismus*, Heidelberg: Winter, 1913.

Wilhelm, Theodor: *Die englische Verfassung und der vormärzliche deutsche Liberalismus. Eine Darstellung und Kritik des Verfassungsbildes der liberalen Führer*, Stuttgart: Kohlhammer, 1928.

Wilhelm, Uwe: *Der deutsche Frühliberalismus. Von den Anfängen bis 1789*, Frankfurt a.M.: Lang, 1995, p. 125.

Williams, Raymond: *Keywords. A Vocabulary of Culture and Society*, London: Fontana, 1976.

Williams, Thomas Harry: *Lincoln and the Radicals*, Madison, WI: University of Wisconsin Press, 1941.

Wingert, Roland: Die marxistisch–leninistische Lehre von der historischen Mission der Arbeiterklasse im Zerrspiegel der Konzeptionen des studentischen Linksradikalismus in der Bundesrepublik Deutschland und in Westberlin im Zeitraum von 1964 bis 1979, Diss. A, Philosophische Fakultät, Martin-Luther-Universität Halle-Wittenberg, Halle, 1972.

Winkler, Heinrich August: 'Extremismus der Mitte? Sozialgeschichtliche Aspekte der nationalsozialistischen Machtergreifung'. In: VfZ, 20 (1972), pp. 175–91.

Wippermann, Wolfgang: 'Extreme Radikale'. In: *Jungle World* (Berlin), no. 10/2009.

Wirsching, Andreas: *Vom Weltkrieg zum Bürgerkrieg? Politischer Extremismus in Deutschland und Frankreich 1918–33/39. Berlin und Paris im Vergleich*, München: Oldenbourg, 1999.

Wolf, Erik: *Griechisches Rechtsdenken*, vol. I: Vorsokratiker und frühe Dichter, Frankfurt a.M.: Klostermann, 1950.

Wolf, Ursula: 'Über den Sinn der Aristotelischen Mesoteslehre'. In: Höffe (ed.), *Aristoteles. Die Nikomachische Ethik*, Berlin: Akademie-Verlag, 1995, pp. 83–108.

Wolgast, Eike: Art. 'Reform, Reformation'. In: Brunner/Conze/Koselleck (eds), *Geschichtliche Grundbegriffe*, vol. 5, pp. 313–60.

Wolters, Gereon: Art. 'Krug Friedrich, Wilhelm Traugott'. In: Mittelstraß (ed.), *Enzyklopädie*, pp. 503 et seq.

Wunschik, Tobias: *Die maoistische KPD/ML und die Zerschlagung ihrer 'Sektion DDR' durch das MfS*, Ed. vom Bundesbeauftragten für die Unterlagen des Staatssicherheitsdienstes der ehemaligen DDR, Berlin, 1997.

Young, Alfred F. (ed.): *Beyond the American Revolution. Explorations in the History of American Radicalism*, Dekalb, IL: Northern Illinois University Press, 1993.

——'Introduction'. In: ditto (ed.): *American Revolution*, pp. 3–24.

Zechlin, Egmont: 'Friedensbestrebungen und Revolutionierungsversuche'. In: APuZ, B 24/1961, S. 325–37, B 25/1961, pp. 341–67.

Zehnpfennig, Barbara: *Hitlers Mein Kampf. Eine Interpretation*, München: Fink, 2000.

Zehntner, Hans: *Das Staatslexikon von Rotteck und Welcker. Eine Studie zur Geschichte des deutschen Frühliberalismus*, Jena: Fischer, 1929.

Zeman, Z.A.B. (ed.): *Germany and the Revolution in Russia 1915–18*. Documents from the Archives of the German Foreign Ministry, London: Oxford University Press, 1958.

Zillig, Paula: Die Theorie von der gemischten Verfassung in ihrer literarischen Entwicklung im Altertum und ihr Verhältnis zur Lehre Lockes und Montesquieus über Verfassung, Würzburg: Univ. Diss., 1916.

Zimmer, Anja: *Hate Speech im Völkerrecht. Rassendiskriminierende Äußerungen im Spannungsfeld zwischen Rassendiskriminierungsverbot und Meinungsfreiheit*, Frankfurt a.M.: Lang, 2001.

Zinn, Howard: 'Abolitionists, Freedom-Riders, and the Tactics of Agitation'. In: Duberman (ed.), *Antislavery*, pp. 417–51.

Zitelmann, Rainer: *Hitler. Selbstverständnis eines Revolutionärs*, Hamburg: Berg, 1987.

Zwahr, Hartmut: 'Von der zweiten Universitätsreform bis zur Reichsgründung, 1830 bis 1871'. In: Rathmann (ed.), *Alma Mater Lipsiensis*, pp. 141–90.

——*Revolutionen in Sachsen. Beiträge zur Sozial- und Kulturgeschichte*, Weimar: Böhlau, 1996.

# Index

284    *Index*

from anti-demorcatism 185–89
anti-totalitarian consensus in FRG,
extremism and 140–44
Antiochus of Askalon 41
*Antiope Fragment* (Euripides) 18–19
*Antiquitates Romanae* (Dionysius of
Halikarnassus) 42
Appelicon of Teos 39
Appleby, R. Scott 169
architecture, art of 36
Archytas of Tarent 17
Arendt, Hannah 5, 154, 156
Areopagus 42
*Aretology* (Krug, W.T) 87
Aristotle 10, 13, 14, 67, 69, 70, 73, 89;
aim of ethics 26–27; architecture, art
of 36; checks and balances 37;
citizens, disposition of 35; democracy,
preconditions for 35; early humanism
and mesotês categories 51, 52, 53, 56;
ethics and methodology 26; extreme
social forces and mesotês categories
66, 67, 68, 69, 70; extremes in mesotês
doctrine and mixed constitution,
theory of 25, 28, 29, 36, 38–39, 41, 42,
46, 49; friendship, virtue of 33;
heritage of 182–83, 184–85; justice,
quantification of 28–29; kingdoms,
causes of fall 35; mean and extremes,
juxtaposition of 25, 36–37; mean and
extremes, relationship between 27–28;
mean term between contrary
opposites in *Topics* 25–26; mesotês
categories and doctrine 76, 77,
175–76, 192, 197n77; middle class
state, liberalism and 33–34; middle in
*First Analytics* 25; mixed constitution,
theory of 25–38, 38–39, 41, 42, 46, 49;
Muslim interpretations of 45; norms,
problem of 29–30; oligarchy,
preconditions for 35; politics of 39,
43–44, 45–46, 47; politology of,
mesotês doctrine, mixed constitution
and 13, 16, 18, 19–20, 23–24;
predictors 25; sociological conditions
32–33, 33–34; state and household,
distinguishing features 30; state
constitutions, typology of 31–32, 34,
35, 37–38; syllogisms 25; terminology
of 172–73, 176, 177, 178; tradition of
38–50, 51, 53–59, 62, 63, 66, 166, 180,
181–82; translation of, importance of
49–50; typology of state constitutions

31–32, 34, 35, 37–38; tyrannies,
causes of fall 35; urban development
35–36; virtue and mean between excess
and deficiency 27, 28, 30, 46, 48–49
Aristotle Phokylides of Milet 16
art and idea of right mean between
extremes 17–18
Augé, Claude 215n54
*Augsburger Allgemeine Zeitung* 81
Augustine 43, 59
Außerparlamentarische Opposition
(APO) 146–47
Austria 75, 87, 108, 114, 119, 150
*The Authoritarian Personality* (Adorno,
T.W., et al., Horkheimer, M., Ed.)
159, 160, 226n52
authoritarianism 158–59; extremism and
167–68; political extremism and 190–91
autocracies 191
*Avanti* 107, 109, 215n72
*Les Aventures de Télémaque* (Fénelon,
F.) 60
Averroës (Ibn Rushd) 43, 45
Avicenna 199n169

Baal, Gérard 8
Babeuf, François Noël 4
Barrès, Maurice 5
*Basic Historical Concepts* (Brunner, O.,
Conze, W. and Koselleck, Eds.) 11, 13
Behaim, Lukas Friedrich 69
Bentham, Jeremy 8, 80
Berkeley group 167
Berlin Wall (antifaschistischer
Schutzwall) 138
Bernholz, Peter 121
Besoigne, Abbé Jerôme 79
Bethmann-Hollweg, Theobald von 104
Bhagavad Gita 98
Blackstone, Sir William 66
Bluntschli, Johann Caspar 93, 121
Blythe, James M. 11
Bobbio, Norberto 170–72, 186–88
Bodin, Jean 55–56, 59, 202n28
Boehme, Jacob 10
Boethius 43–44, 44–45
Bolingbroke, Henry St John, Viscount
58–59, 66, 71
Bolshevism 106, 107, 110, 111, 153, 160,
212n3; fascism and, parallels between
115, 152, 159; France, Bolshevists as
embodiment of extremism in 105; in
ideology of National Socialism (NS)
125, 126–27, 128–29; liberal view of

*Zur Vermittlung der Extreme in den Meinungen* (Ancillon, F.) 82, 83
Victims of Persecution by the Nazi Regime, Association of the 146
violence and political extremism 176, 190
virtue: between extremes, doctrine of 43–44; and mean between excess and deficiency 27, 28, 30, 46, 48–49
*Vita Lycurgi* (Plutarch), 'reasonableness' in contrast to extremes 42
Voltaire 64
Vormärz period in Germany 8, 14, 84, 86, 91, 176, 208n28
*Vossische Zeitung* 113–14
*Voyages de Cyros* (Ramsey, A.M.) 61

war, radicalization in conduct of 127
Washington, George 75
Webster, Daniel 95
Weigelo, Ventino 10
Weimar Germany 118, 120, 129–30, 142, 143, 153, 190; constitutional

system of 2–3; extremes in political language of 111–16; Mann's defence of 115
Weitling, Wilhelm 5
Welcker, Karl Theodor 83, 84
Wells, H.G. 107
Weltanschauung 119
Wieland, Christoph Martin 73–74
Wilkes, John 8
wing terms in political language 77
Winkler, Arno 137
Winkler, Heinrich August 173
Winnig, August 104
Wipperman, Wolfgang 170, 181
workers' movements 105–7
World War I 7, 14, 105, 107–8, 117–18; aftermath of 1
World War II 153–54; loyalty of political groups in US during 159, 160

Zedler, Johann Heinrich 9–10
Zimmerwaldian Conference, Kienthal (1916) 99–100